'44 FOXHOLES IN FRANCE

Projected Series for
AN ALMOST PERFECT WAR

⊕

Book One
BOOKS TO BAYONETS

⊕

Book Two
'44 FOXHOLES IN FRANCE

Present volume

⊕

Book Three
SOME RE-ASSEMBLY REQUIRED

⊕

Book Four
ANNOTATED BIBLIOGRAPHY

⊕

Book Five
POEMS OF WAR

⊕

'44 FOXHOLES IN FRANCE

Book Two

of

AN ALMOST PERFECT

WAR

by

Warren J. Wightman

'44 FOXHOLES IN FRANCE

Book Two of AN ALMOST PERFECT WAR

Copyright © 2014 by Warren J. Wightman
All rights reserved

For *Jean*

…remembering all those perfumed letters

Foreword

'44 FOXHOLES IN FRANCE is an account of my personal experiences and is not intended to be used for factual or historical reference. Other publications, several of which are listed in Appendix A, provide more complete and possibly more accurate information about the military actions described. The *Operational Report 357th Infantry* (Appendix B), however, is a photo-copy of the Army's official record, typed at Regimental headquarters during combat—strikeovers and typos included.

We GIs seldom knew where we were, geographically. I was able to reconstruct our route across Northern France only after considerable research. The maps included in the text are greatly simplified and may not show directions and distances with complete accuracy.

Events are described as faithfully as possible, but because our letters were censored, and because we had orders not to keep diaries in combat, I had no notes to work from. Since I didn't start this account until fifty years after the war, some details and conversations are necessarily approximate.

Day-to-day experiences are in present tense and are expressed in the then-current idiom, as best I remember it. Only information known to me at the time is Included. [BRACKETED MATERIAL WITHIN THE TEXT], INDENTED PARAGRAPHS and Chapter Notes, however, have the benefit of hindsight. *Foreign words, Names* and *Place-names* are in *italics* unless they are also in common English usage.

Poetic sections not credited to others are my own, written retrospectively.

The names of several platoon members have been changed.

GI profanity is kept to a minimum, but to avoid it completely in a book about the Army at war would be conspicuously disingenuous.

'44 FOXHOLES IN FRANCE is BOOK TWO of AN ALMOST PERFECT WAR, a projected five-book series. BOOK TWO begins with Chapter 6 and ends where BOOK THREE begins. The other books of the series have been written but have not yet been published. BOOK FOUR, THE ANNOTATED BIBLIOGRAPHY, will probably be next.

W.J.W. – 2014

Table of Contents

		Page	
Lists of Maps, Photos, Sketches, Quotes.		ii	
List of poems by first lines		iii	

Chapter			Chapter End Notes
6	Invasion of the Continent	1	Page 11
7	A Division in Jeopardy	15	25
8	Patrol	27	38
9	Attacked	45	50
10	July Offensive	55	65
11	The Shelling	71	80
12	*Beau-Coudray*	87	105
13	*St.-Germain-sur-Sèves*	109	120
14	Breakthrough	123	136
15	Breakout	141	153
16	Race to *Le Mans*	157	167
17	Trapping the German 7th Army	171	188
18	Through the Heart of France	193	211
19	Into *Lorraine*	217	228
20	*Moselle*	231	243
21	*Fèves* Ridge	245	264

Afterword..271

Appendices:
- A   Primary References......................... 272
- B   *Operational Report*
  357th Infantry Regiment................... 273
  1st Page of Report............................ 276
- C   Web-links.. 309
- D   Correspondence with Robert Patton... 314
- E   GI terms used in this book................. 317
- F   Foreign words used in this book.......... 327

Acknowledgments....................................... 330

Indices... 331

Addenda (Referenced by superscript [A])........ 345

About the Author.. 349

Maps

		Page
1.	*Cherbourg* Peninsula	iv
2.	Defensive Positions and Patrol Near *Portbail*	32, 33
3.	Attack by B-Company at *Beau-Coudray* – Day 1	62
4.	The "Island" at *St.-Germain-sur-Sèves*	120
5.	*Mayenne*	142
6.	Convergence of American and German Motorized Columns Near *Le Mans*	156
7.	Breakout of American 1st and 3rd Armies and Entrapment of German 7th Army	170
8.	Engagement at *Le Merlerault* Roadblock	184
9.	Northern France – Route of 357th Regiment, 90th Division	192
10.	Route of 357 through *Lorraine*	216
11.	Fire fight Near *Avril*	230
12.	Attack at *Fèves* Ridge	258

⊕

Photos of Weapons

Garand M-1 Rifle and Ammo	14
60-mm Mortar, U.S.	44
Bayonet for M-1 Rifle	44
Thompson Sub-machinegun	44
Fragmentation Hand-grenade	44
Rifle Grenade, Anti-tank	44
Trench Knife	44
Browning Automatic Rifle	69
American M-3 Sub-machinegun	269

Sketches

Sackett at *St.-Germain-sur-Sèves*	108
Shaeffer finds Browny at *Fèves* Ridge	252

Quotes

Winston Churchill	193
Loren Eiseley	270

Poems – First Lines

	Page
There on the beach	5
throbbing the cloud	8
They are out there, out in	21
When I hold my grandfather's violin, taut	35
Soldiers don't shake hands, they stand	53
Each shell a wrapped penile parcel of	70
Lipless and mute from the	86
The soft-faced lieutenant is a	94
Swooping, swittering, trooping, skipperling,	96
They can't…say what's on their minds	104
The multirows of	110
On they came, and they came	124
I was the eye	132
Into shades of shadow that	146
under the wall	149
While we pitched our little fight	151
I step out	159
They jerk and snap in	172
falls, tumbles, twists	182
Dear Jean,	194
bivouac near *la Forêt de Fontainebleau*	195
Worming their way across	209
We moved among	210
Appeared suddenly a man	221
Blossoming like white	235
A wrench tugging at a nut stuck	248
He kept himself clean, I don't	255
each to himself, obeying the	261
The grip of the claw on my	264

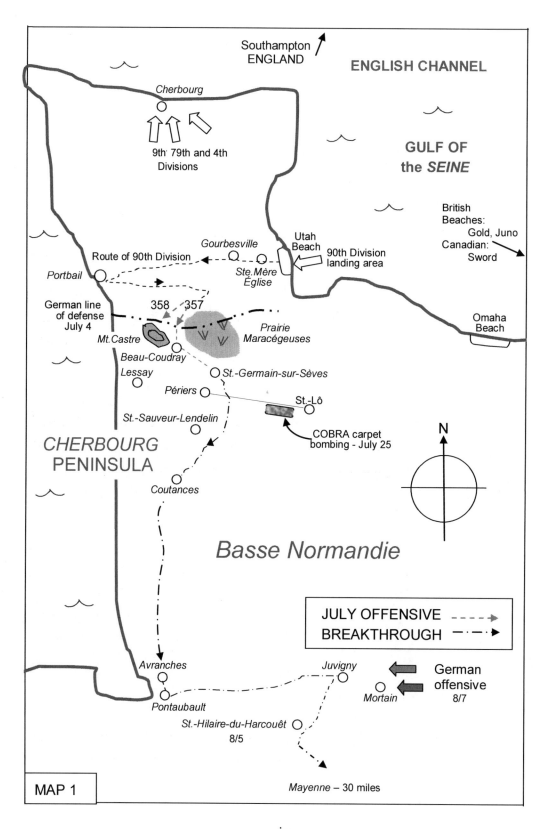

Chapter 6

INVASION OF THE CONTINENT

Tent City – Somerset Hills, England
June 1944

The pace of training revs up. Road marches are longer and more frequent. The roads are lined with hedges, trees and stone walls. I study the vegetation, try to sharpen my powers of observation. In combat a single leaf out of place could betray the enemy's position. Or mine.

All the other infantrymen in the camp are gone—shipped out while I was in sick bay. I'm temporarily attached to the Tank Destroyers. Once again, whatever personal connections I've made with other GIs have been ripped away.

The demeanor of the TDs strikes me as odd. They don't seem to take the war seriously. They joke about "Gerries running around the woods with 88s". A couple of them have plastic recorders and send Morse code signals tooting back and forth between the tents. Again, I wish I'd learned the code as a kid.

Night of June 5

Late at night, almost invisible in the dark sky, a long flight of big planes goes over, flying low and going south. We stand outside our tents to watch. They're cargo planes, C-47s. The planes pass over for many minutes. The drone is hypnotic, mixing the sense of immense power with sobering thoughts of their imagined mission. During a quiet interval we try to get some sleep, but more planes come and we go out again. This time they're towing gliders.[1]

June 6

The next morning we are assembled in a field and told that the Allied assault on the European Continent has begun. Each man gets a printed flyer—General Eisenhower's terse message to the fighting men of the Allied Command:

[Notes for Chapter 7 start on p. 11]

> *SOLDIERS, SAILORS AND AIRMEN OF THE ALLIED EXPEDITIONARY FORCES!*
>
> *YOU ARE ABOUT TO EMBARK ON THE GREAT CRUSADE, TOWARD WHICH WE HAVE STRIVEN THESE MANY MONTHS. THE EYES OF THE WORLD ARE UPON YOU, THE HOPES AND PRAYERS OF LIBERTY-LOVING PEOPLE EVERYWHERE MARCH WITH YOU. IN COMPANY WITH OUR BRAVE ALLIES AND BROTHERS IN ARMS ON OTHER FRONTS YOU WILL BRING ABOUT THE DESTRUCTION OF THE GERMAN WAR MACHINE, THE ELIMINATION OF NAZI TYRANNY OVER THE OPPRESSED PEOPLES OF EUROPE, AND SECURITY FOR OURSELVES IN A FREE WORLD.*
>
> *YOUR TASK WILL NOT BE AN EASY ONE. YOUR ENEMY IS WELL TRAINED, WELL EQUIPPED AND BATTLE HARDENED. HE WILL FIGHT SAVAGELY.*
>
> *BUT THIS IS THE YEAR **1944**! MUCH HAS HAPPENED SINCE THE NAZI TRIUMPHS OF **1940-1941**. THE UNITED NATIONS HAVE INFLICTED ON THE GERMANS GREAT DEFEATS, IN OPEN BATTLE, MAN TO MAN. OUR AIR OFFENSIVE HAS SERIOUSLY REDUCED THEIR STRENGTH IN THE AIR AND THEIR CAPACITY TO WAGE WAR ON THE GROUND. OUR HOME FRONTS HAVE GIVEN US AN OVERWHELMING SUPERIORITY IN WEAPONS AND MUNITIONS OF WAR, AND PLACED AT OUR DISPOSAL GREAT RESERVES OF TRAINED FIGHTING MEN. THE TIDE HAS TURNED! THE FREE MEN OF THE WORLD ARE MARCHING TOGETHER TO VICTORY!*
>
> *I HAVE FULL CONFIDENCE IN YOUR COURAGE, DEVOTION TO DUTY, SKILL IN BATTLE. WE WILL ACCEPT NOTHING LESS THAN FULL VICTORY! GOOD LUCK! AND LET US ALL BESEECH THE BLESSINGS OF ALMIGHTY GOD UPON THIS GREAT AND NOBLE UNDERTAKING.*[2]

Ike's message is an obvious attempt to steel us for the tough times ahead—like English King Harry's exhortation in Shakespeare's *Henry V* on the night before the battle of *Agincourt*: "...this band of brothers". But Ike's words are not from a Shakespeare play. This is the real thing.

I feel a surge of loyalty to Ike, the man, more than to the vague and distant government that sent us here. Ike is believable. Even in a printed flyer he comes across as sincere and determined to carry out his difficult task. Part of that task is to inspire us to put forth our utmost effort, and he gives it a good try. The printed words are tangible, something to hold onto. We don't have much else. I fold the flyer and put it in my pack alongside the undelivered letter to my tent-city CO. They don't belong together, but so be it.

> IKE, IT WAS DISCOVERED LATER, HAD PENCILED A SECOND MESSAGE IN LONGHAND AND TUCKED IT INTO HIS WALLET. IT STATES THAT THE INVASION HAD FAILED, AND THAT THE RESPONSIBILITY WAS "...MINE ALONE".[3] Paul Fussell, A COMBAT VETERAN AND WRITER, WAS SO IMPRESSED WITH IKE'S PERSONAL ASSUMPTION OF RESPONSIBILITY THAT HE ENDED HIS BOOK, WARTIME, BY CITING THE SCRAWLED NOTE AS A "BRIGHT SIGNAL IN A DARK TIME."[4]

Channel Crossing [Foxholes 1, 2, 3, 4]
June 8

I'm still with the Tank Destroyers. A couple of days after D-Day we're trucked to a barracks in the port city of Southampton. I'm issued an M-1 rifle coated with cosmoline, a heavy, sticky grease. The TDs get carbines. I would have gotten a carbine too, but I objected. To Infantry GIs, carbines are "pea shooters", carried by men not actually on the line—artillerymen, engineers, mortar-men—whose primary job is something other than confronting the enemy in person. The carbine bullet itself is .30-caliber like the M-1's, but is shorter, blunt-tipped and the brass case isn't necked down from a larger casing, so it has a smaller powder charge. Even stateside the carbine had a reputation of lacking stopping power. The carbine is a lot lighter than the M-1, but even so, any self-respecting rifleman would prefer an M-1.

We clean off the cosmoline with rags and toilet paper and run patches through the bores. There'd be hell to pay if we fired a round through a plugged bore. We're also issued French "invasion money", colorful paper currency in several different denominations. The largest is as big as a page from a stenographer's notebook.[5] Crap games start up, and a guy comes around who needs money to get in a

[Notes for Chapter 6 start on p. 11]

game, or stay in. He has a civilian hunting knife with a leather sheath and he wants four bucks for it, American money. OK. I'm glad to get the knife.

After two days of waiting, we get the word that we're shipping out. We're issued gas masks, fatigues impregnated with gas-resistant chemicals to go over our ODs, and at the last moment, live ammunition. They didn't want us shooting up the barracks. But we get firm orders not to load our rifles. I get a couple of bandoliers of M-1 ammo clips. It's the first live ammo I've seen since the firing range at Ft. McClellan in Alabama. Then we file onto a troop carrier and after maneuvering through a heavy fog past what seems to be a large island, we head out into the English Channel.[6]

While it's still daylight we see planes coming back from the Continent: American P-51 Mustangs, P-47 Thunderbolts, twin-tail P-38 Lightnings, B-24 Liberators, British Spitfires and Mosquito bombers—along with others I don't recognize. Some are limping back, shot up, trailing smoke.[7]

The channel water is scattered over with an uncountable number of craft of all types and sizes. The magnitude of the water-borne effort is more than I could possibly have imagined. We're still on the ship when it gets dark. Nearby vessels become mysterious looming shapes in the murky night.

In the morning we're lying just off the French coast. Ships and landing craft are everywhere. Tethered barrage balloons float overhead, their cables designed to rip the wings and propellers off low-flying German planes. The shoreline and hills behind the beach show clearly in the bleak morning light. We hear no firing, no explosions, see no enemy planes.[8] But the materiel and machines and men of the American invasion forces are everywhere—dumped, parked, stacked, and scattered over the vast disorderly canvas of war. We are a tiny local item, a minuscule smudge. Our entire ship and all of us on it could disappear and its absence would hardly be noticed.

Loaded down with full gear we disembark at what we learn is Utah Beach—a new military designation for an ancient and storied shore.[9] We clamber down landing nets hanging over the side of the troop-carrier into a small landing craft. If we lose our grip and fall into the gap between the ship and the LCI, we'll go down like a

[Notes for Chapter 6 start on p. 11]

stone. As far as I can tell, we all make it. After crossing several hundred yards of water in the LCI we step off onto a floating steel pier and from there jump down onto the sand. We barely get our shoes wet.[10]

We form a long column, single-file, that snakes its way slowly up the beach through the German minefields. Signs say: "*Minen!*"—mute, ominous. Our first contact with the enemy is through his written language. The touch of it is spooky. They were here a short time ago; they are not here now.

We pass by a large piece of shrapnel lying on the sand. It is two-and-a-half feet long, eight inches across, glistening with hundreds of razor-sharp cusps and cutting edges—a beautiful, lethal, evil, instrument of destruction.

> There on the beach
> the terrible wreckage
> of God's Family gone
> wrong, using our ages-won
> precious skills to
> break and kill on a
> scale never before achieved even
> by God himself. Amidst the
> broken things, and the unbroken—the
> as yet new—things (but bent
> on breaking), soft bodies clothed
> uniformly like packaged
> larvae, edge forward through
> narrow barely mine-rid lanes toward
> personal goals which each
> holds secret: this one to seek
> safety at every turn, carrying the
> secure cocoon from home and
> mother's breast, avoiding the
> search-sear light of courage,
> rejecting it as an unwanted
> feared revelation; another to

> seek that searchlight, urged by
> curiosity and duty, and curiosity about
> duty, and duty to curiosity.
> Another still: to test the
> force of hate, if not reasoned, then a
> boil-hot bursting at being
> trapped in the intolerabilities of
> life and war: dire dilemmas not asked
> for, provings not sought: Perhaps
> that particular one, who
> holds that sense, will, in the blaze of
> Life and Light, end as he solves it. Or by luck
> find himself an unplanned champion filling
> the need for all those less lucky, less
> raged. All the others: with hardly any
> thoughts at all, except feet, food and
> flies buzzing on the dead. They, the
> meek of mind, going along, going
> along and-along, many an one destined to
> inherit soon each his own piece of finally
> quiet earth.

On the scale of things displayed before us one man's death would not cause even a ripple. Anonymity assumes a new dimension. Each of us is a jot, an iota. And it's becoming clear that it will be the job of each of us to look out for our own personal jot, our own private iota. For better or worse I'm in the war; I have no choice but to try to be as effective a soldier as I can manage to be.

We walk several miles, most of it uphill, led off by a TD officer. He's looks soft, overweight, not used to long marches. His musette bag—standard issue for TDs—hangs low and awkward on his back. I have an Infantry pack that sits high on my shoulder blades—as a pack should—and I take a smug pride in my more rigorous Infantry training. I watch the TD lieutenant closely for signs of faltering, but he holds up as well as I do.

[Notes for Chapter 6 start on p. 11]

We move up onto the higher terrain behind the beach and pass through a small town named on a sign: *Ste.-Mère-Église*. Applying my school French with some satisfaction, I tell the TDs near me that it means *Saint Mother Church*.[11]

> ALMOST EVERYBODY KNOWS THE STORY OF THE 82ND AIRBORNE PARATROOPERS WHO JUMPED INTO *STE.-MÈRE-ÉGLISE* EARLY D-DAY MORNING. SOME LANDED IN TREES SUSPENDED BY THEIR PARACHUTES AND WERE SHOT BY THE GERMANS. ONE TROOPER GOT HIS CHUTE SNAGGED ON THE CHURCH STEEPLE AND ESCAPED THE FATE OF THE OTHERS BY PRETENDING TO BE DEAD. HOURS LATER OTHER GERMANS CUT HIM DOWN, THEN ABANDONED HIM—STILL ALIVE—WHEN THEY RETREATED.

First foxhole

I have been shipped to France without an entrenching tool. I dig my first foxhole with the hunting knife I bought from the GI crapshooter at Southampton. I choose the knife instead of my bayonet because I don't want to dull the bayonet. It seems more likely that I'll have to use the bayonet against a German than a knife.[12]

In the field where we stop for the night some holes had already been dug, but they're all taken by the time I get there. As a misfit, I've been marching at the end of the column, so I'm last into the field and I have to dig a new hole. I pick a spot along the hedgerow that borders the road, loosen the dirt with my new knife and scoop it out with my helmet and hands. The soil isn't particularly rocky or full of roots, but the method is awkward and the digging slow. I'm warned that the German planes that regularly appear just after nightfall might strafe the road. If they do, my hole would likely catch some rounds, but I don't switch locations. It's the only spot left unless I dig right out in the open. Daylight fades while I'm still digging. Then it starts to drizzle.

Bedcheck Charlie

I don't know any of the guys I'm with, and I spend my first night in France in the rain, alone, under a piece of scrounged cardboard. As predicted, as soon as it gets dark a German plane drones over the beach—"Bedcheck Charlie". Others follow. What we were told in basic training proves to be true—German multi-

[Notes for Chapter 6 start on p. 11]

engine planes make a throbbing sound—because the engines aren't synchronized as they are on American and British aircraft.

Searchlights seek out the enemy among the clouds and our anti-aircraft tracers go up after them in waving hyphenated streams. We're still close enough to the beach to see the show. The enemy is there....

> throbbing the cloud,
> heard but not
> seen in their lethal winged capsules
> mere multiple feet above our
> darkened field of ear-heightened
> presences waiting for what to come.
> Light shafts wave from the beach.
> Tracers drift in heightening arcs
> yearning to touch the planes with hot fingers. And the
> pilots, dedicated to our
> destruction grip controls with
> expectant hands sailing surely
> into the swarm of beautiful light. Fastened
> to the earth we wait. Rain
> sullies our foxholes. The clean
> beauty of the transactions above
> connects to us we know; would
> our grubbily feeble reply hold the same
> aesthetic clarity? Or are we who are ground-bound doomed
> to a muddied art?

The planes don't strafe the road. During the night I keep waking up because of the rain, shifting the cardboard, trying to decide which part of me, or my gear, to try to keep dry. The cardboard gets soggy, but I'm lucky to have it at all.

I stay with the TDs in the same place for another night. Then we move out of the field into a sunken road bordered by hedgerows with large trees growing up out of them. The road is completely canopied over. It's my first encounter with this

[Notes for Chapter 6 start on p. 11]

feature of the Normandy terrain. Some of the roads in England were similar. The road we took down to the village of Dulverton where we put on our GI kadoodler show was like this—a tree-bordered tunnel, dark and foreboding, redolent with history and legend. In England, Robin Hood might have lain in wait for wealthy travelers in such a place. Here in France *d'Artagnan* may have fought duels defending the Queen; *Jean Valjean* may have used its leafy shadows to escape his nemesis, Inspector *Javert*.

Our holes are along the sides of the road up next to the hedgerows. We're told that although the area has been cleared of Germans we shouldn't get careless. I take the warning seriously, stay on the alert, keep my M-1 handy, look into far shadows. The TDs are less concerned.

A day later, we move on foot to a replacement depot where they say we will be assigned to permanent units. A few copies of the *Stars and Stripes*—the GI newspaper—are available. The headlines are about *Caen*, a name that means nothing to me. "Monty Stuck at *Caen*," is the gist of it.

> ALREADY MONTGOMERY, THE BRITISH FIELD MARSHAL, WAS BEHIND SCHEDULE FOR ENLARGING HIS SECTOR OF THE BEACHHEAD. ACCORDING TO HIS OWN "PHASE LINES" HE SHOULD HAVE TAKEN *CAEN* IN THE FIRST 24 HOURS. BUT MONTGOMERY WOULD BE STUCK SHORT OF *CAEN* WELL INTO JULY. HE LATER MAINTAINED THAT IT WAS PART OF HIS PLAN TO ENGAGE THE BULK OF THE AVAILABLE GERMAN ARMOR AND KEEP IT AWAY FROM BRADLEY'S AMERICAN FORCES ON THE *CHERBOURG* PENINSULA, WHICH COULD THEN SWING LIKE A GATE, WITH THE BRITISH AS THE HINGE. BUT MONTGOMERY SEEMED TOO CAUTIOUS FOR MANY CRITICS.[13]

Also in *Stars and Stripes*: the Germans have started sending flying bombs—"V-1s"—over London. They fly low until they run out of fuel, then nose down and explode on contact.[14]

I find a really nice hole already dug and roofed over with plywood. The floor is covered with a carpet of soft dried grass. Shelves have been cut into the walls. But in the morning a non-com comes by and tells me I have to give up the hole to some TDs who are supposed to stay together. It is a big hole, and there's room

[Notes for Chapter 6 start on p. 11]

for four of them. Maybe they're a gun crew. Or maybe it's just a ruse to get the hole. But it is bigger than one guy needs so I'm ousted. I find another hole, roofless and much less luxurious. Of the two, it is definitely not the better 'ole.[15]

That afternoon an irate French farmer stumps into our field talking loud to anyone who will listen. I quickly learn that my skimpy school French isn't going to get me very far with the natives here. *La Plume de Ma Tante* won't cut much mustard. This one talks much too fast with a rough guttural sound and I catch only a word here and there. It turns out he's complaining that the GIs have taken the hay he needs for his *vaches*, his cows. And his cows got loose because the GIs left a gate open. He doesn't get his hay back, but a non-com tells us not to take any more, and to close any gates we go through. The non-com tells us this because he's been told to tell us, for the sake of international amity. The incident is just an irritation in the midst of more important things on his mind. But I feel better about losing the big hole. At least I'm not guilty of using the French farmer's hay.

At the replacement depot the war doesn't seem very real. No searchlights and tracers at night, no German bombers. As with GIs everywhere, it takes us only a short time to form new habits and routines, come up with new rumors, new words for the GI lexicon. The replacement depot is a *repple depple*. The iodide-treated water we have to drink is *I died* water—"I drank it and I died". *Gourbesville*, the last French town we passed on the way here, is *Goobersville*. The minutiae of the daily experience assume priority over everything else. But we're not camped out on the Somerset hills of England. A wrecked glider is stark proof of that. And a short hike would take us to within sound of the fighting. That's what one of the non-coms says. How far? Five or six miles.

⊕

[Notes for Chapter 6 start on p. 11]

Notes for Chapter 6

1. The C-47s that went over that night were carrying paratroopers of the American 82nd Airborne Division to their drop zones in Normandy. They had taken off from airfields north of us across the Bristol Channel, which we could see as a bright strip of water from our tent city on clear days. We were directly under the paratroopers' route to the English Channel and France. The gliders in the second wave carried airborne infantry and equipment the paratroopers couldn't carry on their persons when they jumped—anti-tank guns and heavy radios, even Jeeps and light artillery. Many of the gliders crash-landed in the small Normandy fields but enough of their cargo got to the troopers to help them succeed in their mission.

   The planes that towed the gliders were the same planes that had carried the troops in the first wave, returned for a second trip. The C-47 was military version of the civilian Douglas DC-3 and was the work-horse of the war. They were also called Skytrains, and by the British, Dakotas.

   Eisenhower was strongly advised against the air drop of the 82nd and 101st Airborne by British Chief Air Marshal Trafford Leigh-Mallory, who predicted it would be a costly disaster. There was quite a lot of confusion due to wide dispersal of the pathfinders (the first to jump), and casualties were fairly heavy, but in the main the American airborne operations succeeded, and Leigh-Mallory had to eat crow. Neither Leigh-Mallory nor Eisenhower, however, anticipated the serious problems that the hedgerows would present, and neither had good intelligence about recently flooded areas in the drop zones along the *Merderet* River where a considerable number of paratroopers became mired, and some drowned.

2. The message was drafted by General Raymond Barker, Eisenhower's Deputy Chief of Staff. It was redrafted several times, changed significantly, and improved, Barker said, by Ike himself. (*Eisenhower at War*, by David Eisenhower, Ike's grandson, page 257) Copies of Ike's message were issued to all first wave participants the night of June 5th.

[Notes for Chapter 6 start on p. 11]

I have not found reference anywhere to the prodigious effort required to print the flyer and distribute it to all troops simultaneously while maintaining tight security. This would seem to be a greatly under-reported aspect of SHAEF's activities, and could well be the subject of a book.

For D-Day there was also a radio message, much shorter, that announced to the world that Allied troops had landed on the European Continent. A German radio announcement of the invasion had actually been first.

British newspapers headlined General Mark Clark's capture of Rome rather than the Normandy invasion because they didn't get the word about D-Day until after press time.

3. This incident has been related in many places. One of the most direct sources is Harry Butcher's *My Three Years with Eisenhower*. The full note read as follows:

> OUR LANDINGS IN THE CHERBOURG-HAVRE AREA HAVE FAILED TO GAIN A SATISFACTORY FOOTHOLD AND I HAVE WITHDRAWN THE TROOPS. MY DECISION TO ATTACK AT THIS TIME AND PLACE WAS BASED ON THE BEST INFORMATION AVAILABLE. THE TROOPS, THE AIR AND THE NAVY DID ALL THAT BRAVERY AND DEVOTION TO DUTY COULD DO. IF ANY BLAME OR FAULT ATTACHES TO THE ATTEMPT IT IS MINE ALONE.

When he showed the note to Butcher, Ike said he'd written a similar note before each of the previous amphibious operations in the ETO—North Africa and Sicily—and had torn them up when they became irrelevant. This one, however has been preserved.

4. Fussell also makes a point of Ike's change from passive to active mode— from "...the troops have been withdrawn." to "...I have withdrawn the troops." The final wording characterizes the hypothetical failure as a direct consequence of his own decision rather than of "...some distant, anonymous agency..." (Fussell, *Wartime*, p. 297)

[Notes for Chapter 6 start on p. 11]

A photograph of Ike's note, complete with the penciled original wording crossed out, appears on Page 88 of Time-Life's *The Second Front*. It is worth looking at for its eerie sense of immediacy.

5. The invasion money caused a flap with General Charles De Gaulle, self-proclaimed head of the Provisional French Government—miffed because he had not been consulted. He said there was no French governmental authority behind the printed money, and that it was therefore worthless.

6. The island was the Isle of Wight, the place of origin for my family name.

7. In basic training our aircraft recognition training consisted of one three-hour session with projected slides of Allied and Enemy aircraft silhouettes in various attitudes. Although the Mosquito bomber's fuselage was plywood, it proved to be one of the most effective aircraft of the Invasion.

8. Most of the German batteries had been overrun, but one remained that continued to bombard the beach sporadically.

9. In 1066 William the Conqueror, AKA the Duke of Normandy, set forth on the *Norman Conquest* of England from Normandy harbors.

10. According to several historical accounts, the "mulberries", artificial piers and harbors constructed in England and floated across the channel, were not used at Utah, but I distinctly remember stepping off onto a steel grid a foot or so above the water and that it moved perceptibly underfoot.

11. *Ste.-Mère Église* was destined to become famous as the first French town liberated by Allied forces.

When I was doing research for this book I found a 1944 *Michelin* map of *Normandie* that shows a town a few miles east of *Cherbourg* labeled *St.-Père-Église*—Saint Father Church. The name struck my funny-bone. It must have been a typo because both *The New York Times World Atlas* and the *National Geographic Atlas of the World, 8th Edition,* show the town as *St.-Pierre-Église*—St Peter Church—which makes more sense.

[Notes for Chapter 6 start on p. 11]

12. The matter of keeping our bayonets sharp was never mentioned in training or in combat, and nothing was ever issued to us for that purpose.

13. Carlo D'Este, in *Decision in Normandy*, has an extended discussion of Monty's inability to make progress. See ANNOTATED BIBLIOGRAPHY, BOOK FOUR, AN ALMOST PERFECT WAR.

14. The V-1 was the first German *Vergeltungswaffen*—Vengeance weapon. Called "buzz bombs" by the Americans, and by the British, "doodlebugs" and "divers", they caused approximately the same number of casualties over time as the D-Day assaults on the beaches. The V-2 was a giant ballistic rocket with an explosive war-head that rose into the upper atmosphere before falling unguided to Earth.

15. *The Better 'Ole* was the name of a PX at Camp Upton on Long Island where I went after induction in Buffalo. A big painting hung over the bar showing a cartoon of a crowded World War One shell hole that a soldier has just jumped into to escape a hail of bullets and shrapnel. When he complains about the conditions, one of the Brits says: "If y'know of a better 'ole, mate, go to it!" The cartoon had been there since the First World War.

M-1 Garand Rifle — .30 cal. — Semi-automatic — 8-round, top-loading clips

Photo - Wikimedia Commons

[Notes for Chapter 6 start on p. 11]

7

A DIVISION IN JEOPARDY

Replacements
for the wounded and dead [Foxholes 5, 6]

I spend most of my time at the repple depple trying to learn how to throw my new knife. I try to throw it flat, overhand, without spinning. If you throw a knife end-over-end, the amount of flip you give it is critical. Knife throwers at side-shows throw from a known distance so they can judge the amount of flip very accurately and can hold the knives by their tips. If I need to throw this knife I won't know ahead of time what the distance will be. So I try to learn a new way to throw it. To keep it flying flat I give the butt end of the knife handle a little tick with my fingers just as it slides off my palm. That way I can throw it overhand as hard as I can without the extra force affecting the way the tip will strike the target. I practice a lot and it's coming along pretty well. It's something to do, and it could prove to be useful. I figure as long as I am here, heading for combat, I should do whatever I can to give myself a better chance of coming out of it alive. Here in the repple depple I can't think of anything else to do toward that end. We can't fire our rifles, even to zero them in. I ask a non-com about it but he doesn't have an answer, just says we can't fire them. So I practice with the knife, and practice some more. Every tuft of grass is a German's throat.

I am still with the Tank Destroyers. The officers and non-coms don't bother us. We're left completely on our own, except for the most basic instructions: We're not to leave the field where our holes are except to get water and chow. We're to use the already-dug slit trenches for latrines, and fill them in with dirt as we go. We may be assigned to dig more trenches. It's OK to smoke. That's about it.

One time I walk past the overweight TD lieutenant, pants down, squatting over a slit trench. He recognizes me as the Infantry guy in his TD outfit, but the acknowledgement is strained on both sides. We're doubly embarrassed—because of the close-up officer/enlisted-man confrontation, and the particular activity I find him engaged in. Officers still have separate latrines, even in combat areas if there isn't

[Notes for Chapter 7 start on p. 25]

actual shooting going on—dug by GIs of course—but here they have to use them out in the open like the rest of us. For all the outward evidence, in the States and in England, commissioned officers never needed to defecate.[1]

We have to go to another field to get water from a big canvas bag hanging under a tripod. The iodide treatment makes it almost undrinkable. Hot chow is ladled out from big GI cans, and we slosh our mess kits around in another one that's full of steaming wash water. Just like home.

There's a glider in the same field, one of our airborne's, crash-landed, nosed into the ground. We wonder if the human cargo fared as badly as the glider itself. It's since been stripped of everything of any possible use—plywood for foxhole roofs and floors, wire. Only the skeleton framework remains.[2]

We get word that American troops have cut off the *Cherbourg* Peninsula. I don't know the geography involved, but the fact is supposed to be important.[3]

"This will not happen again…"

On the fifth day at the repple depple a non-com comes looking for me and takes me to where a bunch of other Infantry guys are gathered. We're told that we've been assigned to the 90th Division as replacements for casualties—wounded, and dead. The thought is unsettling, especially since there are so many of us.[4]

That night we're marched into a dark field and told not to smoke. As German night bombers throb in the moonless sky, a command-grade officer [PROBABLY COL. BARTH] tells us that the 90th Division has not earned a good name in the fighting. Men have refused to obey orders and have run back in the face of the enemy.

"This will not happen again," he says. He has just taken over command of one of the regiments [357] and he makes it very clear that he is determined to build a reputation of success—for himself as well as the units he will be responsible for. It had never occurred to me that American soldiers might run back in combat. It was certainly never discussed in basic, although the *Articles of War* that were read to us twice almost certainly covered such an eventuality. Imagining the circumstances that could cause such behavior casts a sobering pall over all of us.

[Notes for Chapter 7 start on p. 25]

> I HADN'T YET READ ABOUT THE UNION ARMY'S ROUT IN THEIR FIRST MAJOR ENGAGEMENT OF THE AMERICAN CIVIL WAR, WITH WASHINGTON SOCIETY LOOKING ON. NOR STEPHEN CRANE'S *THE RED BADGE OF COURAGE*, WHERE SOLDIERS RUNNING BACK WAS A LARGE PART OF THE STORY.[5]

June 24, 1944

Next morning I find a non-com and tell him that I don't have an entrenching tool. He comes back in a half hour with a small shovel with a wooden T-shaped handle. It's not the all-metal folding combination type the other guys have, that can also serve as a pick. That's OK with me because it's lighter and it looks as if the blade might cut roots better. I can probably also swing it like a hatchet. It has a canvas cover with hooks that fit onto the belt, so it must be kosher.

The next day we're told to get our gear together and we form up into a single column behind a couple of non-coms and start walking west. No "Hup-two-three-four", and nobody talks. After about three hours, with a couple of breaks, we sense a different atmosphere. Are we getting near the front lines? Nobody says so. It's a feeling more than anything else. The clue isn't noise, but silence. The air itself seems different. Strands of wire lie along the ditches and are strung raggedly on trees along the road. We pass several places where someone has cut away the branches of the hedgerows to make guard-posts or roadblocks. Germans, I'd guess, because the camouflaged sides are facing us as we approach them. But the positions are all deserted. The non-coms leading the way don't give them the slightest notice.[6]

We come over a hill and are starting down the other side when we see a couple of soldiers step out into the road ahead of us. They're wearing GI helmets and carrying M-1s. We don't have to be told they've been in combat. They have an instantly recognizable look about them: unshaven, tired; a fatigued confidence—gods of knowledge, power, killing and death. We climb up a small path that goes through the high hedgerow on the right-hand side of the road and find ourselves in a dim orchard, boxed in by hedgerows on all four sides. The apple trees make a continuous canopy overhead. We're told not to smoke.

[Notes for Chapter 7 start on p. 25]

We sit on the ground along the hedgerow nearest the road while a couple of the non-coms talk in low tones. One has a field phone. No rank shows on their field jackets or helmets. After about an hour we're taken to the downhill side of the orchard where we can see out into the bright daylight. A non-com points out a road-crossing. The Germans have it zeroed-in with artillery, and shell it at random intervals. We'll move through the road-crossing running, then break off to the left.

We go back through the hedgerow onto the road and, imitating the non-com in the lead, move forward in crouched positions. It's hard to move crouched over without looking scared. When we get close to the road-crossing we break into a run, get through the road crossing, then go left along a high hedgerow, and peel off two at a time into holes that are already dug. The guys who were in the holes move out, going back the way we came. We pass close and they look tired and dirty and beat, but they're quick to move, eager to go.[7]

The hole I'm assigned to is big, dug deep into the yellow earth of a six-foot high hedgerow. Trees go up another twenty feet. The bank of the hedgerow is partly hollowed out so when we're in the hole we're inside the hedgerow itself. It's also dug down about ten inches, there's a cave-like wing to the left, and a couple of steps dug into the hedgerow so we can look over it when we're watching out front.

There's nobody between us and the Germans. If we look over the hedgerow can they see us? Nobody warns us against it. So I carefully edge up and take a look. There's nothing to see but apple trees. And there's no noise of war, no shooting. No yelling. We're not even told to keep watch over the hedgerow. The field behind our holes is almost unmarked. One place shows some raw dirt, and as we came in we saw some broken trees, split, cracked open. Otherwise, we could be in rural Upstate New York, or Ohio, on a peaceful summer day. But we aren't in New York or Ohio. Men are out there in front of us who speak a dark, harsh language and they will kill us if they can.

The sense of reality is thin. The only connection is through the sober, wearied non-coms. With them there's no bantering, no chickenshit. What they say is bare raw fact. They're not curt, but they're not talkative either. I feel a lot better when there's one of them around.

[Notes for Chapter 7 start on p. 25]

My hole-mate is a tall gawky kid who talks a lot about home and his dog and his mother. He's got a B-A-R. That evening before dark he tells me he sees Gerries running around under the apple trees out front. I look and can't see anybody but he says he's sure he saw Gerries. I tell him he should tell somebody about it. He's apparently not going to tell anyone, so I decide that I will. When a non-com comes by I tell him that my hole-mate says he saw Germans out front, under the orchard trees. I make sure the non-com knows it was my hole-mate who said it, not me. The non-com steps into our hole and looks over the hedgerow. He doesn't say anything, doesn't ridicule the idea, but nothing is done.

Just before dark some German shells come over. None of us new guys know what to expect. The 105s that were fired over us in basic training were so far over our heads we could barely hear them as a faint whisper. The cadre were more worried about the shells than we were. Rumor had it that something had gone wrong on a past exercise.

Here, my first reaction is curiosity, to watch, to see what's happening, and the first thing I learn is that you can't see a shell as it goes over, even when there's enough light. They're invisible spectres. At first the shells land well behind us, coming over with a sort of spiraling whisper, quite high, exploding back of us by a half mile or so. As long as they hit back there it's not so bad.[8]

Then they start getting closer. As the sound of the rush and explosions of the shells gets louder, we try to get deeper into the hole. The cave-like wing is the safest place to be—except that a direct hit could bury you alive—but it's not big enough for both of us. It's not big enough even for one guy's entire body. Part of you has to stick out. The guy who isn't in the cave isn't nearly as well protected.

Our artillery has been firing too, and I begin to tell the difference, whether the shells are ours, going out toward the enemy, or theirs, coming toward us. Finally the German shells are splitting the air close overhead and making angry flashes when they explode, ripping up the dirt and splintering trees, shooting out pieces of metal that hum when they go past. The shells come in groups, salvos, three and four at a time. I forget my curiosity and think only of protecting myself. My hole-mate is out of sight, head-first in the cave. Only his feet stick out. The dirt bank of

[Notes for Chapter 7 start on p. 25]

the hedgerow protects me from out front, and from the right and left, but from behind there's no protection for any part of me that's above ground level, and I can't get all of my body below the surface—the hole is too shallow. When a shell comes close my entire body clamps tight; I can't prevent it. One shell sprays dirt in the hole and cuts leaves off the trees overhead. But after twenty minutes the shells stop coming and we are not hit.

Now I know what a shelling is like. It pounds you down helpless into the soil. But I recover quickly. A non-com comes by in the dark. I've noticed that the experienced men walk around with their mouths[9] slightly open, to hear better, or maybe to equalize air pressure from exploding shells. I'm sitting up in the hole, and I look up at the non-com as he passes. He seems surprised that I'm alert and watching. My hole-mate is still in the cave.

"You OK?" the non-com asks, low-voiced.

"Yeah."

"He OK?"

"Yeah."

"They might try to get through after the shelling," he says. "We have to set up a guard." Do I have a watch? Yeah, the Bullova I bought at Ft. McClellan from Wenner for seven bucks. Not the kind of watch to fit these circumstances, more like a ladies' watch, but the Army doesn't issue us watches and mine is pretty accurate. So far it's been OK. If I can keep the water and dirt out of it.

We have to stand guard "one-on, two-off". That means you stand guard for an hour, then you wake up the next guy and sleep for two hours, then when the third guy wakes you up you go back on guard again. You keep shifting the guard among three guys until it gets to be morning. I go first. My hole-mate still hasn't come out of the cave. I try to tell him about standing guard. He grunts, almost a whine, nearly inaudible.[10]

"I'll wake you up in an hour," I tell him, my head in the cave, not wanting to yell. The non-com tells the third guy, in the next hole, about guard and then disappears

[Notes for Chapter 7 start on p. 25]

back along the hedgerow where he came from. I'm on my own. It only takes a minute for my nerves to get out on the edge—not nervous, but alert, like a mink.[11] What will happen? Was the shelling to soften us up for an attack? Will the Germans try to infiltrate our positions? In the repple depple there were a lot of rumors about snipers, and infiltration. If they do try, which way will they come? Across the field from out front? Along the hedgerow?

> They are out there, out in
> the invisible dark where death
> works. They
> know I am here. They
> are there in the
> night, and in the
> day similarly garbed, but adapted to be invisible in
> different surrounds. They
> are wraiths, but solid wraiths that
> spit, shout shells, single and many
> bullets, spray steel. They
> watch, wait for
> small mistakes and will
> strike when I am not expecting. They may be
> here, already, in unexpected form.
> They…

I check my weapons, pull the bolt of my M-1 part way back till I can see the round in the chamber to make sure it's there and ready to fire—it's almost too dark to see—then ease it home, careful not to let the bolt click when it seats. I leave the safety on. Unfasten the strap on my hunting knife sheath. Get my two grenades ready—partially straighten the pins so they'll pull out easy but not fall out by themselves. Pull off the safety tape from the grenade handles till there's only an inch of it left stuck on. I un-snap one pocket on my cartridge belt, pull a clip out part way, then slide it back. I pull my bayonet out of its scabbard and stick it in the dirt where I can reach it. No, it'll be better to have it on the M-1. I slide it onto the bayonet stud and lock it into place. The small click seems loud enough to alert the entire German army. It's the new short bayonet they told us about in basic. It

[Notes for Chapter 7 start on p. 25]

won't get in the way too much even when I'm in the hole. I put a couple of baseball size rocks on the edge of the hole where they'll be handy. I don't intend to be caught unprepared. And there's my hole-mate's B-A-R. I could use that.

It's dark and very quiet. The sky is clouded over and there's no moon or stars. Looking down along the back of the hedgerow I can see only a few yards. The Germans could be right in among us at any moment without warning. Are they good at night fighting? Will they open up with automatic fire, run at us yelling, or try to garrote us silently, one by one?

I recall the skimpy hand-to-hand training we had in basic training at Ft. McLellan, and the "grapple-grips" Williams taught me on the troopship coming over. Will I have to use those barely-learned skills tonight? My watch has luminous hands. I remember the night field exercise in basic where we were able to see a guy puff on a cigarette 500 yards away. I keep the watch covered under the cuff of my field jacket, and I resist a very strong desire to smoke.

Out front over the hedgerow it's even darker. They could sneak up and toss grenades right into our holes. The hedgerow masks sound from the field out front unless you're standing up looking over it with your head in the gap cut through the branches. Why don't they tell us what to expect, what to do? There's no sound and the hour goes very slowly, dark moment by dark moment. I check my weapons over and over, trying to plan exactly what I'll do if different things happen. But my first guard period goes by and nothing happens. I try to wake up my hole-mate but I can't rouse him. How hard should I poke him? I poke again, jostle him, tell him he's got to get up and stand guard, but he doesn't come out. I don't dare shout. What the hell is the matter with him? He's breathing, so he's not dead. Am I stuck with a psycho? What am I supposed to do?

I decide to wake up the third guy in our guard. He's in the next hole down the hedgerow to the right. When I'm out of our hole I feel naked. I relieve myself as quietly as I can, waving the stream around so it doesn't splash in a puddle. Then I find the third guy and wake him up. He grabs his M-1, rousing instantly. I tell him it's his turn to stand guard. He remembers that he was supposed to be third, not second, but I tell him that I can't get my hole-mate to wake up. "He's psycho or

[Notes for Chapter 7 start on p. 25]

something," I say, feeling that I'm being unfair because I don't know if it's true. But I can't get him up to take his guard, and we've gotta do something. I've got to get some sleep myself.

I give the guy the watch. "OK", he says.

"It glows in the dark," I tell him. "Better keep it covered."

"What'll I do after my guard?" he says. A GI is asking me what to do. How do I know what to do?

"Try to wake him up," I say. "If you can't wake him up, wake me up. Somebody's gotta be on guard." That's the way we leave it. I'm still on the edge, alert, but I fall asleep quickly yielding my fate to Morpheus and the gods of war.

My hole-mate wouldn't wake up for the second guy either so we stand guard one-on, one-off, the toughest kind. You barely get to sleep and the guy's poking you to wake you up again. The next times I'm on guard I have to work hard to stay alert. Sleep rises up from within like warm inky bathwater. But we get through the night and the Germans don't come.

I'm on guard when morning comes. The light sneaks in, there's mist, and I can see somebody moving down at the other end of the hedgerow. A GI. Except for being in a war, and being short of sleep, it's a pretty nice morning.

⊕

Guys start to move around, busying themselves with housekeeping, opening their rations, relieving themselves. Even my hole-mate comes out of the cave. I tell him we couldn't wake him up for guard duty but he just looks at me with a hurt look on his face.

"Nobody woke me up," he says. I let it go. He's beyond reasoning with.

Nobody goes far from their holes, but the morning is pretty much like anywhere else, like the bivouac at Ft. McClellan in Alabama's Talladega National Forest, or Camp Kenan, the YMCA Camp on Lake Ontario. It's hard to believe this is the front line of a real war.

[Notes for Chapter 7 start on p. 25]

I see some wire going past our hole and follow it back with my eye and see that it comes to a loose end. If anybody is depending on a message on that wire he's not going to get it. Was it cut by the shelling? Is it important? I'm too green to know. We've seen a lot of wire lying around, seemingly abandoned. But I go looking for a non-com and find one down a few holes to our left. It's the same non-com who set up the guard last night. Maybe he's our squad leader. There weren't any introductions. I tell him about the cut wire. He seems surprised that I got out of my hole and came looking for him to tell him about it. Why would he be surprised? It's a reasonable thing to do, isn't it, to report something like that? He comes to take a look, warning me not to get careless. There've been snipers in the area.

The wire is a telephone wire, he says. It goes to the Company Commander's telephone. We could hook it back up ourselves, I say. No, they'll send a runner back for a signal corps guy. In twenty minutes one of them comes up and I show him the wire and he splices it back together and checks it with a hand set. I'm not going to get a medal, but I feel I've made a small contribution to the war.

Then the non-com notices the hunting knife on my belt. "That knife isn't GI," he says. I know that, I tell him, but it's come in handy.

"We've got a new hard-ass regimental commander," he says. "He's ordered all equipment to be standard issue. I'll see if I can get another knife for you." He's holding out his hand. Is he serious? I've spend a lot of hours learning to throw this knife. I don't want a different one. But he insists. "I gotta take it." So I unbuckle my belt, pull it through the strap on the knife scabbard, and give him the knife. It's like losing a friend. But he's as good as his word. Late in the morning he comes by with a U.S. Government-Issue trench knife. They took it off a guy who was hit. Killed? He doesn't say.

"Some guys strap it on their ankle," he says. "That way it's easier to get at when you're cramped up in a hole."

I'm glad to get it, and I'm glad he didn't just take my hunting knife for himself, or to sell, but all my knife-throwing practice was for naught. This knife won't throw worth a damn. It's like a two-edged dagger with a protruding hilt at the base of the blade that will catch on my hand if I try to throw it flat. But I buckle on the trench-knife sheath low around my right legging. The non-com was right—it's easy to grab there.

⊕

Notes for Chapter 7

1. This was the first sign I saw of the progressive erosion of the strict officer-enlisted man distinction as both got closer to combat. Another would be the lack of insignia of rank on helmets and jackets, but officers did wear cloth insignia on their shirt collars. When General Patton took over Third Army on August 1st, he required officers in his Army to wear their rank where it could be seen. As for digging foxholes, I don't remember ever seeing a commissioned officer digging his own foxhole. But I don't remember seeing a GI doing it for an officer either. How they got dug I don't know to this day.

2. For details of glider crashes and casualties see *The Glider Gang* by Milton Dank. Also *Night Drop*, by S.L.A. Marshall. American gliders were Wacos; British gliders were mostly Horsas. Both were made of plywood with skids for landing gear. Rough landings were the norm.

3. The *Cherbourg* Peninsula was cut by the 9th Division, General Manton Eddy commanding officer. The importance was mainly that if the line could be held, it would isolate the German troops still defending *Cherbourg*, a major French port at the tip of the peninsula [MAP 1, P. iv]. Such a port was needed by the Allies to get materiel and supplies into France. Even after *Cherbourg* was captured everything still had to come in over the beaches for several weeks because the Germans did such a thorough job of destroying *Cherbourg's* harbor facilities.

4. The designation *replacements* was later changed to *reinforcements* after the negative effect of the former was noted by the brass. For a discussion of this issue see Antony Beevor's *D-Day, The Battle for Normandy*, p. 257.

5. John Ellis, in *The Sharp End of the Fight*, has an entire chapter on routs by ground troops. General James Gavin, then the 82nd Airborne's Assistant Commanding Officer, describes the problems of stopping routs at *La Fière* Causeway in *On to Berlin*, and S.L.A. Marshall includes several graphic descriptions of panic in *Men Against Fire*. His last chapter of *Night Drop* is titled, simply, *"Rout"*.

   Several other frank treatments of routs can be found in the war literature, but at the time, the whole idea that American soldiers might run from the enemy was completely new to me.

6. These could have been GI positions because our battalion's objective was both to keep Germans from moving north to reinforce those holding out at *Cherbourg*, and from moving south to rejoin the main German forces

7. The men we replaced were in G-Company, 357th Regiment (ours).

8. In daylight you can see 105 howitzer shells going away from you through the air if you are standing next to the artillery piece when it is fired. This was demonstrated to us at Ft. McClellan. But when they're going across your field of vision you cannot see them.

9. In Remarque's *The Road Back, the narrator says*: "…we open wide our mouths to save our eardrums." (p. 13)

10. You could get an idea of how serious the situation was by the kind of guard you had to stand. "One-on, three-off" meant that only one out of four guys had to be awake and the situation was not thought to be critical

11. Maybe not quite as alert as a mink. I visited a mink ranch once. As we passed the ends of the long cages, each mink, at the other end near its nest box, emptied its bladder. "They always do that," the mink rancher said, "…to be ready for action."

⌗

[Notes for Chapter 7 start on p. 25]

8
PATROL

Have you ever fired a Thompson sub?

The second day after the shelling, a non-com I haven't seen before and a lieutenant, both about the same build, slim and taller than average, come by and squat down by my hole. The lieutenant holds a short-barreled, lead-colored, deadly-looking weapon.

"Have you ever fired a Thompson sub?" the lieutenant asks me. I tell him no. I wonder why they're asking. Are they looking for information? For somebody who knows something about a Thompson sub-machinegun? No, that's not what they have in mind.

They proceed to show me how it works—how to snap the safety on and off, how to set it for single-shot and for full automatic. How to unlatch the clip and pull it out of the bottom of the receiver. The clip is actually two clips taped together with dirty white adhesive tape to make a single unit, reversible end-for-end, for quick re-loading. Each clip is about eight inches long and holds a dozen or so rounds of .45-caliber ammunition, the same ammo used in the Army's .45-caliber pistol.[1]

"Come on down to the end of the hedgerow and try it out," the lieutenant says. For what, I wonder.

We go down along the hedgerow to the right until we come to an open place where we can see out ahead of our lines. The lieutenant tells another GI to keep watch out front, then hands me the Thompson sub. It is heavy, compact, built of thick chunks of dull pewter-colored steel. The stock is wood, chestnut-colored, nicked and beat-up. The weapon has seen hard use. Some Thompson subs have a forward-mounted hand grip to steady the weapon with the left hand. This one doesn't, but there's a wooden front member under the barrel to hold onto. You've got to hold onto something, the gun jumps up with such force when fired in auto. Even I know that.

[Notes for Chapter 8 start on p. 38]

"Put it on single-shot," the lieutenant says, watching to see how quick I catch on. The tall non-com is just standing by. He seems pleased with himself. I don't know what they're up to, but I've been singled out for something, and it's not for a gig or a reprimand.[2]

The Thompson sub has the ugly beauty of a snub-nosed rattlesnake, but its rattle and venom are a thousand times more deadly than any rattlesnake. Now the lieutenant says:

"See if you can hit that tree out there." He points to an apple tree about twenty yards out front. It's a fair-size tree with a trunk about a foot across.

"Don't use the sights," he says, "Just bring it up and fire."

I bring the Thompson sub up so the butt touches my shoulder, aim by instinct—looking at the tree not the sights—then pull the trigger.

"You hit it!" the sergeant crows. "You got it," the lieutenant says, "I saw the bark fly." I didn't see any bark fly. I didn't see anything fly. I could have missed by a country mile.[3]

What they want is for me to take the Thompson sub out on a patrol in front of our lines.

"When you go out, put it on auto," the sergeant says. "If you have to shoot, aim at the feet. It'll crawl right up a man."

"One round will knock a man down," says the lieutenant.

The gun didn't jump as much as I expected. My M-1 has a harder kick.

The indian, Steel

There'll be another man on the patrol, an indian named Steel.[4] The name could have come right out of American frontier fiction—maybe Altsheler's *Keepers of the Trail*. There's no special significance to Steel's name, of course, but if it's an omen it's not a bad one. Steel has an M-1 and is supposed to cover me.[5] Today is the first time I've seen Steel. He's dark-skinned, shorter than I, built more solid,

[Notes for Chapter 8 start on p. 38]

almost squat. He seems to be in control of himself—the archetypical taciturn American indian.[6]

Ready or not

Steel and I don't discuss anything about the patrol. I just hope he knows what to do and he hopes I do. Neither of us has any reason to trust the other, except that the lieutenant picked us for the patrol. I know how flimsy the basis for picking me was, and it was probably even flimsier for Steel—because I've been picked to lead out.[7]

The instructions for conducting the patrol are equally skimpy:

"Look for bodies, abandoned equipment, vehicles. Don't fire unless you have to. When you come back, run the last twenty yards." That's it. No instructions about how far to go, nothing about taking prisoners.[8] Nothing about trying to help any wounded we might find. Nothing about taking stuff from dead Germans for the intelligence guys. No instructions about whether we should walk, run, or crawl. Nothing about getting word back if we need help or see something important. No password if we can't get back until after dark.[9]

Sniper

We will go out through the gate in the left-hand corner of our field—the same gate where a GI got shot by a sniper yesterday. One of our men was standing just inside the gate when a single bullet went through his body and sailed down along the back of our hedgerow past my hole with a whinging-spanging noise.[10] It happened about one o'clock in the afternoon during a stretch of bright sunshine. I was sitting on the edge of the hole adjusting the straps on my trench-knife when the bullet went past me, probably no more than five feet away.

Because of the sniper, we will go through the gate running. He'll have the gate in the crosshairs of his telescopic sight and if we stop even for a second he'll get us. At least one of us—if he's still there.

As a backup for Steel and me, my hole-mate will be just inside the gate lying prone with his B-A-R. I don't feel good about that *at* all. If we get in trouble he'll be

[Notes for Chapter 7 start on p. 38]

useless. Worse, he might shoot *us*. When we get thirty yards out we might look like the "Gerries" he claimed to see running around under the apple trees the first night we were here. But there will be better heads back where he is, and if he freezes or screws up they could take the B-A-R away from him and use it themselves. Of course I don't know anything about the sergeant and lieutenant either. The fact that they picked me to lead the patrol doesn't get them a lot of brownie points.

And if we don't get back, they'll lose the Thompson sub.

"OK", the lieutenant says, and tips his chin toward the gate. They open the gate a couple of feet and I start out in a semi-crouch, running. I will be in the open with no cover for a hundred yards or so and if the sniper is still out there, and watching, he's bound to see me. I wonder if I should go down on my elbows and knees. Not yet. I have to take my chances and just go. I weave a little, but not much. Dodging back and forth might catch their attention.

I try to see everything. The hedgerow on my right looks undisturbed, no obvious openings cut through, but we can't know if Germans are watching us through the branches from the other side. If any Germans are there, the noise of my running could alert them. I slow to a crouched walk and glance back. Steel is just coming out of the gate.

Small though it is, I am conscious of my role as patrol leader and feel a spurt of satisfaction that Steel is actually following me. He could have objected, as I would have objected if my hole-mate had been picked as patrol leader. I wouldn't follow him anywhere. But Steel is following as if he thinks I know what I'm doing, and I'm trying to act like I know what I'm doing.

After the first open space there will be some cover—a large dirt berm about ten feet high, thirty feet long, with a wide base that tapers up to a ridge about four feet across [MAP 2, P. 32]. The berm is bare of trees but is covered with grass. When I started out I could just see the top of the berm because of the upward swell of the terrain. The berm parallels the big hedgerow on my right, which is an extension of the same hedgerow our holes are in. The berm is separated from the hedgerow by a two-track dirt road that goes out into enemy territory.[11]

[Notes for Chapter 8 start on p. 38]

The berm could be more trap than cover. It's a perfect setup for an ambush. Or the sniper could be there. When I get close I see that the entire space between the berm and the hedgerow is filled with water. The road disappears under the water and reappears at the other end of the berm. To go any farther I will have to either go through the water or go out around the berm. The latter will put me out in the open field again, in full view. The road and the pond are shaded by the tall trees in the hedgerow. An enemy looking toward our lines would surely suspect the road as an obvious route for anyone to come out from our lines, but even so, to venture out into the open field seems to be purely asking to be seen.[12]

I look back and Steel is twenty yards behind me, on one knee, M-1 ready, watching me. I'd rather he'd be watching for signs of the enemy. I decide to go through the water and I signal that's what I'm going to do, and for him to wait where he is.

I start into the water and after three steps it comes over my shoe-tops. The bottom is muddy, but not sucking mud. It takes a couple of seconds for the cool water to get into my shoes. Then my leggings, and the new trench knife and its scabbard strapped to my ankle get soaked with the muddy water. I feel guilty, like a little kid walking in a puddle. In basic when I didn't clean my shoes and leggings after the night infiltration course I got gigged. Here, nobody will care.

Once in the water I find I have to walk very slowly so as not to make splashing noises. A German on the other side of the hedgerow, or behind the berm, not knowing we are there, will be alerted by a splash. Even the water dripping when I lift my feet makes too much noise, so I try to move my feet without lifting them out of the water—the way indians paddled their canoes in the Altsheler books. But it slows me down too much. As long as I am in the water I am a sitting—crouching—duck. Now I'm having second thoughts about going through the water. I feel Steel watching me. Because of the upward bulge of the terrain, we are beyond sight of the others. They cannot help us.

I move ahead very carefully, lifting my feet not quite out of the water, and putting them down slowly. It's like still-hunting deer. If you choose to be quiet you must be absolutely quiet. If you make any noise at all you might as well go crashing through the underbrush, hoping to get a shot as the game bursts out of hiding.

[Notes for Chapter 7 start on p. 38]

When I get to the middle of the pond I stop to listen but hear no threatening or suspicious sounds. I beckon to Steel with my hand and he comes up to the edge of the water. Then I motion with the flat of my hand for him to wait there, and he does. I feel a tick of surprise at the success of my signals. How to make hand signals might seem obvious, but it can easily be screwed up.[13]

I'd rather have Steel on dry land covering me than in the water with me. I don't know if he will go as carefully as I have chosen to go. If he makes noises I want to

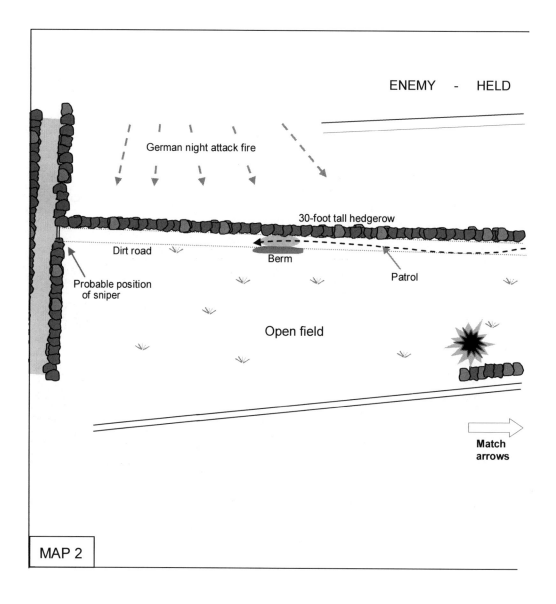

[Notes for Chapter 8 start on p. 38]

be on land myself where I can be more effective if we're discovered. But Steel is an indian isn't he? He can move more quietly than I can, can't he? But will he?

I keep going and get to the other side of the water, and out of the water, and I still can't see around the end of the berm. I pause for a second, then brace my nerves and edge forward. If a German is there I will have to act very quickly. If he's aiming his weapon at me I'll have to shoot or surrender. If I try to surrender he may shoot me anyway. Better to fight it out.

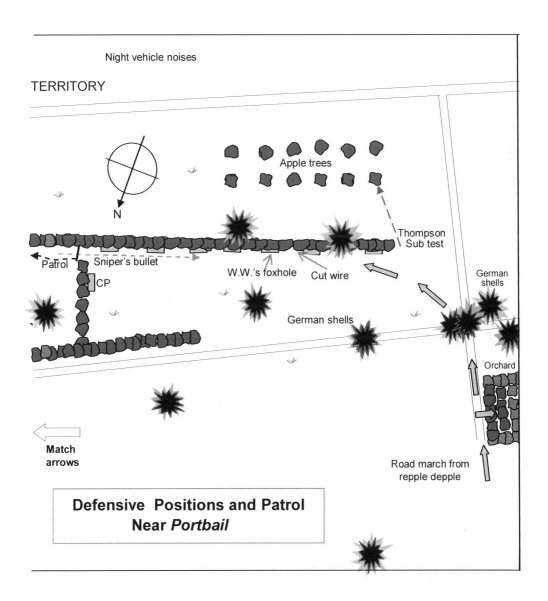

[Notes for Chapter 7 start on p. 38]

If he's not aiming his weapon at me I could try to take him prisoner. The decision will be split-split-second. There is no way to train for this. When the moment comes you do what you do.

I am very conscious of the force of the weapon in my hands. At any moment it may leap into sputtering explosive action. It will be a vicious animal, all claws and teeth. I will have to control it to keep it from expending the clip's total potency in the initial burst. I probably won't have time to switch clips. If there's more than one German I'll have to make decisions even as the bullets are ripping out.

Immediately I see that no German is there. No one is there. There is no sign that anybody has ever been there. My attention flips quickly up to the top of the berm—nobody there either—then forward. The dirt road goes straight for another hundred fifty yards then ends at hedgerow with a gate. Behind the gate is what looks like a crosswise hard-surface road. I crouch lower and listen.

Steel is on the other side of the water waiting to see what I will do. I motion for him to stay put.

What am I supposed to do? We're not on a combat patrol. We're not looking for trouble. We were just told to come out here to see whatever we can see. Especially bodies. Maybe they want to know the effect of our last night's artillery fire.[14]

To get to the bigger road we will have to cross the open space. If there are Germans at the road they are hidden by the hedgerow. Last night I heard noises out in front of our lines. Mechanical, creaking. Tanks? I told a non-com about the noises. Maybe horse-drawn wagons, he said. The Germans used a lot of horses. The noises were spooky. Some of the other guys heard them too.[15]

If the Germans are at the road they are sure to have a lookout watching in our direction. They know where we are. Their artillery knows where we are. The sniper knows where we are.

I can't see how it will help if we get hit or killed out here where nobody can see us. If we get halfway across the open space and are discovered, we'll have absolutely

[Notes for Chapter 8 start on p. 38]

no cover, and nowhere to go. The Germans can rest their rifles on the hedgerow and shoot us like rabbits. If we get all the way up to the road, and are then discovered, our chances will be no better. They can lob grenades over the hedgerow and we'll be wounded, dead, or taken prisoner. We're not prepared to assault the road. That is not our mission.

I become aware of a refreshing sense of freedom. There's nobody out here to make decisions for us. The entire Army of the United States is back behind the gate we came out of. Up to this point, everything we've done in the service has been spelled out in painful detail—by the authority of the Army, Congress and the President himself. Now, abruptly, with our lives on the line, we are completely on our own. It's a heady, exhilarating, liberating sensation. But it leaves me to make the decision.

I decide we've come far enough. Seeing no bodies or equipment or activity will mean something by itself. I decide to watch and listen for a few more minutes, then, if we are not spotted, go back the way we came.

I lower myself down onto my left side, keeping the Thompson sub ready—watching, waiting, trying not to think of anything other than what I am seeing and trying to hear, in front of me and around me, and how to shoot the Thompson sub if I have to.

> When I hold my grandfather's violin, taut
> wood, tight gut ... but
> exquisitely responsive like
> a leather-brown fragile eggshell, capable of
> resonating golden subtlest sound,
> weeping at hearts, spreading into
> the sunny open, or
> dark-doomed places, the all and all of
> people-feel ... then, when I
> hold this lead-and-metal death-er, chunk-
> heavy conceived in spoilage and hurtlust, can I
> hold the one in the one hand and

[Notes for Chapter 7 start on p. 38]

the one other in the other? No,
I must
choose.
Except that if I
choose the viol, they who are at this
time in charge of my bodysoulmind won't
let me play it. If I
choose the
gun, it will play itself by itself at
a very slight invitation
stattering blood and death spelt and
spilt. It's much
easier to lead-shatter hearts than
tease the dance of nuance. I
wonder if there are as many
machine-gunners in the world as
violin players? Probably many
more, at least aspiring ones. It's
just
aim, press: concert; but if I play it well, its
recipient(s) will not
applaud.

The war seems to have come to a stop. There is no firing, no movement, no action of any kind. No natural sounds either. In the woods back home such silence means something is up. When the birds and the crickets and all the slithering and rustlings go quiet it's a time to be especially alert. You may not see anything, but if there's anything out there—a deer, a fox, a bear, a weasel, even a deer-mouse—you can be sure that it sees you, or hears you, or smells you. If the Germans see me they have let me come.[16]

The silence is beautiful. And terrible.

After ten minutes of waiting with nothing happening I get up into a crouch and start back through the water. This could be the moment the sniper has been waiting for—when he sees that I'm not coming any closer. I move sidewise, trying to take steps forward and see backward at the same time, not letting the water from my boots make dripping noises. Steel stays where he is while I'm in the water. We have to be just as careful going back as we were going out. Just because we weren't discovered then doesn't mean we won't be discovered now. The Germans could still be behind the big hedgerow only twenty feet away. The fact that we've been quiet makes it even more likely that they are there.

Ollie-ollie-oxen-free!

When I get through the water I cover for Steel and motion him back toward the gate. The last twenty yards he takes at a run, and just as he gets to the gate it opens and he gets through the gate and there is no crack of the sniper's rifle.

Then I go, running the last twenty yards and I, too, get through the gate. "Home free!" I think of yelling. But I don't want to press my luck.

I tell the lieutenant about seeing the bigger road, but no activity, no equipment, no bodies.

"Did you go all the way out to the road?"

"No."

A flick of disappointment shows on his face, but he has followed his orders to send out a patrol. The fact that we didn't see anything can't be helped. Even that should be useful information. We went out, and we got back. That's something.

For Steel and me it's a lot.

They take back the Thompson sub. I never did find out if it would crawl right up a man.

⊕

[Notes for Chapter 7 start on p. 38]

Notes for Chapter 8

1. The Thompson sub-machinegun was the same weapon as the "Tommy-gun" used in the Chicago Valentine's Day massacre, except that the non-military weapon had a round magazine. I never heard the military weapon referred to as a "Tommy-gun".

   The clips we used held 20 rounds each. Rate of fire was 600 rounds per minute—ten per second—so a full clip fired in auto would last about two seconds. The correct term was *magazine*, but we called them clips.

   The Thompson sub was not a standard infantry weapon. The one I had on the patrol may have originally been carried by a paratrooper in the 82nd Airborne. We fought over much of the same territory.

2. A *gig* in the army was punishment for a minor offense. If you screwed up you might get *gigged* and get put on KP or cleaning latrines. A *gig* in show biz is a job.

3. Using the Thompson sub this way—aiming without using the sights—came naturally for me. On the combat course in basic I did OK snapping off shots with an M-1 at the silhouette targets as we ran through a zig-zag trench.

   And as a kid I'd practiced snap shooting with a wooden gun I made to resemble a Kentucky muzzle-loader—inspired by *The Long Rifle*, a story by Stewart Edward White, serialized in the *Saturday Evening Post* in the 1930s. My father liked the story and my mother used to read it to him at night. My gun shot rubber bands cut from automobile inner tubes.

   I used to crouch with my "Kentucky long rifle" in the dining room, leap suddenly into the living room and snap off a shot at an oatmeal box sitting on the sofa twenty feet away. Snap shooting with a real Kentucky muzzle-loader would have been a lot more difficult because of its length and weight.

[Notes for Chapter 8 start on p. 38]

4. In this account of WW-II, the words indian and negro are intentionally left un-capitalized. Capitalization, as the politically correct and sensibly sensitive practice when referring to ethnic and racial minorities, came later as an adjunct to the Civil Rights movement. No offense or slight is intended, just historical accuracy.

5. To *cover* someone meant being on the alert and ready to fire your weapon to protect a fellow soldier if he was exposed to enemy fire. If the exposed man had to retreat, the covering man could fire at the enemy to try to keep them down or at least make it harder for them to aim carefully.

6. I've since known some American Indians who didn't fit this stereotype at all. Max, a lens grinder at Spencer Lens Company in Buffalo, where I worked one summer between college semesters, was plump, jolly and talkative.

7. As new men, we were still unknown quantities. The only reason I can think of for picking me was that I had shown some initiative in reporting the broken wire next to my hole.

   In the three instances when I led patrols in basic training I did not do well—doubly embarrassing because I was supposed to be one of the cadre's fair-haired boys. In one field exercise my squad got captured almost immediately. In another we missed a check-point on a compass problem. On a third, I called for a loud rushing attack on an enemy outpost that proved to consist of a lone soldier in a pup-tent. A stealthy approach was what the cadre non-com expected.

8. We GI's had never gotten any training about taking prisoners, or more important, being *taken* prisoner. The only clue was that the military tradition of defending one's post to the end was never treated in a derogatory way by the cadre in basic training. We could only assume that we were expected never to surrender.

   Whether to allow the enemy to surrender, or whether to shoot was a different matter, and it became an issue in some divisions of the American

First Army during the Normandy fighting. Unofficial but acknowledged policy was at odds with the Third Geneva Convention of 1929.

The problem arose when the enemy were actively shooting at you right up to the point when you overran them. In the case of a sniper, if he threw up his hands, would you be justified in shooting him anyway? In the First Army, according to some military authors, the word went out from the top—General Omar Bradley—that our guys would not be disciplined if they didn't take prisoners in such cases. In our company I never heard anything on the subject one way or the other.

9. For the patrol with the Thompson sub, the attitude of the lieutenant seemed to be: "Let's send them out and see what they do." This approach to the problems of war, and work and life in general, has taken me years to get used to, even though much of the world operates this way—and apparently always has.

10. You hear a noise like that only when a bullet has been slowed down, or distorted in shape, or set tumbling by hitting something else first—like in a western movie when a bullet ricochets off the rock the cowboy hero is hiding behind. In the movies and on TV, all bullets whine as they go by. In WW-II, high-powered rifle bullets on both sides traveled at more than twice the speed of sound. Our necked-down .30-caliber ammunition for the M-1 had a muzzle velocity of 2,700 feet per second. Sound travels only 1,100 feet per second, so a bullet easily outdistanced the sound made by the rifle it came from. If it went by close, it made a loud sharp POP!—a mini sonic boom. Only after the POP of the bullet did you heard the crack of the rifle itself.

Bullets from handguns, like the Army .45-cal. pistol, and revolvers used in westerns, do travel more slowly, barely over the speed of sound at the muzzle, so if fired from a distance they could be slowed down enough by air resistance to produce sounds similar to those you hear in the movies. Bullets from the Thompson sub, however, though identical with those used in the .45 pistol, traveled faster than pistol bullets because the longer

[Notes for Chapter 8 start on p. 38]

barrel of the Thompson allowed more gas pressure to build up before the bullets exited the muzzle.

11. I saw more berms in the Normandy countryside, but I never learned what they were for. Maybe they helped farmers get on and off wagons that were piled high with hay. That's the best theory I could come up with.

12. Going out through a gate and following a well-marked road was not good Infantry practice. These were exactly the kinds of places that were watched by snipers, and zeroed in on by mortars and machineguns. Advancing soldiers and patrols are supposed to break new paths whenever possible, at least to make the enemy change his point of aim. The problem is that breaking new paths is more likely to be seen and heard by the enemy than taking the easy route—a dilemma for which there is no good solution. On the patrol with Thompson sub, Steel and I were told where to go, and I wasn't prepared to argue with the lieutenant about it, at least not yet.

    I use the word "purely" here, as in "purely asking to be seen," though before basic training I'd never heard it used in this way. A couple of southern Appalachia guys in my hut used the word to mean "downright".

13. Just hang around a small boat launching ramp and watch tempers flare as inexperienced skippers try to back their trailers into the water with the help of their spouses or crew. Divorces have started this way.

    Hand signaling can be a high art, as in pro baseball and in railroad yards. At the Bethlehem Steel Plant in Lackawanna, N.Y. where I worked one summer between college semesters, signals meant the difference between safety and serious injury, or even death. When a big bucket of molten pig iron came swinging down the long noisy floor of the open hearth, suspended from a crane high over your head and dripping fire, visual warning signals were crucial.

14. The most common purpose of a reconnaissance patrol was to locate the enemy, and the surest way to do that was to keep going forward until you

saw them, or got shot at. In basic training, one of the more hard-bitten cadre put it bluntly: "Scouts are out there to get shot at. That's how you find out where the enemy is." I found such a crude statement hard to accept. Soldiers' lives wouldn't be risked that way, wouldn't they? Yes they would. Scouts went out ahead and it was up to the scouts themselves not to get shot. Shot *at*, maybe, but not hit—a neat trick if you could pull it off. Some scouts had a knack for it. Some got hit the first time they went out.

I never heard the term "body count" used in WW-II.

15. The Germans were trying to move reinforcements north to attack the left flank and rear of General Collins's 9th and 79th Divisions as they tried to capture Cherbourg. Our blocking position at *Portbail* was to keep the Germans from getting through.

Seventy years later I can still hear those noises.

16. Drew Middleton, the correspondent who covered WW-II for *The New York Times*, in his book, *Our Share of Night*, writes about an incident when he was lying prone after a sniper took a shot at him in Normandy. Chin pressed to the ground, he watched a tiny bug crawl up one blade of grass and down another a few inches from his nose. I did not see a bug crawling on a grass blade on the patrol at *Portbail*.

I'm convinced that war writers put in things like that to make their work sound "literary", to give it the Stephen Crane touch (*The Red Badge of Courage*), or the Hemingway touch (*A Farewell to Arms*). Ten-to-one Middleton's bug was invented.

Or he might have gotten the idea from *The Road Back,* Erich Maria Remarque's sequel to *All Quiet on the Western Front,* in which, as the first person narrator, *Ernst*, is dreaming of being back in the trenches watching for the enemy: "A beetle with greenish-gold wings crawls up a camomile stalk in front of me... The rim of a helmet shows over the bushes..." (p. 249), and again: "...a ladybird... climbs to the topmost limit of a spray of

[Notes for Chapter 8 start on p. 38]

shepherds purse" (p. 307). Bugs on grass blades and weed stalks seem to be a recurring cliché for war writers, of fact or fiction.

The disjunction of Nature from war's carnage is the point, be it bug or lark, or in the case of the present work, my description of the +the swallows at *Beau-Coudray* (Chapter 12).

In some ways Middleton out-Hemingway'd Hemingway himself in covering WW-II. Hemingway was in France writing for *Collier's* magazine, but some of his writing, collected and published in his book, *By Line*, was, in my estimation, a poor imitation of his earlier work. He might have thought so too. By that time he was worrying about losing his touch. But he still would write *The Old Man and the Sea*, a critical success.

I think A. J. Liebling, a correspondent for the *New Yorker,* did better than Hemingway in WW-II. In one piece his editor almost cut out an especially vivid description of blood mixing with milk in the bottom of Liebling's landing craft at Omaha Beach when it was hit by a German shell. The editor thought the imagery was too contrived. Liebling swears the incident happened just as he described it. I believe him.

CHAPTER 8

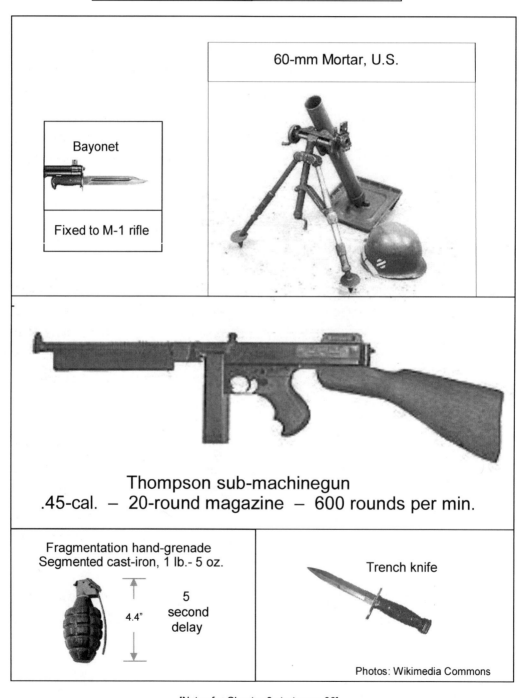

[Notes for Chapter 8 start on p. 38]

9

ATTACKED

I, B-A-R Man [Foxholes 7, 8]

A couple of nights after the patrol, at about eleven o'clock at night, we're hit with an attack. It's over on the left a couple of fields, not directly in front of our hole. It's impossible to tell exactly where the firing is coming from. At first there are just a few rifle shots, then machinegun fire, then the pace increases and there's really a lot of noise with some pretty loud explosions. Not artillery. Maybe grenades or bazookas. It starts while I'm standing guard. My hole-mate is in the cave as usual and won't come out. The non-com comes by to see if we're up and watching. This time he's all business. He wants me to go to another hole down the hedgerow to our left closer to the action. I tell him I can't wake up my hole-mate, and he looks at the pair of legs sticking out from the cave. It's the same non-com I told about my hole-mate seeing the "Gerries".

"I'll take the B-A-R," I say. The non-com goes on past me checking the other guys to my right, and when he comes back I'm in the new position and I've got the B-A-R. He takes note of it with a look but doesn't say anything. The firing keeps up for about half an hour. I can't see anything to shoot at, not even muzzle flashes. Like the first night when I stood guard I try to be ready for anything. I make sure I remember how to work the B-A-R. It comes back to me OK.[1] Finally the shooting tapers off and things go quiet again. The non-com comes by and asks me if I did any firing. I tell him no, and he says why not? I say I didn't see anything to shoot at. He says I should have fired anyway. I don't see why.[2] In the morning I tell my hole-mate that I've got the B-A-R, that the non-com knows I've got it, and that I'm going to keep it. He protests, but I don't pay any attention. The B-A-R is useless if he's the one who's got it. I give him my M-1 and cartridge belt, and keep the B-A-R and the B-A-R ammo belt. I don't intend to give them back.

Except for the shelling and the sniper hitting the guy, and the reconnaissance patrol with Steel, and the night attack, not much has happened. Being on the front line hasn't been so bad. Getting shelled, though, is no picnic. You don't dare get

[Notes for Chapter 9 start on p. 50]

out of you hole, and even when there's a letup you can't go far because it could start up at any time. The only place we need to go, anyhow, is to fill up our canteens at the end of the hedgerow, or to relieve ourselves, or dig a hole to defecate in. So far I haven't had to use my helmet for that.

We've been getting K-rations, single meals packed in green waxed cartons the size of Cracker-Jack boxes. Most of the time we're allowed to heat up water in our canteen cup for instant coffee by lighting the waxed boxes. The best coffee is *Nescafé*. If you cut holes in the box with your bayonet—I use my trench knife—the box burns with almost no smoke. We heat the flat cans of ham and eggs in the same way, but you have to open the can part way with the can-opener key that comes in the box so the can won't explode. You set the box upright with the top cut open, slip the can down into the box and the key keeps it from dropping all the way into the box. Then you light the box. The matches come in the ration boxes with the cigarettes. Cold ham-and-eggs are greasy and tasteless but heated up they're not so bad. Same with the hash in the dinner boxes. You can use an un-burned box to put over the end of your rifle to keep the rain and dirt out.

Being on the line is sort of like camping out. But the weather is rainy for a couple of days, and that's miserable, with no way to get out of the rain, and the hole gets muddy and sloppy.

Late in the afternoon of the fifth day a guy comes sauntering by as relaxed as if we were on bivouac back in the States in the Talladega National Forest. His name is Lancaster, and he's got a twang in his voice so nasal it's almost impossible to understand what he says. He's on special assignment ("spay-shul 'sahn-mn't") he says, gets to sleep in a tent back at 'tallion headquarters, on a cot with blankets. To merit such privileges he goes out nights on patrol, finds enemy guns, and blows them up. He actually does it, I guess, and he likes to talk about his exploits.

After dark when it's good and black Lancaster goes out at the same place where I tested the Thompson sub. The story has gone around that a couple of nights ago somebody from our company was coming back from a patrol and got shot by a GI who thought he was a German.[3] So there's going to be a password tonight, just for Lancaster. He doesn't want a password, but somebody decides there's going

[Notes for Chapter 9 start on p. 50]

to be one anyhow. The password will be "Sweet sixteen". When you see him coming back in you're supposed to say "Halt, what's the password?" He's supposed to say "sweet", and then you're supposed to say "sixteen". If he doesn't say "sweet" (for Lancaster, "sway-utt") you can take him prisoner. If he resists or runs, you can shoot. And if you don't say "sixteen", he can do the same. It's a nervous game, with a possible fatal ending.

"Wha'if ah f'git," Lancaster complains, way up his nose. "Or wha'if y'all f'git? Ah d'wan' no pay-ess wo-wurd."

About a half hour after Lancaster goes out there's a couple of explosions out in enemy territory, then a lot of firing of small arms, and more explosions like a small war is going on.

"That's Lancaster," one of the older guys says. "He's crazy. One of these nights he won't come back."

An hour goes by and when I'm on guard I see a GI coming toward me from my right and it's Lancaster slouching his angular frame along the hedgerow in the dark as though he's just taking a midnight stroll.

"Got two g'ns," he says, nasal as a banjo. "Drapped gruh-nay-udds daown'em. Gotta git back t' 'tallion t' ree-port."

As far as I know the password was never used. But he didn't get shot. Probably slipped right past somebody on guard.

Lancaster is like a secret weapon. But if we've got Lancaster, the Germans probably have somebody like him on their side. It's not a comforting thought.

The next day we hear a rumor that that *Cherbourg* has surrendered. I still can't picture the geography.[4]

Harmonica duet

On the sixth day we move out of the holes and nobody moves in to relieve us. We walk a few miles east to a rear area that's across the road from an artillery outfit.

Somebody says they're 240s. I never heard of 240s. 155 long toms were the biggest we heard about in basic. We're far enough away from the fighting so we don't have to stand guard at night but we dig foxholes. I still haven't seen a German soldier, dead or alive.[5]

A lieutenant tells us that all of us new men will be put in for the Combat Infantry Badge. You're supposed to be on the line for a certain number of days to get it. We were a day or two shy, but the lieutenant says he's going to make sure we get it anyhow. The older guys already have it. Also, Privates will get promoted to Pfc. I will make Corporal for having the B-A-R. Nothing is said about the fact that I took it away from my hole-mate. Maybe they know he's psycho. He shouldn't even be up here.

Steel, the indian from the patrol, comes by and he has a small harmonica. My Hohner Chromatic is still in my pack. I've used the pack for a pillow, scrunched it into tight foxholes with dirt crumbling on it, even sat on it. I get out my harmonica and check it over. It's as good as new. The box isn't even damaged. Steel and I play a duet. No harmony, just songs we both know. The Hohner is still off key a little, but that can't be helped. Steel doesn't complain. I'm surprised we know so many of the same songs. I wonder if he knows "Indian Love Call". But I don't ask him. I can't remember how it goes anyway except for a few notes: "When I'm calling you—ooo—ooo—ooo—ooo—ooo—ooo."

Playing music in a war zone is like an act of affirmation, a gauntlet tossed bravely, and it feels good, but after a while a non-com tells us to quit. He says snipers could still be in the area and the sound could give away our position. I don't believe that's the real reason. Some non-coms just can't stand hearing music played by GIs under their command. Maybe it bothers them because it's a personal expression not held under tight control by army orders.

Some of the non-coms at basic were like that. Jack Reid and I were fooling around one night on the piano in the company rec hall, playing a rinky-dink duet version of Heart and Soul, and Corporal Giella was shooting pool. We kept playing it, with many variations—which is what everybody does with that tune—and finally Giella couldn't stand it anymore and yelled; "Cut that out, it's driving me

[Notes for Chapter 9 start on p. 50]

nuts." I didn't think he had a right to shut us off like that on our own time in our own rec hall. It's the only place we had that was ours. I didn't think he should have been there anyhow, being a corporal. But we quit, and felt lousy and misused and impotent and stupid.

Maybe the non-com here is just taking everything very seriously and doesn't want us to let our guard down. Maybe it's bad luck to act like there's no war going on. Maybe I'll feel that way after a while myself.

In our position near the artillery battery I get a chance to talk with a couple of the guys who've been with the 90th Division since they landed at Utah Beach. They tell me we're in the 357th Regiment. There are two other regiments in the 90th, 358 and 359. They've heard rumors that we're going on the attack.

"Attack is a lot worse than defense," one of the guys says, looking at me sidewise. Why? I want to know.

"Because you have to go out in the open where the Germans can see you," he says. "They're behind the hedgerows, you're out in the open." I hadn't even thought about the difference between defense and attack. We new guys have only been on defense.

I find it hard to believe that in the mid-twentieth century American soldiers are still called upon to make frontal attacks against defended positions, advancing across open ground unprotected by anything except our clothing—just like the first World War and even the Civil War. How can such crude tactics possibly succeed without a lot of guys getting hit—wounded or killed? The answer is that they can't. A lot of guys will get hit—wounded and killed.[6]

What happened to the new world of technology, the "Century of Progress," the world of the Trylon and Perisphere, symbols of the 1939 World's Fair in New York—displayed with optimistic pride on the cover of our 1939 high-school yearbook? And why hasn't the true nature of modern Infantry combat gotten through to me before—that there's nothing modern about it? The cadre officers like Major Green in basic training certainly tried to impress the realities on us, but we weren't ready to accept them. Now, ready or not, we're facing them.[7]

[Notes for Chapter 9 start on p. 50]

As the guy is talking about going into the attack I see a glimpse of the sick smokey fear that swirls behind the eyes of some of the experienced men in spite of their outward look of casual nonchalance. Maybe they were involved in the routs we heard about on our first night with the 90th. Going on the attack is bad. And it's going to happen to us.[8]

⊕

>Soldiers don't shake hands, they stand
>like dogs, waiting to sense
>that careful balance of authority and
>submission that
>all men in all
>armies must seek. Even friends don't shake; they
>punch each other on the arm – "You sonnovabitch! Where
>the hell've you been?" The only shaking is
>deep, a fine tremor:
>(When will the fighting start again?)

⊕

Notes for Chapter 9

1. A somewhat unusual feature of the B-A-R was that it fired from an "open bolt". This meant that special pains had to be taken to keep the receiver area clean. When the need to fire the weapon was not imminent, the bolt could be closed, but the extra motions and noise required to prepare it for firing was a disadvantage, especially on a patrol, or at night. I did feel comfortable with the weapon, however, even with the minimal experience we had in Basic.

2. For a discussion of men not firing their weapons see Chapter 11, Note 16, and Web-link No. 1, Appendix C. Also the entry for S.L.A. Marshall's *Men Against Fire* in the ANNOTATED BIBLIOGRAPHY.

[Notes for Chapter 9 start on p. 50]

3. This incident is documented in the June 27 entry, *Operational Report, 357th Infantry,* typed at Regimental Headquarters during combat. A photocopy excerpt is included in Appendix B, provided to the author by the National Archives.

4. *Cherbourg* was taken by the 9th and 79th Infantry Divisions, backed up by the 4th Infantry Division.

5. This was not unusual, especially in the Normandy hedgerows. Days and weeks could go by without seeing a single enemy soldier. But we knew they were there. If we tried to move forward we often met stiff resistance and counterattacks; in defensive positions we got shelled and mortared. It was spooky. They knew where we were and what we were doing. It reminds me of the western movies where the wagon train is being followed by indians. "They're out there, all right," a grizzled scout says. "But you won't see 'em."

6. There was debate at the highest levels over the tendency of American commanders in Normandy to rely almost exclusively on frontal assaults. Some theoreticians, e.g., the Brit, Liddell-Hart, favored the "indirect approach", such as cutting behind the enemy, or around the enemy, as the Germans did so successfully at the French *Maginot* Line early in the war. Others felt these methods were inferior because they didn't put emphasis on destroying enemy forces. Eisenhower's orders from General Marshall were 1) to destroy the German war machine, and 2) to take the war to the heart of Germany. Generally speaking, Ike favored the frontal assault with "overwhelming force". Great if you've got it. Montgomery favored tricky tactics, perhaps because he didn't have as much materiel at his disposal and was limited in troop strength due to attrition from having already been at war for several years. From early on it became painfully clear that we Americans at least, weren't very good at direct assaults.

At the end of June when we were in the rest area next to the artillery battery, General Bradley ordered commanders to undertake new training throughout First Army designed to better cope with the hedgerows. We

[Notes for Chapter 9 start on p. 50]

had a half-day of training that consisted of throwing grenades—one each—and running across hedgerow-bordered fields simulating assaults against defending Germans. That was our re-training—a minimal token effort. The reason was simple: hedgerow fighting baffled everybody. Nobody knew what to train us to do.

Stephen Ambrose, in his book, D-Day, June 6, 1944, states flatly that the Allied high command, despite all its efforts at gathering intelligence about the beaches of Normandy, simply did not anticipate the difficulties the hedgerows that lay behind the beaches would present.

7. There were quite a lot of people in high places who shared my mistaken belief that by providing an overwhelming superiority in air power and quantity of materiel—explosives in particular—the head-on ground assaults that cost so many lives in the First World War could be avoided. Max Hastings, in *Overlord*, page 12, observes:

    > *In Normandy, the Allies learned the limitations of using explosives as a substitute for ruthless human endeavour. It seems fruitless to consider whether an Allied plan or manoeuvre was sound in abstract terms. The critical question, surely, is whether it was capable of being carried out by the available Allied forces, given their limitations and the extraordinary skill of their enemies.*

    Nevertheless, American artillery, its quantity and quality, and the way it was used, was the only ground weapon system conceded by the Germans to be equal or superior to their own. Considering that an overwhelming preponderance of casualties on both sides was caused by artillery, the role of high explosives was crucial. But following an artillery barrage, ground troops still had to go forward to occupy the territory, and often faced stubborn German resistance in spite of the shelling. After the most intense use of high explosives in support of ground troops in the European war—the saturation bombing for the July 25th COBRA offensive (Chap. 14)—and after turning the terrain into what the German general,

Bayerlein of the *Panzer Lehr* Division, called a barren "moonscape", American First Army troops still ran into stubborn German resistance.

Paul Fussel devotes a chapter of his book, *Warftime*, to the initially held belief of many Americans that WW-II could be fought at a distance with very few casualties.

The Army and Marines in Iraq and Afghanistan provided body armor for ground troops, and body armor was issued to some ground units in the Korean War. Even the "flak jackets" that were used by airmen in WW-II, if worn by Infantrymen, could have saved thousands of lives.

But the idea that Infantry-men's bodies should be protected was a hard one to sell. Ground troops were expected to get shot up. In both World Wars the expendability of Infantrymen seemed to be built-in as an intrinsic part of war itself—as though that's what war should be like. It wasn't uncommon for military people to brag about high casualty rates in their units, as a kind of badge of honor. And to be cynically realistic, how would the more war-like commanders get their sense of awful responsibility without the prospect of death for some of their men? But attitudes may finally be changing in the 21st Century. (See Addendum 7 for a letter about body armor sent out by NY Congresswoman Louise Slaughter, 4/15/14.)

8. In his book *And No Birds Sang*, Farley Mowat talks about the "worm of fear" living inside the men on the line like a malevolent parasite. He didn't have "the worm" at the beginning, in Sicily, but he got it in Italy, where he eventually became completely demoralized and was given a rear-area assignment, the kind of job he despised when he first entered combat.

Several writers have described the look in the eyes of a combat-weary GI as "the thousand yard stare". See entries for Ernie Pyle, and for James Jones's book, *WW-II,* in the ANNOTATED BIBLIOGRAPHY.

⊕

[Notes for Chapter 9 start on p. 50]

Stalled In the hedgerows

By the end of June the American First Army under General Omar Bradley had linked up the two American beachheads—Omaha and Utah—and had made contact with the closest of the three British beaches, Gold. The American 9th Division had cut off the *Cherbourg* Peninsula by pushing through to *Barneville* on the west coast, and, along with the 79th and 4th Divisions, had captured *Cherbourg*, a deep-water port critical for bringing in Allied supplies direct from the United States. The Germans, however, had destroyed much of the harbor and docking facilities so the beaches would still be the only way to bring in supplies for many weeks to come.

Casualties in rifle companies had been high among both enlisted men and officers. In addition to the killed and wounded, cases of combat fatigue clogging the field hospitals accounting for 20% of all casualties. Another type of casualty was even more disquieting: in one hospital near *Carentan* General Eisenhower found 1,100 GIs with SIWs—Self-Inflicted Wounds. Some of the doubts about the ability of American draftees to stand up against the Germans seemed to be justified.[1]

Bradley's plan

Ever since D-Day, American divisions had been crowding onto the beaches but they were too bunched up to be used effectively. A line of departure was needed in terrain that could be exploited by tanks and motorized troops. From such a line, a strong attack might crack through the German forward line and break up the deeper defenses by slicing laterally through their rear areas. The hedgerows did not allow this kind of maneuvering, nor did the large swampy areas in the American First Army sector, some of which had been intentionally flooded by the German defenders.

To launch a decisive breakthrough, a preliminary offensive was needed to get the American forces into better striking position. The 90th and 79th Infantry divisions along with the 82nd Airborne Division were put into the 8th Corps to be commanded by Troy Middledon, with the objective of attacking south out of the dense hedgerow country.

[Notes for Chapter 10 start on p. 65]

10

JULY OFFENSIVE

Rumors [Foxhole 9]

At the rest area across the road from the 240 artillery battery we hear more rumors that we're going on the attack, and the rumors prove to be true. In the evening of July 3rd the word comes down for us to get our gear in order, that we will jump off in the morning. No details, no pre-battle pep-talk, but a non-com comes around handing out D-Ration chocolate bars, one to a man.[2]

"Save it," he says. "Don't use it unless we can't get the rations up."

We check our gear, pick up ammo, fill our canteens. Some of the guys clean their M-1s. I put my harmonica into my combat pack. There won't be any more duets with the indian for a while.

Between the swamp and the mountain [Foxhole 10]
July 4

> ON JULY 4, THE 357TH REGIMENT GOT ORDERS TO ADVANCE IN THE DIRECTION OF BEAU-COUDRAY LE PLESSIS UNTIL CONTACT WAS MADE WITH THE ENEMY. WE MOVED THROUGH 358TH REGIMENT AT THE NORTH END OF THE DRY CORRIDOR BETWEEN PRAIRIE MARÉCAGEUSES AND MT. CASTRE [MAP 1, P. iv], THE 1ST BATTALION TO LEAD THE ASSAULT. THERE WAS NO EXPLANATION TO US GIS ABOUT WHAT OR WHOM WE WERE ATTACKING, WHAT TO EXPECT, OR WHAT TACTICS WOULD BE USED. I DIDN'T EVEN HEAR THE NAME OF THE PLACE WE WERE ATTACKING UNTIL AFTER THE FIGHT WAS OVER. ONE FEAR WAS ALLEVIATED, HOWEVER WHEN WE WEREN'T TOLD TO CHECK ON THE READINESS OF OUR GAS MASKS.
>
> ALTHOUGH WE GIS DIDN'T KNOW ABOUT IT, GENERAL BRADLEY ORDERED EVERY ARTILLERY PIECE IN FIRST ARMY TO FIRE ONE ROUND EXACTLY AT NOON—IN CELEBRATION OF THE AMERICAN FOURTH OF JULY.[3]

[Notes for Chapter 10 start on p. 65]

At about ten o'clock on the morning we move out under the fire of the 240-mm howitzers, the same battery that was across the road from us in the rest area.[4] The fields here are more open than those we've been used to and, in spite of the forebodings about going into the attack, there's a quickening sense of movement and action.

Every time a 240 is fired, a hollow whistling whooming sound follows the blast of the gun. One guy's theory is that the noise is made by metal rings released from the shells just after the shells leave the guns.[5] The shells themselves arch over us invisible, toward enemy held territory. We're still near enough for the 240s to make a great buffeting roar behind us as the guns are fired, but the shells are landing too far away for us to hear them explode when they hit.

> THIS WAS A COUNTER-BATTERY BARRAGE BY THE 240S, PART OF THE BEEFED UP VIII CORPS ARTILLERY. IT WAS INTENDED TO SILENCE GERMAN GUNS ON THE REVERSE SLOPE OF MT. CASTRE. WITH GOOD OBSERVATION AND PLENTY OF TIME TO LOCATE TARGETS ON THEIR FIRING GRID, THE GERMANS COULD PUT THEIR SHELLS WHEREVER THEY CHOSE. THE 240S WERE TRYING TO ELIMINATE THAT ADVANTAGE.

As night comes on we get word to dig in. We dig one-man foxholes along the hedgerows in fairly open fields. The soil is fairly soft and clear of roots and stones so the digging is pretty good. With no shells landing nearby and no guard posted I get a pretty good night's sleep.

Beau-Coudray – **Day One**   [Foxhole 11]
July 5

Early in the morning we leave our holes, cross a road and a railroad track, then advance along the edge of a swamp on our left that is high with lush growth. The air is tight with excitement. I carry the B-A-R which I have never fired. Trees loom through the mist made thicker by smoke [LAID DOWN BY OUR 4.2 CHEMICAL MORTARS, I LEARNED YEARS LATER.].[6] A tall officer who could be our Platoon Lieutenant charges around trying to keep contact with whoever is supposed to be on our left.

[Notes for Chapter 10 start p. 65]

"McConville!" he bawls repeatedly, "Lieutenant McConville!" pushing recklessly through the swamp growth. Contact has been lost, but the attack goes forward nevertheless. I can't help wonder if making all that noise is a good idea. Seems like it will alert the Germans that we're coming.[7]

We move through an opening in a big hedgerow, across a marshy creek, then up a twelve-foot bank covered with large trees. We spread out along the bank that already has foxholes spaced about 20 feet apart. I'm the last man on the left and I have no contact with anybody in that direction. I can't see the guy on my right because of the trees and bushes. By clambering to the top of the bank I can see part way across an open field that swells up the same way the field did on the patrol with the Thompson sub. The tops of a line of trees are visible beyond the up-swell of the hill.

"Get ready to move out," a non-com calls up from the bottom of the bank then disappears. While I'm waiting for the word to go I decide that it's really dumb to go into an attack without knowing if the B-A-R will fire. At the rest area I asked a non-com for permission to test-fire it and he said he'd try to get an OK from somebody but he never got back to me. Here there is no one to ask, unless I get out of my hole and go looking, and with the jump-off imminent I'm not going to do that. It's better that way because I've decided to test-fire it anyway. Nobody can say no. The shouting lieutenant didn't seem to be worried about making noise.

I've been carrying the B-A-R with a full magazine snugged up in the receiver, ready for immediate firing. Flipping off the safety on the left side of the receiver and squeezing the trigger should send the bolt forward to pick up the top round from the magazine, feed it into the chamber and fire the B-A-R. Pressure from the burning powder vented into the gas cylinder through the gas port under the muzzle—like an M-1—should force the bolt back and eject the spent round. Then with the trigger still held back the bolt should fly forward again, pick up the next round from the magazine, ram it into the chamber and fire again—in a repeating cycle until the trigger is released or until the magazine is empty.

I flip the safety, point the muzzle of the B-A-R upward toward German territory, and pull the trigger. The bolt sludges forward and stops with an inch still to go. It

[Notes for Chapter 10 start p. 65]

picked up the top round from the magazine OK, but it didn't push the round all the way into the chamber. The B-A-R will not fire.

I should have tried harder to test-fire the B-A-R back in the rest area. But I've been foresighted in another way. When I swapped my M-1 for the B-A-R I took the oil-and-thong kit out of the M-1's butt compartment and put it in the pocket of my fatigue pants. It's still there. Half of the tubular metal cleaning kit is filled with oil. I take it out of my pocket, pull out the B-A-R's magazine, pull back the bolt to eject the round that didn't fire—taking a quick look at the brass to see if the hang-up was caused by a fouled chamber. The brass looks clean. I unscrew the threaded cover from the oil-and-thong kit and slosh some oil onto the bolt and into the receiver of the B-A-R, trying not to get any oil in the chamber itself. Then I work the bolt back and forth a few times by hand to loosen it up, lock it back, cock it again and pull the trigger. The bolt still hangs up.

If I can't get the B-A-R to fire what should I do? Drop out of the attack? Follow in the rear? I slosh in more oil and exercise the bolt again, then pull the trigger. This time the bolt goes all the way home with a pretty good snap. I jam the magazine back up in place, pull back the bolt, aim the B-A-R upward and once more pull the trigger. BRUPPPP—a burst goes skyward. Not thirty seconds later we get the word to go.

I climb over the bank and out onto the field in a running crouch.[8] The platoon is strung out in a ragged line to my right. There is some shouting. When I get halfway up the hill the lieutenant who seems to be our Platoon Leader tells me in an excited voice to go out on the left and cover the flank. He tells Steel, the indian, to come with me. Steel has an M-1 rifle the same as he did on the patrol back at the roadblock but now he's wearing an ammunition belt for the B-A-R. He must be the assistant B-A-R man, or the ammunition bearer. When I took the B-A-R from my hole-mate I never gave it a thought that a B-A-R team is made up of three men. The third man, whoever he is, isn't with us. I crouch down and move out to the left about fifty yards. Steel follows. Now we're lying on the ground in the open field watching the next hedgerow up the hill. It's a pretty big one, running crosswise about a hundred fifty yards ahead of us. Steel is lying prone a couple of yards back, on my right [MAP 2, P. 62].

[Notes for Chapter 10 start p. 65]

The B-A-R doesn't have a bipod so I just hold it as I would an M-1, except that the B-A-R magazine protrudes from the bottom of the receiver and I have to keep it from digging into the ground.[9]

We're out in the field less than a minute when I hear Steel say: "My finger's hit." He's looking down at his right hand, holding it with his left hand close to his body. Then he says:

"I'd better go back to the aid station."

I don't know what to say. I can't afford more than a quick glance. I don't see any blood. I can't tell how bad it is—or even if he's been hit at all. We haven't been fired on out here. But it's not my finger.

"I better go back," he says again. I'm not going to try to stop him.

"Leave your ammo belt," I tell him. He takes it off, pushes it toward me, then starts to crawl back down the hill.

The rest of the platoon is up ahead along the crosswise hedgerow to my right-front. They took some prisoners on the way up the hill. I was a little behind the others getting up the hill because of my left-most position on the bank. When I got up to the rest of the guys I saw six Germans being held at gunpoint. The loud Lieutenant was bawling at them and the prisoners were standing up in their holes yelling "Ruskie! Kamerad! Ruskie!"[10] They were dug in under some apple trees on our side of the crosswise hedgerow. Only their heads and shoulders showed above ground. With hands stretched high in the air, dirty and scared, the prisoners jabbered for their lives. It was a weird unreal scene. They had cloth caps, and when they clambered out of the holes, their long gray overcoats gave them an awkward chunky look. They didn't look at all like the cocky square-helmeted goose-stepping *Nazis* we saw in the training films back home.

Now I can see the prisoners being run back down the hill by a GI. The prisoners are trying to keep their hands on their heads as they run, their feet almost hidden by the long overcoats. It's almost comical. Everybody is crouching down as though the roof is about to fall in. The GI looks as scared as the prisoners.

[Notes for Chapter 10 start p. 65]

CHAPTER 10

From where I am in the field I can barely see our guys along the back of the hedgerow up ahead, but I do see it when a tall GI—the loud lieutenant, I think, but I can't be sure—strides a few quick yards to the left, heaves a grenade over the bank of the hedgerow then ducks back. The grenade goes off and he waits a few seconds, then heaves another one. Are the Germans right there on the other side of the same hedgerow? That's what it looks like. Then I see a small puff of smoke appear low in the grass at my left front where the hedgerow has a break in it, sort of a gateway, and I hear the statter of a machinegun—too fast to be one of ours—and I aim the B-A-R at the smoke—behind the smoke—and fire.[11]

My first burst stops the German machinegun but I can't see the machine-gunner. Did I hit him? I might have. But I might have just driven him back through the gate.

Once I start firing I don't dare stop for more than a few seconds. I'm out in the open. The grass in the field is just high enough to hide the German machine-gunner from me, and me from him, because of the slight upswell of the terrain. He must have crawled out on his stomach, poked his weapon around the end of the hedgerow and fired along our side—the deadly enfilade fire we were told about in basic. But if any German looks out across the field from a standing position anywhere behind the hedgerow he'll see me. I have to keep them from looking over the hedgerow, or around the end of it. I've got fifty yards of hedgerow to cover from my left-front to my direct front. I don't dare fire toward the right-front where our guys are. I have to chance it that the Germans won't try to look over that part of the hedgerow. They probably won't, after the two grenades went off.

With a B-A-R you can use up your ammunition in a hurry. It fires 550 rounds per minute. That's nine rounds a second. The magazine holds 20 rounds, so if you hold the trigger down you get a little over two full seconds worth of continuous fire per magazine. I'm firing short bursts, five or six rounds to a burst. I want them to know I have an automatic weapon, to intimidate them so they will stay down, but I don't want to shoot off all my ammo unless I absolutely have to. At five rounds per burst, I'll get four bursts per magazine. I'm glad I took Steel's ammo belt.[12]

I fire the B-A-R at the break in the hedgerow where the German machine-gunner was, and along the top of the solid part of the hedgerow, especially where the

[Notes for Chapter 10 start p. 65]

foliage looks thin, trying to guess where somebody might be trying to poke his head up. I look for any disturbance of the leaves that will tell me where to fire. I could be back home in our own woods trying to spot the movement of a deer's ear flicking at a fly. But I see no movement. Even our guys are motionless, down prone because of the German machinegun fire. The air is very still and the big hedgerow stands silent. I'm the only one making the noises of war.

I don't use the rear sight of the B-A-R. It's a leaf-sight and is supposed to be quite accurate, but I never got a chance to zero it in, so I leave it folded down out of the way. All I can do is aim over the top of the fixed sights and fire both a little high and a little low to make sure that at least part of the time I'm hitting where I want to hit. I'm wasting some ammo that way, but the sound of the bullets popping past them will be intimidating by itself. It's an angry aggressive sound; I remember it well from working in the rifle pits in basic. I haven't heard any German bullets "pop" since I've been up on the line, but maybe I will today. The German sniper's bullet I heard go past my hole back at the road block had already gone through a guy so it didn't pop, just made a sort of fizzing twangy noise as it went by.

Ammo is not my biggest problem—at least for a while. What I've got to do is keep the Germans from looking over the hedgerow.

I don't use the B-A-R shoulder rest either.[13] I fire short bursts at both sides of the opening in the hedgerow; I even fire into the solid part of the hedgerow itself, figuring that the AP ammo we were issued might go all the way through and hit a man on the other side.[14] When I switch magazines the second time I accidentally grab the barrel of the B-A-R and sear a piece of skin off my left hand. I won't do that again. At least it's cauterized and doesn't bleed

I started with twenty-four full magazines—twelve in Steel's ammo belt, eleven in mine, and one in the B-A-R. I've used up five. I should save the empty magazines. That's a pain in the tail, and risky, because while I'm putting them back in the ammo belt I still have to watch out front and keep up the firing, but I'd never be able to carry the magazines loose. When the first one is empty I use the magazines from Steel's ammo belt so if I have to move in a hurry I'll have full ones in my own belt. We don't save M-1 clips, but B-A-R magazines are harder to come by. Without them a B-A-R is useless.

[Notes for Chapter 10 start p. 65]

Page 62   CHAPTER 10

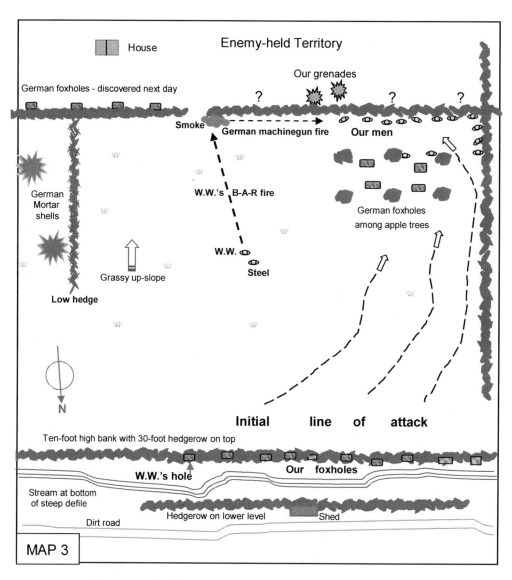

Attack by B-Company at *Beau-Coudray* – Day 1

[Notes for Chapter 10 start on p. 65]

I've been firing intermittently, at random intervals, trying to keep the Germans down, and it seems to be working because I don't hear any more machinegun fire, or any fire at all. I start to wonder what's next. I don't have any further instructions. Maybe I'll be told to get up and move forward to continue the attack. If that doesn't happen soon I won't have much ammo left. Then I see some GIs running back down the hill over at my right. Nobody tells me to go with them—they don't even look my way, they just run, hunched over in that peculiar heads-down-but-looking-forward posture of the running Infantryman—so I stay put.

Everything gets very quiet except for my B-A-R. I don't see any of our guys up at the crosswise hedgerow, and after a while I realize that all of our guys have gone back and that I'm up here all by myself out in front of our lines. Then something explodes off to my left in the next field. The hedgerow going up the hill on my left is low enough so I can see over it. There's a bunch of dirty gray smoke in the field about as big as a Jeep. It takes me a while to figure out what it is. Then I hear another sound, a tunk over in German territory, and after a short pause another explosion and another bunch of smoke, and it's closer. What is happening now gets through to me: they are going after me with a mortar. The mortar is searching for the correct range and azimuth, trying to find me. The first explosions were too far to the left—their right—but they'll correct that. The next one will be even closer. In basic I was in a mortar squad. I know how it works.[15] Now, every time I let off a burst from the B-A-R it helps them adjust the mortar. I don't dare stop firing or a German will poke his head up and spot me, but if I keep firing it's just a matter of time before the mortar finds me and then the B-A-R will stop.

The mortar is like a disembodied mechanical being. I know that men are doing the aiming and firing, but it seems like the mortar itself is trying to kill me. It's not a comfortable thought—the deliberate, impersonal metallic logic, the slow-but-sure inevitability of execution. I've got to get out of here.

But which way? Up to where the guys were at the hedgerow? I don't have any orders except to be right where I am. According to training, without further orders this is where I should stay. But if the guys I saw running back were giving up the attack, then I ought to be able to go back too. I decide that's what I will do.

[Notes for Chapter 10 start p. 65]

I don't dare get up on my feet, or even crawl on my hands and knees—the grass isn't high enough to hide me. And I should keep watching forward so I'll be ready to fire in case a German shows himself, or in case they attack across the field. I try to move backward, flat on my stomach, dragging the B-A-R and the loose ammo belt along with me. I find that I can do it if I dig in with my toes and hook myself back three or four inches at a time. The going is slow and as I drag myself backward my body and the ammo belts flatten the grass making a clear path across the field. It will be easy for the Germans to spot me if they simply look down the aisle of flattened grass. I've got to zig-zag.

I zig and zag a couple of times, backing down the hill like a clumsy crayfish. There is another mortar burst, a lot closer than the last one. The farther back I get, the more protection I'll have from the up-swell of the hill, if they keep the same range. When I get back to where I can see only the upper part of the trees ahead, not the hedgerow itself, I scrunch around and look behind me. The top of a GI helmet is barely poking above the top of the bank where we started out from. A guy's eyes are in the shadow under the brim of the helmet and next to his eyes is the muzzle of an M-1. I wonder if he will shoot.

There is no password. He'd have to be blind not to see that I'm a GI, but if this GI is my old hole-mate from the roadblock I wouldn't give much for my life. I'd be one of his "Gerries". I make a sort of wave with my hand, keeping it low, and he doesn't shoot, and I keep hooking my way back toward him with my feet.

When I get back to him he's in a deep hole dug into the bank—the hole had to be there already, there wasn't time for him to dig it himself. He says there's another hole over to his left.

A moaning in the defile [Foxhole 12]

The platoon has withdrawn to a steep defile bordered by the tree-grown bank we're on. It's the same bank we took off from, but not the same place. We must be farther down the creek that flows though the defile. On the other side of the defile, across from the hill, the bank is lower, more like a regular hedgerow, but it also has large trees in it. After a while German shells start coming in, artillery, probably 105s, and we get a severe pasting, off-and-on, for most of the afternoon. Someone gets hit and keeps moaning, loud, like a desperate bawling calf. The sound fills the defile. Everyone can hear it but nobody does anything about it. The shelling is too severe for anybody to move around. The shelling is worse than it was at the roadblock where I went on the patrol with the Thompson sub. A lot worse.

⊕

Notes for Chapter 10

1. Eisenhower alluded to doubts about the fighting abilities of the GIs in his D-Day announcement on radio and on the flyers handed out to American military personnel on the morning of June 6th, but he emphasized that the clear superiority of the German Army was a thing of the past.

    For a discussion of combat fatigue, see Hastings: *Overlord,* p. 246. For Ike's reaction to the number of SIWs (Self-Inflicted Wounds), see Butcher: *My Three Years with Eisenhower,* p. 645.

    The incident of the SIWs, reflecting poorly as it does on the American forces in Normandy, is nevertheless reported in the *West Point Military History Series, Second World War, Europe and the Mediterranean,* prepared under the aegis of the Department of History, United States Military Academy. It would be interesting to know if these facts are used today in military instruction.

2. D-Rations were thick, hard, almost tasteless chocolate bars, supposedly packed with nutrients that would sustain a man for a couple of days if he couldn't get K-Rations or C-Rations. Rumor had it that the D-Bars were made unappetizing on purpose so we wouldn't eat them like candy. It would be easy to break a tooth on one.

3. This incident is reported in several places. General Omar Bradley's book, *A Soldier's Story,* p. 324, is probably the most direct source. The book

was ghosted by Bradley's aide-de-camp, Chester Hansen, based on a diary that Bradley asked him to keep.

When artillery fire from several different batteries was timed to make impact on the same target at the same time it was called TOT (Time-On-Target). It was perfected by American artillery and was much feared by the Germans. In the Fourth of July barrage the batteries were not all aimed at the same target, so some of the effect was lost. But it was a welcome celebratory event nonetheless.

4. In basic training we learned about our 105-mm howitzers, saw them fired, and went through a field exercise with their shells passing overhead. We heard about the 155-mm "long Toms" and were told (possibly incorrectly) that they were technically called "rifles". 240s were never mentioned. For more on artillery designations see entry for Patrick, Stephen A., *The Normandy Campaign, June and July 1944* in the ANNOTATED BIBLIOGRAPHY.

5. He was apparently right. A description of the bands used with 155s is found in Ernie Pyle's *Brave Men*, p. 115:

> *The shell they fired from those 155-millimeter howitzers had a single metal band around it...those bands would fly off as a shell left the gun. On its own, the band was liable to go in any direction, careening and screaming through the air. They were called "rotating bands", and they made a variety of noises, one of which sounded like a whipped dog yowling in terror.*

The soft metal of the rotating band provided a grip for the rifling inside the gun barrel, giving the shell its twist—needed for accuracy. Once out of the barrel, the band flew off, minimizing the air resistance of the projectile.

6. The 4.2 designation is in inches. They were called chemical mortars because they were designed to fire shells packed with chemicals in case the enemy initiated the use of poison gas. In my experience they were used only to fire smoke shells, as at *Beau-Coudray*.

7. While writing this I realized that there was also a "loud soldier" in Stephen Crane's *The Red Badge of Courage*. This is just a coincidence. I wouldn't be surprised if every military unit had a "loud soldier".

8. We never used the expression "over the top", but for us it was sometimes just like the WW-I doughboys at *Verdun* and the *Marne,* and like the "boys in blue" charging up Marye's Heights at Fredericksburg where my Great Grandfather Alfred Jennings got hit by a *Miniéball*.

    When you got the word, you stood up, moved out into the open and ran forward with just your clothes and your helmet to protect you—until you were shot, or got to some cover, or reached the objective. I was still unwilling to believe that in modern warfare such primitive exposure of unprotected human bodies would be the basic way to gain ground, but it was. Ultimately, when all else failed, it was the only way.

9. A bipod is standard equipment for a B-A-R, serving as a rest to steady the gunner's aim, but using a bipod elevates a B-A-R's muzzle. I'd have had to raise up my head and shoulders in order to hit German machine-gunner because of the up-swell of the hill. I didn't want to get myself any higher than was absolutely necessary.

    Also, because of where the bipod is attached, to move the aiming point meant either lifting the bipod off the ground and setting it down in a new position, or moving my body sidewise to get behind the weapon. That might only take a couple of seconds, but in a situation like this, seconds were crucial. I had no idea where a target might appear.

    Many a B-A-R man conveniently "lost" the bipod. It snagged on bushes and added weight. Whoever threw away the bipod did me a favor.

10. If we thought they were Russians captured on the Eastern Front, brought here and forced to fight for the Germans, we'd have been less likely to shoot them. If they were faking, it wouldn't be discovered until later, and by that time the crisis would be over. It was certainly worth a try on their part. If the ruse caused even a second's hesitation it could save their lives.

[Notes for Chapter 10 start p. 65]

And, of course, they might really be Russians. Not that it would make any difference, if they'd been shooting at us.

11. In basic we were told that the Germans did not have smokeless powder, but that we did have it, and that this would give us an advantage. In his book *June 6, 1944 – Voices of D-Day*, page 357, Gerald Astor says the exact opposite was true. From my experience at *Beau-Coudray*, I have to go with the cadre at Ft. McClellan, at least in regard to the .30-cal. ammo issued to us for the M-1 and the B-A-R. I saw the German machinegun's smoke, but although I stayed in the same position firing intermittently for several minutes, I was not aware of any smoke from my own weapon.

12. On the range back at Ft. McClellan I did OK with the B-A-R, and felt pretty confident with the weapon. We were supposed to try for bursts of three rounds to learn trigger control. I think I actually got a "possible" on my target. The term means that it's "possible" that you got all the shots in the bulls-eye—a perfect score, pending an OK by the range officer. But they didn't give it to me because they couldn't find all the holes. There weren't any holes outside the black so it was pretty obvious that two rounds went through the same hole. A similar thing happened to Patton when he competed in a triathlon in Stockholm in 1912. They denied him a perfect score with the rifle because they found only nine holes in the bull's-eye. (From an article in *The Saturday Evening Post* by Ted Shane, reprinted in *These are the Generals*, published by Alfred A. Knopf, 1943.)

13. A hinged metal strap folds out from the top of the B-A-R's butt plate and is supposed to rest on top of the B-A-R-man's shoulder to keep the butt from working down due to the rise of the muzzle as the weapon is fired. If you're using the bipod, your left hand will be free and you can put it on top of the strap and hold it tight to your shoulder. If you have an assistant he can hold the shoulder rest down. At least that's the S.O.P. we got in basic. I never heard of anybody actually doing it in combat.

14. AP ammo (Armor-Piercing) had silver-colored jackets on the bullets instead of the copper jackets of ball ammo. What made them armor-piercing

[Notes for Chapter 10 start p. 65]

was never explained. I wouldn't expect them to penetrate much armor. Firing .30-caliber ammunition at tanks was a futile exercise, although it would make a racket on the inside and could keep them "buttoned up". I have never found AP ammo for the M-1 mentioned in any of the books I've read on the war, but there are several references to it on the Internet.

15. In basic I was in the 60-mm mortar squad and we carried the mortars, broken down into tube, base-plate and bipod, wherever we went, but we only actually fired them once—two dummy rounds, under tightly controlled conditions. The shells had propellant charges but no HE powder inside. My estimate for the deflection adjustment after the first round was three degrees. The cadre lieutenant second-guessed me with seven degrees. When the shell was fired I was proved right. We got a couple of hours more training on aiming the mortars by adjusting elevation (vertical angle) and azimuth (horizontal angle from North), but without firing any rounds.

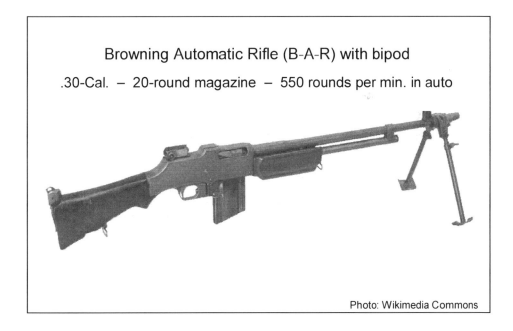

Browning Automatic Rifle (B-A-R) with bipod
.30-Cal. − 20-round magazine − 550 rounds per min. in auto

Photo: Wikimedia Commons

[Notes for Chapter 10 start p. 65]

⊕

Each shell is a tight-wrapped penile parcel of destruction that starts out in a neat and aesthetically beautiful metal container, placed carefully into its propulsion chamber by carefully trained, almost loving hands, then urged forward and upward into the skies by its charge of powder, where it sails free over the fields and trees, over the brooks, over the spotted cows and flapping, prattling magpies, over the roads and paths that meander carelessly like tossed ribbons, until it sees at last the huddled cowering half-men it must try to destroy. Now it has a new persona, roaring alive with a new passion, nearing the fulfillment of its only mission, meeting the earth again in an orgasm of steel—blasting, ripping, tearing the soil and the pitiful creatures that huddle in holes scraped into the earth's integument, ex-ploding at the surface or in the air or in the trees, each of its thousand-razored pieces seeking to loose blood, rip flesh, tear brains, shatter bone, slit eyeballs, smash testicles. Never mind that this one misses you. The next one will have a completely new chance undiminished by the failures of those that came before.

[Notes for Chapter 10 start p. 65]

11

THE SHELLING

A deal with the gods

The big shells are looking for us, trying to break up our attack, and they are succeeding. All we can do is stay low in our holes. The shells come in groups: **Sheeeeew sheeeeew sheeeeew** skimming in over the rise of the hill. Then **KRACKKTTT !!! KRACHT !!! KRHAKKT !!!** in the defile. The holes we're in are well placed to withstand a shelling because it's hard for a shell to make a direct hit—we're under the brow of the bank—but they don't have to score direct hits to get us. When they detonate in the trees, shell fragments spray down from overhead. You can't hide from a tree burst unless you've got a solid roof over your hole made of planks or tree trunks. These holes don't have roofs of any kind. A shell could hit a tree right over your hole, and from that there is no escape. I do pretty well for a while, but the effect of the pounding accumulates. I find that I can keep myself under control for only so long. Then in spite of my best efforts I begin to cringe—flinching from the brutal assault, from the gigantic noise, from the second-by-second suspense, from the random timing of the punishment. Nobody over on the German side is writing my name on a shell before they slide it into the breech of the artillery piece, I know that. It is chance, and chance alone, that will find me out, and everybody has the same chance. But the shells seem personal nevertheless. They seem to be looking for *me* as an individual. It's hard to think of anybody else when you're taking such an intimate pounding.

> *THE PSYCHOLOGICALLY PERCEIVED SIZE OF A 105-MM SHELL GOING OVER CLOSE ABOVE YOU IS—I WOULD SAY—ABOUT THE SIZE OF A BOXCAR, OR THE ENGINE BLASTING ALONG AHEAD OF THE BOXCARS.[1] IMAGINE YOURSELF CAUGHT ON THE TRACKS AS THE ENGINE (THE OLD STEAM STYLE) COMES ROARING OUT OF A TUNNEL. YOUR SHOE IS CAUGHT UNDER A RAILROAD TIE AND YOU CAN'T GET LOOSE. ALL YOU CAN DO IS CRUNCH DOWN TIGHT BETWEEN THE RAILROAD TRACKS AND HOPE THAT THE NOISE-BELCHING MONSTER GOES OVER YOU WITHOUT SNAGGING ON YOUR*

[Notes for Chapter 11 start on p. 80]

BODY, ARMS, LEGS, HEAD. **ROARRRRING** AND **HISSSSSING**, IT **ROCKETS** OVER YOU, **SKKKKIM-SSS** OVER YOU, **MISSSSSING** YOU BY AN INCH, THEN **CATTTTAPULTING** OFF THE END OF THE TRACK TO **PULLLL…VERIZE** ITSELF THIRTY FEET AWAY IN **A GREAT DISINTEGRATING BLAST SHOOTING** PIECES OF STEEL IN EVERY DIRECTION THEN, JUST AS YOU'RE SITTING UP AND DUSTING YOURSELF OFF, CONGRATULATING YOURSELF ON YOUR MIRACULOUS ESCAPE, OUT COMES **ANOTHER MONSTER MACHINE EXPLODING FROM THE MOUTH OF THE TUNNEL ROARING, CRASHING, ROCKETING, CATAPULTING, PULVERIZING**, BEATING YOU DOWN AGAIN WITH ITS CLOSE **IMMENSITY**. YOU BARELY MAKE IT DOWN THIS TIME, THEN COMES **ANOTHER, AND ANOTHER. AND ANOTHER:**SHEEEWWWWW**KRACHTTT!!!**SHEEEWWWW

SHEEEEEWWWW **KRAKKTTT!!! KRACKKKKTTTT!!!**

I can't help feeling a moment's lift when I'm not hit by a close one—but the feeling is a seductress: If I let myself enjoy the relief, I might relax a treacherous iota; the fate that spared me the last time may take advantage of my lowered guard and mark me for the next.

THE SOUND OF A CLOSE-BURSTING SHELL IS A SHARP, INCREDIBLY INSTANTANEOUS AUDITORY ATTACK THAT TAKES PLACE IN A METAL-TIGHT PARTICLE OF A SECOND.

A SHELL COMING OVERHEAD FROM THE ENEMY HAS AN ENTIRELY DIFFERENT SOUND AS IT FORCES ITS WAY THROUGH THE AIR: AT A DISTANCE IT SLITHERS, WHISPERS; CLOSE, IT HOWLS, SHRIEKS—A VICIOUS SMEAR OF NOISE THAT SHREDS NERVES AND SHATTERS RESOLVE.

MANY A WRITER HAS TAKEN A TURN AT DESCRIBING SHELLS COMING AT YOU, OR GOING OVER YOU, OR EXPLODING NEAR YOU. EVEN WRITERS WHO NEVER HEARD SHELLS HAVE WRITTEN ABOUT THEM. STEPHEN CRANE WROTE ABOUT SHELLS IN *THE RED BADGE OF COURAGE*. HE WAS TOO YOUNG TO SEE ACTION IN THE AMERICAN CIVIL WAR BUT BECAME A WAR

[Notes for Chapter 11 start on p. 80]

CORRESPONDENT DURING THE SPANISH AMERICAN WAR. HIS DESCRIPTIONS OF THE CIVIL WAR FIGHTING HAVE BECOME LITERARY CLASSICS:

> *A shell screaming like a storm banshee went over the huddled heads of the reserves. It landed in the grove, and exploding redly flung the brown earth. There was a little shower of pine needles.*
> (*The Red Badge of Courage*, pp. 267-8)[2]

ERNIE PYLE, THE WW-II WAR CORRESPONDENT, WROTE ABOUT THE SOUNDS OF SHELLS—SHELLS HE HAD HEARD PERSONALLY. HIS DESCRIPTIONS HAVE BECOME CLASSICS TOO.

> *You could hear the shells chase each other through the sky...making a sound like the cold wind through the leaves on a winter night.*
> (Ernie Pyle, *Ernie's War*, Ed. by David Nichols, p. 175)

NEW YORK TIMES WAR CORRESPONDENT DREW MIDDLETON WROTE ABOUT SHELLS IN A LITERARY WAY—AFTER THE MANNER OF HEMINGWAY (THOUGH HE WOULD DENY THAT, OF COURSE.)[3] AND MANY OTHERS. I'M DOING IT NOT IN AN ATTEMPT TO JOIN THE LITERATI, BUT JUST TO ADD MY BIT TO SOMETHING I HAPPEN TO KNOW SOMETHING ABOUT.

Various after-effects follow a shell's impact—dirt and stones rain down, branches split off and fall, sharp shards of metal spin past, thrumming like demented bees—with a sting that will slice your leg off.

The shelling of our positions along the defile continues off-and-on for most of the afternoon. During an unusually long lull a guy comes along the bottom of the bank and calls up to me:

"Are you all right?"

"Yeah," I tell him. I don't see why he's singling me out. He doesn't ask the guy in the hole next to mine if he's all right. Then he says:

[Notes for Chapter 11 start p. 80]

"That was a great thing you did up there."

There's an awkward silence. I don't get the full import of his words. Then he goes back the way he came.

> INCREDIBLE AS IT SEEMS NOW, IT TOOK ME YEARS TO FIGURE OUT WHY THAT GUY SAID WHAT HE DID. HE MUST HAVE BEEN A NON-COM AT THE BIG HEDGEROW UP ON THE HILL. BY SILENCING THE GERMAN MACHINEGUN I KEPT IT FROM CHEWING UP THE ENTIRE PLATOON FROM THE SIDE—EVEN IF THAT WASN'T MY CONSCIOUS INTENT. THE MEN HAD NO COVER; A COUPLE MORE BURSTS COULD HAVE GOTTEN THEM ALL. THE GERMAN MG-42 FIRED AT A RATE OF 1,200 ROUNDS A MINUTE—20 ROUNDS A SECOND. IT'S NOT REASONABLE TO EXPECT MEN WITH RIFLES TO RETURN FIRE WHEN AN MG-42 IS TARGETING THEM AT CLOSE RANGE.[4] WHAT I DID WAS THE OBVIOUS THING TO DO, BUT AS I SHOULD HAVE LEARNED AT THE *PORTBAIL* ROAD-BLOCK, WE COULDN'T EXPECT VERY MANY GUYS TO DO EVEN THE OBVIOUS. NOBODY EVER MENTIONED THE INCIDENT AGAIN., BUT THERE WERE CERTAIN CONSEQUENCES.

So now—up on the hill—I've had my first direct contact with the enemy, and I was not stunned into impotence. I didn't have any particular reaction at all. I was just doing what any soldier would be—or should be—expected to do.[5]

Are there atheists in foxholes? I've never thought of myself as an atheist, but I'm not particularly religious either. That doesn't mean I don't believe that there are forces beyond the human. *WEATHER* is a force beyond human power. *LIGHTNING* and *THUNDER* are beyond human power. The *SEA* is a great force far beyond human power. *FATE and CHANCE* are mysterious powers beyond the human. *WAR*—once you're in it—is a force and power beyond the human. *LIFE* itself is a force beyond the human—and beyond human power to comprehend. But not beyond human power to DESTROY. INHUMANITY is a force beyond the human—perhaps kept alive by a DEVIL or a DEMON. If you believe in Devils and Demons.

I figure it this way: unless I do everything I know, and can, and should do, to keep the shells from slicing me up, I'm not doing my part. And somehow the other side of it seems to make sense too—that if I *do* do my part, my utmost, to apply everything I know, from training, experience, common sense, logic, intuition, and hunch, if I keep my part of the unspoken bargain, maybe I can tip the odds of the **GREAT IMPERSONAL CHANCE MACHINE** an inch or an iota or two in my favor.

But what can I do—short of running back from the danger? Even that might not help, because shells fall in rear areas as well as at the front line. They hit command posts, supply columns, tank concentrations, artillery and mortar positions, road crossings. By running back, you could be running into the very shells you're trying to escape. And you wouldn't have the protection of a foxhole.[6]

> I DIDN'T REALIZE IT AT THE TIME, BUT THERE WERE FELLOW AMERICANS BEHIND US WHOSE JOB IT WAS TO STOP US IF WE TRIED TO RUN BACK. RUNNING BACK FROM COMBAT WAS AN OFFENSE FOR WHICH YOU COULD BE SHOT. NOT ON THE SPOT, BUT LATER, BY A FIRING SQUAD. THE GERMANS WERE SHOOTING AT YOU FROM AHEAD, CUTTING YOU UP WITH ARTILLERY OR MACHINEGUNS, TRYING TO BLOW YOU APART WITH SHELLS AND GRENADES, READY TO SKEWER YOU WITH BAYONETS, AND BACK IN THE REAR AREAS WHERE EVERY SANE SOLDIER WANTED TO BE, THERE WAS THIS OTHER LINE OF MEN, YOUR OWN COUNTRYMEN, THE MP LINE, DUTY-BOUND TO TAKE YOU AT GUNPOINT TO THE MILITARY AUTHORITIES WHO WOULD DECIDE IF YOU SHOULD BE EXECUTED, OR CONDEMNED TO SOME OTHER EXTREME AND UNDESIRABLE PUNISHMENT—LIKE TIME IN THE GUARDHOUSE WITH ITS STORIED CADRE OF BRUTAL SADISTS.
>
> IN WW-II ONLY ONE SOLDIER WAS SHOT FOR DESERTION, BUT THE POSSIBILITY WAS ALWAYS THERE.[7] AT THE BEGINNING OF BASIC TRAINING THEY READ YOU THE *ARTICLES OF WAR,* SO YOU WOULDN'T GO AWOL EVEN BEFORE YOU BECAME A SOLDIER. AND THEY READ THEM AGAIN AT THE END OF BASIC TRAINING—WHEN YOU WERE DIRECTLY FACING THE HARD FACTS ABOUT YOUR FUTURE.[8]

In my foxhole on the bank I try to think of everything that might tip CHANCE in my favor. I could dig deeper when the shells aren't actually falling. I could dig sidewise at the bottom to get a roof of earth over my body, or part of it, if only a leg or an arm, but the soil is clotted with tough roots. Efforts, both downward and sidewise-under, prove futile. Whoever dug these holes spent a lot of time at it. All I can do is try to protect the most vulnerable parts of my body with whatever I've got. I can pull my steel helmet down so it covers the back of my neck—as I lie, face turned to the soil, nose to the earth, with the shells screaming down.

I can try to protect my heart with the flat spade of my entrenching tool—it will stop shrapnel better than the helmet.[9] Even the B-A-R provides some steel-stopping protection. The receiver section is a pretty solid chunk of metal, and the stock is inch-thick wood. The ammo belt is a 50/50 proposition. The steel of the magazines and even the brass of the cartridges might stop some small fragments. Even small fragments can do lethal damage. But the ammo itself could go off and some of it would almost certainly end up in my body. Grenades present the same problem. I take the grenades off my pack straps and set them outside at arm's length over the lip of the hole. They're more likely to get hit there, yes, but they're less likely to get me if they are hit and explode.[10] I decide to keep the B-A-R ammo belt strapped on so if I have to get out of the hole in a hurry it will come with me. When the shells are coming down I place the B-A-R itself where it can shield my kidneys and crotch.[11]

Some ancient armies used tightly-woven cloth to cover their shields. Our canvas webwork offers similar protection—the heavy canvas straps, ammo belts, canteen pouch, leggings and pack. Anything, everything, helps. Stories abound about people whose lives were saved by Bibles in their breast pockets, or even decks of cards.[12]

Shhheeeew...Shhheeeew...Shhheeeew come the shells again. **CRAAACK-BRAAACKOTT... CRAAAAKUTKOW**. Dirt falls around me and on me.

SHAKKKKKKKTT! A tree is hit and takes a while to break off, then splits and crashes. Tree bursts are the worst—barring a direct hit in your foxhole. We don't have any protection from overhead.

Shhheeeeew, shhheeeeew, more shells.

[Notes for Chapter 11 start on p. 80]

BANGGGinnnnng...Zumma-zumma-zumma — a big fragment goes spinning down the defile, searching, then—**THUBB**—it hits something, or somebody. The moaning man is still moaning, and there is no new cry. The piece either killed instantly or missed. Or it could have caught someone in the throat.

Sheeeewwww—plupp. A dud plows harmlessly into the earth. It's heartening to hear even this small evidence of German fallibility. Better yet, maybe it was sabotage, a forced-laborer—Polish or Russian prisoner—in an ammunition plant intentionally leaving out the detonator, or one tiny screw.[13]

⊕

After three hours of shelling my spirit has collapsed into a soggy rag, a wet-rotted leaf. Beaten, I lie unresisting, waiting for the final destruction that must come.

But it does not come. The **BEAST** withdraws, satisfied that it has shown its **POWER**. The shells stop. The day is a day again. The afternoon is an afternoon. My body is not visibly damaged. I am not wounded. Nor, apparently, is the man in the next hole—I can see him moving around and his movements are ordinary movements, not desperate movements. It takes us a while to get back to where we can sit up, stand in our holes, feel whole and reasonably human again.

Veterans of all wars

But suddenly there is a new danger. If the purpose of the shelling was to beat us into numbness, to soften us up for a counterattack, the Germans will be coming—down the hill through the apple trees, over the flattened grass where I lay earlier with the B-A-R, coming at us in their gray uniforms, bayonets fixed, *Mausers* and potato-mashers held ready, *Schmeisser* machine pistols triggered to spit out the air-splitting AAARRRRRRUHHH—running at us down the afternoon.

"Keep watch," says a non-com from the bottom of the bank. If he hadn't come by, it wouldn't have occurred to me to watch—so preoccupied am I with my astonishing survival.

I crawl up the bank to where I can see up the hill, and, holding the B-A-R ready, watch and wait—but the Germans do not come.

[Notes for Chapter 11 start p. 80]

CHAPTER 11

About nine o'clock in the evening as the light starts to fade we get the word to withdraw. We come down from our holes to the level of the small stream in the bottom of the defile and I see the others, also down from their holes. We don't linger. The shells may come again. But we glance at each other with a new recognition. A new understanding imbues each word and gesture—or absence of word or gesture—with a meaning that can only come from sharing what we have shared. Rank and background mean nothing in the mutuality of the feeling. We have all faced the same moment-to-moment desperate thoughts, not just of the threat of death and dismemberment, but from the threat of giving up and of giving in. There is a flush of elation, even though we have won no battle except the one against the grim and gluttonous daemon that battered and consumed our selves, and our control of selves, while insidiously insinuating the bodily-manufactured poisons of physiological fear.

We did not leap terror-torn out of our holes to stumble back down the bank in wanton retreat. Nor up the hill, raging, shooting off our weapons in frustrated frenzy. We hung on, and we are all, now, because of it, different beings. Our GI clothes and gear seem cut from leather, buckled with bronze or beaten iron. Our weapons and equipment swing on our bodies like the ageless accoutrements of war—in every time and on every field of battle since war itself began.[14] We are the Huns after beating back the Mongols, Romans after fighting off the Franks, Braddock's men after the ambush—those who got away. It is a close, awful fellowship and we savor it secretly even as we sense that its origins are in evil and weakness of resolve, even as we acknowledge the abjectness of our submission to the forces of contrived destruction and the random devastation of war.

⊞

As we move out of the defile I hear that up at the big crosswise hedgerow on the hill a lieutenant and a sergeant were killed, one of them by a bullet in the head. It was that first and only burst of the German machinegun that got them—the machinegun that I silenced with the B-A-R. I wonder if it was the loud bawling lieutenant who was yelling for McConville, or maybe it was McConville. It was almost certainly the man I saw throwing the grenades over the hedgerow—he was on the left-hand end of the line of men and would have been the first to get

[Notes for Chapter 11 start on p. 80]

hit—but he was too far away for me to recognize. I don't see the loud lieutenant as we move out of the defile.

> WHY DIDN'T FIELD COMMANDERS MOVE TROOPS OUT OF AN AREA THAT WAS BEING HEAVILY SHELLED? THE FIRST PART OF THE ANSWER IS THAT IF YOU MOVED BACK OUT OF THE FOXHOLES WHILE THE SHELLING WAS HEAVY YOU COULD BE CUT UP WORSE THAN IF YOU STAYED IN YOUR HOLES.
>
> SECOND, FROM A TACTICAL POINT OF VIEW, IF THE ENEMY'S PURPOSE WAS TO SOFTEN YOU UP FOR AN ATTACK, YOU NEEDED TO BE THERE WHEN THE ATTACK CAME. IT WAS THE ONLY WAY YOU COULD HOLD WHATEVER GROUND YOU HAD TAKEN.

In spite of the intensity of the shelling, as far as I can tell only two men in our immediate group were hurt. One goes back on a stretcher, but he's conscious and talking. The other walks back with the medics, hit in the right arm and shoulder. I never learn what happened to the guy who was moaning, or whether he was a GI or a German. One of the guys says that if he was a German prisoner he should have been shot to keep him from giving away our position—the sound was loud enough. But I doubt if the man who said it would do it.[15]

We move back across the creek and out of the defile, through a gate and along the back side of the hedgerow that runs along the creek.

"Go in there," a non-com tells three of us, pointing to a low shed.

By this time the sky has clouded over, night is upon us, and it has started to rain. The interior of the shed is too dark to see anything. I'm last in. I have to stoop to step over a high wooden transom to get through the low opening—it's more like a window than a door.

"Watch out," one of the guys says, "There's a dead guy in here." My knee has already pushed against something soft that doesn't move.

How he got dead, or whether he is a German or a GI, I don't try to find out. But I think about lice and try not to touch the body. We huddle in the dark, the rain comes down, the shed leaks. When the rain lets up a non-com comes by and tells

[Notes for Chapter 11 start p. 80]

us to come out and pick up more ammunition. The ammo consists of 8-round M-1 clips in cloth bandoleers, packed in green steel ammunition boxes. Someone has carried a couple of the heavy ammo boxes up to us and set them down in the path by the shed.

Most of the guys don't need more ammo because they didn't fire their weapons.[16] To reload the empty B-A-R magazines I will need to unload the rounds from the M-1 clips and load them round-by-round into the empty B-A-R magazines. But after swapping the full magazines from Steel's ammo belt for my own empty ones, I have to re-load only one magazine to have a full belt. In the dark shed it's hard to see but I manage to get it done, sitting by the opening and trying not to sit on the dead guy. I barely finish when the non-com who told us to go into the shed comes by. He takes Steel's belt. He doesn't know what happened to Steel. He says to get ready to move out. We're going to make a night attack up the hill.

⌗

Notes for Chapter 11

1. I wrote this description of shelling with its train analogy before I found a similar comparison in *Fighting Words*, a collection of writings by war correspondents for *Collier's* magazine reviewed in the ANNOTATED BIBLIOGRAPHY. The fact that many observers and participants describe their experiences in similar ways speaks to the universality of war—one of its timeless attractions.

2. More excerpts from Stephen Crane's *The Red Badge of Courage:*

    > *The skirmish fire increased to a long clattering sound. With it was mingled far-away cheering. A battery spoke.* (p. 265)

    > *The guns squatted in a row like savage chiefs. They argued with abrupt violence. It was a grim pow-wow.* (p. 275)

[Notes for Chapter 11 start on p. 80]

> *Batteries were speaking with thunderous oratorical effort.*
> (p. 276)

> *The shells, which had ceased to trouble the regiment for a time, came swirling again, and exploded in the grass or among the leaves of the trees. They looked to be strange war flowers bursting into fierce bloom.*
> (p. 277)

3. In his novel, *A Farewell to Arms*, Ernest Hemingway wrote graphically about artillery:

> *There was fighting in the mountains and at night we could see the flashes from the artillery. In the dark it was like summer lightning.*
> (p. 3)

> *Outside we ran across the brickyard. A shell burst short near the river bank. We went flat and with the flash and bump of the burst and the smell heard the singing off of the fragments and the rattle of falling brick.*
> (p. 52)

> *—then there was a flash, as when a blast furnace door is swung open, and a roar that started white and went red and on and on in a rushing wind.*
> (p. 54)

And in *Our Share of Night* Drew Middleton took his turn:

> *The bombardment reopened and reached its height. The artillery, hidden around the city, talked all day long. From pine groves and the muddy courtyards of farmhouses the 105s and 155s lifted their voices. The explosions hammered at your head wherever you were along the front. In the early morning we could hear the low rumble of the guns when the Jeep climbed the hills above Spa and turned toward Aachen.*
> (p. 347)

4. The German machinegun I silenced was probably an MG-42, called a *Spandau* by the GIs, but not by the German Army. *Spandau* was the name of the German who promoted its manufacture and its use by the

[Notes for Chapter 11 start p. 80]

German military. The MG-42's rate of fire was much faster than any of our automatic weapons—which was both a plus and a minus for the Germans. The plus is obvious. Its 1,200 rounds per minute gave the Germans a lot more firepower compared to either our B-A-R or our .30-caliber machine-guns, which fired at only half that rate. But the greater rate of fire meant that the MG-42 used up a lot more ammunition. Somebody had to carry all that ammo. And, back home in the Third *Reich*, someone had to manufacture it.

Hearing our .30 cal light machinegun, then the sound of a German MG-42, the comparison was almost laughable. Ours would pop away at a pedestrian pace—tut-tut-tut-tut-tut—each round a separate sound. R-r-r-r-r-r-r-r-r-r-i-p, would go an MG-42, too fast to hear the individual rounds. Or, if it was a German *Schmeisser* MP-40 machine pistol—what we called a "burp-gun"—it would start fast then trail off at the end, the pitch dropping as the rate of fire slowed down for the last few rounds: A-r-r-r-r-r-r-r-uhhh. The sound was distinctive and we got to know it well.

5. U.S. General Ulysses Grant said, about his first battle in Mexico, that he was "not unmanned" by the experience. (John Keegan, *The Mask of Command*, p. 183)

6. As Horace put it (*Odes*, Book Three, 2, line 13):

> *Sweet and proper it is to die for your country,*
> *But Death would just as soon come after him*
> *Who runs away; Death gets him by the backs*
> *Of his fleeing knees and jumps him from behind.*

7. It's said in many places that Private Eddie Slovik was the only American serviceman executed for desertion in WW-II. He was shot by an American firing squad as the Allies were pushing into Germany, an incident reported in great detail in William Bradford Huie's book, *The Execution of Private Slovik* (See ANNOTATED BIBLIOGRAPHY). But Hugh Cole, an official Army historian and the author of *The Lorraine Campaign* (one of the acclaimed

[Notes for Chapter 11 start on p. 80]

Green Book series on the war in Europe), says that General Patton "...had troops hung for rape, just as he had troops shot for cowardice in front of the enemy (this despite all the later business about only one man being executed in World War II)." Cole is quoted in D'Este's *Patton, A Genius for War*, p. 653.

There may be a technical distinction between *desertion* and *cowardice*, but for the shootee it doesn't make much difference.

8. The reading of the *Articles of War* to recruits is discussed in Kennett's book, *G.I.*, p. 34, reviewed in the ANNOTATED BIBLIOGRAPHY.

9. *Shrapnel* is not the correct term for the fragments of metal produced by an exploding shell. Shrapnel was originally ball-shot enclosed inside a metal shell casing, named after General Henry Shrapnel, the British officer who first used it. Later, in the American Civil War, the term *shrapnel* came to be used for all manner of material crammed into a cannon's barrel on top of the powder. Sometimes it was grapeshot, sometimes miscellaneous pieces of junk metal, even stones and rocks.

GIs in WW-II wounded by HE (high explosive) artillery or mortar shells, were hit by shell *fragments*, pieces of the steel shell casing itself, broken and splintered by the explosive force of the powder. Studies were made on how to design shells to break up into the most effective size and number of pieces to wound the greatest number of men on the theory that a wounded man tied up more enemy personnel than a corpse.

10. Most of the guys didn't bother to take off their cartridge belts, grenades or bandoliers of ammo during a shelling, but I never knew of anyone who was killed or wounded by ammo on his body being set off by enemy fire.

The story went around that Lancaster, the battalion's night patrol specialist mentioned in a previous chapter, was wounded when a grenade went off in his back pocket, but how it happened and why he escaped serious injury we never found out. He later returned to duty and I saw him at *Fèves* Ridge (Chapter 21). He'd been promoted to sergeant.

[Notes for Chapter 11 start p. 80]

CHAPTER 11

11. The dust jacket of Paul Fussell's book, *Wartime*, has a photo on its cover of a soldier cowering on the ground with a B-A-R lying across his body. It could be me—except that I would have placed the B-A-R where it could have provided more protection for vital organs.

12. Teddy Roosevelt life was saved in part by a thick sheaf of papers in his pocket when he was shot before a speech in 1912. He insisted on giving the speech anyway. And in the movie, *The Man Who Would Be King*, played by Sean Connery, was thought by natives to be immortal when an arrow failed to kill him because it hit a bandolier hidden under his clothes.

13. See entry for July 4 in the *Operational Report*, Appendix B where the Regimental CP was shelled, and 18 of 26 shells were duds.

14. People in all walks of life seem to feel more in control with things hanging from their bodies. Huge bunches of keys hang from the belts of people who need only two or three keys for their days activities; elaborate tool holsters hang from the belts of workmen in all trades; cops have so much stuff on their belts they can't run fast enough to catch criminals. Women carry designer purses that hold stuff they never use for weeks at a time.

    There's a passage in Hemingway's *Big Two-hearted River*, where Nick Adams was carrying a lot of fishing gear:

    > *Nick felt awkward and professionally happy with all his equipment hanging from him.*
    > (*The Nick Adams Stories*, Scribner, p.190)

    The idea that a soldier in an invasion should be as self-sufficient as possible makes sense because his supply "tail" might not catch up with his unit for days, or weeks. Soldiers were therefore used as pack mules. In some cases, the overloading probably caused men, and missions, to fail.

    The farther up the ladder of authority a person gets, military or civilian, the less he carries. British General Montgomery, carried only a baton. As Supreme Commander in Europe, Eisenhower usually carried nothing at

[Notes for Chapter 11 start on p. 80]

all, though at one time he carried a small pistol given to him by General Patton.

15. In a bridgehead across the *Moselle* River south of *Metz,* where the wounded could not be evacuated, GIs were ordered not to moan for fear of revealing the number of casualties to the Germans. (Cole, *The Lorraine Campaign*)

16. According to Hastings, in *Overlord*, p. 187, "American research showed that, in many regiments, only 15 percent of riflemen used their weapons in any given action."

The research referred to was probably based on interviews conducted by the official Army historian, S. L .A. Marshall and reported in his book *Men Against Fire*. Marshall himself came under fire posthumously in an article printed in *American Heritage* magazine by critics who questioned both his credentials and the reliability of his data. From my own experience 15 percent was about right. For details of the controversy see *Reconciliation Road*. by S.L.A. Marshall's grandson, Douglas Marshall.

William DePuy, our Battalion Operations Officer (S3), and later the first Commanding General of the U. S. Army Training and Doctrine Command (TRADOC), seemed to agree with S. L. A. Marshall's assessment. See Web-link No. 1, Appendix C.

⊕

Lipless and mute from the
clotted extrusion of himself glistening
In the fire streaked
shadows, appealing with
unbelieving eyes: "What
has happened to me?
How much of me is left? Where is
my mouth — my
voice — my face — Who
Am I now?"

12

BEAU-COUDRAY

Night of Day One [Foxhole 13]
The man with the half-face

I find it hard to believe that we're going to attack again after taking such a shelling and losing the sergeant and the lieutenant. It seems like we need more time to recover.[1]

About ten P.M. we start to move out. The rain has stopped and there's some moon along with the clouds. A non-com gathers eight of us into a squad-like unit, takes us back toward the hill through a gate and gets us lined up in the deep shadows under a large tree. We can see out across an open field sloping up to some trees at the base of the main hill. The German shelling has resumed, but sporadically. The non-com says to go out across the open place one at a time when he taps us on the shoulder. I'm third in line with the B-A-R. The first two guys go, and make it across OK, then the non-com taps me. Because of the touch, the personal contact, it seems easier to go. I see the non-com's teeth and eyes glinting in the moonlight filtering through the shadows, stubble-bearded, avuncular, patient with fatigue, doing his tough job.

I run out into the open, crouched down in that awkward way we have all learned, and get thirty yards up the slight grade when a German shell comes roaring over my head skimming close to the curve of the hill. The noise by itself seems big enough to knock me down, efface me with the force of the sound alone, but I don't have time to go down. The shell explodes behind me where I was standing only seconds before. I'm still on my feet, moving, running, and I am not hit. When I get across into the shadows under a line of trees I look back, but I can't see the other men, and nobody follows me.[2] For a while I wait, alone. Then I see some GIs huddled in the shadow of a hedgerow and I see a guy who looks like a non-com and I ask him what I should do. He says to come along with them. I tag on behind as we go up the hill through a couple of fields, then stop. Our own time-fire

[Notes for Chapter 12 start on p. 105]

artillery is cracking overhead, some of it bursting in the air, short, spilling out ragged webs of red and orange as the glowing fragments spin away. A man comes up to me out of the darkness and when he gets close I can see that he doesn't have the bottom half of his face. It's a mass of blood, already partly congealed, shining black in the moonlight. He can't talk, but he can still breathe and he makes grunting noises through his nose. He's holding his bloodied left hand up near where his chin and mouth used to be. He wants to feel himself again, to know what has happened to his face, but is afraid to touch himself, afraid to know what is left and what is gone. He stands in front of me, sagging, completely defeated.

I open the bandage pack that's clipped to the back of his belt and tie the bandage around his face using its tie-strips, making sure not to block what's left of his nostrils, pulling it just tight enough to stay on. The sticky blood helps hold it in place. He doesn't flinch or protest. It doesn't seem to cause him any more pain than he already must be feeling. It won't help much, but it wouldn't seem right not to do anything at all. When the bandage is on, there's a decision to be made. He raises an arm that says what he himself can no longer say: "What should I do?"

I have a hard choice—go back with him and try to find the medics, or stay with the others trying to get up the hill. For a moment I think I will go back with him—but I have the B-A-R, not just a rifle. A Browning automatic rifle is a squad's main firepower. I change my mind and tell him I have to stay with the other men, that if he keeps going down the slope back where we came from he'll find the medics. He seems to be able to walk OK. I don't know for sure where the medics are, but they're always back of us somewhere.

I've never had anybody so dependent on me. I have the sense that he will do anything I tell him. He tries to say something, but only a gurgle comes out and he stops trying. Then he turns and starts down the hill with his half-face and I wonder if I'm doing the right thing, letting him go back alone.[3]

The guys I'm with get up to some buildings at the edge of what seems to be a small town and we lie on the ground in a narrow lane, in the dark, not talking, up next to one of the houses. There is a firefight up ahead—some rifle fire and machineguns—but not a lot of sustained firing. At any minute I expect to be called up front with the B-A-R, but no word gets back to me, and after a while somebody says we're moving back down the hill. I don't see why we have to move back. We certainly didn't use all of our resources. We go back to the field where I bandaged the guy's face and we're told to dig in.

I look for a place that feels right, trying to pick up some sort of feeling or hunch that might tell me where to dig. There's nothing else to go by. It's pure chance as far as the shells are concerned. You might as well go with whatever hunch you get if you get any at all. I'm like a dog looking for a place to lie down. I do get a sort of feeling after a while, and I pick a spot next to a short hedgerow and dig a shallow hole, and when nobody tells me to stand guard I sleep.

Beau-Coudray—Day Two [Foxhole 14]
Seeing the dead, all in a row

In the morning everybody seems relaxed and we're all walking around standing upright. Nobody explains what happened the night before, why we fell back after getting up to the buildings, what the situation is now, or the plan. We move laterally one field to the right and I see that it's the field where we got stopped yesterday, where I lay in the grass with my B-A-R, firing at the crosswise hedgerow. The two dead men are still lying behind the big hedgerow where the German machine-gunner got them. We don't have any assignments or orders, so I go up and look at the dead men. I think they are the lieutenant and the sergeant who sent me out on the patrol with the Thompson sub back at the roadblock. The lieutenant is not the loud lieutenant who was yelling for McConville, because that lieutenant has shown up again and seems to be in charge of whatever group I'm with. Maybe the dead lieutenant is McConville. If I had seen the German machine-gunner before he fired the two men might not be dead. But I didn't see him, and I couldn't have done any differently, or any better than what I did . I don't feel guilt. I don't feel anything.[4]

When I look at the two men there is no blood. Their wounds are not visible. They lie quiet, facing each other, about three feet apart, the lieutenant on the left, fallen

[Notes for Chapter 12 start p. 105]

forward toward the hedgerow, on his left side, his helmet askew exposing his right ear and some brown hair. The left side of his face is on the ground, his right knee drawn up slightly, his left arm crunched under his body. Someone has taken his weapon. The tall non-com lies similarly, facing the lieutenant, expressionless. His helmet has come off and it sits open-side-up about a foot away from his head. If they're the lieutenant and the non-com who sent me out on the patrol with the Thompson sub, they seemed to be friends, maybe both from the 90th in England before the invasion.[5] Maybe even back in the States. If no one moves them and they lie where they are forever it would not be inappropriate.

Late in the morning we go out ahead of our lines through the gate in the big hedgerow where the German machine-gunner was when I silenced him with the B-A-R. In the field to the left of the gate we find an entire squad of Germans, dead in their foxholes—apparently killed by air bursts from our time-fire artillery. Some of them are behind the hedgerow I was firing at with the B-A-R. It's conceivable that I might have killed some of them myself when I fired into—and maybe through—the hedgerow, but I doubt it. The hedgerow looks pretty solid.

At the uphill edge of the field where the dead Germans are is a house with broken-out windows. One of the guys says: "There's somebody in the house!" Everybody looks, and we see a man in the shadows behind one of the upstairs windows. He quickly moves out of sight, but becomes visible again a couple of minutes later. We can't tell if it's a German or a Frenchman. We don't have any Red-Cross arm bands, and we're carrying our weapons, but there are no shots. Then we simply ignore him.

I'm standing over one of the German holes looking down at a crumpled body lying on its left side, knees up to its chest, when I see a slight movement in the fingers of the right hand. The man is alive. I tell the lieutenant and he gets the medics and they lift the man out of his hole and bring him back to our field on a stretcher. We all stand around looking down at him. His lids are barely open. The black eyes behind them move in jerks, apprehensive, among us. He makes some low incomprehensible noises, then in a hoarse whisper, "*Wasser, Wasser.*" We give him some water. I feel nothing but emotionless pity for the poor bastard. Then the medics take him away.

[Notes for Chapter 12 start on p. 105]

I go looking for where I lay on the ground with the B-A-R yesterday and find the empty casings lying in the grass. I know I was there, and I fired all these rounds, but the incident already feels historically remote. There's no point in gathering up the brass, but it seems a shame to waste the metal. On a whim I pick up one empty cartridge—almost surprised that it's not still hot—and slip it into my pocket.

Then I see a pile of GI gear stacked up, apparently from someone who became a casualty—pack, cartridge belt, canteen, entrenching tool, helmet, and, sitting on top, a pair of black binoculars. Whoever he was, his M-1 rifle stands sentinel for him, bayonet thrust in the ground as per custom. It could be the dead sergeant's gear. I think about taking the binoculars. They're not GI. They're covered with black pebbled split-leather. Maybe they're German, taken from a prisoner, or from a dead body. I decide to take a closer look at the binoculars. I reach out, grasp them, lift them carefully off and away from the stack of gear. They are German. On the black enameled frame it says *Dienstglas, PRAG, 6 X 30*. When I look through them I see a grid in the right eyepiece, probably for artillery spotting. I really want the binoculars, but I don't walk away with them right away. I want to give somebody a chance to say I shouldn't take them. Nobody does. After a couple of minutes I put the leather strap over my head and let the binoculars hang on my chest. Suddenly I feel more potent, more capable of knowing where I am and what's going on. One GI told me that if we're captured and found with German equipment on us, we'll be shot on the spot. I decide to take the chance.

Now that we're not attacking, the change of mood is remarkable. We're strolling around the field as though it's Sunday in the park. Maybe it is Sunday; nobody keeps track. I walk past a deep hole and down in the bottom is my ex-hole-mate from the roadblock, asleep.

At night we withdraw again and dig in at the edge of the swamp. The soil is damp and musky from the rotting vegetation. But it's a wholesome smell, pure and earthy. It rains and the hole gets soggy, but it doesn't keep me from sleeping.

Beau-Coudray—Day Three [Foxhole 15, 16]

In the morning I notice that my ex hole-mate is not with us. I ask a non-com but nobody knows anything about him. He must have been left sleeping in the hole

[Notes for Chapter 12 start p. 105]

when we pulled back. But there is nothing to do about it, nor time to do it. We're going to attack up the hill again.

At about nine o'clock we start up at a new place, accompanied by two Sherman tanks. Halfway up the slope is a shaded orchard completely enclosed by hedgerows and roofed over by the branches of the trees. The tanks, along with some GIs on foot, go outside the orchard, around to the left and we lose sight of them. Then we hear some machinegun fire, and some other firing, and in a couple of minutes we get the word that the Company Commander was shot off the lead tank. He was riding on top to spur the attack.

Our movement up the slope comes to a stop. I find a group of men crouching behind a hedgerow just outside the orchard to the right. They're pretty tense. One of the men has been hit in the knee by a bullet. The knee is loose, no longer firmly connected to his upper leg. The guy is in a lot of pain. I decide to try to put a splint on his leg—the way they showed us in first-aid movies in basic training. He doesn't want anybody to touch his leg, but he finally says OK.

I get a couple of guys to help me and when we get working on it the tension eases off little. We do a pretty fair job with a couple of loose branches that had been clipped off the hedgerow by artillery, tied with cloth strips ripped from a discarded field jacket. We just about get it done when a couple of medics come up with a stretcher.

"You did our work for us," one of the medics says, surprised.

They don't do anything different to the guy's leg, just put him on the stretcher the way he is, splint and all, then take him down the hill.

Wanderers in nobody's land

The guys I am with are not the same ones I started out with, so I start looking around to see if I can find my own group. I go into the orchard and see a GI carrying a bazooka.[6] He too is separated from his unit. Then we realize that there's nobody left in the orchard but us. German shells start coming in and we look around for holes to get into. There's just one hole in sight, not quite a foot

[Notes for Chapter 12 start on p. 105]

deep. One man lying down would be able to get his body below the surface of the ground, barely—but there isn't room for both of us. We're staring at the hole and the question is obvious—which one of us is going to get in the hole? We can't take time to make a big philosophical case out of it, so I get in one end of the hole and bring my knees up to my chest, and I tell the guy with the bazooka to get in the other end. "We'll be lower down," I say. He gets in and we sit there scrunched down, staring at each other, me with the B-A-R, him with his bazooka. The shells come into the orchard again and explode around us and the shrapnel and the dirt flies. The bazooka guy has a very doleful look on his face. The situation could be funny, but it isn't. The bazooka tube is peppered with small holes made by shell fragments on some other occasion. It's a wonder it still works. Maybe it doesn't. Branches clipped off by the shells fall from the trees. A twig with a couple of leaves on it falls into the hole between us. The bazooka guy stares at it. I stare at the bazooka guy.

When the shells let up we discover that we are OK but completely alone. We wander around looking for the rest of the platoon. On our side of the orchard's uphill hedgerow we find a couple of dead GIs. When we look over the hedgerow up the hill we can't see any sign of the Germans, or anybody else. Toward the downhill part of the orchard we find another man lying on the ground, an officer, still alive. He has a head wound that has been bandaged but he doesn't have the strength to talk. He's a big man, too heavy to carry. We wouldn't know where to take him anyway. We give him some water, which he can barely sip, and tell him we'll be back.

We figure that in order to find out what's going on it makes as much sense to go back, as forward. We leave the orchard on the downhill side and cross the small creek that runs along the bottom of the hill. It could be the same creek that ran through the defile where our holes were on the first day of the attack.

Coming down the hill was the right decision. The company has pulled back to the initial line of departure. We come strolling in among them as though we've been out seeing the sights. A small boyish second lieutenant is sitting on a log, sobbing out of control. I ask a non-com what's the matter with the lieutenant. He says it's because of the attack that didn't work out, because of the casualties. I know the

[Notes for Chapter 12 start p. 105]

attack didn't work out—we're right back where we started—and I know about some of the casualties because we saw them, but I still don't see why the lieutenant is so disturbed. What did he expect? We're in a war.

> The soft-faced lieutenant is a
> boy, more than I, at least for
> now, bawling like a
> baby. Tears, sobs. The all the
> tensions burst suddenly, loose
> the cataclystic shooting out of the
> all the taut-tightened cramps of
> doubt. No doubts now, the boy is
> disarmed, displayed. Can he
> ever lead again? Perhaps. We, watching, un-
> derstand. We remember when kids we
> broke through suddenly into pure release,
> like this into that uncaring exposure of
> hurt and anguish, betrayal. He
> is learning as he sobs. Men break. If
> he leads again he will remember
> that. Men break.
> Perhaps this boy is the lucky one: all is out,
> here, now. Will my way be silent,
> without a sound, with secret wrenchings of the
> deepest hidden parts, rending and tearing,
> bleeding inwardly, telling no-one?
> Will we all come apart, each in his way?
> The boy bawls, we watch, and wait, as the unseen
> beast
> prowls among us.

I tell a non-com about finding the officer alive and he gets excited.

"It's the Company Commander." Do I know where he is? Can I show the medics where he is? Can I take the medics to him? I find it strange that somebody knew where the man was when they bandaged his head, and it wasn't the medics or they would have taken him back, but now nobody knows where he is. Everyone must have moved back in a rush, not checking, or looking.

[Notes for Chapter 12 start p. 105]

I say, yes, I can take the medics to him, and they come up and I point out where we left the wounded man, but the medics decide not to go. They say they have orders not to go out ahead of our lines. The non-com tries to get them to go anyway, but they won't. Maybe they can go out after dark, they say.

⊕

A guy who says he is Sgt. Yensko assigns me to an already-dug hole on the forward side of a hedgerow looking up a different part of the same slope where our aborted attack took place earlier. It's the first time anybody has bothered to introduce themselves. Yensko says he will share the hole with me, but he leaves, and never does get into the hole. It's a deep hole, shoulder high, yellowish sandy clay, no roots or stones, and when we start getting some heavy shells I think seriously about digging under at the bottom. When the shells aren't actually coming in, though, I'm supposed to be watching. On this side of the hedgerow I'm out ahead of everyone else. To get to the others the Germans will have to go through me. And my B-A-R. That's why I'm here. So I have to stay alert. But I dig when I can, and I get a narrow horizontal cave scooped out under the forward side of the hole, just room for me to squeeze most of my body in if I lie flat. But I don't like being in there. It's too tight. I want to be able to get out of the hole fast. Maybe I'm claustrophobic.

"I want men who can fight!"

Yensko comes back and says he is going to put me in for sergeant. He says he wants "men who can fight". He's a small slim man with a black mustache almost as big as Jerry Colona's. I'm not sure what he means by "men who can fight". It makes me uneasy that he thinks I'm one of them.

Sweet swallows, obscene magpies

We hear rumors that two companies in another battalion are cut off. At about three o'clock in the afternoon two of our tanks with a squad of supporting Infantry go out directly ahead of my hole [TO RESCUE THE CUT-OFF COMPANIES, I LEARNED 50 YEARS LATER], but the attack is aborted because the tank treads slip on the wet

[Notes for Chapter 12 start p. 105]

grass and can't get up the hill. I watch unbelieving as the great machines struggle to make progress up the slight slope. After a few token bursts of their 30-caliber machineguns—I don't think they saw anything—the tanks and the men on foot withdraw past my hole, the GIs' faces tense, but relieved to be giving it up.

We are warned that German tanks may attack us, and I prepare myself mentally for being run over by a tank. In basic we were told that German tanks made a practice of grinding GIs to death in their foxholes, burying them alive—if the tank treads didn't get them first. With the soft earth, it could happen here.

While I'm watching for the German tanks I'm treated to a classy display of French swallows darting past my hole and flipping in and out of the gates of the fields. They're a lot like our American barn swallows as they sail and flutter, dodge and swoop. They don't know there's a war going on. Their beauty and grace contrast sharply with our crude purpose. It's a nice show, but I can't afford to let my mind get diverted. Up the slope some black-and-white magpies are flashing their white wing patches like airborne semaphores, pecking at the external openings of two bloated black-and-white cows—rolled over on their backs, feet in the air.[7]

> Swooping, swittering, trouping, skipperling,
> silky-sheen metallic, but fluid as water.
> Nothing is more graceful than a swallow,
> in any country, any place. And they don't
> stay high above the guns below, as did the larks at
> Flanders Fields. These swapopliong swallows dare look
> guns and tanks and dead cows dead in the eye as they
> flick by, but they let the magpies do the picking.

All afternoon I keep myself ready for the tanks, wondering if I will try to fight them when they come. A bazooka is an anti-tank weapon, but a B-A-R isn't much better than an M-1. .30-cal ammo doesn't hurt a tank. Maybe I could throw grenades into their tracks as we were told to do in basic. But I wonder if I should do anything at all. Maybe just lie low, hope they pass me by, and let our own tanks take them on. All I can do is try to be ready for whatever is going to happen. But nothing happens. The tanks do not come.

[Notes for Chapter 12 start p. 105]

Toward evening Yensko comes by again and says he's going to move me into another field, but I can stay here for the night if I want to. I leave my hole and scout out the field over on my right a little farther up the slope. It's bordered by hedgerows on the right and left sides, and a towering hedgerow across the uphill side. A gate in the upper left corner of the field opens uphill toward the German lines. Guys are standing and sitting by their holes along the hedgerows and I look for a hole for myself. I find one that's already dug, next to the left-hand hedgerow, just inside the field. Nobody is in it and there's no gear around. I can have it if I want it. But I get a funny feeling about it. It looks too good to be true. Why isn't anybody in it? So I come back to my old hole and stay there. There's about twenty minutes of shelling just before dark with a couple of fairly close ones, then it quits.

After dark the medics go out looking for the Company Commander without me. They find him, but he is dead.

Beau-Coudray—Day Four [Foxhole 17]
"We don't go up there for dead guys."

In the morning Yensko tells me to move to the other field so I can guard the gate with my B-A-R. On the way I go by the hole that I passed up the night before. A shell has hit one edge of the hole and dumped a lot of dirt into the hole. I could have been there when it hit. Up the hill by the gate a guy named Alf Green invites me to share his hole with him. He says his family has a horse ranch in Oklahoma. It's an instant friendship. We're behind the giant crosswise hedgerow and have to climb up a short path—using some exposed roots as footholds—to get to the top so we can see over it when we stand guard. At night a burning house in front of our position lights up the sky. Wood sparks drift upward in the heat draft.

When it's completely dark a tall shadow comes quietly through the gate. We're ready to shoot, but it's a GI. He's a slim man with a soft southwestern accent and he has a sucking wound in his chest where a bullet went through and came out his back. He sits on the edge of our foxhole, head sagging. He says that after he got hit he lay in a ditch all afternoon and the Germans kept shooting at him. He's from one of the companies that got cut off. I put bandages over the wounds, front and back, trying to stop the flow of air, but the wounds continue to wheeze, like a

[Notes for Chapter 12 start p. 105]

person with asthma. I find a non-com and say that somebody ought to take the wounded guy back to the aid station, and that I will do it. He says I should get permission first. He tells me where the company CP is and I go back to the middle of the field and find some officers in a deep hole covered with planks and dirt. They've got some kind of a light in the hole that glints eerily off their sober faces. One of them says "OK", reluctantly. And then: "Make sure you come back."

We start out, the wounded guy with one hand hooked into my ammo belt for support, but we get lost. I tell him to sit down on the trunk of an uprooted tree and wait, that I'll come back with the medics. He is fading. The moon comes out and I find a road and finally come to an aid station with two medics. The medics are skeptical. Am I sure the guy is still alive? They're not supposed to go up after dead guys. They went up yesterday for a guy who turned out to be dead. Medics don't take dead guys. Graves registration guys take dead guys. It was a waste of the medics' time, and an unnecessary risk.

The medics have a tent and a lantern and they give me hot coffee while we wait for another litter bearer because one guy has to stay at the tent with the radio. The tent is warm and the coffee is hot. We could be a hundred miles from the front line. We could be on bivouac in Alabama's Talladega National Forest. We could be camping in the Adirondacks.

The second litter bearer shows up and he starts to get himself a cup of coffee but I tell him the wounded guy is pretty bad off and time is important. He grouses a little but puts the coffee pot down and I lead them through the quiet fields and we find the wounded man exactly where I left him. His head is drooping more than it was before, but he is still alive.

"See," I feel like saying, "I told you he was alive," but with the guy hit so bad there's nothing to crow about. I go with the medics as they carry him back to the aid station on the stretcher. His name is Ramsey. They decide they shouldn't try to do anything for him at the aid station and they leave the bandages I put on his wounds just as they are, with some extra adhesive tape to keep them in place. The sooner he gets back to a field hospital the better. They don't give him morphine because morphine is a depressant and they don't want to depress

[Notes for Chapter 12 start p. 105]

whatever life he's got left. They strap his stretcher onto the back of a Jeep, I give him a last word of encouragement, he gets out a barely audible "Thanks," and the Jeep drives away. It's a rough dirt road. No matter how careful the driver tries to be it's going to be a bumpy ride.

"Will he make it?"

"Maybe."

I decide to have one more cup of coffee in the warm tent with the lantern. Then I start back up toward the field and the hole with Alf Green. I get to the place where Ramsey was sitting and sit there for a while myself. I don't sit exactly where he was sitting; I'd feel funny about that. Was he thinking I wasn't coming back for him? I was lucky he didn't wander off. So was he. But like the man with the half-face, he was beyond deciding anything for himself. He would do whatever I told him to do.

Now I am alone in the silent countryside and it's a beautiful night with clouds moving raggedly across the moon. "The moon was a ghostly galleon, tossed upon cloudy seas," wrote Alfred Noyes in *The Highwayman*. And I think of Vaughn Monroe's song, *Racing With the Moon*. With the clouds sliding across its face, the moon does seem to be racing. One of my housemates at Oberlin had some Vaughn Monroe records. He liked the music, but he said Monroe was queer. It was easy to imitate Monroe's voice, nasal but deep. A voice student in the Oberlin conservatory of music who lived in our dormitory said Vaughn Monroe had "good head tones". Whoever wrote that song must have been thinking about a night and a moon like this one.

There is no sound of the war. There are no sounds at all. Not even crickets. It's spooky. The B-A-R is leaning against the log, touching my leg. The B-A-R could have been in a lot of fire-fights before I got it. Maybe it was involved in the action the officer at the repple depple was talking about—the fighting, or lack of fighting, that gave the 90th Division the poor reputation he mentioned. I sit for about ten minutes, wondering how I got all the way to here from the house on Bailey Avenue in Buffalo, from our rubber-band-gun wars in the back yards and the side streets and over the garage roofs, from our little neighborhood gang all the way to

[Notes for Chapter 12 start p. 105]

this real war. And what will happen next? I know I have to go back up to the hole. There's nobody here telling me I have to go. The Army doesn't even know I'm here. Nobody in the entire world knows I'm here. But I know I have to go back. Alf Green is a decent guy, and that makes it easier, so I go back.

Beau-Coudray – Day Five
The Map

In broad daylight a German with a white armband walks around the smoking house in front of our positions acting as though he's searching for wounded. He keeps looking up in our direction. We think he's trying to spot our positions, but we're told not to fire at him.

Things are somewhat relaxed in our field and we can walk around as long as we don't expose ourselves through the gate. The change from the tensions of attacking, and being shelled and fired on, is abrupt and in an odd way, unnerving.

I see a lieutenant squatting down studying a map and I ask if I can look at the map. He seems surprised that I would be interested, maybe surprised that I can read a map. I tell him I had a course in cartography at college. Cartography? Am I trying to make points? Maybe, but not knowing what is going on, or where we are, is hard for me to accept. I feel I should make an effort to find out. It might be easier to be kept in the dark, just doing what we're told, but I don't feel that way, at least not for myself.

The officer with the map is the loud-talking lieutenant. He lets me look at the map but I can't make any sense out of it. It shows only a small area with a lot of contour lines. Hedgerows are not shown, and everything is the same color – green or brown—I'm color-blind enough not to be able to tell the difference. I can't figure out where we are. The lieutenant points with his finger: "We're here." I can't match the map to the terrain but I don't let on that I can't. What the hell, I had a course in cartography didn't I?

I spend another night in the hole with Alf Green. We stand a 1-on 2-off guard. The house out ahead of our hedgerow is now just a pile of embers. Alf wants me to

[Notes for Chapter 12 start p. 105]

come out to his horse ranch after the war. He smiles a lot in a scared sort of way, white teeth gleaming out of a black stubble beard. He's a good guy to be with.

Beau-Coudray – Day Six [Foxhole 18]
"Who's there?"

We're moved to another field and I'm in a hole by myself behind a medium-sized hedgerow looking out over an open field. No other hedgerows are in my forward line of sight. There's nobody on my left, and I don't know the guy on my right. He has a small dark mustache and pale skin. A little pudgy and unusually clean, maybe a fresh replacement. We don't talk. We're warned to watch on all sides. German infiltrators have been spotted, and there may be snipers. But, we're told we can have fires during the day to heat coffee.

At night it is very dark and the air gets very tense. I hear a click from the next hole—it's the sound of an M-1's safety being snapped off, a common fault of the M-1. The safety should move quietly, but many don't. There are some very uneasy moments. Finally I hear a whisper: "Who's there?" I can feel the guy's M-1 aimed straight at me, from fifteen feet away. Jeezus, what's the matter with the guy? He knows I'm in the hole next to him, If he panics I'm a dead duck. Very carefully I talk him out of shooting me.

Night of Day Seven

Around 2:00 in the morning while I'm on guard I hear a noise on the other side of the hedgerow. It's a scuffling sound, like somebody walking. It could be a German. Or a cow. But I didn't see any cows in the daytime. I can't make up my mind what to do. There's no one to ask. The noise stops, then starts up again. Someone, or something, is moving around, close. I don't dare move, myself, for fear of giving away my position. Finally, very quietly, I unhook a grenade from my pack strap, ease off the tape from the spring handle, wait, and when I hear the noise again, pull the pin and toss the grenade over the hedgerow. It goes off with the hollow metallic bang our grenades make. Absolutely nothing happens. But there are no more noises.

[Notes for Chapter 12 start p. 105]

In the morning I look over the hedgerow but there is no sign of anybody or anything out front, and nobody mentions the grenade going off. I wonder if I really threw it. [I STILL WONDER.]

Day Eight—Stragglers

In mid-morning a non-com comes by and says to get ready to move out, we're going to attack again. I check over my gear, test the action of the B-A-R again without firing it. I've still got the D-Ration chocolate bar we were given back at the rest area by the 240s. My canteen is almost full. I'm as ready as I'll ever be. But the non-com never comes back. So we stay put.

> THE ATTACK WAS ANOTHER ATTEMPT TO RESCUE THE COMPANY THAT WAS CUT OFF. THE REGIMENTAL OPERATIONAL REPORT SAYS IT FAILED BECAUSE OF stragglers.[8] IF I WAS A STRAGGLER I DIDN'T KNOW IT.

Beau-Coudray at last [9] [Foxhole 19]

There's a rumor that the enemy may have pulled back and we get the word to be ready to advance directly ahead of our holes. At about 11:00 A.M. we move out across fairly open fields. At first we crouch down as we are used to doing even behind the hedgerows, then when there is no firing or shelling, we start walking upright. It feels strange to be walking this way out in the open and at first I feel uneasy and guilty, but we don't take any fire.

I see a light brown binocular case lying out in the open. It could have a pair of binoculars inside. But it's too inviting. It could be booby-trapped. Anyhow, I have the German *Dienstglas* binoculars. They don't have a case, but there's a leather tab with a slit that buttons to the front of my fatigue jacket to keep them from flopping around, and a rubber cap that flips over the eye-pieces to protect the lenses. I don't need another pair of binoculars, or a binocular case, so I skirt around the case on the ground and keep going.

We go through the outskirts of a very small town with just five houses [BEAU-COUDRAY] and come to a road. A German soldier lies on his side in the ditch. His mouth is slightly open, teeth showing like a dead animal's—not because he's German, just because he's dead.

[Notes for Chapter 12 start p. 105]

We move off along the road to the right, then cut back into the fields. When we stop at night we dig holes. Anyone shot in the foot or leg or arm or hand by a bullet will be put up for court martial, we're told. A couple of shots do go off and the word goes around that two guys "accidentally" got shot with their own rifles.

The lieutenant who had the map comes by and tries out a "potato-masher"—a German hand grenade first used in World War One. He gives it a good wing out into the field in front of the hedgerow and it goes up in an arc, the handle spinning around the heavier end, then goes off with a flat POP! Not very impressive.

We don't have any action with the enemy but just after we came into the area we heard the *arrrrrruhhh* of a German burp-gun a couple of times. We didn't pay much attention to it—just exchanged looks.[10]

"I never get used to the smell" [Foxhole 20]

The next day we move to a place where there are some German holes. Personal papers and equipment lie scattered around. An issue of *Völkischer Beobachter*— the newspaper of the *Nazi* party—has been used for toilet paper. I'm afraid of lice in the German holes so I dig a new one.[11]

At this location I first smell a ripe dead human body. It's a compelling odor, not pleasant certainly, but hypnotic. I find myself sniffing, to get a distinctive whiff, to smell it more clearly. I find the source and get near enough to see that it's a GI, left where he was hit, crumpled on the ground. I don't go up to look at him close.

When I come back I go past a GI machine-gunner in one of the German holes near my fresh one. He says he never gets used to the smell of a dead guy. He was in the fight on Hill 122 [MT. CASTRE]. It was *bad*, he says, with that odd look I've come to recognize—sober awareness of personal vulnerability, mixed with the fragile elation of survival. I wonder if it was worse than at *Beau-Coudray*.[12]

There's a slight breeze and when I'm ready to sack out in my hole the odor of the dead man is still in the air, a faint, distracting miasma, intermittent, like wafts of warm smoke. When I do get to sleep I dream about training in Alabama and the brush fire on bivouac in the Talladega National Forest. Major Green is waving his

[Notes for Chapter 12 start p. 105]

arms, giving an impassioned speech in the middle of the smoke of the burning pine plantation—"When the chips are down across the pond…" We trainees didn't really believe we were going to go "across the pond", but here we are. When I wake up the smell is still in the air. Dead men, it seems, don't get up and walk away.[13] They can't… say what's on their minds…

    We don't know if they
    have anything to
    say at all. They speak the only
    way they can, slumped and
    sagged into the
    soil, sending forth their
    sour essence to linger in the
    hollows, catch in the grass, one
    last message—though not in any
    language known to them, or us, unable to
    articulate, released upon the
    air—published, thither-blown, wafted with
    no purpose known. Vapor trails of
    final pheromonic phrase, unlinked to
    codified vocabularies; wraiths of inchoate
    encryption, left for us to
    sense, interpret if we can—the last
    epistle, telling of the last condition, even as
    Living told Life. His, now, the
    Secret Cipher of the
    Dead.
    …
    We
    cannot answer, cannot
    speak, cannot understand the
    primal tongue.
    We
    leave him there, move on,
    forget.

[Notes for Chapter 12 start p. 105]

BY JULY 16TH THE CASUALTY RATE FOR ENLISTED MEN IN THE 90TH DIVISION WAS 100%. FOR OFFICERS IT WAS 150%.[14] IN FIRST ARMY'S JULY OFFENSIVE EVERY EIGHTEEN INCHES OF GROUND GAINED COST A MAN'S LIFE (MY CALCULATION).

Notes for Chapter 12

1. I had never heard the word *reorganize* used in any of our training, and it was never discussed or considered as a factor in any of our field problems. This was one of our training's greatest weaknesses. Whenever there are significant casualties the need to reorganize is obvious. Somebody has to take stock of the remaining men and their weapons and ammo to see if they still constitute an effective fighting unit, and to move men into vacant leadership positions by on-the-spot promotion. The formal paperwork would follow—unless those who did the promoting became casualties themselves. If that happened, the promotions sometimes never got documented.

   Without leaders, soldiers normally do nothing. This is not a criticism or indictment. Without orders, they simply don't know what they are expected to do. Doing something could be worse than doing nothing.

   To effect a reorganization, a unit—usually a company or platoon—was pulled back from contact with the enemy, even if only a couple of hundred yards, so someone could move around among the survivors to count heads. In the hedgerows, reorganization was a common experience. See the *Operational Report 357 Infantry Regiment,* Appendix B, for instances of reorganization in the fighting at *Beau-Coudray* (July 5 ff.) and "The Island"—*St.-Germain-sur-Sèves*—(July 23).

   That night at *Beau-Coudray*, we got more ammo, but no replacements. If there were changes in leadership we didn't know about them; we didn't know who our non-coms and officers were when the attack began.

2.	I found out later that the men directly behind me were killed by the shell.

3.	In Colby's *War From the Ground Up*, a man with the lower half of his face shot off is described by a medic at the battalion aid station at *Beau-Coudray*. If it was the same man, I'm relieved to know that he found the medics OK. I didn't discover the book until 1982. Colby's book, and Blumenson's *Breakout and Pursuit*, are the only places I've found the *Beau-Coudray* fighting described in any detail. Both of these references are reviewed in the ANNOTATED BIBLIOGRAPHY.

4.	In basic training nobody tried to tell us what to feel when we saw dead GIs. In combat, they were usually left lying where they fell. If the fighting moved on past them, days went by, and in some cases weeks, before they were found by the graves registration people. No doubt some were never found, and lie mouldering still in the copses and hidden byways waiting for French children to come upon them in their play.

	We learned new values and feelings only by becoming absorbed into the army, combat and war, by actually participating in the fighting and the killing. Nobody back home could have told us what to feel, or what we might feel, and they didn't try—until after it was over. Then, a lot of people claimed to know what it had been like, and what we felt. And they told us.

	In basic, the closest they came to preparing us for the odor of dead men was simply to tell us to be ready for it. They didn't try to simulate the actual conditions, at least not at Ft. McClellan.

5.	At Cardiff, Wales.

6.	The original *bazooka* was a homemade musical instrument consisting of a stovepipe and a funnel that was used and named by the radio comedian, Bob Burns in the forties and fifties.

	For WW-II a portable weapon resembling Burns's bazooka was devised that allowed one man to launch a self-propelled rocket. The rocket had a *shaped charge* in its head that gave it the ability to penetrate medium-weight armor. The explosive force focused at the center of impact melted a hole through the armor and sprayed a tank's interior with molten steel. The weapon was also used against concrete pillboxes, machinegun positions, mortar emplacements, and anything else that needed high explosives delivered at relatively short ranges. Somebody dubbed the new weapon a "bazooka" and the name stuck. The German *Panzerfaust* was copied from our bazookas picked up on the battlefields of Sicily.

7. Thousands of cows were killed by artillery fire. They swelled up because the grass they'd eaten continued to ferment inside, producing gas, much of which couldn't escape. Freshly dead cows were sometimes butchered by GIs for steaks, but I, myself, never saw this happen.

8. Effective strength of B-Company was reduced to "about ten men and two officers". (357 Regiment's *Operational Report,* entry of July 10, 1944)

9. The hamlet of *Beau-Coudray*, sometimes written as *Beaucoudray*, is found on American military maps in Blumenson's *Breakout and Pursuit*, and in Colby's *War From the Ground Up*, but not on French civil maps. As far as I have been able to determine, we were attacking what shows on French maps as *Le Plessis-Lacaille*. When the hamlet was damaged by earlier military action some of its functions were moved to the nearby *Beau-Coudray* farm, leading to the confusion.

10. The *Schmeisser* MP-40 machine pistol—GIs called it a *burp-gun*—was a very fast-firing hand-held German sub-machinegun. Because many of its parts were steel stampings with little or no machining required in their manufacture, it could be mass-produced quickly and relatively cheaply. It proved to be so effective that an American version was designed and introduced as the M-3 sub-machinegun—dubbed "grease-gun" by GIs because of its shape. It fired the same ammunition as the .45-cal. pistol and the Thompson sub. A photo of an M-3 grease-gun is on p. 270.

I didn't think of it then, but maybe the burp-gun we heard was left behind by the Germans and one of our guys was trying it out—the way our lieutenant tried out the potato masher.

[Notes for Chapter 12 start p. 105]

11. Lice were not a significant problem for the American Armed Forces in WW-II because of recently developed production methods for DDT which made it available in commercial quantities. For the Germans, however, lice were extremely bothersome, and when they were taken prisoner, DDT powder was often dusted inside their clothes. Even General *von Schlieben*, the German commandant of *Cherbourg*, got a dusting after he surrendered—treatment which he strongly resented—or pretended to.

12. After reading Blumenson's *Breakout and Pursuit*, I think the fighting on *Mt. Castre* was probably worse. At *Beau-Coudray*. I didn't fire the B-A-R after the first day. We apparently won the battle, but who did the winning? Not the guys I was with. But two companies did get cut off, and one of them surrendered en masse. It was just luck that I wasn't in the worst action.

13. It seems strange now that we weren't told to report the location of dead bodies. We just left them where we found them. How did the graves registration guys find them? Probably the same way I found this one.

14. Hastings, *Overlord*, p. 246.

Sketch of Sackett at *The* "Island" (Chap. 13)

[Notes for Chapter 12 start p. 105]

13

ST.-GERMAIN-SUR-SÈVES

The "Island" [Foxholes 21, 22]
July 13

We move ahead a couple of miles and take defensive positions on the northwest bank of a stream [MAP 4, P. 120]. It's more like a swampy creek than a river. From the looks of it we could probably wade across. A row of forward foxholes has a view of the river and the terrain on the other side, and some of our guys are always up there on watch. The rest of the company is back up a slight slope, spread out over four or five fields. We're mostly hidden from the other side of the river by hedgerows but there are some exposed places and we're supposed to stay away from them so we don't bring in artillery or mortar fire from the Germans.

Curiosity gets the best of me and I find a place where I can see across the river, but I'm careful to follow the warning about snipers:

> *Don't stay where you can be seen by the enemy for more than two seconds.*

We've started to call the other side of the river the "Island". It just looks like a low hill with the usual fields and hedgerows. Somebody had to look at a map to know that there's another branch of the stream on the other side that makes it an island. I use my *Dienstglas* binoculars and see a German exposed from the waist up behind a low hedgerow. It's my first sight of a German in enemy territory. I don't get any particular feeling from it, but it is a strange twist, using the captured German binoculars to spot a German soldier. He follows the same rule about exposing himself that we've been given—then disappears behind the hedgerow. If I'd been a sniper I wouldn't have had quite enough time to get him lined up in my sights. But if he appeared again in the same place I could be ready. It's a good object lesson.

We haven't seen any GI snipers, I don't know why.

[Notes for Chapter 13 start on p. 121]

CHAPTER 13

    The
multirows of
hedge, each silhouetted against the one
behind, as the hillside rises, layered, each as
cut from leafy paper, each differ-toned stepping
away and up from the near to the
far, those farthest cutting their
line against the sky. My
optical attention drifts, then: without
announcement of any kind, the form, the shape, the
movement of one of they-whom-we-swear-our-
enmity-against, one of them, he, for seconds only, seen. Did I
see him? Yes, I did. And he is there still, now, hidden behind the
layered collage. His manner was not a threat; he paid no
heed to me his watcher, nothing about him to show
his and his people's deadly intent. A man who took a few
steps into the open day, square-helmeted, yes, but otherwise,
as far as I could see, merely like one of us.
But if I can, I must kill him, and he me. Can he, will he, will/can I?
And if he is there, are there there his fellows? Will they, at any moment, all
rise abruptly running at us down the hill? Should I shout:
"I saw a German, I saw a German!" No. But
Such loaded knowledge cannot stop with me. The
Army of the United States must know. When I tell, will
our powers and bombs and packeted explosions rain down upon the
man I saw, and his fellows?
I must tell: "I saw a German…"

I make a sketch in my notebook showing where I saw the German. It's like the drawing I made from the tree on our field problem back in basic training in the Talladega National Forest, with some hedgerows and terrain features roughed in.

We were told in basic that one man is not a good target for mortars or artillery, but when I show the sketch to the lieutenant—the one who had the map, and threw

[Notes for Chapter 13 start on p. 121]

the potato masher—he says he'll tell the Company Commander and maybe the mortars will put in a few shells. I tear out the page and hold it out to him. He seems surprised, the way he was when I asked to look at the map at *Beau-Coudray*—surprised that I *could* make a sketch? Or surprised that that I *would* make it. He hesitates, then takes it. But I don't hear any of our mortar shells explode over on the Island. Maybe they don't want to start a mortar duel just for one German soldier. Of course where there was one there could be more, unless he was a lone forward observer or an outpost.[1]

> WHEN TO ENGAGE THE ENEMY, AND WHEN TO LET THINGS BE, WAS A BAFFLING PART OF COMBAT FOR US GIS. SOMETIMES WE'D BE AT IT HOT AND HEAVY ON BOTH SIDES. AT OTHER TIMES THERE'D SEEM TO BE SOME KIND OF A TRUCE. WHO DECIDED WHAT WAS GOING TO HAPPEN AT ANY PARTICULAR TIME, OR WHY, WE NEVER KNEW. THE UNIT COMMANDERS PROBABLY GOT DIRECTIVES LIKE: "PATROL AGGRESSIVELY", OR "AVOID FIRING UNLESS ATTACKED", OR "KEEP OUT OF SIGHT." AT OUR LEVEL WE HAD TO TRY TO FIGURE OUT THE SITUATION FROM THE MOOD AND ACTIONS OF THE NON-COMS AND OFFICERS. IF THEY WERE RELAXED, WE RELAXED. IF THEY KEPT LOW IN THE INFANTRYMAN'S CROUCH AND STUCK STRICTLY TO BUSINESS, SO DID WE. AFTER A WHILE IT BECAME AUTOMATIC—YOU READ THE SITUATION FROM SMALL CUES OF ATTITUDE AND TONE OF VOICE. SOME GUYS NEVER DID FIGURE IT OUT.

We get shelled every day, usually for about twenty minutes at a time. If they're not close it's no big deal, we just get in our holes and wait it out. But a couple of times the shells land in our field, and one of the guys' canteen gets peppered with shell fragments. It was sitting on the ground just outside his hole. All the water leaked out and he shows it around like a prize he'd won at a carnival.

We rotate between the holes we've dug back in the fields and the ones at the forward outpost. Up ahead we have to be alert—maintaining a lookout but keeping out of sight—not an easy thing to do.

In the rear we can pretty much relax if the shells aren't coming in. I take out Jean's last letter from my combat pack and sniff the perfume she always dabs on

[Notes for Chapter 13 start p. 121]

the envelope. Back in basic at mail call I always got ribbed about the perfume. The mail clerk would make a big deal of sniffing the envelope, then pass it back through the hands of several GI's, each one sniffing and rolling his eyes. I didn't really mind. I was getting letters from my girlfriend—that was more than a lot of them were getting.

I write a letter to Jean, and for lack of anything else to write about, I go through the differentiation procedure I remember from a calculus course at Oberlin. It looks strange on the V-mail in place of the usual light chit-chat. Maybe they'll think it's some kind of coded message and censor it out. Jean won't understand the math, but I figure it won't hurt if the officer who censors our letters knows that I had some math in college. It's probably the tall loud lieutenant. Somebody said he went to Lehigh University for engineering. If he did, he'll know what my letter is about. Am I trying to score points, like with the map? Well, why not—as long as I'm doing the job I've been assigned to, which is being a GI on the front line fighting the Germans.

Just over the hedgerow from my hole is a dirt road with an abandoned German half-track painted yellow and green. It's the first German vehicle we've been able to look at close up. There's a charcoal storage bin on the back. The engine apparently runs on gas generated from the charcoal. I've heard of that, but I don't know how it works. Are the Germans running short of gasoline? We hope so.

⌗

On the third day Sgt. Yensko comes over to my hole and wants me to volunteer for a one-man patrol over to the Island. I haven't thought about patrols since the one with Steel at the roadblock. I hesitate a couple of seconds, then tell Yensko I'll go if he tells me to, but I don't want to volunteer. I'm surprised at my ability to say no. If yesterday you'd asked me what I'd do, I couldn't have told you.[2]

I really don't feel that I'm particularly good at what Yensko wants me to do. I used to spend quite a lot of time out-of-doors back home, yeah, but I don't have any special abilities that would help on this patrol. At Ft. McClellan I failed miserably when I was supposed to lead my squad on a night patrol through enemy lines. I

[Notes for Chapter 13 start on p. 121]

got the whole squad captured in the first ten minutes. And I was never a very good hunter. Animals are crafty. Some are very smart. We have to assume that the Germans on the Island are at least as smart as animals.[3]

And I'm no Lancaster. On the patrol with Steel I was too cautious. Yensko doesn't offer any reason for this particular patrol. My response to Yensko is literal. I will go if somebody orders me to go, but I won't be a volunteer. On the patrol with Steel I wasn't even asked if I'd volunteer. I was romanced into it. A slick job.

Yensko isn't the patient type. I half expect him to tell me I have to go on the patrol anyway. He doesn't, but he doesn't hide his disappointment either. I've let him down. His instructions were to get a volunteer and he thought I'd be his man.

The next morning I hear that a non-com went on the patrol and got shot in the arm. He had to lie in the swamp until dark but got back, otherwise OK.

A couple of days later Yensko himself is hit by a shell, bad, in the leg, and is evacuated—probably out of the war. He was hit while lying in his foxhole during a shelling. Secretly, I'm relieved. I've been uncomfortable at not volunteering for the patrol. It was going to be awkward running into Yensko. Maybe he'd change his mind about putting me in for sergeant. Now I won't have to face him.

When I get a chance I go over to the next field to look at Yensko's hole. It's partly covered over with planks but it's not caved in anywhere. The shell that got him must have been a tree burst. Some of the branches in the hedgerow over the hole are split off. His leg must have been sticking out from under the planks.

⊕

I discover that I have, in fact, been made a sergeant. I will be Assistant Squad Leader of 3rd Squad, 2nd Platoon, B-Company, 1st Battalion, 357th Regiment, 90th Division. It's the first time I've known what unit I'm in—other than the 90th Division. We also learn the names of some of the officers and non-coms.

Yensko will be replaced as Platoon Sergeant by a new man with no combat experience, Tech. Sgt. Barrett. The Platoon Guide is a guy named Shaeffer, with combat experience. A Platoon Guide is like an assistant Platoon Sergeant.

[Notes for Chapter 13 start p. 121]

CHAPTER 13

Among other things, he's supposed to bring up the rear of the platoon to collect stragglers. As the new Assistant Squad Leader I'll be expected to do the same thing for the squad.

The Platoon Leader is 2nd Lieutenant Chuck Liebau. He's the tall loud lieutenant from *Beau-Coudray*—the one with the map and the German potato-masher, and the one I gave the sketch to of where I saw the German. I finally get to know his name. The Company Commander is First Lieutenant Stevens [NEW TO THE COMPANY—AND TO COMBAT—HAVING TAKEN OVER THE JOB FROM A CASUALTY DURING THE LAST DAYS AT *BEAU-COUDRAY*]. THE Squad Leader will be Pulczak, an experienced man from *Beau-Coudray* and maybe before that, though I don't remember seeing him anywhere.

A bunch of green replacements have come up to fill in for casualties and you can spot them immediately. They're cleaner than we are of course, but it's mostly their manner that gives them away. They don't know what's going on—what's dangerous and what isn't. They've been told to stay low, and most of them do—very low. But a few of the new guys don't seem to take the war seriously.

Shaeffer introduces the new men to Pulczak and me. They are: Brown, Bruthiers, Gervase, Logan, Russell, Sackett, Sankey, Sartori and Seace. Bruthiers was born in Quebec and speaks French, but it's harsh and guttural, even harder to understand than the few local French people I've tried to talk to. Pulczak and I are the only combat-experienced men in the 12-man squad.

The question of why I was made Assistant Squad Leader comes up. "You don't know what Wighty did," Shaeffer says. Wighty was my nickname in college, and I've been tagged with it here.

> AT THE TIME I DIDN'T KNOW WHAT SHAEFFER MEANT, BUT IT'S CLEAR NOW THAT MY ACTIONS ON THE HILL THE FIRST DAY AT *BEAU-COUDRAY*—WHEN I STAYED OUT AHEAD OF OUR LINES WITH THE B-A-R AND UNKNOWINGLY COVERED THE PLATOON'S RETREAT—HAD BECOME A SMALL LEGEND. THAT'S PROBABLY WHY YENSKO SAID WHAT HE DID ABOUT "MEN WHO COULD FIGHT", AND WHY HE PUT ME IN FOR SERGEANT. THAT, AND THE

[Notes for Chapter 13 start on p. 121]

PATROL WITH STEEL, AND MY WILLINGNESS TO GO OUT AFTER THE WOUNDED COMPANY COMMANDER. BUT ANY SATISFACTION I MIGHT HAVE DERIVED FROM THOSE OCCASIONS—IF I'D KNOWN ENOUGH TO HAVE ANY— WOULD HAVE BEEN TEMPERED BY MY UNWILLINGNESS TO VOLUNTEER FOR YENSKO'S PATROL. THE SCORE, IN MY MIND AT LEAST, WAS ABOUT EVEN.

Pulczak starts giving the men assignments. The B-A-R I have been carrying will be given to a new man yet to be assigned. I'm find I'm reluctant to give it up. They're probably looking for somebody who's been a B-A-R man before, if only back in basic training. They go by the book on things like that when they have time. It's a wonder they let me carry the B-A-R as long as they did.[4] As Assistant Squad Leader I get an M-1 with a grenade-launcher on it, a handful of blanks, and a bag of rifle-grenades. I have never fired a rifle-grenade. They're supposed to give you a real jolt if you fire them from the shoulder. You can also fire them with the butt of the rifle on the ground, like a mortar.

The bag of grenades isn't as heavy as the B-A-R ammo belt but it's awkward to carry, and the grenades are just joggling around loose in the bag. That doesn't seem safe even if they do have arming-pins that have to be pulled out before the grenades will detonate. Maybe I can find something soft to wrap them in.

I'll have to carry the regular ammo for the M-1 too—a cartridge belt with 8-round clips in the snap-pockets, and a couple of cloth bandoliers filled with clips that hang diagonally across the chest.

Pulczak says Seace and Sackett will be scouts. Whenever Seace's name is mentioned he comes back with: "...firing", a trademark he probably has carried since he first got into the Army—when the drill sergeants didn't tell him to can it.

Seace accepts the assignment without comment, but Sackett objects. He says he doesn't think he should be a scout. He says he only had artillery training, not Infantry training. He does have a different style of field jacket, and he's got camouflage netting over his helmet, which none of the rest of us have.[5]

His objections sound lame to me, and I think to some of the others too. Somebody else will have to take the job if he doesn't. Anyhow, the only thing you do as a

[Notes for Chapter 13 start p. 121]

scout is go out ahead of the rest of the guys and try to avoid getting shot. Getting shot *at* is OK, because even if you blunder into the enemy's position you're still doing your main job—which is to find out where they are.[6]

And since when does a GI have anything to say about what job he's given? Once you accept being drafted, they tell you what to do and you do it. After a while it becomes a matter of pride, even a perverse point of honor, to do what you're told. You may bitch—but not to the person who tells you to do something, and after a while you even stop bitching. Especially in combat. You just do what you're told. Everybody's in the same boat.

Now here's this new guy, Sackett, trying to get out of an assignment because he thinks it's too hazardous. At least that's the way it looks. I don't let on, but the incident makes an impression, and I tuck it away in my head.

Pulczak goes looking for Shaeffer. When he comes back, Pulczak picks another guy for scout—Sankey. Maybe it's better that Sackett isn't a scout. A too-cautious and unwilling scout wouldn't be much good. I don't know if I'd make a good scout myself. Like Seace, Sankey accepts the job without comment.

The roster for third squad—in the order of march—is now as follows:

1.	Seace	-	1st Scout
2.	Sankey	-	2nd Scout
3.	Pulczak	-	Squad Leader
4.	(Unassigned)	-	B-A-R Man
5.	Russell	-	Assistant B-A-R Man
6.	Logan	-	B-A-R Ammunition Bearer
7.	Brown	-	Rifleman
8.	Bruthiers	-	Rifleman
9.	Gervase	-	Rifleman
10.	Sackett	-	Rifleman
11.	Sartori	-	Rifleman
12.	Wightman	-	Assistant Squad Leader

[Notes for Chapter 13 start on p. 121]

> AT THE TIME I DIDN'T SEE A PARALLEL BETWEEN SACKETT'S RESISTANCE TO BEING MADE A SCOUT AND MY UNWILLINGNESS TO VOLUNTEER FOR YENSKO'S PATROL. I REALLY DID THINK THEY COULD FIND A BETTER MAN FOR THE PATROL—SOMEBODY WHO HAD A KNACK FOR IT. MAYBE THAT'S THE WAY SACKETT FELT, TOO. IN DEFENSE OF BOTH OF US, CONFIDENCE, IN COMBAT, COUNTS FOR A LOT—SOMETIMES EVERYTHING.

On the very first day Brown tries to test me out to see what I'm going to be like as one of their non-coms.

"Is it OK if we call you 'Whitey?'" he asks, with the trace of a smirk. "Or do you want us to call you 'Sergeant?'"

Brown is from near a small town in the north-west corner of Pennsylvania with the seemingly inappropriate name of North East. The "town" itself is a traffic light and a gas station. I mentioned to Brown that I'd been through North East several times on my way hitchhiking from Buffalo to Oberlin College in Ohio. That was probably a mistake. A lot of people think Oberlin is just a music school. Next thing he'll ask is if I'm learning to play the triangle.* Oberlin itself is in the boondocks. Without the college, there'd be nothing.[7] But where Brown comes from has to be the real boonies. Maybe he and his small-town buddies made fun of guys who went to Oberlin. I can't help wondering how things are going to work out between us.

"Doesn't matter to me," I say, aware that the others are listening. I could make a joke of it—*Call me anything you like, as long as you don't call me late for chow.* But Brown's attitude isn't helpful. It's a distraction from the business at hand. We're not back in Pennsylvania hunting woodchucks. I handle things OK, I guess, at least for now. I didn't ask to be a non-com. I'm not even sure I want the job.

July 17

While we're at the Island we hear that German Field Marshal *Erwin Rommel* has been severely injured by Allied fighter bombers.[8]

I didn't even know *Rommel* was in France. Lt. Liebau is jubilant. Now the *Desert Fox* of North Africa and *El Alamein* won't be able to use his cunning against us.

---

* Not to minimize the skills and athleticism of percussionists.

[Notes for Chapter 13 start p. 121]

It's probably a lucky break for us, and I suppose it makes sense to be happy about it. *Rommel* has a formidable reputation. Even I have heard of him. But I find that I'm not eager to rejoice at his injuries. At *Beau-Coudray* I never saw the German machine-gunner I shot at, and possibly killed, or wounded, and I had no sense of satisfaction seeing all those dead Germans in their foxholes. What will happen when I come face to face with a German soldier at close quarters?

July 20

Another rumor bursts like an artillery shell:

Hitler is dead, assassinated by one of his own generals!

For a couple of hours we're excited and euphoric. With *der Führer* gone, a lot of the fight is bound to go out of the Germans. The war can't last much longer. But the report is soon amended: *Hitler* was injured, but he is still alive. I find myself much more willing to wish death on *Hitler* than on *Rommel*. *Hitler* is evil incarnate. That's what we were told in the training films. *Rommel* was respected for his military abilities by both sides.

The squad gets assigned to the forward foxholes for the afternoon. It's a fine summer day and nothing is happening. We take turns watching and in one of my off periods I try making a pencil sketch of Sackett in the small notebook I've carried with me since leaving England. He's a good subject, with regular, almost chiseled features. He's from South Carolina and talks with a soft, but definitely southern accent. I can imagine him in a gray Confederate uniform with a black leather belt and a cavalry sword. The sketch is a pretty good likeness and I put it away in my fatigue jacket pocket. He didn't know I was doing it. I'll show it to him sometime.[9] We get to talking and Sackett says he was in college planning to go to law school when he was drafted. At first he was put in the artillery, then got transferred to the Infantry. He obviously thinks he got a bad deal.[10]

At the Island when we're not being shelled we get to move around the area if we're not up in the forward holes. The day after my squad is brought back to the rear again I'm walking past a hole with a partial roof over it and a guy calls up to

[Notes for Chapter 13 start on p. 121]

me from the shadows down in the hole. He recognizes me from somewhere, maybe *Beau-Coudray*. He seems to be in hiding. There's nothing going on, no shells, no firing. Things have been pretty quiet. It's a nice day. He could be up and around like me, enjoying a little freedom. But he's hole-bound, with that same smoky dark look some of the original 90th Division guys had back at the rest area near the battery of 240s. Only this guy is worse. All he can talk about is how bad things are going to be when we move out. His white eyeballs and teeth gleam out of the dark hole the way Alf Green's did the first night by the burning house at *Beau-Coudray*, but this guy lacks Green's grin. And it's daytime with the sun shining. I don't see why this guy is so scared. The rest of us aren't reacting that way, not here, not today. Hell, *Rommel* is out of it, and *Hitler* was almost killed. There's talk of a complete German collapse. The war could be over in a week.

"I don't think so," the guy says.

I try not to let his mood bother me but it's hard to shake off. Maybe he's right. He's had more experience than I have. Maybe things will get bad again.

> THINGS AT THE "ISLAND" GOT VERY BAD FOR A BATTALION OF 358. IT WAS ORDERED TO ATTACK AT NIGHT ACROSS THE RIVER, DOWNSTREAM (NORTH-EAST) FROM OUR POSITIONS. TWO COMPANIES GOT ACROSS, THEN WERE COUNTER-ATTACKED. A WITHDRAWAL ATTEMPT BACK ACROSS THE RIVER TURNED INTO A ROUT. ACCORDING TO ONE ACCOUNT AN OFFICER PULLED HIS .45 AND THREATENED TO SHOOT ANYONE WHO RAN BACK, BUT WHEN AN 88 HIT CLOSE HE GAVE UP THE HEROICS AND DISAPPEARED.[11] THE MEN WERE SURROUNDED ON THREE SIDES, TRAPPED AGAINST THE WATER. IF THEY'D TRIED TO WITHDRAW BY WADING BACK THROUGH THE MARSH THEY'D HAVE BEEN EASY TARGETS. WHEN A GERMAN TANK APPEARED AN ENTIRE COMPANY SURRENDERED. THE BATTALION COMMANDER WAS RELIEVED OF DUTY ON THE SPOT WHEN IT WAS DISCOVERED THAT HE HADN'T GONE ACROSS THE RIVER WITH HIS MEN.[12]

CHAPTER 13

THE "ISLAND" AT ST.-GERMAIN-SUR-SÈVES

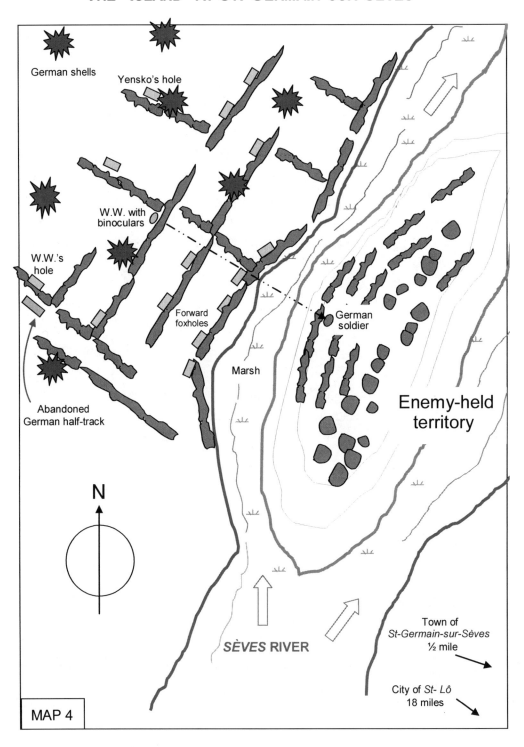

MAP 4

[Notes for Chapter 13 start on p. 121]

Notes for Chapter 13

1. An order to conserve mortar ammunition may have been the reason. See *Operations Report*, Appendix B, entry for July 21.

2. When I left for overseas, the only advice my father gave me was that I shouldn't feel that I had to do anything "out of the ordinary". In other words, I didn't need to try to be a hero. Such feelings on a father's part are certainly understandable. I didn't have any clear idea of what I wanted to do, or be, in the war, but I didn't want to be restricted by cautionary advice from my father. His words didn't influence my decision about Yensko's patrol. I made up my own mind, for my own reasons.

3. A kid in my neighborhood back home was much better than I was at out-foxing the rest of us guys in search-and-pursuit type games. He had an instinctive talent of some kind, I guess. But he wasn't very good at team games like softball and touch football. I've wondered how he might have done in combat. Maybe he'd have been another Lancaster.

4. Our records followed us around and were periodically updated, probably in regimental headquarters.

5. According to Max Hastings, in the spring of 1944 only 37% of Infantry replacements in Normandy were trained as riflemen (*Overlord*, p.167). Sackett's claim may well have been true.

   Netting on helmets was for holding leaves and small branches of foliage for camouflage. Our company didn't have the nets and I never saw one actually used for camouflage. I always thought that foliage waving around when you moved your head would give away your position. But bare helmets did tend to glare in the sun even with their metal surface dulled with grit-containing OD paint, and the netting cut down on the glare.

[Notes for Chapter 14 start p. 136]

CHAPTER 13

6. Some combat guys might disagree with me that anybody could be a good scout. Exceptionally good scouts were, no doubt, rare. You had to keep a sharp lookout for ambushes and booby-traps, move quietly so you'd see the enemy before they saw you, and be ready to make quick decisions.

7. Not quite true. Oberlin was a station on the Underground Railroad during the Civil War and a substantial African-American population still exists.

8. The Infantry grapevine was remarkably efficient. Unlike the wild rumors that flew around the troopship on the trip over from the States, most battlefield rumors turned out to be true. We heard about *Rommel's* accident the day it happened. His command car was attacked by British Typhoons and landed in the ditch. Rommel suffered a serious brain concussion, facial fractures, and temporary loss of vision in one eye.

9. I lost the notebook, but many years later I re-drew the sketch from memory and sent it to Sackett. He said he framed it and put it up on the wall.

10. In William Bradford Huie's *The Execution of Private Slovik*, he notes that the decision was made in the summer of 1943 to make preparations for assaulting both Germany and Japan with ground troops. It had been hoped that such an all-out commitment of Infantry would not be necessary. A vast "combing out" of men from other branches ensued. Riflemen were in special demand. This was the period when I was drafted out of college and when Sackett was transferred out of the artillery. Private Slovik was reclassified from 4-F to 1-A. They didn't want him at first, but when their needs escalated they changed their minds.

11. An eye-witness recalls this incident in Colby's *War From the Ground Up*. See also Web-link No. 2, Appendix C for another instance of an officer threatening troops with a weapon.

12. Grim accounts of this event are found in Martin Blumenson's *Breakout and Pursuit,* and in the entries of the *Operational Report 357th Infantry* for July 22 and 23, Appendix B. See Also Web-link No. 7, Appendix C.

[Notes for Chapter 14 start on p. 136]

14

BREAKTHROUGH

COBRA

July 25

We move back a half mile from our holes across from the "Island" and spread out along a dirt road. The company clerk brings us mail and I get a package from home wrapped in the usual brown paper cut from a grocery bag. Inside are broken cookies and a whole, though badly dented orange. I go around crowing: "Hey look, an orange!" We haven't had any fresh fruit since landing in France. There are plenty of apple trees, but the apples are still green and hard. I offer half of the orange to Liebau but he declines—because it looks so beat up, or because he doesn't want to deprive me of any of my prize, or both. I also get a letter from Jean, perfumed as always, but faint now from its long journey. I eat the orange and read Jean's letter—savoring both. She says she may start taking voice lessons from somebody named Werrenrath.[1]

Ring-side seats

Late the next morning our attention is drawn to the east by the deep drone of many planes. We stand along the road and watch as wave after wave of Allied bombers appear, moving from left-to-right across our front, only a few miles past the Island. Soon we hear the rolling roar of their bombs pummeling the earth. They're being dropped on an area quite close, to the southeast. Clouds of dust and smoke boil up. It's a spectacular show. Something really big is going on.

German anti-aircraft fire dots the sky with dirty puffs of poisonous black carnations, but the bombers drone on without changing course. Two of our B-17s are hit. They falter, break apart, the pieces falling slowly, sliding smoothly, then, as they catch the air—flipping and swooping crazily. Another B-17 is hit, trails smoke but holds together, spirals down majestically, burning. We glance at each other. Men are dying in full view, and those in the doomed planes have clear foreknowledge of their fate. A few chutes pop out, tiny dots can't get out, or are

[Notes for Chapter 14 start p. 136]

already dead, or are wounded too severely to escape, or prefer to ride their ships into the ground.

Back in civilian life, our leaders—parents, teachers, church, government, newspapers, radio—tried to interpret catastrophic events for the rest of us, a duty that went with their positions. Here, officers and non-coms are the only leaders we have—and I'm one of them. But we need as much guidance as anybody else.[2]

> On they came, and they came
> on: swarms, flights, inundations,
> dronings, rumblings, thrummings,
> powering, pounding, pummeling, then
> their issue dropped free, the
> bombs, and the Earth
> heaved, shook. Ack-ack drifted invisibly
> upward, burst, spiked destruction into
> the summer sky, but the great
> planes paid not heed.
> When one of their own in virtuous arrogance
> ventured, caught flack, tore itself into
> shards that fell like flipping leaves—the great
> planes paid not heed. Nor when their
> crews, some pluffling out into silken chutes,
> swinging, settling, waiting to be
> shot; others plummeting from the start—the
> great planes paid not heed. On they came, and they
> came on. Nature displays her shows of awful
> might—tidals, quakes, excrescences of the Earth's
> own flowing blood-ma; men, too, do,
> determined, grudgeful, striking: chaos from
> chaos, chaos from ordered havoc, havoc from
> ordered chaos; impotent anger in the face of the
> fearful force of war.

[Notes for Chapter 14 start on p. 136]

THIS WAS THE GREAT COBRA "CARPET BOMBING" A DETERMINED MOVE TO BREAK OUT OF THE HEDGEROWS. 2,200 ALLIED PLANES SATURATED GERMAN POSITIONS IN A SMALL AREA JUST SOUTH OF THE HIGHWAY BETWEEN ST.-LÔ AND PÉRIERS [MAP 1, P. iv]. ON THE PREVIOUS MORNING THE MISSION HAD BEEN POSTPONED BECAUSE OF POOR WEATHER, BUT THE ADVANCE PLANES DIDN'T GET THE WORD IN TIME AND SOME OF THEIR BOMBS FELL SHORT KILLING AMERICAN TROOPS. ON THE 25TH, THE FULL COBRA MISSION WAS CARRIED OUT AND MORE AMERICANS WERE KILLED. GENERAL LESLEY MCNAIR, WHO HAD BEEN CHIEF OF AMERICAN GROUND FORCES AND ONE OF THE ARCHITECTS OF THE NEW AMERICAN ARMY, WAS ONE OF THEM. HIS BODY WAS BLOWN APART, IDENTIFIED ONLY BY HIS WEST POINT CLASS RING FOUND ON A SEVERED HAND.[3]

AS WITH ROMMEL'S ACCIDENT, WE HEARD OF MCNAIR'S DEATH THE SAME DAY IT HAPPENED, BUT IN THIS CASE THE EFFICIENCY OF THE GI GRAPEVINE WAS NOT APPRECIATED. OFFICIALLY, MCNAIR WASN'T EVEN IN FRANCE. HE WAS SUPPOSED TO BE BACK IN ENGLAND AS THE COMMANDING GENERAL OF FUSAG—FIRST UNITED STATES ARMY GROUP. THIS WAS THE PHONY AMERICAN INVASION FORCE POISED FOR WHAT HITLER THOUGHT WOULD BE THE MAIN INVASION EFFORT AT THE PAS DE CALAIS—THE PLACE ON THE FRENCH COAST CLOSEST TO ENGLAND. MCNAIR HAD TAKEN OVER FUSAG FROM PATTON WHEN PATTON WENT TO FRANCE TO ORGANIZE THE THIRD ARMY. SOMEONE OF MCNAIR'S PROMINENCE WAS NEEDED AT FUSAG TO MAINTAIN CREDIBILITY AFTER PATTON DROPPED OUT OF SIGHT. EVEN AS LATE AS THE 25TH OF JULY, THE GERMAN HIGH COMMAND THOUGHT THE INVASION IN NORMANDY WAS ONLY A FEINT.

TO AVOID PUBLICITY AND KEEP THE FUSAG FICTION ALIVE, MCNAIR WAS BURIED IN FRANCE IN A SECRET NIGHT CEREMONY WITH ONLY A HANDFUL OF WITNESSES. EVEN SO, THE WORD GOT OUT—AT LEAST TO US GIS.

Suddenly there is a terrific roar overhead as a fighter plane blasts over us at tree-top level. It's a German *ME-109*. Tight on its tail is an American P-47.[4] The chase is almost laughable. I can see where the term *dogfight* comes from, but this is more like a dog going after a cat. The planes tear furiously out of sight and a few seconds later we see a plume of black smoke. The word is passed quickly—the *Messerschmitt* went down. Everybody cheers.[5]

> COBRA SEEMED TO BE A FAILURE WHEN COLLINS'S VII CORPS TROOPS TRIED TO MOVE INTO THE BOMBED-OUT TERRAIN AND STRONG RESISTANCE WAS PUT UP BY THE REMNANTS OF THE GERMAN *PANZER LEHR* DIVISION. BUT ON THE FOLLOWING DAY RESISTANCE CRUMBLED. TWO OF COLLINS'S ARMORED DIVISIONS BROKE THROUGH AND SLICED LATERALLY THROUGH GERMAN REAR AREAS. THE OBJECTIVE OF THE WESTERNMOST OF THESE DIVISIONS, THE 3RD ARMORED, WAS THE CITY OF *COUTANCES*.
>
> PART OF OUR OWN VIII CORPS ALSO HAD *COUTANCES* AS AN OBJECTIVE. THE 4TH ARMORED DIVISION HAD BEEN BROUGHT UP ON THE LINE WEST OF OUR POSITIONS AT THE *SÈVES* RIVER ISLAND AND WAS POISED TO PUSH DOWN THROUGH THE MIDDLE OF THE *CHERBOURG* PENINSULA. PART OF THE 90TH'S MISSION WAS TO PROVIDE INFANTRY SUPPORT FOR THE 4TH ARMORED. TANKS NEEDED INFANTRY WITH THEM TO PROVIDE PROTECTION AGAINST GERMAN *PANZERFAUSTS* AND OTHER CLOSE-ON WEAPONRY.
>
> ON JULY 26TH, VIII CORPS STARTED MOVING. SPREAD ACROSS THE CORPS FRONT WERE THREE INFANTRY DIVISIONS: THE 90TH ON THE EAST; THE NEWLY-ACTIVATED 8TH IN THE MIDDLE (TAKING THE PLACE OF THE 82ND AIRBORNE WHICH HAD GONE BACK TO ENGLAND FOR REFITTING); AND THE 79TH ON THE WEST. BY THIS TIME THE 90TH DIVISION HAD A NEW COMMANDING OFFICER, GENERAL LEONARD MCLAIN—THE THIRD SINCE THE DIVISION DISEMBARKED AT UTAH BEACH.

On the day after the big bombing we wade across the *Sèves* River north of the island and move through an area that shows signs of heavy fighting. A GI helmet with a bullet hole centered just over the front rim has been carefully placed on a log. Nobody disturbs it.[6]

My first assignment as Assistant Squad Leader is to take half the squad through the fields along the right-hand side of the road to mop up as the company moves forward. Pulczak has the other half on the left side. We move off the road into the first field and find ourselves face to face with a stack of dead GIs. They must have

[Notes for Chapter 14 start on p. 136]

already been stiff when they were put there because the bodies don't sag down on themselves as soft bodies would have done. Legs protrude at awkward angles, hands and arms reach out. The stack is chest high. The faces are black, and at first I think they're negroes, or that they were burned in a tank. Then I realize their uniforms aren't charred, and they're not negroes. They're just dead, and have been for some time. For some reason, the dead GIs are less disturbing to me than the helmet with the bullet hole.

We finally got a new B-A-R man, Paull. "Two ells," he interjects whenever his name is mentioned. He's a green replacement and I'm concerned about his lack of caution. I try to give him some advice—to be more alert and not expose himself unnecessarily, but he shrugs it off. He's a big man with a shambling way of moving. The B-A-R is heavy, almost twenty pounds. Paull cradles it in his arms like a bird hunter with a shotgun. It's a standing joke that the B-A-R is usually given to the smallest man in the squad, but that didn't happen this time.

Chances are the Germans are gone because some of our guys must have been here to stack up the dead GIs—I doubt if the Germans would have done it. Even so, I still think we should use caution approaching each hedgerow. Before I can set up a plan, Paull strolls out in front of the first hedgerow and walks right up to it. No shots are fired and the rest of us follow. The hedgerow has been hollowed out from the back with gun ports cut through. They aren't visible until we get right up to the hedgerow. The dead GIs could have been shot from these very positions. The hedgerow is abandoned, but Germans stragglers could have been here and killed us all. I've got to find a way to control the guys better, especially Paull.

Pulczak told me to keep contact with him across the road but that's hard to do because of the hedgerows. We have to climb over them, or force our way through them. A few have openings between fields, but most of them don't, at least not near the road. I tell the man closest to the road, Logan, to keep the rest of the squad in sight, but that proves to be impossible and we lose touch. I send Seace up the road to find the other guys. He comes back and says we're behind and are supposed to catch up. The only way I can see how to catch up is by going out on the road, so that's what we do. When we get even with Pulczak's men we start checking the fields on our side again, but quickly lose contact just as before. I

[Notes for Chapter 14 start on p. 136]

don't know how the other guys can get so far ahead of us unless the hedgerows aren't as thick over there. The only way we can maintain contact is to continue the leapfrogging, which leaves some of the territory unchecked. But it can't be helped. I feel that I should discuss the problem with Pulczak, but that is not going to be possible. Everybody is trying to keep up with whoever is up front, and nobody is going to stop just to talk things over. Luckily nothing happens due to the unchecked fields, and after another half hour our flanking assignment is over.

This has been my first experience as a non-com, and although it was a simple assignment, it wasn't easy—keeping contact, providing some kind of leadership, keeping everybody alert, checking the fields and hedgerows, trying to keep the guys from getting shot—mainly Paull—watching for booby-traps, trying to decide if I'm making each small decision correctly. When I was playing football at Oberlin we had the plays memorized and we all knew exactly what to do. The only time I had any freedom to make my own decisions was when I was running downfield with the ball trying not to be tackled. Here, nobody knows from one moment to the next what to do. I'm not sure I'm going to be very good at this.

> THE COMMANDERS OF THE GERMAN 7TH ARMY REALIZED THEY COULD NO LONGER HOLD THE WESTERN END OF THEIR DEFENSIVE LINE AND HAD GIVEN THE WORD TO PULL BACK TO THE SOUTH AND EAST. THERE WAS NO WAY OF KNOWING WHERE GERMANS MIGHT BE ENCOUNTERED.

> THE THREE AMERICAN DIVISIONS IN VIII CORPS HAD WIDELY DIFFERENT EXPERIENCES MOVING DOWN THE CHERBOURG PENINSULA. THE 8TH INFANTRY DIVISION, FOR WHICH THERE HAD BEEN HIGH EXPECTATIONS, PROVED DISAPPOINTING AND THE DIVISION COMMANDER WAS QUICKLY REPLACED. THE NEW MAN DID BETTER, USING WHAT ARE DESCRIBED BY BLUMENSON IN BREAKOUT AND PURSUIT AS "INDIRECT" TACTICS RATHER THAN DIRECT FRONTAL ASSAULTS.[7] THE 79TH DIVISION ON THE WEST RAN INTO A LOT OF MINES AND STIFF RESISTANCE IN ITS ATTEMPT TO REACH LESSAY. THE 4TH ARMORED MADE GOOD PROGRESS DOWN THE CENTRAL HIGHWAY, AND THE 90TH, THOUGH ONLY SPORADICALLY IMPEDED BY ENEMY RESISTANCE, WAS HARD PUT TO KEEP UP.

[Notes for Chapter 14 start on p. 136]

We keep moving and come to the tiny hamlet of *Raids*. I've got half the squad out on the left flank this time. As we emerge from a dark sunken road I send Brown and Bruthiers ahead and to the left to check out two small farm buildings. I tell them we'll cover them—exactly how I don't know. We'll do whatever we can, depending on what happens. This is the first time I've told Brown to do anything when he wasn't simply going along with the rest of the guys. He has sobered down a lot since that first day when he got a little smart-ass. Maybe the shellings at the Island did it. We got enough of a pasting to give the new guys a taste of things. I don't think there are any Germans in the buildings—based only on hunch—but I don't want to take the chance of being ambushed, or sniped at. Brown and Bruthiers go up the slight rise to the buildings, Brown first, both in the GI combat crouch—it didn't take them long to learn that. They go around the back of the buildings to the left. Three minutes later they come into view again around the right side, walking erect—so they didn't run into any problems, unless a French farmer waving his arms and shouting can be called a problem.

"What was that about?" I ask Bruthiers when they get back, thinking the farmer might have been offering some important information about the enemy.

"Just about his cows, or somethin'."

"Did he say anything about the Germans?" He shrugs, negative. He could have asked the farmer if any Germans had been there, how many, how long ago. He can speak French—it would have been an obvious thing to do. But he didn't. I can see I can't count on much initiative from Bruthiers.

Out of the hedgerows [Foxholes 23, 24]

The company reaches a pretty good-sized stream [THE *TAUTE* RIVER] and we cross on a small bridge with no opposition. Late in the afternoon we reach a sizable paved road running east-to-west [THE WESTERN PART OF THE *PÉRIERS*-ST.-LÔ HIGHWAY] and dig in. The platoon straddles the road—my squad on the north side. Bruthiers is assigned to a big hollowed out position to watch the main road to the west. The Germans apparently used it for the same purpose. Bruthiers won't be very effective at the assignment because he has a lousy cold. When he goes back to the aid station I have to fill in for him. They send him back up with some

APC pills but he isn't going to be good for much, so another guy is moved into the hole with him. There's plenty of room.

The next day we go south through the fields past a town called *St.-Sauveur-Lendelin*. The hedgerows are becoming more widely spaced, and smaller. There's a rumor that a big entrapment of Germans is underway. Disorganized groups of Germans are moving east, cross-country, trying to hook up with the rest of the German 7th Army. We might come onto them anywhere. Resistance in our area is spotty. My squad hasn't fired a weapon. In the evening we stop in a field that borders another paved road. I've been feeling punk all afternoon, probably the same thing Bruthiers had. I dig in alongside a hedgerow, then lie in the damp hole shivering and miserable with what seems like the flu. I finally go over to the Platoon Sergeant's hole and tell him I'm sick. He talks to Liebau, then says for me to go to the aid station. I walk back in a fog, my head jangling with every step. I finally find the aid station and sit on the ground and suck on a thermometer for a while but I don't have the full degree of fever needed to take me out of the line so I'm sent back up with a packet of APCs. I take a couple, then climb into my clammy hole and spend a rotten night. The only thing worse than being in a foxhole when you're sick, I guess, is being in a foxhole when you're wounded, or when you're dead.

I manage to get some sleep, and the next day I feel better. In the afternoon a runner comes over to tell me to come over to Liebau's hole. Liebau tells me that the next morning I'm going to be a map-reader. My interest in his map at *Beau-Coudray* apparently stuck in his mind. The prospect of doing something interesting for a change gives my spirits a big boost. My small but persistent initiatives seem to be paying off. Not that reading a map requires much skill. You don't need a college course in cartography to be able to read a map. But it is surprising how many people can't read maps with any degree of confidence. I recall that I couldn't make sense of the one he had at *Beau-Coudray*. I ask Liebau what kind of a map it will be. He doesn't have it yet so he doesn't know.

At night there's a lot of GI traffic on the road going south—trucks, Jeeps, half-tracks, command cars, tanks, self-propelled guns—rattling and clattering past by the dozens. By the hundreds. The impression of sheer power is staggering. I

[Notes for Chapter 14 start on p. 136]

never imagined we had so much heavy equipment. If the Germans knew we had all this stuff seems like they'd just give up. I can't see how any force could stand up to such a body of military might. In spite of the noise I finally fall asleep. At 3:00 A.M. I wake up and the column is still going past.

On the point of a combat team [Foxholes 25, 26]

Early in the morning I find out what I'm supposed to do. I'm going to lead an entire column of motorized infantry sitting in the front seat of the point Jeep. I'll be following a map on my lap and telling the Jeep driver which way to go at every intersection. I'm really pleased to have been picked for the job, but if we run into any Germans the Jeep driver and I will be the first to confront them. That, I discover, is the peculiar nature of advancement in Infantry combat. The better the job—in the sense of it carrying more responsibility—the more dangerous it is. Up to a point, anyway. Above Company Commander you're probably safer unless you go out of your way to take risks. Some do, I guess, and some officers have paid for their bravado by getting killed, like the Captain who got shot off the tank at *Beau-Coudray*.[8]

The map-reading turns out to be just as easy as I expected. I could have done it when I was in third grade. Our objective is near the city of *Coutances*. The Battalion Commander, Major Hamilton, is in a command car within sight behind us when the road is straight. Everything goes OK for about an hour. My flu is forgotten and the day is bright with interesting prospects.

As we're rounding a curve to the right the Jeep suddenly swerves onto the road-shoulder and skids violently to a stop. I grab my M-1. The driver spotted something ahead. The entire column shudders to a stop. A Jeep with a mounted .50-cal machinegun comes up fast and pokes around the curve, gunner ready, but they find only an abandoned German roadblock. A few cut limbs are bunched together on the bank of the ditch as camouflage for a one-man outpost. Not too good a job, because the driver spotted it. Some time earlier it had concealed a German soldier—with a machinegun or a burp-gun, or maybe a *Panzerfaust*. I was looking at the map, my job. The driver could see around the curve farther than I could, but when we start up again I'm more alert to what may be ahead.

[Notes for Chapter 14 start on p. 136]

CHAPTER 14

This is our first evidence of the enemy since we started out. A German soldier was here, maybe as late as this morning. Maybe only an hour ago, maybe only minutes ago. The leaves on the branches aren't wilted yet. Maybe he took off when he heard us coming. Road blocks are usually outposts for larger units. Maybe there's a German tank around the next bend of the road.

After another hour without any further sign of the enemy we come to an intersection where a side road goes off to the left. The driver stops and looks to me for directions. I check the map. There's no question in my mind that we should keep going straight, and I wave him ahead. We're barely in motion when we hear a shout from back in the column: "Hold it up!" Somebody doesn't think we should be going this way.

A lieutenant comes up in a Jeep and I show him the map. Then Liebau comes up. Then they both go back to confer with somebody back in the column, probably Major Hamilton. Then the first lieutenant comes back up again, says to turn *left* instead of right, then falls back into the column behind us.

I am absolutely sure it's the wrong way to go. The only possible way anybody can think we ought to go left is if they're looking at a map with a different scale, showing different roads. But we go left.

It isn't long before the road starts to narrow. We're been going through farmland all morning, but this is the real boonies. The road becomes a single-lane dirt track. We are obviously going the wrong way.

> I am the eye
> of the great caterpillar that crawls on
> rubber legs, and steel,
> wriggling its creaking way through
> the hedgerow'd narrow roads as the men, mostly
> hidden on covered trucks give their complete
> trust to those who make the plans. I
> know the planners are
> wrong. I tried to guide the wriggling
> monster toward its

[Notes for Chapter 14 start on p. 136]

> proper destination as requested, but my carto-
> graphic eye was
> extinguished, inviting, now, destruction and
> attack. We inch along. I hold the map, but un-
> used now, as before. When will the enemy discover us, bomb
> shoot, strafe, destroy? We can but wait as we
> crawl belly down deeper into the threatful unknown.

Finally somebody yells up the column to stop—it's too narrow to send up a Jeep. So we stop right out in the open country, vulnerable to any German plane that cares to make a strafing run, or to enemy tanks, or artillery. The column is strung out behind for over a mile. We're sitting ducks. An officer I've never seen before comes up striding quickly, climbs into the back seat of our Jeep and takes over giving the driver directions. We turn to the right at the next road-crossing. It's another dirt track, but the column can't turn around and go back the way we came—the road isn't wide enough.

I've lost my job through somebody else's mistake. And I don't get it back. Worse, I'm made to think that I'm to blame for leading us into un-cleared territory. Not by words, but by silence. The long column snakes its way through the countryside at an agonizingly slow pace. I'm still in the lead Jeep but now I'm just a GI riding shotgun. Finally we get back on a good road, I get called back to ride in the truck with the rest of the guys, and we start to make progress again.[9]

In mid-afternoon a lone German plane goes over high and fast. It looks like a *ME-109*—snub-nosed, with wings placed farther forward than on most of our planes. Because of the clouds we see it for only a few seconds against a piece of blue sky. We're warned to be ready to jump off the trucks and run for the fields if we're strafed but it doesn't come back.

The sun is low on the horizon when we and dig in for the night. Nobody asks me anything about my map-reading assignment, or the screw-up, and I don't bring it up. I can't put it in a letter. I can only swallow my pride and forget it.

> ONE OF THE STRANGE THINGS ABOUT COMBAT WAS THAT AT LEAST ON THE LEVEL OF THE FRONT-LINE GI, NOBODY EVER TALKED ABOUT ANYTHING

[Notes for Chapter 14 start on p. 136]

AFTER IT HAPPENED. THE ONLY THING ANYBODY EVER WANTED TO KNOW WAS IF ANYBODY GOT HIT. THERE WERE NEVER ANY TACTICAL CRITIQUES— WHY SOMETHING SUCCEEDED, OR FAILED. AND THE GUYS NEVER ASKED QUESTIONS. THAT WAS EQUALLY STRANGE.[10]

ONE THEORY WAS THAT THE LESS WE KNEW, THE LESS WE COULD REVEAL TO THE GERMANS IF WE WERE CAPTURED. IF WE DIDN'T KNOW SOMETHING, EVEN TORTURE COULDN'T GET IT OUT OF US. I CAN SEE SOME VALIDITY IN THE IDEA, BUT I THINK THE VALUE OF KNOWING WHAT WAS GOING ON FAR OUTWEIGHED THE SMALL RISK TO SECURITY.

In Third Army [Foxhole 27]
August 1

In the morning we climb on trucks again and head south. We see a couple of German tanks abandoned in a field. They're the first of a vast charnel-house of vehicular destruction that begins to spread out before us. The road and fields become littered with disabled and burned-out German tanks, half-tracks, command cars. Only a few are American. Most have been pushed off the roads with bulldozers. Many are tipped onto their sides, some turned completely over.[11]

THE 4TH ARMORED HAD BEATEN GENERAL COLLINS'S 3RD ARMORED INTO COUTANCES. WE WERE NOW HEADED FOR AVRANCHES, A GOOD-SIZE CITY LOCATED AT THE BASE OF THE CHERBOURG PENINSULA—CALLED THE COTENTIN PENINSULA BY SOME GEOGRAPHERS AND HISTORIANS. SOME ACCOUNTS HAVE THE COTENTIN EXTENDING ALL THE WAY TO AVRANCHES; OTHERS PUT ITS SOUTHERN LIMIT FARTHER NORTH NEAR LESSAY.

AVRANCHES WAS OF STRATEGIC IMPORTANCE BECAUSE IT WAS THE GATEWAY TO BOTH BRITTANY ON THE WEST—WITH A MAJOR PORT AT BREST—AND, TO THE EAST, THE ENTIRE CENTRAL REGION OF FRANCE.

Liebau tells us we are now in the Third Army. He's excited by the news but it means nothing to us. We didn't know what army we were in before.[12] But after struggling in the hedgerows so long, now, sitting high on the trucks we can't help enjoying the exhilaration of movement and the signs of success.

[Notes for Chapter 14 start on p. 136]

> IT WAS ON THIS DRIVE TO *AVRANCHES* AMIDST THE WRECKAGE STREWN ABOUT THE COUNTRYSIDE THAT GENERAL PATTON IS SUPPOSED TO HAVE MADE HIS FAMOUS REMARK, DRAMATIZED IN THE MOVIE, *PATTON*: "THERE IS NOTHING IN THE WORLD LIKE WAR. GOD HOW I LOVE IT!"

Traffic jam at *Avranches* [Foxhole 28]

We inch through the traffic jams at *Avranches* and cross a bridge at *Pontaubault* [WHERE PATTON IS SHOWN IN THE MOVIE DIRECTING TRAFFIC PERSONALLY]. Then we turn east, go a couple of miles, and dig in for the night. The *Luftwaffe* has gotten active again and German planes attack our forces at *Avranches* with a vengeance. From our positions we can see the show—our anti-aircraft fire against the German planes, flares dropped by the attackers—like the beachhead revisited.

All the guards are asleep [Foxhole 29]

The next day we go east on foot along the road to *St.-Hilaire-du-Harcouët*.

> THIS IS WHERE PATTON SAW US STRUNG OUT ON THE ROAD AND COMMENTED THAT WE WERE A "BAD DIVISION". SEE APPENDIX C, WEB-LINK NO. 8 FOR REFERENCE TO A SUMMARY OF THE 90TH'S EARLY TROUBLES.

At night we establish a blocking position north of *St.-Hilaire-du-Harcouët* near the tiny hamlet of *Juvigny*, but before we have a chance to dig in we hear that we're moving to a new position south of *St.-Hilaire*, facing east. We're tired, and grouse about the move, but at least we didn't dig holes for nothing.

Again we are warned that Germans could be anywhere. I'm supposed to check on the squad's guards during the night. Each time I make the rounds I find the guys asleep. I'm not sure what I should do—other than wake them up and tell them they have to stay alert. I can see my words alone aren't going to keep them awake. To make an impression I'd have to threaten to turn them in. Sleeping on guard is a serious military offense. But we've had a long march. So I just caution them and hope for the best.

[Notes for Chapter 14 start on p. 136]

Notes for Chapter 14

1. It's a wonder the name, *Werrenrath* got through the censors. Though born in Brooklyn to a Danish father, Reinald Werrenrath made his name as a Wagnerian tenor in *Die Meistersinger*—about as German as you can get. He taught voice in his later years. Was Jean sending me a cryptic message about an Allied bomber strike, passed along from her uncle in Army Intelligence in Washington? Apparently the censor didn't think so. That a Wagnerian tenor like Werrenrath would be giving voice lessons to a coloratura soprano like Jean, though, does seem odd. Maybe the principles of voice training are universal, regardless of range or gender.

2. War is *existentialism* wrenched down to its most primal essence. Nobody who is a close participant in war pontificates about its meaning. Things are what they are, no more no less.

3. The saturation bombing was carried out by 1,800 heavy and medium bombers—American B-17 Flying Fortresses and B-24 Liberators—and 400 low-level fighter-bombers—American P-47s and British Typhoons. The fighter-bombers made the first run, followed by the heavies and mediums. It took three hours for the planes to pass over the target area.

    Bradley had flown to England to make sure that the bombers would fly parallel to the highway to avoid the chance of hitting our own troops, and he was assured that this would be the case. When the bombers came, however, they approached the target at right angles to the highway to avoid a longer run over enemy frontline positions—and the increased anti-aircraft fire this would provoke. Wind blew the dust and smoke from the bombs northward obscuring the road that marked the target area, resulting in some bombs being dropped in the smoke-covered areas where troops were poised to exploit the bombing.

    A vivid account of the "short" bombing by Ernie Pyle is included in the book *Ernie's War* (Random House 1986, edited by David Nichols, p. 330).

[Notes for Chapter 14 start on p. 136]

Pyle was with one of the companies hit by the bombs but he himself was not injured. On hearing of the casualties, Eisenhower said he would never use the carpet bombing technique again. When COBRA proved to be a success, however, his views changed and saturation bombing was later used for the *Rhine* crossing.

4. The P-47 Thunderbolt was an American fighter-bomber manufactured by Republic Aviation, a few by Curtiss-Wright. It was the only American fighter plane in the ETO with a radial air-cooled engine. One might think the blunt nose would cause too much aerodynamic drag for the P-47 to be really fast, but it was a match for the German fighters in the early years of the war. An excellent chapter on the P-47 can be found in *Fighters of World War II*, by Charles Cain (Exeter Books, NY, 1979). According to this account, more P-47s were produced than any other WW-II fighter plane. It was used extensively in all theaters of the war except Alaska.

5. In August 1997 in Rochester, NY, an ex-bomber pilot, Maj. Roy Beany, told me there were no "dogfights" in WW-II. He said the fighters were so fast that one run at an enemy plane was all that could be expected. "Hit-and-run", he called it. Dogfights, he said, took place only in WW-I where the planes were much slower. As a Captain in the 8th Air Force and first pilot of B-24s, Beany flew 35 missions deep into Germany over *Berlin*, *Munich*, and *Frankfort*. I have never heard anyone else make the same statement about dogfights. From what I've read, there were dogfights in both wars, though the tactics were necessarily different.

A photo in the book *Finest Hour, The Battle of Britain,* by Tim Clayton and Phil Craig, is captioned: *Winston Churchill watching a dogfight over Dover with the town's mayor.* Of course the caption may not be accurate. Photo captions in war books seem to be afterthoughts, written by the publishers' interns. They're often ludicrous, lame, or just plain inaccurate. Many photos are obviously posed. A caption in *Code Talker* by Chester Nez and Judith Schiess Avila, actually states that one of the photographs was posed—a rarity. Kudos to Berkley Hardcover, the publisher.

[Notes for Chapter 14 start on p. 136]

CHAPTER 14

6. This was where 358's failed night attack across the *Sèves* River took place. We didn't know about it at the time, or the rout of GIs that followed. I first read a detailed account of what happened fifty years later in Martin Blumenson's *Breakout and Pursuit*.

7. Utilizing an indirect approach, when circumstances allowed, seems to be such a logical part of any tactical repertory that it is almost beyond belief that a policy to try to exploit its advantages hadn't been developed long before the breakout from the hedgerow country, but top commanders, including Eisenhower and Bradley, had no plans for using other than head-on tactics against the Germans defenses. General Collins, Commanding General of VII Corps, did consider other methods and discusses them in his book, *Lightning Joe*. Granted, the upper *Cherbourg* Peninsula didn't offer much opportunity for anything other than direct assaults, hedgerow by hedgerow, and even Collins was stymied in his attempt to set up a line of departure for the post-COBRA breakthrough. Once through the German first line of defense, however, his armored divisions sliced laterally and made rapid progress.

   When VIII Corps moved south down the *Cherbourg* Peninsula following COBRA, the 8th Infantry was put in the middle where the 82nd Airborne had been, and the 8th's oblique tactics initiated by its new Commanding General were so innovative that historians like Martin Blumenson have underscored their uniqueness. The terrain where the 8th came through was more open than farther north, however, and their success in actually gaining ground was no better than the other divisions in VIII Corps.

   See also Author Robert Daley's comments in on tactics at *Verdun* in WW-I and Note 18, both in Chapter 18. Also Web-link No. 3 for General William DePuy view's on frontal assaults, Appendix C.

8. A significant number of Battalion and Regimental Commanders were killed or wounded in the course of the war even though they could usually stay in comparatively safe areas if they chose to—an option not available to the GIs on the line. In my opinion, a lot of the officers—majors and up—

who did get hit were "showing themselves to the troops." For some it was a point of honor and good for morale—theirs as well as the men's on the line. I'm sure that commanders at battalion level and higher had a hard time keeping abreast of the action, since they were dependent on second- and third-hand information, and felt they could make better decisions if they saw things with their own eyes. And many no doubt felt it a duty to be near the action. But the terrain didn't always provide convenient hilltops where commanders could stand as they watched the battles below. This wasn't the Civil War.

From what I've read, field commanders who obviously avoided risks were replaced—like the Battalion Commander in the failed night attack by 358 at the *Sèves* River Island. Policy differed, though, from unit to unit. Patton, though a stickler for correctness of uniform and equipment, was less likely to replace poorly performing combat leaders than some others.

There was nothing as convincing as a wound to validate an officer's intrepidity. In World War One, Patton was hit by a bullet that passed through his groin—and out through the buttocks. According to his grandson's account, the general took pleasure in showing off the scar by pulling down his trunks at the beach (Robert Patton, *The Pattons*).

9. The trucks were the famous 2-1/2- ton "6-by-6s", in this case commandeered from the battalion's kitchen company. Some say our 6-by-6 trucks won the war. The Germans were using a lot of horse-drawn vehicles for supplies, even for troop transport.

10. There was one exception. We did have a post-action session about a week after the road-route mistake. Our platoon was assembled and Liebau read an account of what had happened since the "Island", then asked if anything had been left out. I spoke up about the road-route snafu but Liebau said he didn't think it ought to be included in an official history. I said, "But it happened." Liebau wrote something down, but I thought it was just to mollify me and to appear honest. I was apparently right, because the incident isn't mentioned in the Regimental *Operational Report*.

[Notes for Chapter 14 start on p. 136]

Here was a clear example of intentionally inaccurate reporting. It may seem trivial in retrospect, but it wouldn't have been trivial if we'd been spotted by a German dive bomber looking for a target, or if we'd blundered into one of the German units still in the area. If that had happened, there might have been even less chance of the true account getting into the books. Truth is indeed a fickle mistress.

Using different maps may have been the cause of the route problem. An incident where the use of inaccurate maps resulted in confusion is reported in the *Operational Reports* for August 29, page 301.

11. The scarcity of knocked-out American tanks along that road is probably explained, at least in part, by the efficiency of our tank retrieval crews. They had an excellent record for salvaging damaged tanks and getting them back into service quickly. And, since we were moving forward past the battle sites, the Germans didn't have the same opportunity to re-fit their tanks even if they had the capability.

12. We had been in First Army. Third Army was activated on August 1st with George S. Patton as its Commanding General. Liebau may have known this but he didn't mention it to us. Patton's name was being kept under wraps because he was still supposed to be back in England in command of the decoy army group, FUSAG, set up to mislead the Germans in regard to where the main invasion would be made..

The name Patton wouldn't have meant anything special to me anyhow. Although he had figured significantly in the battles of North Africa and Sicily I knew almost nothing about those campaigns beyond what I had read in *The Battle is the Payoff,* a *Reader's Digest* condensed book by the journalist, Ralph Ingersoll. If he mentioned Patton I don't recall it.

⊕

[Notes for Chapter 14 start on p. 136]

15

BREAKOUT

August 5 [Foxhole 30]

After three days at *St.-Hilaire* we get on trucks and barrel down the road, east. Some tanks are in the column farther back.

> THIS WAS TASK FORCE BARTH, A SELF-SUFFICIENT MOTORIZED COLUMN GEARED FOR QUICK MOVEMENT LED BY COL. GEORGE BARTH, 357'S REGIMENTAL COMMANDER. AFTER THE COSTLY STALEMATE IN THE HEDGEROWS OUR ASTONISHING PROGRESS MADE BIG HEADLINES BACK IN THE STATES:
>
> ## THIRD ARMY ADVANCES 30 MILES IN ONE DAY!
>
> WITH MONTY STILL HUNG UP AT CAEN THE NEWS WAS ELECTRIFYING. TO PATTON'S CHAGRIN, NEWS STORIES COULD NOT MENTION HIS NAME. ALTHOUGH GEN. MCNAIR [KIA AT COBRA] HAD BEEN PUT IN CHARGE OF FUSAG, PATTON WAS STILL SUPPOSED TO BE BACK IN ENGLAND PREPARING FOR WHAT HITLER STILL THOUGHT WOULD BE THE MAIN INVASION.

We see the outskirts of a city ahead and pile off the trucks. Signs say it's *Mayenne*. A German tank has been defending the city's main bridge across the *Mayenne* River.[1] The bridge was wired with explosives, but on his own initiative a GI engineer ran out ahead of advancing American tanks to try to cut the wires. He succeeded, saving the bridge, but was killed by fire from the German tank. The word spreads among us quickly.[2]

We approach the city on foot through the fields on the south side of the main road. When we get to the edge of the city the platoon moves toward the river through the backyards, avoiding the main street, climbing over walls and fences as we go. We're slowed down climbing the fences by all the stuff we've got

[Notes for Chapter 15 start on p. 153]

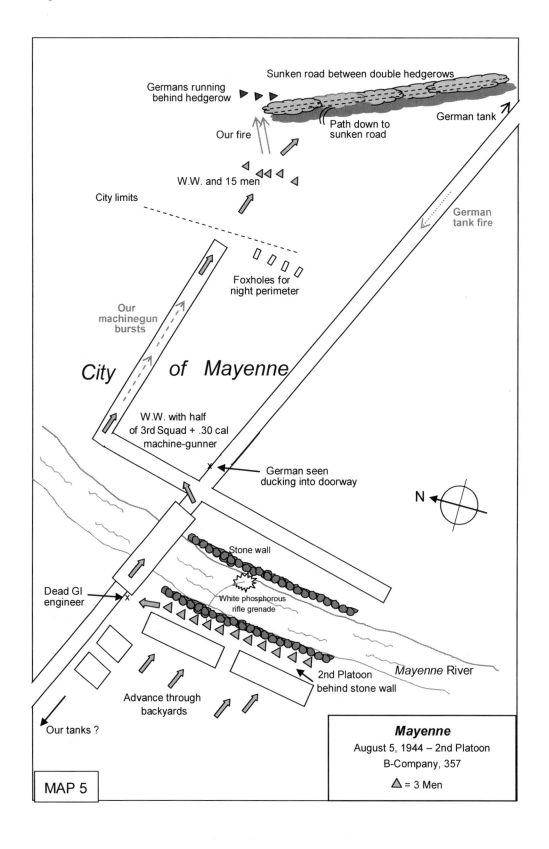

hanging on us. As Assistant Squad Leader I'm supposed to bring up the rear and keep everybody moving forward. Gervase is directly ahead of me, lagging behind the rest of the squad. I see him stop and do something to his shoe. I don't want to get ahead of him, but I don't want to make a big deal out of my responsibilities either. If it's clear that he's hanging back intentionally I'll have to urge him to keep up. It's an awkward situation. I'm not used to getting guys to do what they don't want to do. When we get up to the river, Gervase and I are noticeably behind the others. Liebau sees it but says nothing.

A two-foot stone wall runs along both sides of the river [MAP 5]. We spread out behind the wall on our side, keeping low so as not to expose ourselves. One of the guys spots a German ducking in and out of a doorway on the other side of the river. I take a look, and see him too, but he's too battle-savvy to stay in the open long enough for anybody to get a shot at him. After a while Liebau tells me to fire a white phosphorus rifle-grenade across the river. As Assistant Squad Leader, I have the squad's grenade launcher on my M-1 rifle and have been carrying a canvas bag of grenades.[3]

I try to arc the grenade up so it will fall just beyond the wall on the other side of the river—a logical place for the Germans to be taking cover. I put a propellant cartridge in the chamber, slip the grenade over the launcher, set the butt of the M-1 on the ground and fire it like a mortar—but I misjudge the angle and the grenade falls short, hitting the bank in front of the wall instead of going over it. It might not have gone over the wall even if I'd angled it a few degrees lower.[4] When the grenade goes off it makes an unsatisfactory sizzle, shooting out a few spindly streaks of the burning white phosphorus.[5] Rifle grenades have been a big disappointment and we're learning not to count on them for much—though we do need something to fill the gap between hand grenades and 60-mm mortars.

A row of buildings rises up along the street behind us with windows looking out over the river. Three of us go up to the second floor to see if we can spot anything in enemy territory. It's dangerous because it's an obvious place a German sniper would be watching. Liebau warns us to be careful, and we stay in the shadows well back from the windows. We don't see any Germans, or the German tank, but it feels good to be up high for a change instead of being stuck close to the ground.

[Notes for Chapter 15 start on p. 153]

Across the bridge

At about one o'clock we get the word that B-Company will attack across the bridge.

"Whenever they've got a tough assignment they give it to B-Company," Liebau says, pride mixed with complaint. He warns us that the German tank could still be zeroed in on the bridge. We have a couple of tanks too, but they're out of sight somewhere behind us. I don't see how they can cover us if they're not out where they can see what's going on. We can only hope they'll be able to help us if the German tank opens up.[6] "The dead engineer is still on the bridge," Liebau tells us. "Don't stop when you get there, just keep moving." Whitey Merrill's squad goes first, keeping as low as they can and still be able to run. Then my squad goes. We go past the dead GI and get across the bridge without being fired on. I see Liebau and he yells for me to take half the squad over to the first street on the left. A machine-gunner comes with us cradling his .30-cal. machinegun in his arms, ammo belt strung over his shoulders. He's the same machine-gunner I talked to about the smell of dead guys after we left *Beau-Coudray*.

We get to the first street over and dodge across it, expecting fire. When the machine-gunner gets in the middle he stops and faces down the street, then lets go with his machinegun, firing from the hip. There's nobody in sight but he fires anyhow, three good bursts, the ammo belt snaking across his shoulder.

Maybe the machinegun fire has an effect, just the intimidation of the angrily popping and snapping bullets. The only person we see is an elderly French woman poking her head out a doorway. She ducks back when she sees us coming. Maybe she's deaf. You'd think she'd have heard the machinegun.[7]

We advance along the street all the way to the eastern outskirts of the city without seeing a single German. The open countryside begins abruptly. I'm the only non-com among fifteen men. When we started out there were only five of us. I don't know where the others came from.

"Follow Wighty," someone shouts. Whitey Merrill isn't with us—the guy must mean me. I'm surprised by my sudden appointment as leader. If they're going to

[Notes for Chapter 15 start on p. 153]

follow me, though, I'd better do something. I lead out across the first field and when we get out about a hundred yards we see several Germans up ahead running to our right, trying to get behind a big hedgerow. Some of our guys kneel and start firing at the running Germans. They know what to do better than I do. But despite my lack of assertiveness nobody tries to take over whatever authority I have just acquired. There was just a vacuum and I was picked to fill it.

I'm aware of a new feeling: I've been chosen as a leader not by THE AUTHORITY OF CONGRESS AND THE ARMY OF THE UNITED STATES, but by my fellow GIs. I've never sought to be a leader. The feeling is unexpected. It's made up of some satisfaction, I admit, and a sense of responsibility.

For a while, at least, these are *my men*. Not because I say so—not the way the basic training cadre said we belonged to them (at least our *asses* did), and not because anybody else says so, but because *they* say so themselves. They look to me for some kind of guidance and example. But I've got to do more than just watch them fire their rifles.[8]

We don't see any of the Germans go down from our firing or even falter. They just run faster and scrootch lower. They're about a hundred fifty yards in front of us when they disappear behind the big hedgerow. Will they keep going, or stop and put up a fight?

We keep moving forward without getting fired on and as we get closer to the hedgerow we see that it's a double hedgerow concealing a sunken road that probably joins the main road coming from the bridge. The junction of the two roads would be a logical place for the German tank to be, but there isn't a line of sight between us and the road crossing—the trees of the big double hedgerow block it off.

Even if the tank can't see us, the sunken road is a perfect place for the Germans to set up a rear-guard machine-gunner. Sometimes they leave an MG-42 gunner behind, sometimes a man with a burp-gun. It's pretty much SOP.

I hesitate to send in scouts—I'm not used to sending guys into danger. So I find a path leading down to the sunken road, tell the guys to stay put, and go in alone...

[Notes for Chapter 15 start p. 153]

CHAPTER 15

> Into shades of shadow that
> dance in gloom, portents
> dodge, duck around crags of
> trunk and branch, unbroken
> heritage, since swordsmen,
> carriages carrying nobles and
> the King, dashing headlong
> to outrun cut-throats,
> assassins, pistoleers, or
> peasants with carts grinding
> sloggily, root-laden
> or casks, faggots for warming
> bones. Sheep, driven,
> violent or peaceful traffic,
> lovers,
> under the green canopy that
> hides their tryst, fatal
> ambush, or only the cool
> silence of a summer's day.

In the shadowy tunnel I make my eyes look everywhere, see everything, try to catch by surprise whoever might be there. It's dead quiet, dark and spooky. But there is no enemy to be found. M-1 ready, I probe to the right about twenty yards, cautious, but find nothing. I ease up the opposite bank and look out over an open field. There is nobody in sight. Back down in the road again I'm about to rejoin the guys where I left them when I hear Lieutenant Liebau's bawling voice, chewing them out for stopping in the open. I did leave them in an exposed position, no question about that. When I come strolling up the path out of the sunken road into the daylight I'm Laurence Olivier making a stage entrance. Liebau is astonished.

We all move down into the sunken road, spread out, and stand watch on the opposite bank expecting a counterattack,. We stay there until nightfall but don't see any more Germans, and don't hear any fire from the German tank. Then we get orders to give up our positions and move back because our flanks are open on

[Notes for Chapter 15 start on p. 153]

both sides. C-Company has not kept up with us on our left, and on our right the rest of B-Company is still back in the city. I express my disappointment to Liebau that we have to give up the ground we've gained, but I'm overruled.

> THE 82ND AIRBORNE WAS NOT UNIQUE FOR WANTING TO HANG ONTO WHAT THEY HAD FOUGHT FOR AS GENERAL GAVIN IMPLIED IN *ON TO BERLIN*. AT *MAYENNE* WE DIDN'T FIGHT VERY HARD FOR WHAT WE GOT, BUT EVEN SO IT DIDN'T SEEM RIGHT TO GIVE IT UP.[9]

We dig our holes in the backyard gardens of some homes at the edge of the city. The soil is rich and loose—if a shell lands here it will make a deep crater and a big spray of dirt. We don't get shelled, but later in the night there is some commotion to the north of us. In the morning we hear that a couple of German command cars with some officers drove right into one of our roadblocks and were captured. They hadn't gotten the word yet that *Mayenne* was in American hands.

> IN *WAR FROM THE GROUND UP*, COLBY WRITES THAT COMPANY COMMANDER STEVENS SAID THAT B-COMPANY'S 2ND PLATOON BALKED WHEN ORDERED TO CROSS THE BRIDGE AT *MAYENNE*. MY SQUAD WAS IN THE 2ND PLATOON BUT I DON'T RECALL ANY PROBLEM. PLATOON SGT. BARRETT SHOULD HAVE BEEN UP FRONT. SOMEBODY JUST SAID TO GO, AND WE WENT.[10]

Ste.-Suzanne [Foxhole 31]
August 6

At mid-morning we get on the trucks again and Task Force Barth continues to roll eastward.

> GENERAL WEAVER, ASSISTANT DIVISION COMMANDER UNDER GENERAL MCLAIN, HEADED A SEPARATE TASK FORCE ON A TRACK ROUGHLY PARALLEL TO OURS A FEW MILES TO THE NORTH. TF WEAVER RAN INTO SOME GERMAN RESISTANCE THAT HELD THEM UP A FEW HOURS, SO WE IN TF BARTH MADE MORE RAPID PROGRESS AND A RIVALRY DEVELOPED BECAUSE OF IT. THE TWO TASK FORCES EVENTUALLY CAME TOGETHER, BUT NOT BEFORE TF BARTH REACHED *STE.-SUZANNE*.[11]

[Notes for Chapter 15 start p. 153]

CHAPTER 15

Late in the afternoon B-Company enters *Ste.-Suzanne,* a very small town sitting picturesquely on high ground. Parts of the city are very old.[12] Germans had been there earlier in the day but had disappeared into some woods to the east. My platoon digs holes in the fields along the road just west of the town and settles in for the night.

Early next morning we're roused vigorously. We grab our gear, climb on tanks and ride into the center of town. Our Sherman tanks don't have good handholds on the outside and we have grab on tight so as not to slide off. The Germans had tried to retake the town during the night and almost succeeded. The CP of Task Force Barth had set up in the town square but had to pull out in a hurry—backward. [SEE APPENDIX B, *OPERATIONS REPORT*, ENTRY FOR AUGUST 7.]

Paull, our new B-A-R man since the *Sèves* River Island, has been sent out to watch the road that leads down to where the Germans were last seen. Liebau thinks Paull may have been hit by a mortar shell and he sends me out to check on him. When I find him, he's lying slouched up against a high stone wall along a road that dips down abruptly to the valley. He's still gripping the B-A-R—the same one I used to carry—its muzzle in the dirt.

The land drops dramatically away toward an extensive forest to the southeast. It's a magnificent view.[13] Paull and I are by ourselves outside the town's fortress wall, visible to anyone in the valley. The mortar shell probably came from the edge of the trees. They could send another one at any moment.

"Is he dead?" Liebau asks me when I get back.

Yes, he's dead. I wonder how I'm so sure. I didn't see where he was hit. I didn't see any blood. I did see where the mortar shell hit the road fifteen feet away. It made almost no crater because of the hard surface. The spray of fragments would have gone out very flat. That's why it got him.

All I did was look at Paull but I am sure. There's a look of deadness you come to recognize—a frizziness around the mouth, lips slightly open, flecks of dirt on the face from the mortar blast, slitted eyelids, un-blinking.

[Notes for Chapter 15 start on p. 153]

Paull was dead, and I got the B-A-R and we left him where he lay…

>under the wall
>where once the
>Conqueror William
>sieged and failed to
>breach, or break the will
>of staunch *Suzanne*.
>Out by the wall
>where fell a hundred
>others once, finding ends to
>trails of life and love and loss.
>Paths must end
>at some such certain
>place. Here is Paull's
>sure place…under the,
>out by the storied
>wall at
>*Ste.-Suzanne*.

A couple of hours go by and when the Germans don't try to come back we relax and begin looking around. Sackett and I start to go up the steps of a stone tower that has a notched parapet. Liebau warns us that a GI who went up onto the tower earlier in the day was killed by a sniper. But there hasn't been any more sniper activity since, and things seem pretty quiet, so we go up. Three dozen stone steps take us to the top. It's a perfect spot for a lookout—and for an enemy sniper to be zeroed in on. We try to find where the GI was shot but there's nothing to show where he was. The view is really great. With my German *Dienstglas* binoculars I look down across the open fields to the edge of the woods where the Germans withdrew, but can't spot any activity.

I examine the cracks between the stones where some small plants are growing. I'm always on the lookout for small rock ferns, like Wall Rue. I never found any back in New York State when I was doing research at the Buffalo Museum of Science. Since we're in an exotic place—for us—it seems as though the plants

[Notes for Chapter 15 start p. 153]

ought to be especially interesting, but they aren't. They're just small ragweed-like plants trying to get a roothold in the spaces between the stones—just as they'd be doing back home on a railroad abutment in Buffalo, New York, U.S.A. They do look a little like the pictures I've seen of Wall Rue, but they're not even ferns. I've gotten to know Sackett a little more than the other guys in the squad. He was drafted out of college, the same as I was. Some guys might rib me about my interest in wild plants and ferns, but Sackett doesn't. He says they have a rock-garden in their back yard at home.

I think of that poem from high school English Lit class, something about "Flower in the Crannied Wall…If I could understand you all in all…" That's the only part I can remember. Maybe If I could understand something like a leaf or a flower "all in all" I might be able to understand how we all happen to be here in this war.[14]

After ten minutes on the tower and seeing no Germans we go back down. There's a small pear orchard in the yard of one of the houses butting up to the town square. The pears are filled out but they're green and hard. Like armies everywhere, I suppose, we don't even stop to think that whosever the pears are will be upset when they find they've been taken. The fact that they're green doesn't stop us. Fresh fruit is fresh fruit, ripe or not. The French people have been welcoming and generous; if they were here they'd probably give us the pears. Even so, in peacetime, taking them without permission would be theft.

When Browny—he's acquired the obvious nickname—finds me by myself, he tells me he's the one who shot the GI on the tower. He thought he was a German sniper. Nobody saw what happened, it was just assumed that a German sniper had shot him. I'm touched in a strange way that Browny would tell me. I decide not to tell anybody else. What's done is done. And telling Pulczak or Liebau could do more harm than good—in several ways. And to be absolutely honest, in the back of my mind is the not-so-noble thought that keeping the knowledge to myself could give me an advantage with Browny. I haven't gotten along too well with him since his smart-ass remark on the day he came up with the new replacements. This could be a chink, an edge. If he wants to tell Liebau he can. But I won't. I don't say I won't, I just don't. And I don't tell anyone else.

[Notes for Chapter 15 start on p. 153]

⊕

While we pitched our little fight
there was a wind went by
to the west, a great threatening
rush of gutterals as the
turbid black and clanking
tide raced through the valley's gap and
swept the all and everything before…
but only at the start. The flow
slowed, blocked, then sat in
collected stagnancy as bolts and
strikes came from the
sky. Rumblings unrumbled;
mutterings ceased. Now the
backflows have begun, seeking
riverways and escape,
backward among the
rocks.

⊕

[Notes for Chapter 15 start p. 153]

By leaving ST.-HILAIRE and racing east to MAYENNE we missed Hitler's big counter offensive through MORTAIN by a day. On the night of August 6th, five PANZER divisions and at least two Infantry Divisions began a thrust south through MORTAIN with the objective of cutting through Third Army's supply lines at AVRANCHES, where we'd come through less than a week before One of the PANZER spearheads attacked JUVIGNY, where we'd first stopped for the night north of ST.-HILAIRE.

Eisenhower and Bradley were alerted to the offensive by ULTRA, but instead of keeping us back to help stop the German thrust, they decided to keep us going east. We GIs didn't even hear about the big German attack.[15]

The German's MORTAIN offensive is not familiar to very many Americans, even veterans, but it was a major threat comparable to the German's December offensive that became known as the "Battle of the Bulge". Web-link No. 4 in Appendix C of the present volume refers to a detailed account of the MORTAIN Offensive. The book, SAVING THE BREAKOUT, by Alwyn Featherston, is dedicated entirely to the MORTAIN offensive. A summary is included in the ANNOTATED BIBLIOGRAPHY.

Stopping the MORTAIN offensive was left to the American First Army. German armor surrounded a battalion of the 30th Infantry Division on Hill 317 just east of MORTAIN and the battalion won fame for its heroic stand. For three days bad weather kept American and British fighter-bombers away from the advancing German columns, but while the beleaguered battalion waited for help from the air their artillery observers were able to direct deadly fire on the German armor and slow their advance. Artillery also delivered medical supplies to the defenders packed inside shells. I can't help wonder how our battalion would have fared on Hill 317.

[Notes for Chapter 15 start on p. 153]

Notes for Chapter 15

1. We were told it was a tank, but the regimental *Operational Report* says B-Company was held up by assault guns and mobile 88s (entry for 5 August, Appendix B).

2. We heard later that the engineer who cut the wires was posthumously awarded the Distinguished Service Cross. The exact circumstances are reported differently in different places.

3. I carried the rifle grenades loose in a canvas bag on a strap slung over my shoulder. I should have wrapped each one in something soft, but never did. Once when I looked in the bag I found the pin of a rifle grenade half-way out. The grenade might not have gone off even if the pin had come out because, unlike a manually thrown fragmentation grenade, a rifle grenade needed to hit something solid for it to explode. And, if I recall correctly from basic training there was an inertial safety device inside the rifle grenade that armed it only when it was blown off the end of the rifle. Even so, with the safety pin out of the grenade, if something banged hard enough against the bag it might have gone off—setting off everything else.

   With the grenade-launcher mounted on an M-1 rifle we could still fire regular ammunition through the launcher—as long as there was no grenade in place. But there was no fail-safe device to prevent firing a live round into a mounted grenade by mistake. You had to be clear-headed and know what you had in the chamber of your M-1 at all times.

4. I recalled from physics class that if air resistance is not taken into account, the angle for getting the greatest distance with a ballistic projectile is 45°. The best angle in practice, however, is a few degrees less.

5. White phosphorus burns fiercely in air, and once ignited, cannot be put out by ordinary means. Why it was not banned along with poison gas I don't understand. The phosphorus stuck to anything it touched, including

[Notes for Chapter 15 start p. 153]

human skin, and kept on burning. It seemed like an especially inhuman way to wound people.

6. American Sherman tanks had good reason to be shy. German Panther and Tiger tanks, armed with 88-mm guns were formidable. In the first months of the war, Sherman's had only 75-mm guns. It wasn't prudent to challenge the German tanks head-to-head if it could be avoided. We probably had only a couple of Shermans attached to our battalion, and with the kill ratio at five Shermans for one Panther or Tiger, there was no point in sacrificing them unless they could do some real good. But to us Infantrymen, our tanks seemed too timid to be much help.

7. How the French people got out of the towns so quickly, and where they went, was a mystery to us GIs. We never saw them on the roads or in the fields. Each town must have had spotters watching both the Germans and Americans, trying to guess where we'd go next. Many townspeople took everything of value with them, leaving their homes stripped almost bare.

   One of the few books that covers civilian problems and casualties in the war is Antony Beevor's *D-Day, The Battle for Normandy*. A summary and critique will be included in the ANNOTATED BIBLIOGRAPHY for this series. ANOTHER IS SAVAGE CONTINENT, BY KEITH LOWE (SEE ADDENDA).

8. In the American Civil War some units elected their leaders. Ulysses S. Grant became commander of his first Civil War troops in this way, but as a West Point graduate he was already an officer.

9. At the end of the 82nd Airborne's assignment in Normandy, General Ridgway wrote what was to become a famous division slogan: "No ground gained was ever relinquished and no advance ever halted except on the orders of Corps or Army." (*Ridgway's Paratroopers,* by Clay Blair, p. 297) Blair points out that this pronouncement wasn't strictly true because after they had "gained" *La Fière* causeway over the *Merderet* River on D-Day, the 82nd had to give it up, albeit temporarily, before regaining it in the fighting that followed.

[Notes for Chapter 15 start on p. 153]

10. Considering what happened later at *Hayange*, where Platoon Sgt. Barrett didn't keep up with Liebau, Stevens could have been right. But years later when Sackett saw the "balking" comment in Colby's book he wrote an indignant letter to Stevens, and Stevens replied in apologetic terms.

11. According to General Collins, in his book, *Lightnin' Joe*, on his (Collins's) recommendation Barth had been made Regimental Commander of 357 at the same time General Landrum replaced General McElvie as 90th Division's Commanding General. By the time we were approaching *Ste.-Suzanne* Landrum had been replaced by General McLain. For more on the Weaver/Barth Task Forces see Web-link No. 5, Appendix C.

12. *Ste.-Suzanne* had been an ancient walled fortress. In the 11th Century William the Conqueror laid siege to the town but after three years, abandoned efforts to take it. There is now an "old town" and a "new town". The old town is still strikingly medieval in appearance.

13. This view is highlighted in the *Michelin Green Guide*.

14. The poem I was trying to recall from English Lit class was by Tennyson:

> *Flower in the crannied wall,*
> *I pluck you out of the crannies;—*
> *Hold you here, root and all, in my hand,*
> *Little flower—but if I could understand*
> *What you are, root and all, and all in all,*
> *I should know what God and man is.*

15. The *Mortain* offensive was Hitler's personal project. Plans were discovered by the ULTRA code-breakers at Bletchley Park, England. Some Allied generals were reluctant to acknowledge ULTRA's usefulness but they did take note of the warning, and elements of First Army were repositioned to contain the thrust. Patton, on his own, left XV Corps' 35th Division behind in case they were needed.

[Notes for Chapter 15 start p. 153]

Page 156   **CHAPTER 16**

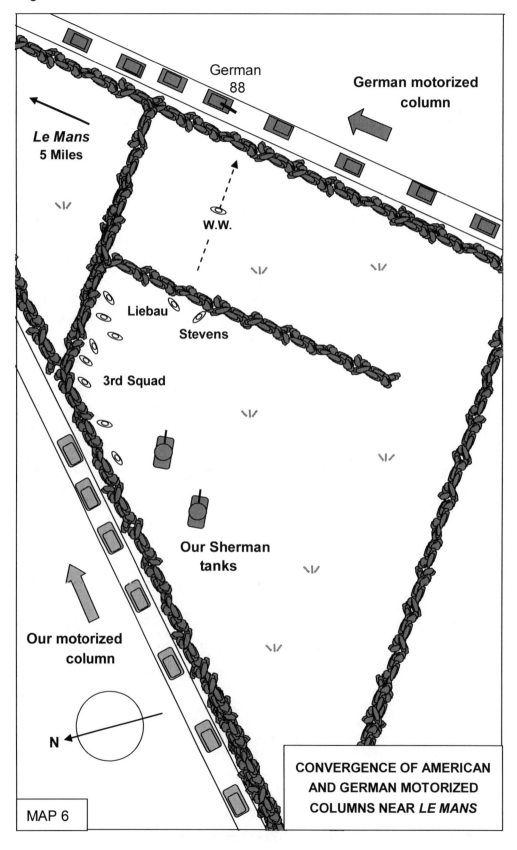

MAP 6 — CONVERGENCE OF AMERICAN AND GERMAN MOTORIZED COLUMNS NEAR *LE MANS*

16

RACE TO *LE MANS*

Assault [Foxhole 32]
August 7

Task Force Barth rolls on eastward. A Cub-type spotter plane is bird-dogging for us ahead of the column.[1] A couple of times it banks and dives violently. The pilot is obviously very edgy. There must be something up ahead to be edgy about.

A German plane appears, low, boring in on us. It ignores the spotter plane. We jump off the trucks but can't get through the thick hedgerows along the road so we go for the ditch—not a good place to be. If the plane strafes the vehicles some bullets will hit the ditch. Some of the guys fire at the plane but it swoops by undamaged. When it doesn't come back we get back on the trucks and keep going.

> FIRING AT FIGHTER PLANES WITH RIFLES SEEMS FUTILE, BUT IT WAS PART OF OUR TRAINING IN BASIC. THE IDEA WAS TO GET A CLOUD OF BULLETS GOING UP FOR THE PLANE TO FLY THROUGH. WITH A WHOLE COMPANY FIRING YOU MIGHT GET A HIT IN A VITAL SPOT. THE PRESCRIBED TECHNIQUE WAS TO LIE FLAT ON YOUR BACK AND FIRE AS THE PLANE CAME AT YOU, OR WENT AWAY FROM YOU. EVEN WITH THE SPEED OF A FIGHTER FLYING AT 400 MPH, A RIFLE BULLET COULD EASILY CATCH UP AND HIT THE PLANE. YOU HAD A CHANCE TO CAUSE SOME DAMAGE BUT I NEVER HEARD OF A FIGHTER PLANE BEING SHOT DOWN THAT WAY. SLOW LIGHT PLANES LIKE OUR L-4 SPOTTER PLANE, HOWEVER, WERE VULNERABLE TO GROUND FIRE.

About noon the trucks stop abruptly. We jump off again and move quickly off the road through a break in the right-hand hedgerow and into the first field. In less than a minute we get a lot of small-arms fire from a couple of fields over—machineguns and rifle fire. The earth banks of hedgerows here aren't high enough to give us much protection and everybody hits the ground. All we can do is keep as low as we can while somebody figures out what to do [MAP 6].

[Notes for Chapter 16 start on p. 167]

CHAPTER 16

Two Sherman tanks come up next to my squad, but a German 88 opens up and the tanks scuttle back. The effect of the 88's flat-trajectory fire is paralyzing.[2] Pulczak, our squad leader, is hit in the arm. He can't be sure what hit him because of the noise of the bullets popping around us and the stupefying sound of the 88s. There might be some grenades, too, we're close enough. Liebau crawls over on his hands and knees and tells me I'm going to take Pulzy's place as Squad Leader. He tells me to pick an Assistant Squad Leader. There's no time to think about it. I decide on Sackett and tell him he's the new Assistant Squad Leader. He's the only one of the new men I've gotten to know at all. Sackett stares at me with no sign of comprehension. I can't be sure he even hears what I'm saying.

Things quiet down for a couple of minutes then Liebau comes over again and says for me to get the squad up to the hedgerow.

"Wighty, you lead out…"

What is now *my* squad is going to attack across the small field separating us from where all the fire has been coming from. I tell Sackett to pick up the rear, and when we get up to the hedgerow Liebau says, "Wighty, you lead out." The squad is behind me on their hands and knees, with Sackett last. He's supposed to make sure the rest of the squad moves forward ahead of him—although in this case Liebau can do that for him. Next ahead of Sackett is Gervase, as far to the rear as he can get and still be with the squad—just as he was at *Mayenne*.

The bank of the hedgerow is only three feet high. A thin screen of brush and small trees grows from the top. Liebau and Lieutenant Stevens get ready to pull back some branches to make a new place for us to get through—so the Germans won't be zeroed in on us even before we move out. They pull back the branches, Liebau nods, and there's nothing for me to do but go. When I stand up I get a quick look at the space I must cross—just another open field boxed in by hedgerows like a hundred others we've seen. As I step over the bank and down into the field my brain is empty, and everything in the field is very clear. My heart is not pounding. My past does not race before my eyes. But I am aware that this may be my last moment on earth. There is nothing else, ever, anywhere, but this moment…

[Notes for Chapter 16 start on p. 167]

I step out
on the crystal cusp
clear as morning air
sharp as crystal sight
I step,
enter the crystal world
of all and everything forever.
My brain an empty glass,
sight and sounds clear,
a struck bell.
I step, urged by a wall
of obeyance, a flood
of linking blood that connects me
to all my fellows, and
disconnects me from all
their enemies. I am not drawn
to vengeance, but
thrust, urged
to a vengeance
sensed as a sweet
sauce that makes palatable
all the dry and sour
pablum we have
been forced by sameness
and anonymity
to consume.
The vengeance is not mine.
My fellows wait.
The enemies wait.
Fate waits.
I step
out onto the crystal cusp
of nothing and
forever…

[Notes for Chapter 16 start on p. 167]

To get to the other side of the field I must first get to a spot ten feet in front of me. Everything else drops away and I go, and I get past the ten-foot spot without sensing that I am hit and run forward down the middle of the field in a crouch, not even zig-zagging, trying to get to the other side as fast as I can. I expect at every second to hear the bullets, or feel them without hearing them, or feel whatever you feel when you are killed instantly, but hoping for the luck of surprise.

When the firing starts will I keep on running or fall prone and fire back? Keep running. Nobody gave us any instructions but I know that is what we should do. The closer we get to the hedgerow the harder it will be for the Germans to keep us in their sights. Unless we're running directly at one of them, in which case we're *kaput*. I keep running and halfway across I'm still on my feet and I'm not aware of any firing, I don't feel as though I'm hit and now I'm almost across and I get to the other side of the field and scrunch down behind the low hedgerow, ripping the tape off a grenade. My eyes and ears are honed to their ultimate sharpness. I'm ready to pull the pin and throw the grenade over the hedgerow but I don't hear anything except the noise of our own guys' feet and knees and elbows and rifle butts scrubbing the earth as their bodies go down. I wave to the squad to spread out along the hedgerow—we aren't supposed to go through it yet. Then I realize that Gervase and Sackett aren't with us. I see Liebau and the other two squads come across the field over on our right. Gervase and Sackett must be with them. Still there is no firing. I ease my eyes up over the bank and stare at a German motorized column stalled dead on the road. Minutes ago they were throwing heavy stuff at us us; now there isn't a German in sight.[3]

Liebau motions for us to go through the hedgerow. As I cross the road I pass directly in front of the drooping muzzle of a long-barreled 88 staring at me with its menacing eye. Lying in the middle of the paved road is a German compass, and in spite of a twinge of caution about booby-traps, I crouch down to pick it up.

There couldn't have been time for a German to rig anything, could there? But it could have been rigged ahead of time. I turn my head, close my eyes and pick it up. Nothing explodes, so I open the cover. It's harmless. It's a lot like one of our own GI lensatic compasses and I put it in my pocket. [SEE THIS BOOK'S COVER.]

[Notes for Chapter 16 start on p. 167]

> IN BASIC WE HAD A FIELD PROBLEM WITH GI COMPASSES VERY SIMILAR TO THE GERMAN ONE. THEY BOTH HAVE A SIGHTING DEVICE FOR TAKING BEARINGS WITH MARKINGS THAT GLOW AT NIGHT. OUR COMPASSES ARE FILLED WITH OIL TO KEEP THE NEEDLE FROM JIGGLING. COMPASSES WERE NOT ISSUED TO US GIS IN FRANCE. THIS ONE MIGHT COME IN HANDY.[4]

Across the road we spread out in a defensive perimeter. Gervase and Sackett are back with us but I don't find out why they didn't follow us across the field. Liebau was there, but he doesn't say anything and I don't ask him.

> THE PERCEPTION THAT SOMEONE IS LAGGING BACK IS AT FIRST ONLY A VAGUELY-FELT HUNCH, BUT IF THE BEHAVIOR IS REPEATED, THE HUNCH GETS A LOT STRONGER. YOU SENSE IT—IF YOU HAVE ANY EMPATHY AT ALL— THE WAY A KINDERGARTEN TEACHER KNOWS WHICH KID LEFT THE WATER RUNNING IN THE BATHROOM. GERVASE HAD LAGGED BACK AT *MAYENNE*, AND DIDN'T KEEP UP WITH THE SQUAD HERE AT *LEMANS*. I COULDN'T HELP THINKING THERE WAS MORE TO IT THAN COINCIDENCE. WHAT ABOUT SACKETT? MAYBE HE STAYED BACK TO SWEEP IN GERVASE—AS I HAD DONE AT *MAYENNE*. BUT I REMEMBER AT THE ISLAND WHEN SACKETT DIDN'T WANT TO TAKE THE JOB AS SCOUT. MAYBE THERE WAS SOMETHING THERE TOO.

The Germans could still be in the fields across the road and might counterattack to take back the column of vehicles. We push on through a couple more fields into a scrubby woods without meeting any resistance. I get word from Liebau to dig in. The guys let me know that they don't feel like doing it. I'm beginning to see that my greatest weakness as a non-com is that I don't like to beat on guys when they don't want to do something. But I'm not going to argue about digging the holes. Arguing and losing is worse than just letting them get away with it.

I tell them once, and why it's important, especially here, because of straggling Germans, and let it go at that. I remind them to keep their rifles close. Half of the guys dig pretty good holes. The rest just scrape out a few inches and quit. The soil is actually pretty good digging, soft and black on top, sandy underneath, not many roots.

[Notes for Chapter 16 start on p. 167]

I post the guards and In the middle of the night make the rounds. Two of the three guards are asleep. I wake them up and repeat the warning that the Germans could be wandering around the countryside, but nothing like that has happened since the new guys came up so it's like crying wolf.

At my own hole, which I didn't dig very deep because of setting up the guard and checking on the other guys, I wake up in the dark and hear some shooting. It's not close but I think I hear a spent bullet thud close next to me and feel around with my hands. It seems like there's a warm spot and I dig a little with my fingers, but I don't find anything. Must be my imagination taking over. It's been a long day.

⌗

In the morning we cross to the other side of a river [THE SARTHE]. One of the GIs in another squad comes over to me and tells me that Alf Green was shot. I don't recognize the man who tells me, but he seems to know that Alf and I were in the same hole at *Beau-Coudray*. He says Alf was sitting on the edge of his foxhole last night when three Germans appeared. Alf grabbed for his rifle but they fired first. He was hit in the side of his back near the kidney and died before the medics got to him. If that guy hadn't told me, I never would have found out. My concerns about straggling Germans proved to be justified, but that doesn't help Alf Green. I haven't seen him since *Beau-Coudray*, but he was the only one of the guys I've felt close to at all.[5]

We march through the city of *Le Mans* and the streets are lined with French people of all ages, smiling, waving, laughing, walking along beside us handing us drinks—water and *cidre* and wine. Winning is pretty heady stuff. "Easy on the booze," we're told, and after a while we're told not to take any more.

This is a day when we have to walk. Our bedrolls were brought up to us early in the morning and dumped in a pile. They must need the trucks for something else. Liebau commandeers a small civilian car, a sporty open roadster, and gives me the job of driving it with the platoon's bedrolls piled on the back. I'm game. The car has English words on the dashboard, a stick shift on the floor, and a right-seat

[Notes for Chapter 16 start on p. 167]

steering wheel. It doesn't take any time at all to get used to. It's a pretty nice assignment. But the guys don't fare too well because once we clear the city limits of Le Mans the road isn't paved. When I drive up to the head of the column between the two files of men—one on each side of the road—the car throws up a cloud of dust, and they have to eat it. They start to bitch, at first just kidding me about my soft job, but it's an extra discomfort they don't need. Whitey Merrill is serious about his complaints. He's squad leader of First Squad—"Whitey" because of his light blond hair. I haven't had much contact with him but I sense the relationship from his side is not the warmest. I don't know why.

I try to stay at the back of the platoon, but the Third Platoon is coming up behind us and their bedrolls aren't even on the car. They're getting the dust for nothing. I can't win. The whole thing is one of those ideas that sounds good but doesn't pan out when you actually do it.

We go all day, with a few breaks, the guys walking and me driving the classy little car, and it's hot. In the evening the column turns off into a wooded area and I'm about to turn off behind them, but an MP stops me and says I have to take the car to the motor pool. I protest, explaining that I've got the guys' bedrolls, but he stands in my way unmoved, pointing in the direction to the motor pool.

"Tell them about it," he says. If they let me take the car to the platoon area, OK, but he can't give me permission on his own. Cripes, I thought we left that kind of chickenshit behind.[6]

But that's what I have to do. When I get to the motor pool it's in a shadowy grove of trees. Some of the trucks are jacked up and being worked on. I find the officer in charge and tell him what's going on, and he says OK, take the car to my company area, it's not one of his vehicles. He doesn't care what happens to it. Unless "Old blood-and-guts" sees it, but that's our problem.[7]

Can I have some gasoline? Why not? Compared to his big stuff, my little car has the appetite of a hummingbird. "But no lights," the captain says. OK, no lights, but I need something to get me past the MP. OK. He scrawls something on a scrap of cardboard from a ration box.

[Notes for Chapter 16 start on p. 167]

CHAPTER 16

I head back, trying to remember the way. It would be easy to get lost and wind up tooling around the French countryside. It is a temptation. It's pretty nice driving the car by myself out in the cool night with the just the stars to keep me company. I can see the Big and Little Dipper, and Polaris, and Cassiopeia.

It's reassuring to see the familiar patterns, but disturbing too. Seems like I ought to be looking at the sky from my own backyard in Buffalo, New York. But that isn't where I am. I'm in a foreign country half a world away, in war, and I've got to take the bedrolls back to the guys.[8]

When I finally find B-Company the MP is gone. I drive in with the bedrolls and the guys are already sacked out on the ground without them. Liebau gives me a chewing out.

"Where the hell have you been, Wighty?" he bawls in his loud voice.

Everybody hears me getting my ass reamed. Maybe that's his plan, to let them know that it was my fault, not his. Except it wasn't my fault. I explain what happened and Liebau cools down, then I help the guys find their bedrolls.

But I feel misused. Using the car was Liebau's idea, and I only did what I was told by the MP. I don't think he should have jumped on me like that before I had a chance to explain. Harboring resentment is one of my character flaws I guess. I don't like to be yelled at. And Liebau should be trying to help me in my new job as Squad Leader, not undermining me. I don't forget that kind of thing easily.

To top everything off, my own bedroll is missing. Identifying your own bedroll is questionable anyhow. We're not supposed to put our names on them, or serial numbers. If the Germans got them they might glean some useful information. So we tie special knots, or make personal marks or use wacky names. And what difference does it make if we get somebody else's bedroll? They're all the same, just a blanket and a shelter-half.[9] We know better than to put anything valuable in them because we might not get them back for weeks, or ever.

When all the guys have taken their bedrolls from the car there's none left for me. It's not a particularly cool night, and I've got a raincoat rolled up and tied to my

[Notes for Chapter 16 start on p. 167]

combat pack, so I unroll it and start looking for a place to lie down in the dark. Nobody has dug any holes. Then I hear a voice say, "Wighty, c'mon, share mine."

It's Sartori, one of the new guys, one of the replacements that came up at the "Island". He's a mild-mannered guy, amply built, and he somehow manages to keep a little cleaner than most of us. I haven't learned anything else about him. I don't know his first name, or where he's from, except it's from a city somewhere I'm quite sure, and up to now I haven't even spoken to him except for the simple routine stuff. But he has found exactly the right time to make a friendly gesture.

I take him up on it. We lie on top of his blanket with his shelter-half under it crosswise, each with a raincoat over us. I lie awake for a while, looking at the stars through the trees. My resentment from Liebau's unjustified chewing out still festers, but after a while it fades away and I sleep.

More chickenshit [Foxhole 33]

In the morning the little car is left behind—because of an order from higher up Liebau says. [SEE OPERATIONAL REPORT, APPENDIX B, P. 297] In a way I'm relieved. It was awkward to be traveling in comfort while the guys slogged it out chewing on the dust from the car.

We walk a few miles to another location carrying our bedrolls, dig holes, but not very deep, and get the word that we'll be here for at least a day. It's a reserve area, which means our battalion, maybe the whole regiment, is not at the advancing edge of the division—if the division is in fact still advancing. We never know what's going on.

Being in reserve, they'll set up the kitchen and we'll get hot chow. Maybe that's why they needed the trucks. And we'll have a little more freedom to walk around. Not far, but the feeling is welcome, not being tethered together with unseen ropes like mountain climbers.

So I'm doing that, walking around and I'm doing it with my head bare, another part of the freedom, but that turns out to be a mistake. A shrimpy second lieutenant I've never seen before accosts me, scowling mad.

[Notes for Chapter 16 start on p. 167]

"Where's your helmet, soldier?" he rasps, as though it's a personal affront to him that I've left my steel helmet back at my hole.

I'm caught completely by surprise. This is a war, and we're combat fighters, and we're winning. We're conquering warriors, and we just beat up on a German column and chased their asses out of *Le Mans* [IT HAD BEEN THE HEADQUARTERS FOR THE ENTIRE GERMAN SEVENTH ARMY]. What the hell does it matter where my helmet is? I'll wear it if I feel like it. That's what shows on my face I'm sure, but I'm actually speechless, staring.

"I mean it," the bratty second looey snarls. "Go get it, and if I see you without it again I'll report you to your commanding officer!"

So report me!, I snap, but keep it inside my throat. I find it hard to believe what's happening. It's like basic training again, crotch-deep in chickenshit. Where has this guy been? Not near any flying bullets, I'll bet.[10]

> THE LIEUTENANT COULD HAVE BEEN A GREEN REPLACEMENT EXERCISING HIS RANK TO CALM HIS NERVES, OR MAYBE PATTON HAD LAID DOWN THE LAW AGAIN ABOUT BEING IN PROPER UNIFORM AT ALL TIMES. PATTON WAS A FANATIC ABOUT GIS BEING "GI", PROCLAIMING THAT PROPERLY DRESSED TROOPS WERE BETTER TROOPS, THAT MORALE WAS HIGHER WHEN THE MEN WERE CLEAN AND NEAT AND FOLLOWING REGULATIONS TO A "T". WITH FIFTY YEARS TO SORT IT OUT I THINK HE WAS WRONG.
>
> THE GOOD COMBAT INFANTRYMAN IS NOT NECESSARILY THE NEAT COMBAT INFANTRYMAN. UNKEMPTNESS CAN BE A BADGE OF PRIDE AND COURAGE WHEN IT RESULTS FROM HARD SLOGGING AND SLUGGING IN CONTACT WITH THE ENEMY. SEASONED COMBAT TROOPS CAN DERIVE PRIDE FROM THEIR SLOPPINESS AND FROM THEIR CONTEMPT FOR USELESS REGULATIONS. KILLING IS A DIRTY BUSINESS AND TO ME, IT SEEMED IMMORAL FOR PROFESSIONAL KILLERS TO LOOK TOO CLEAN. I DON'T THINK PATTON UNDERSTOOD ANY OF THIS.[11]
>
> FURTHERMORE, PATTON BENT THE REGULATIONS HIMSELF. AS THE STORY GOES, A CLOSE FRIEND OF PATTON'S IN NORTH AFRICA WAS DECAPITATED

by the chin-strap on his steel helmet when the blast from a bomb blew the helmet off. After that, nobody in Patton's command was allowed to buckle the chin-strap under his chin. It was, instead, to be buckled neatly over the top of the front edge of the helmet. But chin-straps often did dangle, at all levels of rank. Some photographs show General Ridgway's chin-strap dangling. Patton's ivory-handled revolvers weren't regulation either.[12]

Notes for Chapter 16

1. The Piper Cub J-3 was one of the first airplanes manufactured in America for the civilian aviation market and many are still flying, rebuilt or re-covered. A military version, the L-4, "L" for liaison, was used in WW-II. It was a small single-engine fabric-covered monoplane with two-seats, one behind the other. Dual controls allowed a pilot in either seat to fly the plane by means of a stick positioned between the knees.

2. The German 88-mm artillery was the most talked about, and feared, of all German weapons. The guns were dual-purpose, used against both aircraft and surface targets such as tanks and other armored vehicles. They were often mounted on German Panther and Tiger class tanks. Muzzle velocity was 3,200 feet per second, almost three times the speed of sound, and 22% faster than the bullet from an M-1 rifle. The 88 shell made a sonic boom as it went past; the explosion of the shell itself came a split-second later: **POW**-KRASHH You never heard the shells coming.

   Kinetic energy is what gives a projectile its penetrating power. It is proportional to the mass of a projectile but to the *square* of its velocity. It was the great velocity of the shells from the long-barreled guns that gave the 88s their awesome advantage against American tanks.

3. The fire had been coming from a German motorized column heading for *Le Mans* on another road parallel to the one we had just left. The two roads came together about a half-mile ahead of us just short of the city

limits. Task Force Weaver was pounding at the rear of the German column and our fighter bombers had knocked out some German vehicles up front, blocking the road and trapping the column. At the place we got off the trucks the converging roads were only two small fields apart.

4. The German *Dienstglas* binoculars were stolen back in the States. The German compass is my one souvenir—except, of course, myself.

5. I finally contacted Alf Green's family 68 years after the war. I was given their e-mail address by Fabrice Avoie, a French author who grew up near *Le Mans.* His book, Sarthe-août 1944 - Histoire d'une Libération, describes the battles around *Le Mans* in detail. It is currently out of print, but a second edition is expected in 2014. I recommend it.

6. *Chickenshit* is a term used throughout the armed forces referring to excessive emphasis on petty authority and bureaucratic detail. I have no idea about its origin, but it has nothing to do with being "chicken", i.e., timid. Paul Fussell, in his book, *Wartime*, devotes an entire chapter to the subject, headed, simply, "Chickenshit".

7. "Old Blood-and-Guts" was the GI's name for General Patton. It was bitter sarcasm, meaning that he had the guts—to plan audacious moves—and the GIs provided the blood.

    We in the 90th Division didn't refer to him in that way, though. In fact, we didn't referred to him at all. I never heard his name spoken while I was in France.

8. When I was driving the little sports car at *Le Mans* I had never heard of the *Le Mans* road race, or the "*Le Mans start*"—where the drivers run to their cars when the starting flag drops—or even the term *sports car.* It wasn't until the early fifties that *bona fide* sports cars were manufactured in America—the 1953 Corvette and the 1955 Ford Thunderbird—unless the early racing cars like the Stutz Bearcat could be put in that category. In 1962 I bought a second-hand 1959 Corvette and enjoyed it immensely.

[Notes for Chapter 16 start on p. 167]

9. A shelter-half was one half of a two-man pup tent. In combat we used them as ground-cloths and ponchos, but not for tents. I never saw a tent of any kind while we were in France.

10. The job of a Second Lieutenant as Platoon Leader in a combat rifle company was one of the toughest and most hazardous jobs in the war. Statistics show they had very high casualty rates.

    When a 2nd Lieutenant came up on line as a replacement for a casualty, the job was especially demanding. He had to take over a platoon that contained experienced men, prove that he knew what to do and how to do it, and provide an example of aggressiveness and courage, all with no experience of dealing with the enemy or with troops under fire. A description of such circumstances is found in Paul Fussell's *Doing Battle.* He had that kind of experience. I don't necessarily recommend the rest of his book, but this part seems realistic and honest. The chickenshit 2nd looey may have been reacting to the stress of past, or anticipated, responsibilities.

11. Bill Mauldin's *Up Front* characters in the *Willie and Joe* cartoon were the epitome of unkemptness. Patton threatened to ban the *Stars and Stripes*—in which Mauldin's cartoons appeared—from the Third Army but with the backing of General Eisenhower, Mauldin won out. See entry for Bill Mauldin in the ANNOTATED BIBLIOGRAPHY; also Appendix C, Web-link No. 6.

12. The decapitation story may be apocryphal. Other accounts have Patton's GI audiences pointedly buckling their straps under their chins—long after the African campaign. As for Patton's revolver handles, many writers say they were mother-of-pearl, but Robert Patton, the General's grandson, says in his book, *The Pattons,* that the handles were ivory, adding that "Georgie" thought pearl handles would be effeminate. Clay Blair, author of *Ridgway's Paratroopers*, writes that the revolver handles were bone.

⊕

[Notes for Chapter 16 start on p. 167]

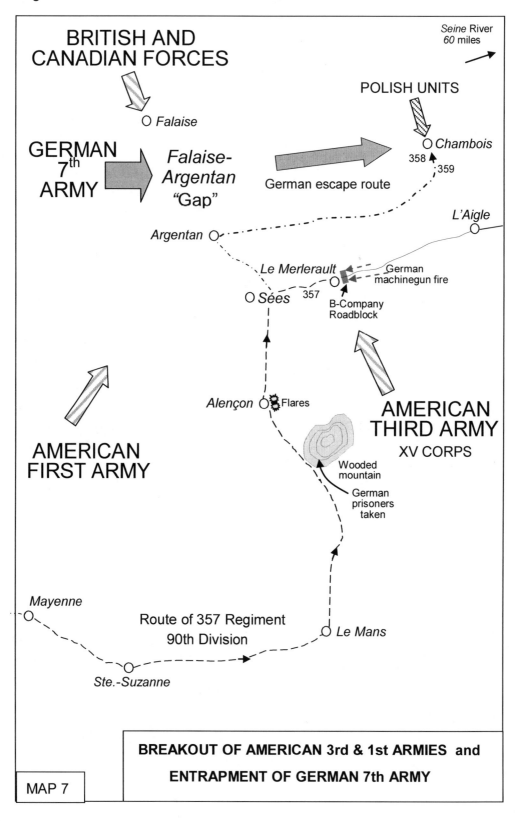

17

TRAPPING THE GERMAN 7ᵀᴴ ARMY

Prisoners [Foxhole 34]

Late the next morning we get on trucks again and head north. At one point we have to move off the road to let a motorized column go by—GI vehicles driven by members of the 2nd French Armored Division now attached to the American Third Army. They're excited to finally be in the fighting, and from what we've heard, are boisterous and reckless with patriotic zeal. Their driving bears it out.[1]

We stop for the night on a dirt road running along the side of a small wooded mountain [MAP 7]. Following instructions from Liebau I take Sartori with me on a reconnaissance patrol up the mountain. It takes only a few minutes to get to the top. The view is spectacular. We watch one of our P-47s make a strafing run a couple of miles to the northwest. The sun catches the plane's wings as it banks and sweeps down into a valley already filling with shadows. Two strings of puffs pop out from its wing-mounted cannon. The sound never does reach us.

The top of the mountain on the north is open and grassy with scattered clumps of small bushes. The rest of the summit is covered with a dense grove of tall pines. As in many pine forests there is no underbrush. Branches begin about twenty feet up. We peer in under the trees and down the dim aisles of pine trunks lined up like a battalion in review. If any Germans are hiding there they'll be watching us with their weapons ready. I decide not to go into the pines. Reconnaissance has to stop somewhere.

When we're back with the platoon Liebau says to pick two men from my squad to go back up the mountain as an outpost for the night. I choose Sackett and Russell, and give Sackett my watch. I warn them about the light from the watch showing in the dark and tell them what Sartori and I found, and where to set up the outpost. They take off and we start digging holes a little way back from the road, but there doesn't seem to be any real need, so we don't give it more than a half-hearted effort.

[Notes for Chapter 17 start p. 188]

CHAPTER 17

A half-hour later I'm astounded when Sackett and Russell show up again with a squad of German prisoners in single file—Russell in the lead, Sackett bringing up the rear. The Germans are young and cocky, and a couple of them are smiling. On Sackett's "Halt!" they stop instantly and snap to attention in a perfectly spaced perfectly straight line— mechanical like marionettes on strings.

> They jerk and snap in
> puppetized response, trained
> like circus seals. Kids. But
> lethalized. *Nazi* soldiers. Their
> early blood tainted by Hitler's
> and cronies' demented plan. They
> don't know that man, the one
> with the black tooth-brush moustache, they,
> boys, plucked from families, schools, from
> peaceful lives (as were we), funneled
> into military habits and ways (as were we),
> but they, when
> we were at their—unbeknownst-to
> -us—mercy, perhaps even centered in their
> Mausers' sights, they, let us
> Live, Sartori and me. We live at their
> pleasure. Some deep inner
> twitch said to at least one of them: "Wait!" A
> twinge of reason, encouraged perhaps by a
> clamp of hunger. (Where will we find a meal tonight?)
> "Let's take a chance," one said, as they looked
> at each other in wild surmise: "Let's surrender."
> Now we are all the same, they, us. Except that
> for them, the war is done.

Sackett is taut, nervous as a cat, concentrating completely on his task. I don't blame him. But the prisoners don't cause any trouble. They look embarrassed. Our guys cluster around, take a couple of the Germans' watches. I don't feel quite right about that, but if we let them keep the watches somebody else will just get

[Notes for Chapter 17 start on p. 188]

them down the line. Taking prisoners' watches is pretty much SOP. We might as well have them. GIs weren't issued watches so our guys can make good use of them, mostly for standing guard.

I feel some pride for Sackett. He could have really screwed up. He could have misread the Germans' intentions, got into an unnecessary firefight, maybe got himself and Russell killed. But they did OK. I feel some satisfaction for myself, too, picking Sackett for Assistant Squad Leader back at Le Mans. I had no idea whether he'd be any good at the job. I didn't have time to think about it, just chose him because he was nearby and the only guy I knew anything about. I did have some lingering doubts, though, remembering how he dodged the assignment as scout when he first came up with the other replacements.

He tells me the Germans were in a slight hollow in the grassy area on the summit, hidden by some bushes. When they surrendered they just stood up and put their hands in the air. I've wondered what I would do in a situation like that. It could have been a trap. A German with a burp-gun could have been off to the side ready to mow them down. I have to admit a twinge of envy. I've never brought in any prisoners. Why should I care? Maybe I'm starting to think like a soldier.

My guess is that the Germans gave up because they were cut off from their outfit and were hungry. All they'll get tonight, though, is K-Rations—I hope. That's all we got. The prisoners aren't abused in any way. Nobody taunts them. Someone takes them back to the rear, wherever that is. The regiment must be strung out behind us for miles. We're just about to sack out in shallow holes—though some of the guys dig them a little deeper because of the Germans being in the area—when Shaeffer comes by with the word that we're going to move out. Yes, tonight.

Caught in a flare [Foxhole 35]

We've been ordered to go to a place called *Alençon*, Liebau says, to help defend it against a possible German attack. The guys who dug good holes bitch, but you can't take your foxhole with you. We get our stuff together, move down to a bigger road, pile back on the trucks, and head out. It's eerie because the trucks' headlights and taillights are masked over almost completely leaving only small points of faint light in the darkness.

[Notes for Chapter 17 start p. 188]

CHAPTER 17

WHEN THE GERMAN OFFENSIVE AT *MORTAIN* SHOWED SIGNS OF BOGGING DOWN, BOTH THE ALLIED AND GERMAN COMMANDS BEGAN TO SEE THE POSSIBILITY OF A GIANT ALLIED PINCER MOVEMENT BETWEEN MONTGOMERY'S CANADIANS ON THE NORTH AND OUR THIRD AND FIRST ARMIES ON THE SOUTH. IF SUCCESSFUL, IT COULD TRAP THE ENTIRE GERMAN SEVENTH ARMY—FIVE ARMORED DIVISIONS INCLUDED. ALTHOUGH HITLER HAD FORBIDDEN THEM TO GIVE GROUND, THE MORE RATIONAL OF THE GERMAN GENERALS—WHO HADN'T APPROVED OF THE *MORTAIN* OFFENSIVE FROM THE START—WERE ALREADY LOOKING FOR WAYS OUT OF AN ENCIRCLEMENT.

THREE POSSIBLE ROUTES OF ESCAPE EXISTED THAT HAD DECENT ROADS [MAP 7]. ONE WAS THROUGH *ALENÇON*, THIRTY MILES NORTH OF *LE MANS*. THAT'S WHERE WE WERE HEADED. *ALENÇON* WAS THE SUPPLY CENTER FOR ONE OF *EBERBACH'S PANZER* DIVISIONS STILL INVOLVED AT MORTAIN. ANOTHER POSSIBLE ESCAPE ROUTE WAS THROUGH *ARGENTAN*, TWENTY MILES NORTH OF *ALENÇON*. A THIRD WAS THROUGH *FALAISE*, TWELVE MORE MILES NORTHWEST OF *ARGENTAN*.

WORD GOT TO BRADLEY THROUGH ULTRA, THE BRITISH CODE BREAKING CENTER, THAT *VON KLUGE* AND *EBERBACH* HAD CHOSEN *ALENÇON* AS THEIR FIRST CHOICE FOR A WAY OUT OF THE TRAP. THE 90TH DIVISION WAS RUSHED TO *ALENÇON*—LEAVING A THIRTY-MILE GAP BETWEEN *MAYENNE* AND *ALENÇON* WITH NO ALLIED TROOPS.[2]

I WAS SO IGNORANT OF FRANCE'S GEOGRAPHY I CONFUSED *ALENÇON* WITH *AVRANCHES*, AT THE BASE OF THE *CHERBOURG* PENINSULA. I THOUGHT WE WERE BEING ORDERED BACK TO WHERE WE'D BEEN A WEEK BEFORE.

We get to *Alençon* a little after midnight and dig in along the east bank of a river [THE *SARTHE*]. A German plane comes over and drops a couple of flares that drift down on parachutes. Sackett and I are caught out in the open. We don't know whether to freeze, as we were taught in basic, or to ignore the flares. When lit by a flare, movement on the ground is supposed to be easy to detect from reconnaissance planes, and faces reflect light. But a motionless person who keeps his face tilted down looks like just another bush. We stay stock-still for a couple of minutes, staring at the ground, hardly daring even to talk. But no more planes come over and feeling both foolish and guilty we start moving again. After a while the flares burn themselves out.

> THE AFTERNOON BEFORE WE GOT THERE GERMAN GENERALS *VON KLUGE* AND *EBERBACH* CAME TO *ALENÇON* TO LOOK THINGS OVER. THEY FOUND GERMAN ADMINISTRATIVE PERSONNEL PACKING UP AND LEAVING AS FAST AS THEY COULD. AN AMERICAN ARMORED DIVISION WAS ALREADY BATTERING AT THE CITY'S SOUTHEASTERN EDGE, AND FRENCH GENERAL *LE CLERC'S* 2ND ARMORED HAD ALREADY CROSSED THE *SARTHE* RIVER NORTH OF THE CITY. THE PLAN FOR A GERMAN PULL-OUT THROUGH *ALENÇON* WAS ABANDONED. IF IT HAD BEEN CARRIED OUT, WE IN THE 90TH WOULD HAVE BEEN DIRECTLY IN ITS PATH.[3]

We post a one-on, two-off guard, and we're told to keep a close eye on the river in case the Germans try to come across, but nothing happens.

The "Gap" [Foxhole 36]

The next day we're trucked farther north to a place near the city of *Sées*. Incredibly, a movie is going to be shown and we can go see it, half the company at a time.

I don't go. I've gotten myself into a sober mood. I don't want any diversion from the war. The war is serious stuff, and I'm convinced now there's going to be a lot more of it. My optimism at the *Sèves* River has been tempered. *Hitler* wasn't killed, and the war isn't over.

Maybe I caught some of the gloom from that guy in the dark hole back at the "Island". I feel I've got to keep my mind focused on the realities around us, not the fantasies of a Hollywood movie. Watching a movie won't change what's ahead..

I spend the time writing a long fairly bitter letter to Sgt. Harper at Fort McClellan, criticizing the way the cadre in basic came down so hard on us for trivial stuff while neglecting the really important things. [HARPER WAS THE NON-COM WHO GIGGED ME AND MADE ME STAY UP ALL NIGHT CLEANING MY GEAR WHEN I WAS SICK—*BECAUSE* I WAS SICK.] I'm not happy with my letter. I can't seem to say what I mean. Maybe I don't know exactly what my beef is. It's mixed up with my personal disagreement with the Army's entire way of doing things. But I get some stuff off my chest, keeping the censor in mind—it's probably Liebau—and turn in my three pages of V-mail.

> I wasn't just bitching. I was trying to identify what I thought were serious weaknesses in the training. Many military people, later acknowledged that important weaknesses did exist. S. L. A. Marshall had a lot to say about the subject. So did General "Lightning Joe" Collins, Commander of First Army's 7th Corps. For a discussion of their views on training, see the *Annotated Bibliography*.
>
> Considering everything, though, I think the training the Army gave us was quite good. They crammed a lot into thirteen weeks, and although it was hurried and superficial, a surprising amount of it stuck. To their credit, the cadre, though sometimes crude, were never cynical about what they were doing. They took their job seriously and did the best they could.
>
> The one thing the training could not provide was a realistic sense of combat. One consequence was that they had no way of sorting out guys who would or wouldn't make effective combat soldiers. But there never has been a good way to do that.[4]

While we're at *Sées* we hear rumors that something big is going on just a few miles to the north of us. "It's awful," a guy from another outfit who'd been there says. What's awful? He's talking about the "pocket" north of *Argentan*. The Allies' attempt at encirclement of the German 7th Army is in full progress, and the 90th is part of it. Entire divisions of trapped Germans are getting pulverized by our artillery and fighter bombers, but the Germans won't give up. As usual, we GIs in B-Company haven't been told anything about the bigger picture.

> This word-of-mouth report was the only information we ever got about the *Falaise* Gap, also called the *Falaise-Argentan* pocket. When we were at *Seés* the trap was already closing, but the Germans resisted with suicidal stubbornness. One of the 90th's

[Notes for Chapter 17 start on p. 188]

> OTHER REGIMENTS INITIALLY TOOK A STRATEGIC RIDGE JUST SOUTH OF *ARGENTAN*, WAS FORCED OFF, BUT REGAINED THE RIDGE AND MANAGED TO HOLD ON. THE RIDGE COMMANDED THE 12-MILE GAP THROUGH WHICH THE DESPERATE GERMANS WERE STREAMING EASTWARD. UNOPPOSED AMERICAN ARTILLERY AND FIGHTER BOMBERS POURED IN DEVASTATING FIRE. GENERAL EISENHOWER WENT TO VIEW THE CARNAGE AND SAID THERE WERE PLACES WHERE A MAN COULD WALK ON FLESH FOR A HUNDRED YARDS WITHOUT HIS FEET TOUCHING THE GROUND.[5]
>
> AT SÉES OUR GUYS WERE WATCHING A MOVIE, AND JUST A FEW MILES NORTH FROM THERE A BIG BATTLE WAS GOING ON WITH ENTIRE DIVISIONS OF GERMANS BEING ANNIHILATED. WE WERE ALMOST CLOSE ENOUGH TO HEAR THE BOMBS AND GUNFIRE, WHICH MEANT THAT THE SOUNDTRACK OF THE MOVIE MIGHT BE HEARD WHERE THE FIGHTING WAS GOING ON (PERHAPS A SLIGHT EXAGGERATION).

At *Sées,* one of the few things occurs that has struck me funny since I've been overseas—since I've been the Army, actually. I'm sitting on the edge of my foxhole in a field along the north-south road, writing the letter to Harper, when I become aware of a pounding sound coming toward me on the road to my left.

There's a thundering roar as a cloud of dust goes by and I get a glimpse of our own man, Gervase, riding bareback on an immense gray horse. He has a wild look on his face as he gallops like crazy down the road.[6] I don't know how to ride a horse with a saddle, let alone bareback. Here's Gervase—the reluctant, hang-back infantryman—flying across the countryside like a horseman out of history. I want to laugh, but I can't—in my mind I'm still staring straight-on at the war.

> THE FACT THAT I COULDN'T LAUGH, OR LET MYSELF BE DIVERTED EVEN FOR A SHORT TIME TO ENJOY A MOVIE OR A FUNNY INCIDENT WAS, I COULD SEE MUCH LATER, AN OMEN OF THINGS TO COME. I TOOK MY RESPONSIBILITIES VERY SERIOUSLY—NOT JUST THE NEW JOB AS NON-COM, BUT WHAT I CONSIDERED AS MY PERSONAL JOB—DOING AS WELL AS I COULD AT WHATEVER I HAD TO DO.[7] NORMALLY, A CAPACITY FOR HUMOR IS A SIGN OF A WELL-BALANCED PERSONALITY. WITHOUT HUMOR, THINGS TIGHTEN UP.

[Notes for Chapter 17 start p. 188]

Roadblock [Foxhole 37]

After a couple of days in reserve at Sées we're taken by truck to set up a roadblock just past *Le Merlerault,* a tiny hamlet on a hard gravel road going east [TO *L'AIGLE*]. Beyond our roadblock is German-held territory [MAP 8, P. 184].

> OUR MISSION WAS TO PREVENT GERMAN REINFORCEMENTS FROM BREAKING BACK INTO THE *FALAISE-ARGENTAN* POCKET FROM THE SOUTH AND EAST, OR FROM CUTTING OFF THE TIP OF OUR PINCER THAT HAD BEEN THRUST NORTH-EAST FROM *ARGENTAN*.

The First Platoon is assigned to man the roadblock, with a couple of Sherman tanks to back them up. The rest of us can relax. Sackett and I take a hike through the woods on the south side of the road where our platoon is dug in. We're going to be here for a couple of days and I want to know what's behind us. We find ourselves in about fifteen acres of open woods. Part way in we come upon what looks like an honest-to-gosh rabbit warren [LIKE *WATERSHIP DOWN*]. When I was a kid somebody at school looked up all our first names in a dictionary and I got teased because my name meant a rabbit colony. In Western New York where I come from, rabbits don't live in colonies. Here, about a dozen holes go into a mounded-up area some forty by fifty feet, bare of vegetation and packed smooth by the traffic. When we first see the place, we can't be sure what kind of animal made the holes. When we find their droppings we decide it's rabbits—"sign", as hunters say.

After making a circuit of the woods and seeing only empty fields beyond the trees we swing back to the eastern edge closest to German territory. I scan the fields with my German binoculars but don't see anything threatening so we step outside the trees into a faint path along the edge of the woods going south toward some distant buildings. I check out the buildings for enemy presence or activity, but see nothing, and have just put the binoculars away when a young boy appears in the path seemingly out of nowhere. We're wary, and so is he, but he seems friendly and harmless, and is apparently alone. I try out some of my school French on him and it works pretty well after I get him slowed down (*Lentement, s'il vous plaît*). We have a pleasant though limited conversation. I mention the holes in the woods and ask him if he knows what kind of animal made them.

[Notes for Chapter 17 start on p. 188]

"*Les lapins*," he says, the rabbits. So we were right.

"*Pour manger?*" I ask, for eating? He shrugs. Apparently not, or too hard to catch, or all trapped out. Or maybe he wants to save them for himself.

When I ask him if there are any Germans around, his face goes sober. "*Non, monsieur, pas ici.*" No, Sir, not here. It's a safe answer. Maybe his family has warned him to be careful of what he says to *les Américains*. Maybe the Germans themselves have warned him.

"Are they down the road?" I point to the east. "How far?"

"*Je 'n sais pas*," he shrugs. He almost certainly knows, but I don't press him.

"Do you want some wine?" he asks in French. "I will bring you a bottle of very good champagne."

"OK", I say and he starts to go, but I stop him. "When will you be back?" I want to set a definite time and place to meet. I don't want him to get the idea that he can just walk into our positions whenever he feels like it. He might have German friends. But he probably knows exactly where we are anyhow. Kids his age everywhere have a knack for finding out whatever is going on.

"I will return in ten minutes."

"OK", I say, "*Ici*," pointing down to the path. He runs off toward the distant buildings and we sit down to wait, but we don't let ourselves get too relaxed. I still think about Alf Green.

The boy is prompt getting back and he has a big dusty bottle of champagne. He says it came from his father's wine cellar. [THAT COULD EXPLAIN IT BEING CHAMPAGNE, BECAUSE WE WEREN'T IN CHAMPAGNE COUNTRY.] He wants a good price. "*Pour mon papa*," he says, intimating that *papa* will get whatever payment we provide. That the wine is his father's we don't doubt; whether *papa* will see any of the payment is another matter. Chances are the kid took it without permission. We negotiate, give him some cigarettes—*pour papa*—half a bar of *chocolat*, and a little of our fancy invasion money. He's satisfied with the deal and scoots off.

[Notes for Chapter 17 start p. 188]

I inspect the bottle's neck and cork carefully. Nobody would try to poison us would they? The seal doesn't look tampered with. I pry out the cork with the tip of my trench knife and we each take a swig. It's sweet but dry, tingling, perfect—the best champagne I've ever tasted [I HADN'T TASTED MUCH, TRUE, BUT I'VE NEVER HAD BETTER SINCE].

"Kommen zie oudt!"

On the third day at the roadblock Liebau tells me to pick four guys from the squad for a reconnaissance patrol. We all pile onto a jeep and take off down the road toward enemy territory. Hedgerows line both sides of the road. We've gone about three quarters of a mile at a pretty good clip when a single German in a cloth cap and dark gray uniform steps out into the road ahead of us from the hedgerow on the left. He motions for us to stop. I jump off with Seace and Sankey; the Jeep spins around to face where we came from, tires spitting stones. The German has already stepped back out of sight. The timing of the German soldiers, showing themselves like that without allowing time to get a shot off at them, is uncanny.

Where we jump off the Jeep, the hedgerow along the left-hand side of the road has a break in it opening into a field. Once In the break, Sankey, Seace, and I are protected from the German's fire. To get a shot at us he'd have to step out and expose himself. The Jeep is on the shoulder on our side of the road and is also out of the German's view—as long as he stays hidden. For once the Germans have screwed up—their roadblock doesn't have a good field of fire [MAP 8, P. 184].

I grew up hearing some German spoken by our next-door neighbor, so I shout:

"Nicht scheitsen! Kommen zie oudt mit der hands oop!"

Nothing happens so I shout again: *"Nicht scheitsen! Kommen zie oudt mit der hands oop!"* Just saying the German-sounding words makes me bristle inside.

> I THOUGHT I WAS SAYING "DON'T SHOOT, COME OUT WITH THE HANDS UP!" WHAT I ACTUALLY SAID, I FOUND OUT MUCH LATER, WAS "DON'T DEFECATE."—IN ITS CRUDER FORM. "COME OUT WITH THE SOMETHING SOMETHING." THE WORD FOR SHOOT IS *SCHIESSEN*, NOT *SCHEITSEN*. I DON'T KNOW ABOUT THE FIRST PART, BUT HE DIDN'T DO THE SECOND PART.

[Notes for Chapter 17 start on p. 188]

There's no way of knowing how many more Germans there might be at the outpost. If there's another one on the other side of the road we're in a bad spot.

"Use a rifle grenade," Liebau yells from the Jeep.

I still have the grenade-launcher on my M-1, though by rights Sackett should have it because he's the Assistant Squad Leader now. With the launcher in place I can fire regular ammunition through it—as long as there isn't a rifle-grenade mounted on it. To use a rifle-grenade, I have to eject the regular round from the chamber by pulling the bolt back by hand, insert a special powder-only cartridge into the chamber, then ease the bolt forward without picking up another live round from the clip. With the propellant cartridge in place I can't use the M-1 as a regular rifle—even without a grenade on the launcher—until the special cartridge is fired, or ejected.

I tell Sankey to be ready to fire at the place the German disappeared, then I slip a green anti-tank rifle grenade onto the launcher, and pull out the safety pin. I nod to Sankey, and when he starts firing I step out onto the road to get a better angle and fire the grenade from my shoulder. It kicks like a sledgehammer. But for it to detonate, the grenade's round nose has to strike something solid. Barring a lucky hit on a tree trunk, there's nothing solid for it to hit, just loose branches. It flies through the air in a slightly arched trajectory, wobbling slightly, and disappears into the branches where the German was last seen, but it doesn't go off.[8]

Liebau shouts for somebody to go up the inside of the hedgerow. I don't think this is a good idea because it will be going right into the lion's mouth. At least one German is there, and when he sees or hears someone running at him on the inside of the hedgerow he'll have the advantage. There's a crosswise hedgerow going to the left from where the German is—he can use it as a parapet to fire over, or lob grenades over. I glance at Seace. He's in the nearest position to do what Liebau wants. With just my glance, not even a nod, Seace starts up the inside of the hedgerow.

With the spent powder-cartridge ejected and a live round back in the chamber, my M-1 is a rifle again, I try to shoot along the inside of the hedgerow into the corner where the German must be. For some reason that is never explained,

[Notes for Chapter 17 start p. 188]

we're still being issued "AP"—armor-piercing—ammo for the M-1s. Maybe they don't have enough of the regular "ball" ammunition available.[9]

But Seace is in my line of sight, running, crouched, close along the inside of the hedgerow, I have to hold my fire. I yell at Sankey to keep firing, and he shoots into the corner of the hedgerow from the outside. Suddenly there's a burst of machine-pistol fire on the inside of the hedgerow and Seace...

> falls, tumbles,
>
> twists
>
> > regains
> >
> > fires – a life
> >
> > in mid-
> >
> > > precipice,
> > >
> > > off balance
> > >
> > > for two fractioned
> > >
> > > seconds, loosed, then
> >
> > re-balanced, back
> >
> > in control, poised on
> >
> > the caprice of an
> >
> > ugly-beautiful
>
> bullet, the icon and
>
> symbol of our
>
> best. Two million years of
>
> upward striving to
>
> produce: this
>
> lead thing,
>
> and yet
>
> we are here, its hostage...

I see immediately that Seace went down intentionally. Now he's firing at the corner of the hedgerow from the ground, and with him out of my line of sight I can put some shots past him, and I keep firing, and an empty clip goes *whinging* out of my M-1 and I jam in another one, and fire some more. The burp-gun stopped after the one burst and Seace comes scrambling back and dives and rolls into a very slight hollow in the ground, twisting around to face the German.

[Notes for Chapter 17 start on p. 188]

The burp-gun fires again and I see a line of dust blobs just ahead of Seace, hitting short by ten feet. I can't see how the German can miss—unless he's just pushing the burp-gun over the hedgerow and firing without aiming. I get the weird feeling that he's not trying to hit Seace—but that's a dangerous thought and I force it out of my head.

I pump in a few more rounds, and then Liebau yells, "Let's get out of here," and with Sankey and me firing into the corner of the hedgerow, Seace scrambles back and we run for the Jeep. I see a string of dust blobs peppering the road short of the Jeep by twenty yards and hear the statter of another machinegun from down the road, and again I'm surprised they're missing. From where the machinegun is firing, the Jeep is a sitting duck. The Germans will see the dust blobs too, and can quickly adjust their fire. The Jeep is already moving and the guys grab us as we clamber on and we ram back up the road the way we came.

Actually the German soldier did us a favor, stopping us where he did. If we'd kept on going down the road we'd have run right into a trap.

Back with the rest of the platoon there is very little talk about the patrol, even by the guys who were on it. And nothing from Liebau. No rehash, no critique. That always surprises me. But the word will get around. It takes me a while to calm down and get back to normal, though I try to act as if not much happened. And there are some things to think about. The way Seace hit the ground and rolled was exactly what they taught us in basic training—he looked just like the guys in the training films—but I'd never seen anybody do it in combat. The fancier points of training and tactics get dropped quickest. What if Seace had been hit? Could we have gotten him back to the Jeep? A tough question—without an answer.

Another thing to think about: In the first couple of minutes we had the edge, the advantage of surprise. Then the tide of the fight turned quickly against us and we were put on the defensive.

> MANY MILITARY OBSERVERS AND PARTICIPANTS HAVE COMMENTED ON THE ROLE OF MOMENTUM IN COMBAT. PATTON, ESPECIALLY, KNEW, AND PREACHED, ITS IMPORTANCE. WHEN YOU'VE GOT IT, KEEP IT, WAS HIS MAXIM—EVEN AT THE RISK OF OUT-STRIPPING SUPPLY LINES OR LEAVING

[Notes for Chapter 17 start p. 188]

Page 184 **CHAPTER 17**

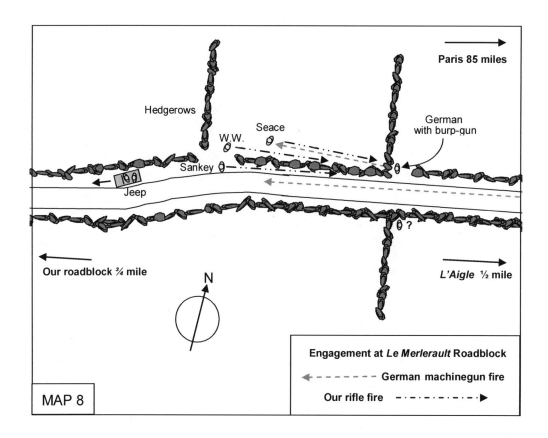

AN OPEN FLANK. A SMALL SCALE EXAMPLE ON THE TACTICAL LEVEL WAS BACK AT *MAYENNE* WHERE THE GUYS AND I GOT GOING AND JUST KEPT MOVING RIGHT THROUGH THE TOWN AND OUT THE OTHER SIDE—UNTIL LIEBAU FINALLY CAUGHT UP TO US AND STOPPED US. I WANTED TO KEEP GOING EVEN THEN, BUT HE SAID WE HAD AN OPEN FLANK ON BOTH SIDES—SO WE HAD GO BACK TO THE EDGE OF THE CITY WITH THE OTHERS.

ON A MUCH LARGER SCALE, IT WASN'T UNTIL THE BIG BREAKOUT AFTER COBRA BY VII CORPS THAT ANY OF THE COMMANDERS WERE ABLE TO BUILD UP AND SUSTAIN MUCH FORWARD MOMENTUM. WHEN GENERAL COLLINS'S ARMOR BROKE THROUGH ON THE SECOND DAY AFTER THE

[Notes for Chapter 17 start on p. 188]

CARPET BOMBING, HE DECIDED ON HIS OWN TO TURN HIS COMBAT TEAMS LOOSE BEHIND GERMAN LINES—WITHOUT PAUSING TO CONSOLIDATE THEIR GAINS. HIS DECISION PAID OFF, SETTING THE STAGE FOR THE FULL-SCALE BREAKOUT FROM THE HEDGEROWS.[10]

The next afternoon a Frenchman appears at our squad's position. There's a dirt road just inside the front edge of the woods behind us, parallel to the highway. It's pretty well screened over with branches—not quite a typical sunken road, but on the way to becoming one. The squad is set up in a defensive line of foxholes facing the woods. The Frenchman just comes walking out of the hidden road and before anybody realizes it he's in the squad area. We all have our rifles within grabbing distance—that's one thing I'm strict about—so he's not going to make any trouble, by himself at least. He's about fifty and looks a lot like *Jean Gabin*, the French movie actor—cloth cap, dark clothes, typical French *nonchalance*. Now he knows exactly where we are, at least where my squad is, but I'm not going to just let him walk around and see where the rest of the company is.

"*Il est défendu à faire une promenade,*" I try on him, sweeping my arm, "It is forbidden to walk around,"—or something like that.

"*Mais certainment,*" But of course, he says, dipping his shoulders slightly and turning up both palms in the universal gesture of acceptance. I talk with *Mon. Gabin* for a while as best I can, wondering if he's part of the French resistance, and whether our intelligence people might want to talk to him, or whether he's just a local person trying to see if we've wrecked the house we're dug in behind. We haven't, but we have been through it, checking for Germans.

He says he's not the owner. Everything of value had been removed, probably when soldiers were first sighted far down the road. Maybe when the Germans first came. I've wondered where the French people take all their things when they clean out ahead of an advancing army, and how they know where to go to be safe. They seem to know as much as the generals do about where the war is going to be going next.

We GIs feel we have a right to go anywhere, and the French people seem to accept that we can, and will, do pretty much as we please. We have to take our

[Notes for Chapter 17 start p. 188]

weapons along, of course, in case something happens, and what French citizen is going to criticize, or start an argument with the United States Army? We feel our power, and probably misuse it even without meaning to. Everybody yields to us, and nobody tries to stop us no matter where we want to go. But so far we haven't misused our status as the conquering army in any serious way. We're not sackers and looters. We don't go into houses unless they've been abandoned, or we think there might be Germans inside. There's never anything of any value and they're always unlocked. Outdoors, we go where we please. And if there's fruit on trees, we pick some. But I'd say we're a pretty well-mannered bunch, at least in our platoon. I can't help wondering how we compare with the Germans.[11] In the house I did find a blank greeting card with paper lace on it among some loose things that had been spilled out onto a counter, and I sent it home to Jean.[12]

Mon. Gabin doesn't seem to be a person of importance, or to consider himself such, or have any special knowledge, and he doesn't ask to see anybody else, but he does provide some information about our skirmish with the Germans the previous day. The townspeople down the road are disturbed, he says, because we killed one of the Germans. This is our first knowledge that a German was killed. It had to be the one at the roadblock—he was the only one we saw—or somebody with him, killed by our shots fired blindly into the corner of the hedgerow. But why would the townspeople be disturbed? Some of them think it was not *nécessaire,* he says very cautiously, humbly. They think that when we saw there was a roadblock, we should have just turned around and gone back—as the German was gesturing for us to do. It's not his opinion, *Mon. Gabin* tries to make clear, it's just what he heard. He, himself, does not have an opinion. But is he someone's messenger? I give him a cigarette—maybe that's all he wants—he thanks me, we smoke and talk a little, and after a while he goes back the way he came. Maybe I was right about the German not trying to hit Seace after all.[13]

Booby-trap

That night I figure we're being dangerously careless if we don't take more precautions against being infiltrated. I consider setting a booby-trap with a hand grenade, but the chances of killing or injuring an innocent civilian, or even a GI, decides me against it. So I collect a lot of C-Ration cans, put them in the open-

[Notes for Chapter 17 start on p. 188]

topped cardboard box the cans were packed in, and just after dark, with some twine as a tripwire, I set up a noise-making booby-trap in the dirt road along the edge of the woods where the Frenchman had come from. Anybody coming along that road in the dark will run into the twine and dump the junk.

We set up a light guard for the night, one on, three off. I tell the four guys nearest the booby-trap that if they hear the box dumped, to fire a couple of rounds in the direction of the noise. I figure whoever sets off the trap will be scared off, or at least temporarily halted, and I will be alerted and can take it from there.

In the morning I ask the guys if anything happened. Logan says yeah, the trap went off while he was on guard. I ask him why he didn't fire his M-1 according to plan. He says he didn't want to wake everybody up. I go down and look at the junk-trap, and it's spilled all over the road, but there's no way of telling what did it. The Frenchman? The boy? A German? An animal? The question is never answered. But I learn that I can't count on Logan to follow my instructions.[14]

THE GAP BETWEEN BRADLEY'S AND MONTGOMERY'S FORCES KEPT SHIFTING EASTWARD AS THE GERMANS REFUSED TO GIVE UP. FIGHTING WAS FIERCE. THOUGH THEY LOST 60,000 MEN—DEAD, WOUNDED, OR CAPTURED, AND HAD TO ABANDON THEIR HEAVY EQUIPMENT, SOME 40,000 GERMANS ESCAPED, AMONG THEM THEIR TOP COMMANDERS.[15]

THE GAP WAS FINALLY CLOSED AT *CHAMBOIS* ON AUGUST 19 WHEN A BATTALION OF THE 90TH'S 358TH REGIMENT MADE CONTACT WITH A POLISH ARMORED DIVISION FROM THE NORTH.

EVEN BEFORE THE TWO PRONGS OF THE PINCER MET, PATTON WAS ORDERED EAST WITH A LARGE PART OF THE THIRD ARMY TO TRY TO HEAD OFF THE ESCAPING GERMANS BEFORE THEY COULD CROSS THE *SEINE*—AN EFFORT THAT WAS ONLY PARTLY SUCCESSFUL.[16]

THE GERMAN WITHDRAWAL, IN THE FACE OF OVERWHELMING ALLIED SUPERIORITY BOTH IN THE AIR AND ON THE GROUND, IS REGARDED BY SOME HISTORIANS AS A SINGULARLY REMARKABLE MILITARY FEAT. HITLER CALLED IT "THE MIRACLE IN THE WEST". FAILURE TO CLOSE THE TRAP COMPLETELY PROBABLY KEPT THE ALLIES FROM ENDING THE WAR IN 1944.[17]

[Notes for Chapter 17 start p. 188]

CHAPTER 17

The 90th is relieved and we get a day off. Field showers have been erected. We get clean underwear and socks. It's the first shower I've had since leaving England. But "Stay alert and don't dawdle," we're told. Small groups of Germans are still straggling through the countryside. Again I think of Alf Green.

> PATTON LEFT ORDERS FOR EVERYBODY IN THE 90TH TO BE ISSUED INSIGNIA OF RANK, AND FOR THE INSIGNIA TO BE PUT ON AND WORN. SO I FINALLY GOT MY STRIPES, BUT I CAN'T REMEMBER IF THEY ACTUALLY GOT SEWN ON. IF THEY DID, WHO DID IT? WE NEVER SAW ANY USO PEOPLE, AND WE DIDN'T GET SEWING KITS WITH THE STRIPES. I KNOW I DIDN'T HAVE ANY STRIPES ON DURING CERTAIN LATER EVENTS

⊕

Notes for Chapter 17

1. At least 15% of the 2nd French Armored Division—the *Deuxième Division Blindée*—were Moroccans, Algerians or Spanish Republicans. Both the 2nd French Armored and the American 79th Infantry Division bore the *Croix de Lorraine* on their shoulder patches, causing confusion among the French citizenry. The 79th acquired that designation in World War One.

2. Few Allied commanders wanted to admit that ULTRA was of much help. Bradley gave it some credence, but depending on anything as technologically sophisticated as ULTRA was thought to be too fancy for conducting a serious war. Further, if the Allies repeatedly anticipated the enemy's intentions the Germans would use even deeper encryption, or avoid using radio altogether. ULTRA intelligence was therefore utilized only for the most critical situations, and even then with reservations.

3. My own feeling is that they could have rolled right over us. The 90th hadn't done well on the *Cherbourg* Peninsula. Patton called us a "bad division". The replacements that came up at the *Sèves* River "Island" were still pretty green. I wouldn't have expected my own squad to make much of a showing against a determined German thrust through *Alençon*.

[Notes for Chapter 17 start on p. 188]

4. In the States there seemed to be little concern over whether Infantry trainees would be effective combat soldiers. If you met the minimum physical standards and didn't show overt psychological problems you were shipped out. This was especially true in 1943 when it was realized that vast numbers of ground troops would be needed to reclaim Europe.

   Volunteer units like the Rangers and Paratroops could use more rigorous screening procedures. Whether the screening and special training actually resulted in better performance in combat is another question, though it's widely assumed that it did. Predicting a man's actions under great stress is an iffy business and I don't think military people or psychologists are any better at it than anybody else. [But see: Addenda, page 345, Item 1.]

5. In the interests of journalistic accuracy, many of the corpses were horses; the Germans used a lot of horses. The stench was said to have reached the pilots of the L-4 reconnaissance planes.

6. We were in the *Perche* region in France, home ground for the internationally renowned *Percheron*, a breed of big dappled gray draft horses. Percherons are featured in "The Horse Fair", a painting by the French artist *Rosa Bonheur*—a favorite of my mother's because of its pictorial realism. A long-format print hung in our upstairs hallway. Where Gervase went galloping was near *Le Pin Stud*, a famous horse breeding farm. How he got the horse I never found out, nor what happened to it later.

7. More on this subject in *Book Three* of *An Almost Perfect War—Some Reassembly Required*.

8. Rifle grenades had two arming devices. One was an external safety pin, similar to the safety pin on a fragmentation hand grenade; the second was an inertial device that was released by the forward jolt of the propellant. And to detonate, the nose had to hit something solid.

   We had two types of rifle grenades—HE (**H**igh **E**xplosive), and white phosphorous. Both were housed in thin sheet metal which produced relatively non-lethal fragments. In basic, the HE grenades were touted as *anti-tank* grenades but I never saw one used effectively for that purpose. Some apparently did have shaped charges capable of penetrating armor.

9. Whether AP (Armor Piercing) ammo would penetrate branches better than ball ammo is problematic. Either type would be deflected by glancing off a branch, but the AP would have been better at penetrating anything solid.

10. Contrary to many writers, it was not Patton who first broke the hedgerow stalemate, but First Army's "Lightning Joe" Collins. Patton didn't have a command until August 1st; Collins broke through the German defenses following the COBRA bombing on July 25th. Following Collins's success, Bradley turned Patton loose with the newly activated Third Army which included the 90th Division. For a couple of weeks we went hell-bent-for-leather. Patton's detractors said we were mostly just "taking real estate".

When Bradley ordered Patton to stop at *Argentan* it seemed like a prime example of giving up the advantages of momentum. Patton voiced his frustration by saying that if given the go-ahead, he could drive Montgomery back into the English Channel. This was not well-received by Bradley and Eisenhower, and Patton was back in the doghouse.

One reason Bradley gave for stopping us was that as the gap narrowed, the Americans and Canadians might mistake each other for the enemy. More reasonable, to me, was that Bradley doubted our ability to keep the Germans from breaking out of the pocket. Until First Army came up on Third Army's left flank, our forces were stretched very thin. I believe the latter assessment was realistic and prudent, but stopping Third Army at *Argentan* remains one of the most controversial decisions of the war.

11. The American Army's S-5 staff officers handled Civil/Military relations, but we GIs never heard of Americans contacting French officials. Who was in charge of French affairs was problematic, with the country under the puppet Vichy Government. Even General *De Gaulle* was ignored until we reached Paris. The Allied armies simply did what they had to do to win the war. (See also: Addenda, Item 2.) They did work closely with the *FFI*, but we soldiers in the foxholes heard only rumors of the *FFI's* existence.

[Notes for Chapter 17 start on p. 188]

12. *Alençon* and *Argentan* were traditional centers of lace-making, each with its own unique and protected patterns. I didn't notice whether the card's pattern was labeled but I might still find out; Jean might still have the card.

13. In WW-I there were many examples of "understandings" between Allied and Germans soldiers. Robert Patton tells of an incident described by his grandfather, then Col. George S. Patton, on a night patrol into no-man's-land at *St.-Mihiel.* They had come out on the enemy side of some barbed wire when they heard a whistle. Their French patrol leader said it was a warning from the Germans that if they went any farther they would be fired upon. At that point Both sides were anxious to avoid an exchange of fire so the patrol crawled back the way they had come. (*The Pattons,* p. 178)

14. This is an example of the reluctance of many GIs to fire their weapons. For an extended discussion, see entry for S. L. A. Marshall's *Men Against Fire* in the ANNOTATED BIBLIOGRAPHY. See also William DePuy's comments in the *Leavenworth Papers Number 16,* referenced in Web-links 1 and 2, Appendix C in the present volume. It's a controversial subject, but from my personal experience I agree with Marshall.

15. Statistics from Ambrose, *The Supreme Commander*, p. 477.

16. In this maneuver Third Army was allowed to move into Montgomery's territory, a privilege denied Patton at *Argentan*.

17. The destruction wreaked upon the German forces at the *Falaise-Argentan* Gap was pivotal in the battle for France. Who planned the entrapment, Montgomery or Bradley, and who was responsible for its lack of more complete success, are questions still being argued. One of the most detailed analyses by a reputable historian can be found in Carlo D'Este's *Decision in Normandy*. A discussion of his, and others', views is included in the ANNOTATED BIBLIOGRAPHY for the present series.

CHAPTER 18

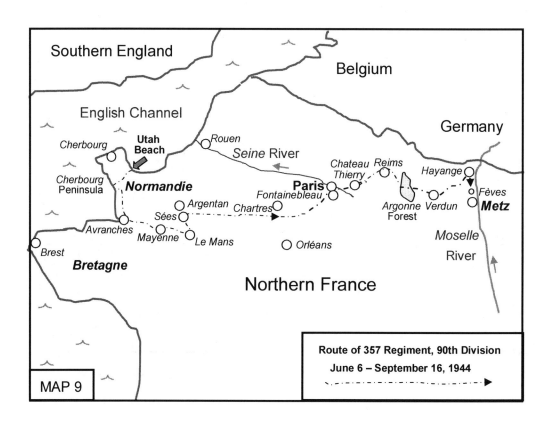

18

THROUGH THE HEART OF FRANCE

HISTORY, WITH ITS FLICKERING LAMP STUMBLES ALONG THE TRAIL OF THE PAST, TRYING TO RECONSTRUCT ITS SCENES, TO REVIVE ITS ECHOES, AND KINDLE WITH PALE GLEAMS THE PASSION OF FORMER DAYS.

Winston Churchill, in a speech shortly after becoming Prime Minister—*1940*

Jeep Patrol [Foxhole 38]

After the shower break we get on trucks again and barrel east, stopping for the night in the middle of nowhere—somewhere in the heart of France. The night is dark, but with a lot of stars. Liebau sends me out on a Jeep patrol, just the driver and me, down the road on our right flank, to make sure it's clear. All I have is my M-1 and a couple of grenades, and the driver has a carbine. We spin along in the dark, smelling the sweet smells of the August countryside, expecting anything, hoping for nothing, and finding nothing. In spite of the tenseness and heightened awareness we always feel on a patrol, it's a nice ride in the open Jeep. When we get back to my squad area I hear loud strange noises: Brackkkkt! Spbraaachttt! A wild night creature? Not unless our man Bruthiers fits that description. The poor guy has got a whopping case of the GIs, in the exact middle of our field, squatting bare-assed in the starlight, vociferously evacuating his bowels. If the Germans are near and are trying to locate us they'll have a clear auditory beacon.

Bruthiers by starlight, and Gervase galloping bareback on the big horse at Sées are the only things that have struck me as funny in the entire war. I shouldn't laugh. The GIs are no fun, and they make a man almost useless for combat.[1]

The second day on the trucks we see road signs for *Chartres* pointing to our left, and *Orléans* to our right [MAP 9].

> WE DIDN'T EVEN GLIMPSE THE *CHARTRES* CATHEDRAL, BUT ORDERS FROM SHAEF HAD SPARED IT FROM OUR BOMBERS AND ARTILLERY.[2]

[Notes for Chapter 18 start on p. 211]

CHAPTER 18

ORLÉANS WAS WHERE JEANNE D'ARC, IN ARMOR CLAD, LED HER ARMY TO LIFT THE ENGLISH SEIGE OF THE CITY.

THOUGH NOBODY BOTHERED TO TELL US GUYS ON THE LINE, AFTER THE FALAISE GAP WAS CLOSED, THE 90TH WAS TRANSFERRED FROM GENERAL HAISLIP'S XV CORPS TO GENERAL WALKER'S XX CORPS ALSO IN THIRD ARMY. OTHER UNITS OF XX CORPS WERE ALREADY SLICING SOUTH AND EAST OF PARIS TOWARD THE SEINE.[3]

We go through *Étampes* and as the second night approaches stop on the western edge of an extensive forest [THE *FORÊT DE FONTAINEBLEAU*]. We're not under fire and I write Jean a long letter about the scenery. It's like the pictures in a tourist guide but even more romantic and picturesque seen first-hand. I take a walk around the platoon area in the thickening twilight and go past several odd-looking farm buildings, no lawns around the houses, everything left with a natural, ragged look.[4]

The houses, many with ponds beside them, the poplar-lined lanes, tall trees that disappear into the purpling sky, are from a separate, incredibly beautiful world. Yet the hard metal of my M-1 presses against my hip, and the grenades taped to my pack-straps bump obscenely on my chest—reminding me that I'm not here for beauty; I'm here for the grit-grisly business of war.

> Dear Jean,
> I am sitting here holding
> a small pineapple, 40
> segments of cast iron
> packed with powder, power,
> waiting to burst anonymously
> when asked. I have been
> carrying this quiescent volcano
> hung bumpingly on my breast
> (where your head should be),
> as I run or as I am lying, it heavy on my
> chest (where your head should be).
> Carrying it thus is by itself an act of
> defiance. I am willing to risk splitting my

[Notes for Chapter 18 start on p. 211]

>breast through some mistake: See, I am not
>afraid. I live with destruction bouncing
>intimately on my
>chest (where your head should
>be), earning thus my right to
>participate
>in this grim
>business.

I vow I will return when the war is over and explore France as a humane being, someone other than a destroyer and a purveyor of death. I will search for the art and the music and the language and literature, and the science and the mathematics, and philosophy that are surely still alive in these cities and villages, fields and forests—to which we give such offhand and superficial notice.

> THE NORTHERN EDGE OF THE FORÊT DE FONTAINEBLEAU WAS THE SITE OF THE FAMED *BARBIZON* SCHOOL OF PAINTERS—*MILLET*, *COROT*, *DAUMIER*, *ROUSSEAU*, AND OTHERS—NAMED FOR A SMALL TOWN NEAR WHERE WE WERE BIVOUACKED. COPIES OF *MILLET'S* WORK, *THE ANGELUS* AND *THE GLEANERS,* WERE HUNG PROMINENTLY IN OUR SUNDAY SCHOOL WHEN I WAS A BOY. THE FORMER SHOWS A PEASANT COUPLE IN THE DAWN FIELDS WITH BOWED HEADS; IN THE LATTER, PEASANTS ARE STOOPING TO PICK UP GRAIN LEFT BEHIND BY THE REAPERS—POSSIBLY IN ONE OF THE FIELDS I WAS LOOKING ACROSS. ANOTHER EVEN BETTER KNOWN PAINTING BY *MILLET* WAS *THE SOWER*. *MILLET'S* PAINTINGS REPRESENTED A NEW RECOGNITION OF ROUGH-LIVING RURAL FOLK AS SUITABLE SUBJECTS FOR SERIOUS ART—PORTRAYED AS THEY LIVED THEIR SIMPLE LIVES DOING THE HARD WORK OF THE WORLD. THAT WAS US, TOO, IN OUR…

>bivouac near *la Forêt de Fontainebleau*.
>In these fields *Millet* heard the *angelus* in his
>heart, probed his
>canvas even as his peasants probed the straw-
>strewn ground, each
>seeking sustenance, theirs in errant grain, his in
>crumbs of

art. *Millet*, then, inspired Homer's Song of the Lark,
still
bravely singing, as at *Flanders Fields*. Too, here,
Bonheur pranced her horses to the fair, and others
of *L'École de Barbizon*. We too
dig in these fields, learning a crude and simple life,
not for gleanings, not for Art, but for
the obscene, insatiable, destroyer of worlds, war.
The painters'
assuagement did not prevent the First, nor Ours.
Needed: new gleaners and healers to spread their
quiet emollience on
this raw and bleeding land.

Crossing the *Seine*

The next day we roll through the forest into the city of *Fontainebleau* itself, glimpsing what looks like a great château [THE *PALAIS DE FONTAINEBLEAU*], then cross the *Seine* on a Bailey bridge.[5]

> THE ORIGINAL BRIDGE WAS BOMBED OUT BY THE ALLIES' TRANSPORTATION PLAN, AN EFFORT OVER A PERIOD OF SEVERAL WEEKS PRIOR TO AND DURING THE NORMANDY INVASION INTENDED TO CURTAIL THE MOVEMENT OF GERMAN REINFORCEMENTS AND SUPPLIES TO THE ATLANTIC WALL DEFENSES. EISENHOWER INSISTED ON IMPLEMENTING THIS PLAN AGAINST THE WISHES OF OUR OWN AIR COMMANDER, GENERAL SPAATZ.[6] THE LONG RANGE SUCCESS OF THE PLAN DEPENDED NOT ONLY ON LIMITING THE GERMANS' ACCESS TO THE BEACHES, BUT ALSO ON OUR ENGINEERS' ABILITY TO REBUILD THE BRIDGES WHEN WE NEEDED THEM.
>
> JUST OFF OUR ROUTE TO THE RIGHT AS WE CUT NORTH AND EAST FROM *FONTAINEBLEAU* WAS THE CATHEDRAL TOWN OF *PROVINS*, AND NOT FAR BEYOND *PROVINS*, *NOGENT*, A SMALL TOWN NEAR THE RUINS OF THE ABBEY OF *PARACLETE* WHERE *HÉLOÏSE* AND *ABÉLARD* CONDUCTED THEIR SCANDALOUS AND TRAGIC LOVE AFFAIR—ONE OF THE MOST CELEBRATED IN EUROPEAN HISTORY.

[Notes for Chapter 18 start on p. 211]

Crossing the *Marne*

At *Château Thierry, a few miles* east of Paris, road signs point to *Compiègne*, seventy *kilometres* to the northwest.

> THE ARMISTICE AT THE CLOSE OF WORLD WAR ONE WAS SIGNED AT *COMPIÈGNE*. HITLER, SYMBOLICALLY, CHOSE *COMPIÈGNE* FOR ANOTHER SIGNING AFTER FRANCE CAPITULATED IN 1940.
>
> TOWARD THE END OF THE HUNDRED YEARS WAR BETWEEN FRANCE AND ENGLAND, JOAN OF ARC WAS TAKEN CAPTIVE BY THE *BURGUNDIANS* AT *COMPIÈGNE*. THEY TURNED HER OVER TO THE ENGLISH WHO TOOK HER TO *ROUEN* AND BURNED HER AT THE STAKE.

Sackett knows a lot more about World War One than I do. He says the name *Belleau Wood* fascinates him.[7] We're fairly close, but it's not on our itinerary. We cross the *Marne* on a bridge that the Germans had tried to destroy to impede our progress; it was saved by the *FFI*—the French Forces of the Interior. Then we head northeast.

> NOT FAR OUT OF *CHÂTEAU THIERRY* WE PASSED WITHIN 20 *KILOMETRES* OF THE WW-I AMERICAN CEMETERY AT *FÈRE-EN-TARDENOIS*. HERE THE AMERICAN POET, JOYCE KILMER, AUTHOR OF THE POEM *TREES*, WAS BURIED, KILLED IN ACTION IN THE GREAT WAR. ACROSS THE ROAD FROM THAT OFT-VISITED PLACE WAS ANOTHER CEMETERY, HIDDEN AND UNKNOWN TO TOURISTS, WHERE THE REMAINS OF PRIVATE EDDIE SLOVIK WOULD LATER LIE IN SHAME—WHOSE SHAME IS A MATTER OF OPINION—HIS BODY RIDDLED BY THE BULLETS OF AN AMERICAN FIRING SQUAD.[8]
>
> AS WE MOVED RAPIDLY SOUTH AND EAST OF PARIS, NO ONE TOLD US ANYTHING ABOUT WHAT WAS HAPPENING IN THE "CITY OF LIGHT". PARIS WAS, IN FACT, ALREADY IN ALLIED HANDS, SAVED FROM DESTRUCTION BY THE SURRENDER OF GENERAL *CHOLTITZ*—THE SAME COMMANDER WHO HAD BEEN IN CHARGE OF THE GERMAN DEFENSES ON THE *CHERBOURG* PENINSULA. IKE ORIGINALLY PLANNED TO BYPASS PARIS, BUT GAVE IN TO GENERAL *DE GAULLE AND ALLOWED LECLERC'S DEUXIÈME BLINDÉE DIVISION* TO PARTICIPATE AT THE FOREFRONT OF THE CITY'S LIBERATION.

[Notes for Chapter 18 start on p. 211]

CHAPTER 18

We stop in late afternoon on the edge of a small hamlet in the middle of open country. My squad takes over a hay-shed and we gloat over the soft dry beds we'll have for the night. We're told we'll be here for at least a day and we don't get any instructions to stay put or stand guard. Soon after we get here a French girl ducks into the shed. Russell is nearest to her, but he doesn't take any initiative, so I say *bonjour* to her *en Français* and she comes over to talk to me. I feel I have to act the part of a leader in this matter, to demonstrate a little *savoir faire, n'est-ce pas*? So I try to engage her in conversation. She says her name is *Nicole*, and I tell her mine, including the Sergeant part. We're getting along OK, and the guys think I might have something going, and they disappear.

Nicole has a sore at the edge of her mouth, and that cools my ardor somewhat, but we spend some time together on the hay. She lets me know right away that she is not a professionally wanton woman, volunteering the information vehemently: "*Absolument pas!*" After a while she says she has to go, but she'll be back in half an hour. Will I wait for her? Sure. She's calling the shots.

When she returns she has a different dress on, prettier, and her dark hair is done up with a white flower-bow, but the biggest difference is that she now has a baby carriage, and in it is a baby. Her baby. Where is her husband? She says she doesn't have *un mari*, and then changes the story a bit—"*Il n'est pas ici...*" He is not here. She looks a little wary and I leave it alone. Maybe he's in the *FFI*—the *Maquis*, or maybe in a German labor camp. Or maybe he *is* a German.

Then she asks if I'll go with her for a walk. Why not? So we start out down the road toward the houses that make up the village. I start to feel embarrassed, to be seen with her and the baby carriage, with a little baby in it, being escorted by a *sergeant Americain*, and I become acutely aware of the villagers watching us as we go by. They don't speak to her, just watch. We finally get to a big house with a portico and stairs leading up to an ornate front door, and she says she lives there with relatives and she has to go in, but she'll meet me later in the evening. She has to help with the evening meal and then get somebody to stay with her baby. So I go back to the hay shed and some of the guys are there, and we eat our K-Rations, and I shrug off the whole thing. Yeah, she's going to meet me tonight, but nothing serious is going to happen. They're OK about it, not making smart

[Notes for Chapter 18 start on p. 211]

remarks, or commenting on my taste, or that I'm robbing the cradle. If any of them gives me a hard time I figure it'll be Browny, but ever since the incident at *Ste.-Suzanne* he's been pretty sober. Maybe shooting that GI is bothering him. Neither of us has brought it up since.

Of course if the guys don't even acknowledge my success, so far, I'll be disappointed. A couple of knowing looks and a sly grin or two is all I get. I'm not against a little recognition. I have a leadership role to play, don't I? I don't feel any great attraction for Nicole. I'm just doing what's expected of me, taking the opportunity to have a romantic interlude with a French *mademoiselle*. It's almost a duty. And this is the first chance that has come along. So it's my obligation to try, *n'est-ce pas?* If I don't, somebody else will, or should. Maybe Sackett, or maybe even Bruthiers. He should have an advantage, with his French, but I have to wonder if his guttural mutterings would even be understood by *la belle jeune fille*.

At the agreed-upon time, *huit heures et demi*, I go to Nicole's house and rap the knocker and she comes to the door. She says she can come out for a while, and we walk around—without the baby carriage. We talk, as best we can. She says she wants to be an artist. I show her my sketch of Sackett from the "Island". She says it is *très beau*, but asks for my pencil, and quickly copies it, keeping the likeness but sharpening it up and giving it a definite style. She's very good.

It gets dark. I can see she isn't going to make anything easy, anything heavy or serious. Whenever we get to a road that could lead to the hay shed she steers me in another direction. We wind up an hour and a half later back at her house outside the big knockered door. What can happen out here in the public courtyard? Not much.

And I'm beginning to see the picture—that I have served a special purpose for her. Once I start thinking in that direction, everything becomes clear. The baby's father is probably a German soldier. That would make her a *collaboratrice*. Now that the Germans are gone she needs some insurance so she won't be treated badly by the villagers—like being paraded through town with her head shaved.

The more I think about it the more it makes sense. Walking around town with an American sergeant isn't going to do her any harm, unless the father is a village

[Notes for Chapter 18 start on p. 211]

boy, and he apparently isn't, because of her open association with me in public. Maybe her family in the big house encouraged her, or even put her up to it. Maybe she was lukewarm with me because she's in love with *Hans*, or *Helmut*—the German father. "Go out there and make friends with an American," maybe they told her. It might help protect the family if they were cooperating with the Germans in doing whatever they were doing here. It couldn't hurt to have the American Army on their side.

I figure that's the end of it, and it is. I have likely been used very cleverly by a maid. To be honest I'm relieved that things didn't go any farther than they did. And probably lucky. The guys? I shrug, noncommittal. Let them think what they will.

Armies have always had camp followers but we're moving too fast to collect any. The next morning we move out on trucks and my brief romantic dalliance is forgotten.

Champagne country

We were entering the *Plaine de Champagne*, a région of northern France lying between the *Île-de-France* (Paris at its center) and *Lorraine* to the east. The name *Champagne* originally had nothing to do with the sparkling alcoholic beverage. The land here was called *Champagne* long before the farmers found they could make a living, and an international reputation, by growing grapes and bottling the fermented juice. Nothing much else would grow here because the land is underlain with chalk. Water drains right through it. Only grapes had the determination to send their roots deep enough to reach moisture.[9]

The lower part of *Champagne* is where Napoleon Bonaparte first studied the art of war, in battles that seasoned him for bigger things. Here, too there have been great religious wars, and over the centuries the land had been ravaged by successive armies forced to live off the countryside. *Champagne* is also a region of many cathedral towns, but we didn't get to see any of them.

[Notes for Chapter 18 start on p. 211]

When we get on the trucks again some of the GIs in the other companies are wearing scarves made of German parachute silk printed with a random camouflage pattern of greens and browns.[10] Somebody in the battalion liberated a railroad car full of German supplies but we in B-Company don't get a chance to get any of the silk and we feel left out. One of our guys does gets some by trading for it—cigarettes, a hand-full of Nescafé packets and some invasion money. He's says he's going to send the silk home to his girlfriend. The parachute silk doesn't have the ugly stark look a lot of the German things have. It will make a nice souvenir, and will probably pass the censors.

I don't have the temperament to be a souvenir collector myself. It takes a certain aggressiveness and sometimes a little of the con man. I feel inadequate in this respect, not so much for myself, but for the guys in the squad. Because I can speak some French, and being a non-com, I feel an obligation to try to get stuff— if there's anything to be gotten—short of out-and-out plundering. But I haven't done very well. There's a guy in C-Company I cross paths with every so often who speaks better French than I do, and is more assertive than I am, and manages to work his way into the more productive situations. I guess I do resent the competition, but I'm not really interested in souvenirs.

I don't think of my German binoculars as a souvenir. They're more of a necessity, almost like a weapon. Thinking about souvenirs, and trying to get them, and getting them sent home, is too much of a distraction from the business we're here for. Things are pretty peaceful right now, yeah, but what's down the road? Like the guy at the "Island", I have a feeling our war isn't over.[11]

We cross the *Vesle* River at *Vismes*, then, riding on trucks and tanks parade through the streets of a small town in the hilly country west of *Reims*. None of us know where *Reims* is, geographically, or what its role has been historically.

The welcome we get in the little town is tumultuous. Everybody is out in the narrow streets, waving, laughing, the women blowing kisses, trying to catch our hands, handing up fruit and pastries and wine. I'm riding on a tank enjoying it all, except that if the place is not really empty of Germans we're dangerously exposed to snipers from the windows of the buildings that rise up in a wall on both sides of the street. When the tank behind mine stops, one of the guys grabs a girl's hand

[Notes for Chapter 18 start on p. 211]

and pulls her up on the tank and she rides along, laughing, and kissing every GI she can reach. Everybody cheers like crazy. She's lucky she doesn't fall off and get ground under the tank treads, which could happen easily enough. That would sour the whole celebration. Tanks aren't easy to ride on. There aren't any good hand-holds unless the tankers have jury-rigged them on their own.

The girl finally jumps off and we keep going through the town and out into the open country and spend the night bivouacked near *Guignicourt,* a small town on the *Aisne* River on the hills above the city of *Reims.* We can just see what we think is the top of the *Reims* Cathedral, the only cathedral in France that I know anything about—except Paris's *Nôtre Dame* where *Quasimodo* in Victor Hugo's novel held forth as *The Hunchback of Notre Dame.*

Reims has an airfield and we see American C-47 cargo planes going in on their landing runs, disappearing behind the hills just before they land.

> REIMS WAS THE CITY HISTORICALLY CHOSEN FOR THE CORONATION OF KINGS. CHARLEMAGNE WAS CROWNED HERE, AND CHARLES II—BY JOAN OF ARC IN DEFIANCE OF ENGLISH RULE.
>
> GERMAN DIRIGIBLES BOMBED REIMS IN WORLD WAR ONE AND THE CITY WAS DESTINED TO MAKE HISTORY AGAIN AS THE SITE OF THE FINAL GERMAN CAPITULATION IN WW-II.

The hills are very peaceful, it's a mild night, and we don't dig in, just lie on our blankets under the sky. Sackett comes over and we talk a while about home and school. I try to sing one of the songs I learned at Oberlin, and manage to recall the words of one of the verses:

> *Come and let our swelling song Mount like the whirling wind,*
> *As it meets our singing throng, Blithe of heart and mind,*
> *Care and sorrow now be gone,*
> *Brothers in song sing on!*
> *Bro...ther r r r r r s... in song, sing on!* [12]

I try to remember how the harmony goes, singing first one part then another. At Oberlin I didn't make it into the men's glee club, but one of my roommates did and

[Notes for Chapter 18 start on p. 211]

he sang some of their songs around the dorm. This was one of them. I was completely captivated by it.

Out of gas [Foxhole 39]

> In the last days of August Third Army was in full stride chasing after the fleeing Germans. Patton's "kitchen cavalry"—small fast-moving reconnaissance teams with light armored vehicles—had already probed ahead as far as the *Moselle* River. Then suddenly the entire Third Army stalled for lack of fuel. Patton fumed. He ordered the tanks and trucks to keep going until their fuel tanks went dry. He wanted to push the Germans across the *Rhine* before they had a chance to re-group. History suggests that we might have succeeded if we'd had the gas.
>
> The fuel shortage was due both to the lack of a good port—neither *Cherbourg* nor *Brest* was fully operational—and to our extended supply lines. Our headlong progress had stretched them perilously thin. In contrast, as the Germans retreated, they were getting closer to their supply bases. To add to Patton's pique, the British General, Montgomery, lobbied SHAEF vociferously and successfully, with the result that his troops in the north got most of whatever POL—Petrol, Oil and Lubricants—was available.

Next day we move, walking, to *Witry-les-Reims* a few miles northeast of *Reims,* and dig in. We can move around we're told, but the usual precautions apply—don't go too far, and stay alert.

Not far down the road there's a very small crossroads hamlet with a half-dozen houses. Sackett and I go exploring and run into Lt. Liebau and Sgt. Barrett standing with a Frenchman outside his modest but well-kept house. The man speaks some English, and invites us to come inside.

We stand around a table and our French host pours each of us a very small glass of what looks like brandy. Not knowing our politics, except that we're *les*

Americains who are beating the Germans, he raises his tiny glass and says: "*À la victoire!*" That's safe enough. We raise our glasses. I watch as he sips his, so I sip mine, but Liebau and Barrett knock theirs back in a single gulp.

Monsieur l'hôte is somewhat nonplused. From my sip I can tell it's a lot more refined than the rotgut swallowed wholesale by cowboys in the saloons of American westerns. Sackett also has enough sense to go slow, but our host has to pour two more for Barrett and Liebau so they won't be standing empty while we continue to savor ours.

I feel I ought to intervene for the sake of French-American relations—and our host's brandy supply—so I say to the Frenchman, "*Le plus meilleur cognac, n'est-ce pas?*"—"The best brandy, isn't it?"—to which he replies, relieved that somebody appreciates what he has offered to the conquering troops, "*Vraiment*," truly, and using our small conversation in French as an opening, I say to Liebau, who doesn't speak any French at all, "This is the best brandy you can get...worth taking some time with." Pretending I know something about the subject of good brandy I give it an appreciative sniff.

The Frenchman nods, "*Oui, le plus meilleur,*" yes, the best. Liebau gets the point, and we all sip the brandy and try to find something intelligent to talk about.

I happen to say something about *les Russes,* the Russians, and a cloud drops over the Frenchman's face. He seems to fear the Communists as much as he feared the Germans. Maybe more. He's some kind of official for the *départment*. In his village they have been fortunate, he says carefully. The Germans were not really oppressive, thank *le bon Dieu,* but he is very glad that the Americans have come, of course. To us GIs, politics is simple: Germans are the enemy, Russians are our allies. We're both trying to destroy *Hitler* and the *Nazis*. What comes after that, none of us has any idea. That some of the French might be afraid of the Russians has never occurred to us.

> EVEN FARTHER FROM OUR MINDS WAS THE POSSIBILITY THAT SOME OF THE FRENCH MIGHT HAVE BEEN COMMUNISTS THEMSELVES. OUR S-5 GUYS WOULD HAVE TO SORT THAT OUT; IT WASN'T OUR PROBLEM.

[Notes for Chapter 18 start on p. 211]

When we get back to our holes the First Sergeant comes by with a man named Soussignard. He's going to be in my squad for a while. He's a friendly sort, dark complexioned, black hair, black shiny eyes, smiling but subdued, taller than I, a couple of years older. Speaks good French. The scuttlebutt is that he's up for court-martial for desertion, or stealing, or rape. We never get the real story. He's got an M-1 and ammo, just like the rest of us. Am I supposed to watch him? No. And why me? No reason. Like that guy they put in my tent at the Talladega National Forest during basic. Maybe it's just because we're the third squad, the last in the platoon. It's certainly not because I'm a tough disciplinarian.

There's going to be a Catholic mass on Sunday morning and Sartori invites me to go with him. I hesitate. What does one do at a Roman Catholic mass? I feel a certain sense of companionship for Sartori ever since he offered to share his blanket-roll with me north of *Le Mans*, and I want to be sure not to hurt his feelings. It's a genuine gesture of friendship on his part—he's offering the best thing he has—and I don't want to seem unappreciative. He sees me wavering, and helps me decide.

"You won't have to do anything, like kneeling, or take communion. You won't feel out of place, it's just like a lot of other churches." How would he know? I thought Catholics weren't supposed to even go inside other churches.

But I go with him, and he's right, it's completely un-embarrassing for me. There aren't any seats, so everybody sits on the ground. When Sartori kneels I just stay the way I am. I'm glad he mentioned that part ahead of time. There is no offering, no tithing. What would the money be used for? The priest is a chaplain and his robe and cross make the occasion seem a little less war-like. I'm glad I came.

A small revolt

At *Reims* we get the word that we're going to get some additional training. Something that might be useful? No, close-order drill. Jeeezus! The guys hear about it and start to bitch. I go to Liebau and complain, but I find it hard to express myself without flat-out saying I think it's stupid. I haven't gotten quite that bold. I never did like close-order drill. Its fundamental purpose is to get troops to forget their individuality and to get in the habit of obeying commands without thinking.

[Notes for Chapter 18 start on p. 211]

That's exactly what I don't like about it. We ought to be able to think about our actions and possibly contribute something from our own heads. Except, of course, when such a luxury can't be afforded because of immediate, clear, and dire danger. Even then, maybe especially then, individual initiative should pay off. But all I can think of to say is that the guys in the squad are capable of more than just drill, that drill would be demeaning, a reduction to the status of basic trainees again. We're way past that, aren't we? There are some smart guys in the squad, I say. That isn't what I wanted to say, and it sounds lame, and Liebau sensing my uncertainty, of expression if not conviction, jumps in: "Who?"

My argument is weak, and anyhow, Liebau got his orders from somewhere above him, so we have to do close-order drill. It's obvious that the army brass doesn't know how to conduct effective and useful training of experienced combat troops in the field. They fall back on close-order drill because it's the only thing they know how to do. And it's the easiest. One reason I'm against it, here, I admit, is that I might have to conduct the drill myself. I've never really done it. I'd look pretty stupid screwing up in front of the guys that I'm supposed to be the squad leader of. And I'm disappointed with Liebau. When he challenged me with "Who?" I took it as an insult. Maybe he does think we're just a bunch of robots. Or should be.

The upshot is that I take the guys—except for a couple who conveniently disappear before I get the word to them face to face—to where we're supposed to do the drill, and we sit around waiting for some kind of further orders or instructions. We don't get any, so we do nothing. Sgt. Barrett, the Platoon Sergeant, was supposed to come over and either conduct the drilling, or have me to do it while he observed. I'm relieved when he doesn't show up. So after a while we just wander away, each to his own devices. So much for training.[13]

⊞

I poke around the area and run across a Frenchman in a garden behind his house. We talk as best we can, me with my school French, which, as we get farther from Normandy, is more like the way the French people actually talk. He says his name is *Henri* and invites me to a rabbit dinner. Remembering how my mother used to fix rabbit with biscuits and gravy, I accept with enthusiasm. When I come back at supper time *le lapin* is prepared almost the same way. We have the

[Notes for Chapter 18 start on p. 211]

rabbit, and some potatoes *au gratin*—in the country where the dish was named—and *gateau,* cheese, and sparkling wine, the genuine article. It's a good home-cooked meal, my first since coming to France. Remembering Alf Green, I keep my M-1 with me, and lean it against the wall near my chair. "*Les régulations,*" I say apologetically. I don't want to insult him and his family by suggesting that I don't trust them. *Henri* shrugs a good-natured acknowledgement.

I meet his wife *Janine*, their cute-as-a-flower-bud three-year-old *Aimée*, and their dog *Venez*. The dog is a nondescript houndish anybreed that is wary, but wagging his tail, which probably means the Frenchman himself is genuinely friendly. The dog got his name as a puppy, they tell me, from having to call him repeatedly to get him to come: "*Venez, venez!*" After a few dozen repetitions, he thought that was his name. This is supposed to be a joke, and they laugh. Little *Aimée* giggles. A glorious sound—compared to the sounds of death and destruction our experience in France has provided us.

The house isn't an old-style farm manse where the farm animals live in the same building as the humans, as some we've seen, but it's not a modern house either. They're just simple home folks, and we avoid the war and politics and why he's here at home with his family instead of in the French underground, or at a German labor camp. We have a nice meal together and an after-dinner smoke with American cigarettes—Lucky Strikes scrounged for the occasion, traded one-for-three for the tasteless Chelseas everybody hates. I leave a D-Ration *chocolat* bar and some cigarettes. He invites me back, but after days of inaction Third Army's fuel is restored as suddenly as it was cut off.

> IT WAS DELIVERED PARTLY BY AIR, SOME OF IT TO THE *REIMS* AIRFIELD WHERE WE'D SEEN THE PLANES LANDING, AND BY THE TRUCKERS OF THE RED BALL EXPRESS. THE LATTER WAS A 'ROUND-THE-CLOCK ALL-OUT EFFORT CARRIED OUT LARGELY BY NEGRO TRUCK DRIVERS TO GET FUEL FROM THE BEACHES TO THE ARMIES NEARING THE GERMAN BORDER. THE GASOLINE WAS CARRIED IN *GERRICANS*, RECTANGULAR METAL CANS, RIBBED FOR STRENGTH, WITH HANDLES ON TOP, PAINTED NON-REFLECTING OD, EACH CAPABLE OF BEING HANDLED BY ONE MAN. THE ALLIES TOOK THE DESIGN FROM THE GERMANS, THE *GERRIES*—HENCE THE NAME.

[Notes for Chapter 18 start on p. 211]

On the third of September we get marching orders. Liebau comes by our holes in a dark field by a hedgerow, squats down and tells us that our new objective is *Frankfurt,* Germany. *Nazi* Germany. I don't know where *Frankfurt* is, but it sounds both optimistic and ominous. And it sounds like the war is not going to be over tomorrow.

Ghosts of the Great War [Foxhole 40]
September 5, 1944 – Through the *Argonne*

After what seems like weeks of sitting at *Reims*—it was five days—we get on trucks and head out again, east. Another battalion investigates a German supply dump in the southeast corner of the *Argonne* Forest, but we go straight through [MAP 9, P. 216]. The word *Argonne* brings to my mind vague associations with the First World War, but I was never interested enough to read about it. Now, interested or not, I'm in it. But we get through and out the other side without contacting any of the enemy.

> IN THE *MEUSE-ARGONNE* OFFENSIVE OF WW-I, GENERAL PATTON SAW ACTION HERE AS A COLONEL IN CHARGE OF A TANK BRIGADE. HE WAS AWARDED THE DISTINGUISHED SERVICE CROSS FOR VALOR.[14] HIS TOTAL COMBAT TIME IN THE FIRST WORLD WAR, HOWEVER, WAS ONLY TWO DAYS, IN TWO SEPARATE INCIDENTS. THE FIRST WAS AT *ST.-MIHIEL*, THE SECOND HERE IN THE ARGONNE WHERE HE WAS WOUNDED BY A BULLET THAT PASSED THROUGH HIS GROIN AND OUT THE LEFT BUTTOCKS. BY THE TIME THE WOUND HEALED THE ARMISTICE HAD BEEN SIGNED.
>
> THOUGH NOT A PATTON FAN, I CAN UNDERSTAND THE EXCITEMENT HE MUST HAVE FELT, AND THE SENSE OF DESTINY—A BIG THING IN HIS LIFE—WHEN, IN WW-II AS THE COMMANDING GENERAL OF AN ENTIRE ARMY, HE REVISITED THE PLACES WHERE HE'D SEEN ACTION IN 1918. HIS FAMILIARITY WITH THE TERRAIN OF THE WW-I BATTLES—WHICH HE HAD STUDIED BETWEEN THE WARS—GAVE HIM A DEGREE OF CONFIDENCE MOST OF THE OTHER ALLIED COMMANDERS COULD NOT ENJOY.[15] EVER SINCE THE COBRA BREAKOUT, THIRD ARMY'S SPEED OF ADVANCE HAD OUTSTRIPPED SHAEF'S ABILITY TO PROVIDE MILITARY MAPS, SO PATTON USED

[Notes for Chapter 18 start on p. 211]

ORDINARY MICHELIN ROAD MAPS. TO MOVE ARMOR QUICKLY HE RELIED ON THE ROAD NETWORK, SO WHAT BETTER TO USE THAN A ROAD MAP?

ACCORDING TO GENERAL COLLINS, IN HIS BOOK, LIGHTNING JOE, THE 90TH DIVISION FOUGHT WITH DISTINCTION IN THE MEUSE-ARGONNE OFFENSIVE IN WW-I. COLLINS SAYS HE USED THIS FACT TO TRY TO INSPIRE—OR SHAME—SOME 90TH DIVISION LAGGARDS IN THE EARLY DAYS OF HEDGEROW FIGHTING ON THE CHERBOURG PENINSULA, BUT HE SAID IT DIDN'T WORK. TWO OF THE 90TH'S COMMANDING GENERALS—MCELVIE AND LANDRUM—HAD TO BE REPLACED BEFORE THE 90TH STARTED TO DEVELOP INTO AN EFFECTIVE UNIT UNDER GENERAL LEONARD MCLAIN.

Verdun
Where half a million mortals died[16]

Verdun is another name that has vague historical meaning for me, but its enormity was never impressed on me. I'm beginning to wish there'd been a required course in high school or college on the First World War. When we get to *Verdun* the trenches still twist across the landscape and the cratered fields look like a bad case of terrestrial smallpox.

>Worming their way across
>the raped land the
>trenches, stench of
>carnage still attached, lingering
>fringe of futile folly—exploiting the
>fatal frailties of the flesh; no
>flesh remains on bones
>stacked in bins catalogued
>carefully to no reasonable
>purpose except to show
>us, the later ones, where and
>how we too may be
>remembered.

[Notes for Chapter 18 start on p. 211]

CHAPTER 18

> What happened at *Verdun* verges on the unthinkable. Almost 800,000 men died there. The very name *Verdun* came to represent senseless carnage.[17] The commanders knew no tactics beyond bombardment and frontal assault. Robert Daley says in his book, *Portraits of France*, "Neither side attempted to improvise any new scenario."[18] Forty-six years later, alternatives to this simplistic approach were still woefully lacking.
>
> The Allies won here in 1918, but winning "the war to end wars"—in which ten million young men died—did not end War. Here we were again, in 1944, American troops in *Verdun*, led by a man who lived for, and loved war, whose sister echoed his entire family's feelings (with the exception of Robert Patton, the general's grandson) when she said "[war] ...is terrible, but grand."[19]
>
> In 1918, a few miles south of *Verdun* near *St.-Mihiel*, Patton, as a Lt. Colonel, experienced his first day of combat. While commanding a tank brigade, in his attempt to keep the attack moving he got out ahead of his men but finally, finding himself alone in a shell hole, gave up the heroics because it was clearly suicide to go farther. Furthermore, there would not have been anyone to see him do it.[20]

Even though I know very little about the First World War, in some ways it seems more real than the one I'm in, probably because its events are known and fixed in history. The facts and events of our war are still being made—by us. But I ought not indulge in such mental meanderings. More of our war is surely down the road.

In *Verdun* we cross over the *Meuse* on a bridge that's still intact. Others in XX Corps have preceded us and we see no fighting here.

> We moved among
> The swirling mysterious memories of other times and
> Other wars:
> *Château Thierry*, Belleau Wood, Ypres,
> Argonne – a pair of faded canvas leggings in

[Notes for Chapter 18 start on p. 211]

my neighbor's attic. *Over There,*
Mademoiselle from Armentiers, parlez vous? Doughboys,
Limeys, tin hats, The Great War still steeps its nostalgic legend and
perverse romance: Big Bertha, The *Kaiser*, the
Lusitania. Tomb of the Unknown
Soldier. Taps. No-man's-land. *In Flanders Fields (where*
poppies blow). More real theirs than ours. Can we
match it with fresh redolence? What
will be the new *Verdun*, the new *Marne*? We
crossed the *Marne*, today, through the forest *Argonne*—
toward What? Our own fresh-cut, dog-
faced, not-so-secretly-dreaded fate. That's
what.

⊕

Notes for Chapter 18

1. "The GIs" is yet another usage of the term "GI". In the plural with the definite article, its universal meaning was diarrhea—thought to be caused by the film of grease left on mess kits that were not washed thoroughly in the big galvanized GI-cans of boiling water after we got hot food. The kitchens had been set up in the rest area so this might have been the origin of Bruthiers's discomfort. Or maybe eating green apples.

   I wasn't unsympathetic, but the bizarre scene punctured the tension from the patrol and laughter was the natural relief.

2. According to a seemingly authentic account on the Internet, the elaborate stained glass windows of the *Chartres* Cathedral were removed in small sections and stored out of harm's way in both World Wars. The windows tell stories that read from left to right and from bottom to top (i.e., heavenward). Visitors are given an interpretive booklet explaining the iconography. A labyrinth is inlaid in the floor of the nave.[A5]

3. Nobody had told us GIs when we were moved into Haislip's XV Corps from Middleton's VIII Corps either, or the name of our new Corps Commander. In fact, we never knew we were in VIII Corps in the first place,

[Notes for Chapter 18 start on p. 211]

nor the Corps Commander's name. "Corps" was too abstract for us GIs to comprehend. We barely knew about battalion, and only because guys who were hit or sick went back to the battalion aid station. And we occasionally heard mention of the Battalion Commander, Major Hamilton.

On the *Cherbourg* Peninsula, with General Troy Middleton as our Corps Commander, the 90th Division didn't do much to distinguish itself, but in Third Army and Haislip's XV Corps—with General McLain as our new Division Commander—the 90th got in on some important action making headlines back in the States, as we raced east to *Mayenne* and *Le Mans*, then north to *Alençon* and the *Falaise-Argentan* Gap.

When we were first put in XX Corps, the 90th was not in the vanguard so we missed several sharp engagements across northern France.

4. In 1947 when I drove by the writer Louis Bromfield's country house near Mansfield, Ohio I noticed that he left his grounds similarly untrimmed, by choice. The French may have left their grounds untended because of the disruptions of war.

5. A Bailey bridge was constructed of steel sections that could be transported by truck. Sections could be added from the river bank, extending the span out over the water as far as 200 feet. A finished bridge could support tanks. They were available for use by D-Day and Donald Bailey, a British engineer, was knighted for their design.

6. I was dismayed when I learned that top air people, British and American, did not believe in using their planes to support ground troops. Spaatz felt strongly that the strategic bombing of German industry should be his primary mission; direct support for ground troops was not part of it, and fighter planes like the Mustangs and Thunderbolts were solely for shooting down German planes. The Brits held similar views. Ike strongly favored the *Transportation Plan*—bombing roads, bridges and railroads to prevent German reinforcements from reaching the beachheads—and at one point threatened to quit if air resources could not be used for that purpose. He finally prevailed, and the plan was carried out with notable success.

[Notes for Chapter 18 start on p. 211]

7. In 1918, American Marines at *Belleau Wood* stopped the Germans advance only thirty miles from Paris. Fearing the city would be overrun by the Germans, officials relocated the government's archives. Lasting through July, it was the Marines' most costly battle until Tarawa in WW-II. The site was renamed by the French in honor of the American Marines.

8. See entry for William Bradford Huie, *The Execution of Private Slovik*, in the ANNOTATED BIBLIOGRAPHY.

9. In France, wine cannot legally be labeled as *Champagne* unless the grapes were grown in *Champagne* country, so the borders of the *Région de Champagne* are important. It is generally supposed that *Champagne* country is limited to a triangle between the *Marne* and the *Vesle* rivers with *Reims* at the northern apex, *Châlons-sur-Marne* at the south-eastern apex, and *Épernay* at the south-western apex. But according to Robert Daley, author of *Portraits of France* (see ANNOTATED BIBLIOGRAPHY), *Champagne* country extends as far south as *Troyes,* and wine made from the southern grapes can legally use the *Appellation Champagne*. The grapes, however, are often shipped north before they are made into wine.

10. This was our first look at camouflaged fabric. The 82nd Airborne's parachutes that we saw at *Ste-Mère Église* were solid OD. I have used the term "silk" for parachute fabric, but ours were probably nylon, which accounted for the scarcity of women's nylon stockings during the war.

11. Artillery Capt. Harry S. Truman, in WW-I, heard a Frenchman remark that "Germany was fighting for territory, England for the sea, France for patriotism, and Americans for souvenirs." (Aida Donald, *Citizen Soldiers*[A6])

12. A favorite of many men's choruses, the music was written by Edvard Grieg; Norwegian lyrics by Sigvald Skavlan, English by Herbert Dalmas.

13. I was pleased to read, in General J. Lawton Collins's autobiography, *Lightning Joe*, that when he was at West Point he, too, "loathed close-order drill." For more on this subject see comment at the end of Collins's entry in the ANNOTATED BIBLIOGRAPHY.

[Notes for Chapter 18 start on p. 211]

14. Robert Patton, the General's grandson, in *The Pattons*, describes the behavior of "Georgie"—as he was known to his family—that led to his being wounded and getting the DSC. Georgie himself told how, when he found himself alone and under fire out ahead of his tanks, he withdrew in long slanting sidewise moves that looked less like retreating from danger.

    Patton's emphasis on the importance of appearances was shown also in WW-II by his advice to his sub-commanders—that they ride in open command cars on the way *up* to the front lines, but use planes on the way *back*. It was good for the troops to see them going *toward* the action, but when they were going *away* from the action they should stay out of sight.

15. Eisenhower, too, familiarized himself with the terrain of WW-I during several visits to France between the wars when he was a staff officer based in Washington. Ike nursed a yen to "command troops". (Source: address by David Eisenhower, the General's grandson, at the Strong Museum, Rochester, N.Y. December 7, 1991). In the light of subsequent events, Ike's interest in French terrain seems almost spooky.

16. Figures differ from one source to another. The figure, 800,000, is from Robert Daley, *Portraits of France*, 1991, p. 80. For moving descriptions of *Verdun* and its place in history I recommend Daley's book.

    At *Verdun,* modern-day tourists can see the Ossuary, filled with the bones of thousands of unidentified soldiers, segregated in bins according to where they were found, mixed irretrievably in final anonymous intimacy.

    Daley walked over many of the battle grounds and visited many of the cemeteries and memorials, but the terrain itself, he says, is "...the true monument to the battle of *Verdun*." Relics from the war—human and non-human—litter the landscape. Unexploded shells erupt out of the fields every spring. Plaques on monuments to individual shells tell where they exploded and the destruction they wrought. At one site 10,000 men (or their parts) disappeared into the mud, and in repeated bombardments were disinterred and buried over and over again. As it was for Daley, the effect on the reader is cumulative—monstrous and depressing.

[Notes for Chapter 18 start on p. 211]

Daley writes: "In those days, and into my lifetime as well, men believed absolutely in duty and honor, which were considered not vague obligations but articles of faith, as holy as belief in God. Today one does them from nine to five, five days a week. Maybe. One does them if convenient. It is as if the world saw in which direction duty and honor could take nations, never mind individuals, and gave them up at last." (*Portraits of France*, p. 82).

Compare these sentiments with Farley Mowat's epilogue for his book, *And No Birds Sang*. Mowat quotes from Wilfred Owen's poem, *Dulce et Decorum Est*, written during World War One. The part in Latin is from Horace's *Odes* iii 2.13:

> *My friend, you would not tell with such high zest*
> *To children ardent for some desperate glory*
> *The old lie: Dulce et decorum est*
> *Pro patria mori.*

17. Daley, *Portraits of France,* page 91.

18. For a discussion of Allied reliance on frontal attacks, see Chapter 9, Note 6 and Chapter 14, Note 6; also Web-link No. 3, Appendix C, and the entry for General J. Lawton Collins's book, *Lightning Joe*, in the ANNOTATED BIBLIOGRAPHY.

19. Quoted in *The Pattons*, by Robert Patton, the General's grandson.

20. This incident is also described in *The Pattons,* referenced in Note 19, above.

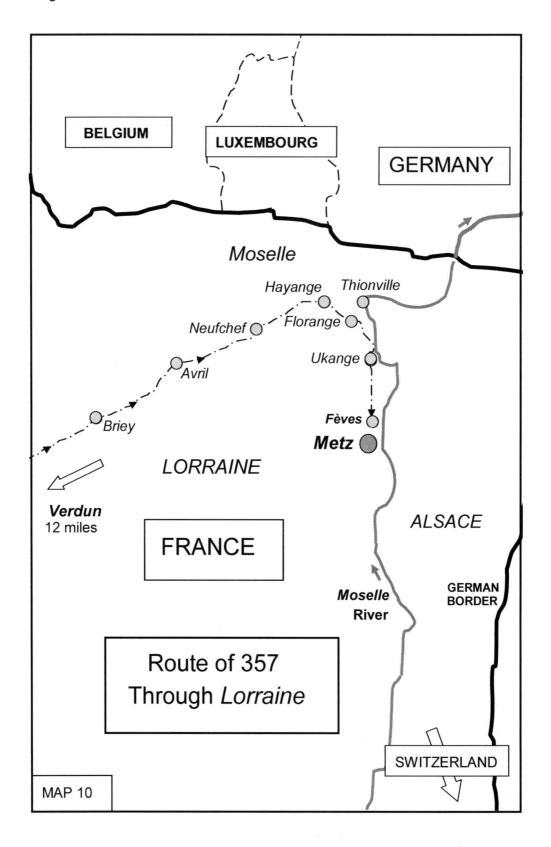

19

INTO *LORRAINE*

On the Point of Third Army [Foxhole 41]

Northeast of *Verdun*, the 90th Division is out in front again with 357 as the lead regiment. If there are Germans in our path we are the ones who will encounter them first. We go through a series of small towns—*Étain, Gondrecourt, Fléville* ("Fleaville" to the guys). When the advance units of 357 reach *Briey* there is a fight. Germans defend it stubbornly [MAP 10]. The 2nd and 3rd battalions surround the town while we in 1st Battalion bypass it and dig in astride the road beyond the town to block reinforcements from the north. The Germans hold *Briey* overnight but In the morning give it up. We hear that a lot of prisoners are taken.[1]

When we get the word to move forward 1st Battalion is in the lead, B-Company first, on foot, our platoon on point. We leave the road to take a dirt track through some woods, then abruptly come out into the open overlooking a small valley, a natural amphitheater about three quarters of a mile across. [MAP 11, P. 230]. A group of farm buildings sits below us—where a stage might be. We're in the balcony. At our left a ridge with bushes along the top forms the left-hand rim of the amphitheater. The ridge stretches away from us then dips down to a road that goes across our front on the other side of the farm buildings. Across the road is a pine forest. Forming the amphitheater rim on the right is another ridge, roughly parallel to the one on the left. The dirt track we're on descends to the farm buildings, and we get the word to proceed. The rest of the company follows.

Three alert, alive

Shortly after reaching the farm buildings, Liebau tells me to take my squad up to the top of the ridge at the left. With all of B-Company exposed in the valley, and the other companies coming in behind us, we'd be wise to have somebody up there as an outpost, I can see that. It's not steep going up but it is a definite grade. The slope is covered only with meadow grass and the hill gets steeper near the top. When we get there it rounds off and we look through the screen of

[Notes for Chapter 21 start on p. 228]

bushes and see that the land falls away on the other side, and off in the distance, about a mile away, is a small town. We have a perfect view. Liebau and Stevens and Major Hamilton must know about the town, but Liebau didn't mention it to me. I get the men spread out behind the row of bushes along the crest of the ridge. We're not at the exact crest, but a little below it on our side, so the ridge gives us some cover if fire should come from the direction of the town, and the bushes keep us from being seen. A hundred feet along the ridge to the right the bushes give out. There's a bare gap, then a final small clump about twenty yards farther along the ridge. Seace says he'll go out to the separate clump of bushes. OK. A good idea. He dips well below the ridge until he gets to the clump, then comes up to the crest and disappears in the bushes.

The rest of the line of bushes is continuous except for an opening about eight feet wide, near the left end. At the left end, the line of bushes takes a sharp left turn and goes part way down our side of the slope, so there's a sort of corner made by the bushes. The main line of bushes may extend farther to the left, but we can't see clearly where it goes without getting out in front and exposing ourselves.

I can see a small building farther up the slope of the hill to our left. It's about fifty yards into a woods that is a continuation of the same woods we came out of when we first came into the valley. The building is on a line extending to our left from our line of bushes. I look it over with my *Dienstglas* binoculars. I tell Sackett to take Russell with him and go up to scout out the building and they start off. When I put my binoculars on the town below, being careful to look through a screen of bushes rather than from out in the open, I see a German soldier at what seems to be the town's main crossroads. He's doing something to what looks like an anti-tank gun emplacement at the side of the road that comes out of the town in our direction. He seems to be covering the gun with a tarp. When he gets finished, I can't see the gun. The road the gun is on is the same road we first saw going left beyond the farm buildings in the amphitheater. We can't see the whole road because the rise of our own ridge blocks it off. If our guys are going to go down that road, from the farm buildings to the town, they will come up against that gun. I tell Gervase and Logan to go back down to the farm houses in the valley with a message for Liebau that I can see a gun position in the town on the other side of the hill. I want Liebau to know that we've got a good view of the town. They

[Notes for Chapter 21 start on p. 228]

should know what town it is from their maps [ST.-PIERREMONT] unless they botch their map-reading again the way they did on the way to *Coutances.*

Gervase and Logan take off leaving Logan's B-A-R ammo belt with us. I send two of them so there'll be less chance of a screw up. Halfway down the slope they break into a run for the farm buildings. Sackett and Russell are back already, too soon for them to have gone all the way up to the house. Sackett says they saw a German at the house so they didn't go any farther. I look again with my binoculars and it does look like a man crouching next to the house, looking in our direction, but it's hard to be sure if it's a German, or even a person.

"I saw him before, he's by the house," Halpern, our new B-A-R man, says. He saw somebody but didn't said anything to me about it. That tells me something about Halpern—and it is not encouraging. The bushes don't give us real cover from the house if we're standing up, and the German, if it is a German, must have seen us when we first came up. And he probably saw Sackett and Russell. So they know we're here. From the house they can see down into the whole amphitheater, though their view is somewhat screened by the trees. More of our guys are streaming into the valley from the same dirt track we came in on. I see Major Hamilton in his command car. It looks like battalion headquarters is down there now. If it's a German at the house, and if he has communication with their mortars or artillery, he can direct fire on all of our guys in the amphitheater. Probably not machineguns, because of the trees, but he might be able to get machinegun fire on us where we are, and maybe drive us off the ridge. From the ridge they'd have a clear field of fire on everybody in the amphitheater.

I tell Halpern if he sees anybody at the house to fire his B-A-R at them. I look again with the binoculars and see what I saw before, what looks like a man still crouched by the side of the house. A civilian wouldn't crouch there like that. "He's still there, right by the house, on the right side," I say. But Halpern doesn't want to fire the B-A-R. The best firepower we've got is his B-A-R, but it's useless if he won't fire it. But I don't push it, right now, because I want to see how the other guys are doing and I start down the line. Alongside Halpern is Sackett, and Russell, then just past the opening in the bushes, Sankey, then Fullard—new since the "Island"—and Sartori and Browny together, and at the right-hand end of

[Notes for Chapter 19 start on p. 228]

CHAPTER 19

the bushes, Bruthiers and Logan, and out in the isolated clump of bushes, Seace. Sartori has worked himself into the bushes so he can get a pretty good view across the open top of the ridge, and he's dug himself in a little. Not much—the roots of the bushes make digging almost impossible—but any little bit helps. Browny has become Sartori's sidekick and is right behind him. There are three guys who are reasonably dependable—Sankey, Sartori, and Seace. Halpern will probably be useless; Fullard is over forty years old. His heart isn't in any of this stuff. Bruthiers is almost not here at all. He comes along, but is a very neutral element. Sackett and Russell were stopped by the one German they thought they saw at the house. I wish they'd gone further, but to be fair, they didn't have instructions to get into a fight or to keep going until they got fired on. And when Gervase and Logan get back—if they come back—Gervase will find a way to keep away from anything dangerous. Logan, like Bruthiers, is here, but barely. Halpern, Fullard, and Logan theoretically make up the B-A-R team and have ammo belts for the B-A-R. I should give the B-A-R to somebody else. I can use it myself if it comes to that, but I can't do everything. I can't be a one-man army.

Gervase and Logan do come back and Gervase tells me they delivered the message to Liebau. There was no way for them to avoid coming back because they were in full view from the farmhouse in the valley, a fact which I had taken into account. They barely get into position behind the bushes, Gervase behind Browny behind Sartori, and Logan at the other end with Bruthiers, when we get raked with machinegun bullets. Everybody who isn't down already goes down flat. The machinegun, not just a machine pistol, more like an MG-42 from the steady rate of fire, is coming from the direction of the house. It's hard to tell if the up-swell of the hill gives us any real cover, and the bushes aren't protection from the machinegun bullets, but nobody is yelling "medic" yet, and we get raked by a few long bursts and the bullets are popping excitedly through the air but they're going over our heads, ripping through the leaves of the bushes but not hitting anybody. Then they stop. Then they start up again and keep coming for another group of long bursts. Then they stop again. That's both good and bad. I get up into a crouch and see that the three guys at the left end are OK, and start to go to my right, past Sankey, but just as I start down the line I catch a movement out of the left corner of my eye and swing around to my left, and in the eight-foot opening in

[Notes for Chapter 21 start on p. 228]

the bushes I see a German soldier in a camouflage cape holding a pistol running past the opening from my left to my right. He is about fifteen feet away. Just as he gets to the middle of the opening he sees Sackett, Halpern, and Russell lying prone in the corner with their heads down, and he stops and swings around to his right (my left), his arm outstretched moving in an arc to point the pistol at Sackett at close range. My rifle rises without thought or effort and I fire into the upper middle of the German's body which, by turning toward Sackett, he has opened up to me. He sinks down without a sound and falls face forward into the grass.

> Appeared suddenly a man
> running, cloth-capped
> camo-caped, caught
> Sackett in the
> corner of his
> eye, stopped mid-strided,
> wheeled, cape-flared, swung
> arm sweeping, flung
> arc-at-its-end the black
> semi-auto 38, P-, and then in
> less, second, fraction thereof, than
> an Olympic sprinter spends
> dashing one two-hundredth of a
> stride, eyes my, saw; M-1 whipped,
> finger tripped, bullet leapt, closed
> space to
> zero: the wheeling man
> a careless pile
> a-top
> the hill that overlooks the place they
> call *Avril:* April,
> the spring of Life…

There was no interval between my shot and his collapse, the two events took place at precisely the same instant, and there is no motion or sound from the

German on the ground.[2] But something is haywire with my rifle. When I fired, it didn't feel as though it ejected the spent cartridge case, which usually snaps out of the receiver from the rearward motion of the bolt, and flips away to the right. It's a helluva time to have to monkey with my weapon, to take my eyes away from the surroundings even for a second, but I absolutely have to know if there's another good round in the chamber—or not—so I pull the bolt back by hand and when the cartridge gets far enough back, there isn't any bullet on the end of it and the empty case flips out and spins away the way it should have in the first place, though not with as much force because of my doing it by hand. With the bolt all the way back another round comes up in position to be loaded into the chamber, and I let go of the bolt and it snaps forward loading the round into the chamber. Great. I am fighting the war with a bolt-action rifle. I can't keep looking each time so I will just have to assume the rifle is not working properly and work the bolt by hand after each shot and if I waste half of each clip of eight cartridges, so be it. If my rifle does eject the empties, and if I eject the next good one each time, I'll have only four shots instead of eight before I have to reload with another clip, but it's better than pulling the trigger on an empty round when I absolutely need it to work. And if it didn't eject the first empty maybe it won't eject the rest and I'll still get eight shots out of a clip. I'll know when the clip is empty when I pull back the bolt by hand and the clip whings out after the last round.[3]

I have to make sure the German is dead and no threat to us in any way. I remember the warnings from basic. Fanatical *Nazis* sometimes throw grenades even after they're down. So I step to where I can get a good view of him on the ground. The German non-com is sprawled motionless and out of the fight. Then I fire another round, past him just over the crest of the hill, and keep firing because if there are more Germans coming up the other side of the hill I want the noise of bullets popping over their heads, to make them know they can't just run up the hill at us without getting shot at. To emphasize our presence even more, and our will and ability to fight them off, I unhook a grenade from my pack strap and rip off the adhesive tape and pull the pin and heave the grenade as far as I can, hoping it will discourage anybody coming up the hill from the other side. It explodes with the peculiar metallic tinny sound our grenades make, then I yell "I'm going to throw another grenade," and heave another one, and it goes off like the first. I

[Notes for Chapter 21 start on p. 228]

probably should have yelled before I threw the first one, the way we were trained to do, because there's a chance that fragments of the grenade could hit our own guys if they're not lying flat, but I took the chance and nobody got hit.

I hurt my shoulder some, throwing the grenades, throwing them overhand like a baseball or a football, because I never did get the knack of throwing them the right way, which is either like a modified shot-put, or sidearm like throwing a discus, which I did some of on the Oberlin track squad.[4]

I take a quick look to see what's happening with the squad. The three guys at the left end are all prone, heads still down. I've been firing pretty close over their heads through the bushes so I don't blame them for staying down.[5] Sankey is flat down too, but OK, from the little I can see of his face. The German attack seems temporarily stalled, so I start down the line to the right again. I stop where Sartori and Browny and Gervase are, and I tell them to watch in all directions, even behind them. I say that I just got a German right in front of the bushes, and that they might come right in among us, and Browny's face is turned to me close as I'm telling them this but he doesn't look scared, or not scared. The expression on his face is the non-expression of a mind in arrest. Sartori tells me he got a German too, coming over the top of the hill. He says it quite calmly.

Gervase is doing something with his wrist. "I think I'm hit," he says. I take a quick look but I can't see anything. The way he's acting is identical to the way Steel acted when I had the B-A-R on the hill at *Beau-Coudray*—a sort of preoccupied picking and examining, as if at a pimple, or a sliver. I keep going down the line of bushes to where Bruthiers and Logan are and they're OK. And I get a glimpse of Seace and he seems OK. Then I come back to Gervase and if he's hit I can't see where, so I assume he isn't. Or if he is, he'll tell me again. I get back to the left end and the guys aren't quite so prone and their heads are up a little more.[6]

"They were trying to surrender," Halpern says, looking up at me with scary innocence. I think of my hole-mate at the roadblock my first day on the line, claiming he saw "Gerries" running around out front, and not waking up to stand guard. There's a similarity, an inability to face the truth of the situation. But I can't take time to get into it.

[Notes for Chapter 19 start on p. 228]

Then we see a man coming up the hill from behind us from the amphitheater and it's a lieutenant with a walkie-talkie. "Where's the gun emplacement?" he wants to know. Then I know my message to Liebau got through and is having the desired effect. I take the lieutenant to where we can see through the bushes and point out where I saw the German just outside the town covering up the gun. He looks through his binoculars and says "Oh," with a disappointed tone, as though he's miffed at coming up here for nothing. I don't know why he should react that way unless the German gun is too far for whatever kind of weapons he's observing for. Seems like mortars ought to go that far, at least 81s. If the battalion goes toward the town they will have to face that gun.

Then the lieutenant sees the dead German on the ground through the opening in the bushes and tells me to crawl out and get the German's pistol and field glasses. I hadn't noticed the field glasses. They're the long straight-barrel type. I don't want to do it, and I come close to refusing, but the lieutenant stares me down. I'm not used to arguing with commissioned officers, and we need this one's help, so like a jerk I crawl out to the dead German, exposing myself to anybody who might be where he came from, probably the machine-gunner, because he'll still be back there, and I take the pistol out of the dead German's hand where it is still being grasped, and pull the strap for the field glasses over his head trying not to pull off his cloth cap—I don't know why I should worry about that. What does it matter? I get a close look at one side of the guy's face—he's about my age—then I crab back through the gap in the bushes where the lieutenant is waiting.

The pistol is a Walther P-38, a nice souvenir. He thrusts it in his belt, and takes the field glasses and puts the strap over his head, then goes down to where Bruthiers and Logan are, and starts looking out over the valley beyond the ridge using the German field glasses instead of his own. I go along with him, and we both see some Germans coming from the direction of the town, running out from behind a row of trees, coming toward our hill, toward the house in the woods. The Germans haven't given up the attack. They are bringing more men up for another attempt. They have decided that they really want this hill. The lieutenant asks if we've got any men in the woods by the house, and I say no, and he starts talking into the walkie-talkie, and pretty soon some mortar rounds start landing off to our left near the house and where we saw the Germans coming up. [HUGH COLE, IN

[Notes for Chapter 21 start on p. 228]

HIS BOOK *THE LORRAINE CAMPAIGN*, SAYS THE OBSERVER LIEUTENANT WAS WITH THE ARTILLERY, BUT THE SHELLS HE CALLED IN SOUNDED LIKE MORTARS TO ME.] Then we see a couple of the Germans who were running toward the house now running back, but not all of them, and I go back down to the left end of the bushes again to see how the guys are doing. When I get there I look back at the lieutenant and he's standing right out in the open looking through the German field glasses. I think maybe I should caution him about exposing himself like that, but hell, he's the lieutenant, he should know what he's doing.

The guys are OK, and no more Germans have got up to us, or in among us yet, and after a few minutes Bruthiers comes to me from the other end and says the lieutenant is shot. I go back to the right end of our line and the lieutenant is lying on his back with a bullet hole in the middle of his chest. I kneel down over him and he says in a weak voice to get a morphine syrette from inside his helmet where it's taped. I find it and he says to stick it in his leg. I remember hearing somewhere that a person with a chest wound shouldn't be given a sedative, but I do what he says, ripping through his pant leg with my trench knife to get at his thigh. I unscrew the cap from the Syrette and force the tip of the needle into his thigh and squeeze but nothing comes out. I don't tell him, but I can't get the damn stuff into him. And I can't spend any more time trying. He is fading, not saying anything, just lying quietly with his eyes closed, but still breathing.

I take his walkie-talkie and try to figure out how to work it. There isn't time to sit down and study it. I glance at Bruthiers and Logan, but they're not offering any suggestions. So I push the biggest button and say into the mouthpiece that the lieutenant is hit. Nothing comes back to me out of the walkie-talkie, so I talk into it again, and I realize my voice is starting to show my anxiety—from not knowing how to work the damn walkie-talkie. We had one brief run-through in basic but if anything stuck to me it isn't coming back to me now. I don't know if my message is getting through. But I try once more: "The lieutenant is hit, bad," and then I add: "We need help up here." I repeat it a couple of times, emphasizing the last part, and I realize that my anxiety must be showing to Bruthiers and Logan, listening, but their faces don't show much of anything. Then I put the walkie-talkie down, and go back to the other end of the bushes to check on the guys. I'm sorry the lieutenant is hit, but we aren't out of this thing yet. I can't see anybody at the

[Notes for Chapter 19 start on p. 228]

house, but we saw Germans coming toward it, so we can expect another attempt to brush us off the hill. If they do, and if we try to retreat down the slope toward the farm house, we'll be in the open and it'll be a rabbit-shoot.

"They're not surrendering," I tell Halpern and Sackett and Russell. "A sniper got the lieutenant. You gotta keep watching, and if you see any of them, shoot."

Halpern is a little less giddy now. Sackett and Russell have that frozen non-expression on their faces that Browny had, that everybody except Sartori has. Then after a few minutes without anything happening somebody comes up the hill behind us from the amphitheater and it's a stretcher team and they ease the lieutenant onto the stretcher. I tell them I tried to give him the morphine but that the Syrette didn't work, but that he probably thinks he got it. In any case, he's lying quietly, not talking or moving, but he's still breathing slightly, and they start down the hill with him. It can't be easy carrying a man on a stretcher down a hill. The fact that they came probably means my message got through—the whole message, I hope, including about needing help.[7]

It apparently did. About fifteen minutes later some GIs come in view at our left rear, coming out of the woods where we first came into the amphitheater, crouching and scrambling up the hill on our left where we haven't been yet, except Sackett and Russell, at least part way, on their recco patrol. The German machinegun opens up again, this time at the new guys coming up the hill. The new guys go down, and luckily there is a line of shallow cover across the hill where they are, and I don't see any of them get hit. Another lieutenant, younger, with the new guys, crouches his way up to where we are. He's with C-Company come to help us out. The lieutenant sees the opening in the bushes and the German on the ground and he wants to know if I can see the machinegun by crawling out through the opening. I've been out there before. I'm not going out there again. Not when there are a lot of the lieutenant's own men available to do it. We did our part. This time I stare him down and he gives it up. He's not my lieutenant, though going by the book any commissioned officer can give orders to anyone of lower rank and they're supposed to follow them. He stops short of actually ordering me to go out and look for the machinegun, and I don't.

[Notes for Chapter 21 start on p. 228]

Then a runner comes up from Liebau and says our squad is supposed to come down off the hill. I signal to Seace and he comes in from the flank on the right, scrooching along below the brow of the hill. He says he got a German coming up over the hill too. There is the briefest moment of eye-to-eye acknowledgement, then we go back down the hill, running. We get back to the farm houses and Liebau asks if any of us are hit, and I tell him no. I tell him about the mortar observer, and Liebau says he saw me throw the grenades, and wants to know how many Germans we got. I count mine, and Sartori's, and Seace's, which could have been the same one Sartori got, which makes three, but I tell Liebau five. Five sounds better than three. And a lot better than two.[8] Tallying the count seems important to Liebau. Recently he has gotten more intent on killing more of the enemy, and shows anger when he talks about it. It's the first time I've heard anybody do this. The enemy is there to be driven back, shot at, and, if necessary, killed, but to be angry at the enemy as you express the need to see more of them taken out of the fight is, to me, a new thought.[9]

Gervase doesn't say anything more about getting hit, and he doesn't go back to the aid station. Overall I think we did pretty well. At least three of us in the squad were alert and effective. The moment I had been wondering about since the summer of 1943—when I would confront the enemy up close—has come, and in spite of my reservations about the war and my role in it, I was able to do what was expected of me. I did get a little flustered when the radio didn't respond,[10] and I couldn't get the morphine into the lieutenant's leg. Why I exaggerated the number of Germans killed I can't say, except that I guess I wanted to tell Liebau what he wanted to hear. I don't know what happened to the lieutenant's souvenirs.[11]

While I'm talking to Liebau I look up at a ridge beyond the amphitheater to the right where there is a long straight line of trees on top as if bordering a road, and I see some vehicles silhouetted against the late afternoon sky. Liebau sees them too, but does nothing. They're not GI vehicles, but I can't be sure whether they're German military vehicles or even if they're carrying military personnel. Our guys must have seen them, and done whatever they are going to do.

The short discussion with Liebau about my squad's fight on the hill is all that's said about it. Combat actions don't get critiqued. But we were in view of everybody in the amphitheater, and we held onto the hill, and all of our guys got back OK, and I feel pretty good about that.

⊕

Notes for Chapter 19

1. As we penetrated deeper into *Lorraine* and neared the *Moselle* Valley, mining and steel-making became significant in the local economies. *Briey* was an iron mining town important to the German war effort.

2. The M-1's .30-cal. bullet left the barrel at 2700 feet per second. It would have taken $1/180^{th}$ of a second to go the fifteen feet to the German.

3. Counting rounds as you fired them, in my experience, was almost never done. In the excitement of combat you just fired until the empty clip sprang out of the rifle's receiver. If clips and cartridge casings had been retrieved it would have saved tons of metal, and untold hours of factory work. All that steel and brass got sprinkled wantonly over the soils of France—for kids and farmers to collect as we still collect American Indian arrowheads.

4. After the war, I tried to throw a stone across the Genesee River gorge from the top of the "high banks" at Letchworth Park and the old soreness returned. My shoulder is still sore when I throw anything with any force.

5. I think it was a mistake for the cadre at basic to keep telling recruits "Keep your head down!" Some learned it so well they never looked up to see what was going on. You can't win a fire fight by keeping your head down.

6. By rights, Logan, as the ammunition bearer, should have stayed near the B-A-R. I don't think this ever occurred to me. As it turned out, it didn't matter because Halpern wouldn't fire the B-A-R anyhow.

7. In Cole's *The Lorraine Campaign* he says the artillery (not mortar) lieutenant's name was McDonald and that he was awarded the DSC posthumously—for whatever he did, or whatever they say he did, on that

[Notes for Chapter 21 start on p. 228]

hill near *Avril*. Our Battalion Commander, Major Ed Hamilton, wrote glowingly of McDonald—I can't remember where I read it—and the hill now has a plaque on it commemorating his role in defending "McDonald Hill". If I had been hit while crawling out to get him his souvenirs, and lived to tell about it, instead of getting a medal he could have been court-martialed.

8. S.L.A. Marshall, as official historian for the Army, interviewed GIs immediately after combat action. He claimed to get accurate descriptions of what happened. My exaggeration of the number of German dead casts doubt on Marshall's claim. For more discussion, see *Men Against Fire*, by S.L.A. Marshall, and *Reconciliation Road*, by his grandson, Douglas Marshall.

9. Paul Fussell, in his book *Doing Battle*, says: "To survive in the infantry, I had mastered the technique of productive anger, the impulse required for effective close-combat killing." (p. 211)

   I, myself, did not experience such anger. The usual advice is that in a fight, anger gets in the way of cool-headed action. I do remember, though, as a kid wrestling with my neighborhood friends, when caught in a hold that was hard to get out of, I could summon a sort of frenzy that gave me extra strength and quickness—probably from a rush of adrenaline.

   Both Fussell and Liebau were Second Lieutenants. Their anger may have derived from the frustration at the difficulties inherent in their greater responsibilities. In Liebau's case, at least, I think it was also a way of letting the men know that he was not unfeeling about our casualties.

10. It didn't occur to me that the volume of the *listen* function on the radio was probably turned down or off, because an artillery or mortar observer would not want it to come on at the wrong time, possibly giving away his position. I never found out how much of my message got through, or to whom. Or what led to C-Company coming up to our relief, or what the lieutenant may have said on his radio before he was shot.

11. German P-38 pistols were prized souvenirs, but some GIs wouldn't carry anything German for fear of being shot if they were captured. Our

CHAPTER 19

Company Commander, 1st Lt. Burrowes Stevens, is quoted in Colby's *War From the Ground Up* saying that at *Mayenne* the only weapon he had was a P-38 given to him at the *St.-Germain* "Island" by Sgt. Yensko, the non-com who put me in for sergeant. Stevens had taken over the company at *Beau-Coudray*. It's hard to believe he wouldn't have been issued a .30-cal. Carbine, the standard weapon for Infantry officers, or at least a GI .45 pistol. I know he carried a carbine later. Long after the war he sent me a photograph of himself alongside his father, a senior officer, visiting him at the "Island". In it, Stevens was holding a German burp-gun.

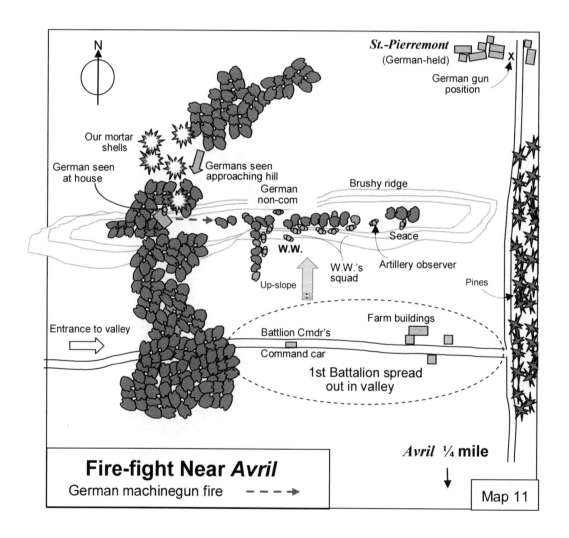

Fire-fight Near *Avril*
German machinegun fire - - - - ▶
Map 11

[Notes for Chapter 21 start on p. 228]

20

MOSELLE

ATTACKED...
But we're not there

We cross the road on the other side of the farm buildings and are told to get in under the pine trees and stay out of sight. When it's dark we come out and move along the road toward *Avril* and take up positions on the reverse slope of the ridge that forms the south rim of the amphitheater where we were earlier in the day. We get instructions to dig in, and we get shelled—not too bad, but bad enough, because we don't get time to dig very deep. One of the shells hits somebody off to our left, but nobody in our platoon gets hit.

Liebau comes over to my hole and says that contact with the battalion on our left flank has been lost and a runner is needed to go out looking for them. He's thinking about asking me to volunteer for the assignment. The runner will try to find somebody in the other battalion, an officer if possible, who knows where they are on a map. The runner will determine the other battalion's location, tell them where we are, then return with any messages they want to send back. The runner will avoid a fight. If captured he will tell the Germans only his name, rank, and serial number—S.O.P. according to the Geneva Conventions.[1] It's the kind of assignment that appeals to me. I have exceptionally good night vision and I've always been comfortable alone in the woods at night. I am just about to tell Liebau that I will volunteer to go, when a messenger comes over to us and says a guy in battalion headquarters will go instead.

At about one A.M. we move off the hill, go back across the road again that goes to *Avril*, and head into the deep forest on a good hard-surface highway. Dark pines loom up on both sides of the road. Before we go very far we stop, get in under the trees and bed down on a deep layer of pine needles. We don't bother to dig holes. "Don't go out on the road," we're told, there could be German traffic. We get sacked out without hearing any, and get a good night's sleep.

[Notes for Chapter 20 start on p. 243]

CHAPTER 20

> Cole, in *The Lorraine Campaign*, describes a battle near Avril that same night in which the Germans attacked a hill they thought was occupied by Americans. All of our men who had been on the hill had moved off and our guns were zeroed in on the hill—with the result that considerable damage was inflicted on the attacking Germans. At the time I knew nothing of this action except that while we were getting shelled there was a lot of firing going on from our own artillery. We in B-Company were not directly involved. From the description in Cole, it sounds as though the hill where the Germans got clobbered was the same one my squad had defended earlier in the day. After the war, Sackett and I referred to it as "Little Roundtop".
>
> In Colby's *War From the Ground Up*, Major Hamilton, our Battalion Commander at the time, gives his account of what happened, referring to the various hills by number, but his description is not accompanied by a map so it's impossible to figure out which hills were which. Hamilton took credit for luring the Germans into the trap.[2]

In the morning we get going again deeper into the forest and it's a beautiful day for a hike. It's hard to get geared up for a war on such a bright September morning. After a half-hour we hear firing up ahead—a few shots—and we stop and get in under the pines again. Our advance scouts were fired on, or had fired first, at some Germans at a roadblock. We don't get the whole story. After a few minutes a Jeep goes by us toward the head of the column but we don't see any medics and we move out again. When we come to the place where the firing took place a large tree is lying across the highway forming a roadblock and our Jeep is trying to pull it off the road. It's a big tree, and looks like a job for more than just a Jeep. There are no bodies that we can see, ours or theirs. The tree was dropped at a good place because it is impossible for a vehicle to get around it even by going off the road—the pine trees are too big and too close together. We guys on foot aren't stopped by the felled tree, though, and we keep going, knowing that any vehicular support we might need won't be coming for a while.

[Notes for Chapter 20 start on p. 243]

The terrain changes from flat to hilly, with the road cutting a clean swath through the forest between two ridges. I am sent out as flanker along the ridge on the right. I take Sankey with me and we're out on the ridge in the forest by ourselves, trying to keep pace with the rest of the company, but going carefully, trying to see whoever might be ahead of us before they see us. There were Germans at the roadblock, and they went somewhere, maybe up here. But we don't come across anybody and we finally come to the edge of the trees, still on the ridge. Below us is a tiny post-card type town, and we can see the rest of our guys down on the road. Keeping an eye on the buildings, we go down and join the others.

The *Moselle* [Foxhole 42]

The little town is *Neufchef*. We bivouac on the open-topped hills to the left, a short distance beyond the town. On the hilltop we are up close to the sky and the view is panoramic. We can see the terrain getting more rugged to the east.

Sackett and I are assigned to scout the woods ahead of us at the bottom of the hill we're going to bivouac on, and it turns into a nice evening stroll. We don't see anybody or find anything, so we go back up to the top of the hill and start digging in. After walking all day nobody is in the mood to dig deep. We scrape out a few inches then sleep on the ground outside the holes. We watch what looks like lightning flashes on the northwestern horizon and hear rumblings that are not thunder. There's a fight going on over there, but we're not in it, and after setting up a one-on-three-off guard, we go to sleep looking at the sky. War has its pleasures.

> THIS WAS THE NIGHT WHEN A GERMAN LUFTWAFFE DIVISION[3] BLUNDERED THROUGH A GAP BETWEEN THE 90TH'S OTHER TWO REGIMENTS, 358 AND 359, RUNNING SMACK INTO THE 90TH'S DIVISION HEADQUARTERS. THERE WAS A BIG FIGHT THAT LASTED ALL NIGHT, WITH THE SURPRISED GERMANS GETTING BEAT UP PRETTY BADLY BY THE HEADQUARTERS DEFENSE PLATOON—WITH A LOT OF HELP FROM 358 AND 359. COLE HAS A DETAILED DESCRIPTION OF THE FIGHT IN *THE LORRAINE CAMPAIGN*, AND SEVERAL PARTICIPANTS PROVIDE FIRST-HAND ACCOUNTS IN COLBY'S *WAR FROM THE GROUND UP–THE 90TH DIVISION IN WW-II*. THE GUNS THAT LULLED

[Notes for Chapter 20 start on p. 243]

us to sleep were the 90th's divisional artillery called in to bail out the brass.

In the morning we can see a river valley in the distance to the east [THE *MOSELLE*]. We set out again on foot. The terrain looks a lot like pictures we've all seen of Switzerland and the German *Tyrol*, but the hills aren't as jagged and there aren't any lakes or snow-capped peaks, or ski chalets. In late-afternoon we come to a fair-sized town lodged between hills, and the mood changes. Trouble is expected. My squad goes through backyards to the right of the main street leading into the town and we have to scramble over fences and walls and have a hard time keeping up. When we get back on the main street again I see Liebau up ahead, dodging from doorway to doorway, and I follow him. Pretty soon I'm right behind him, and he turns around and sees me and says, "Where's Barrett?" Tech Sgt. Barrett is our Platoon Sergeant, but I haven't seen him, and I say I don't know.

"He's supposed to be covering me," Liebau says with some heat.[4] We've left everybody else behind and Liebau decides we'd better go back. Later we get into the center of the city without a fight and set up guards for the night. The place seems empty of Germans, but they were here earlier in the day. We in the 2nd Platoon are given a street to watch—the guard guys will watch it—and we find a place to sleep inside a building in a hallway on the second floor with windows onto the street. We don't have beds or mattresses, but just being inside is a luxury. At least we won't get wet if it rains. We hear some firing northeast of the city, but B-Company is in reserve and we are not involved. We have to be ready to move out at any time if we're needed, but we're not.

Flags *pour les Americains*

In the morning the city is considered to be secure. We are in the city of *Hayange*, in the northeastern corner of France near the border of *Luxembourg* just a few miles west of the *Moselle* River. Overnight, dozens of American flags have sprouted like flowers all over town. The inhabitants have made the flags out of anything they could get their hands on. It's a joyful sight. All the people are smiling, proud of what they have done to show us that they are on the side of *les Americains*, not *les Allemands*, the Germans, and that we are welcome. Some of the larger flags, carefully made and accurate as to the number of stars and stripes, had to have been made earlier and been kept hidden. It strikes me that they have taken a big risk doing this. Other flags have been hurriedly sewn together, maybe since we got here. Many are not good replicas of Old Glory, but we get the point, and there is a lot of good will being spilled in both directions.

> Blossoming like white
> daisies and blue and red petunias from
> window-boxes and doorways, our
> flag, Betsey's pride, still there through the
> perilous night.
> All sizes, crafted from
> petticoats, stockings, blouses, sheets,
> shouting all the joys of freedom – to us who
> freed them. Or
> are they currying our favor, switching
> allegiance as circumstances
> require? Take care. A flag is only a
> symbol. Truth lies deeper. *Hyange* is also
> *Hyangen*. A flag may be the cape of the matador that
> hides the sword. But Hooray! We're here! Laugh, proffer wine.
> Don't
> lurk sullen behind the blinds. And as
> far as we can see, they don't,

Our alert has been relaxed and we are free to move about, but as usual, we have to be careful. Even I know that *Lorraine*, along with *Alsace*, has see-sawed back and forth between France and Germany for centuries. Sovereignty over the territory was an issue at the start of in World War One. Some of the people here may be German sympathizers, or have German relatives, or *be* German. The town itself has two names: in French it's *Hayange*; in German, it's *Hayangen*. We are definitely on our way to *Frankfurt*.

Halpern and I take a stroll down the main street and come to what could be the town hall. We go inside feeling that we have a perfect right to do so, to poke around, pull out file drawers. Anything important will probably have been stashed elsewhere, and anything incriminating will probably have been destroyed, but I look through some of the stuff imagining that I might find something of great value to Army intelligence. A French citizen shows up as we're poking through the papers. He's a small nervous man, and I get from him the information that this is where the vital statistics for the regional populace have been stored, and still are stored, and he lets me know that he doesn't think I should be messing with the files. I ask him about *Monsieur le Maire*, the mayor. Is he around? He is hesitant answering, but no, he isn't here, not in *Hayange*, not now. I try a dangerous route: Is he with the Germans? This makes the little man very nervous.

"*On ne sais pas,*" he says. "One does not know." Which tells more than just the fact that he does not know. The government of the town is not in the government building, and that seems odd. Just because the Americans are here and have caused the Germans to leave hurriedly, is that reason for the government to go out of business? Did the government people all leave hurriedly too? "One does not know," he says again.

Halpern and I move into what looks like a meeting room with a long table and straight chairs around it. Yesterday the members of the governing body might have met here and decided to leave, not hurriedly, of course, but just so as not to be in the way of whatever military activity might ensue.

The man follows us in. Behind the head of the table, on the wall, is a large photograph of Adolf Hitler, framed, but with no glass. I have my bayonet on my rifle and holding the rifle with one hand like a pointer, I reach up to the photograph and touch Hitler with the tip of the bayonet, watching the minor government clerk, as I have figured him out to be. He stares transfixed as I dig the point of the bayonet into the photograph and deliberately tear it open with a foot-long gash from *der Führer's* breast bone to his forehead, splitting his face in two. The poor little man is terrified. I am being intentionally cruel, enjoying his consternation. A small noise comes out of him, then he leaves quickly.

Halpern finds some blank typing paper and takes two reams of it. I find some small envelopes, suitable for cards, and take a half-dozen.

[Notes for Chapter 20 start on p. 243]

The impulse to take things—simply because they can be taken—is insidious. What will Halpern do with two reams of typing paper? Why does he feel that he has to have it? Did he come from a home where paper was scarce, as I did? Why do I want the envelopes? The V-mail paper we get through regular channels folds into its own envelopes. Everyone has his own reasons, I guess.

> THE ENVELOPES I TOOK WERE BORDERED IN BLACK. I DIDN'T REALIZE THAT CONDOLENCES FOR DEATHS ARE CONVENTIONALLY SENT ON BLACK-BORDERED STATIONERY. I USED ONE OF THE ENVELOPES TO SEND A LETTER TO JEAN. WHEN I LEARNED OF MY *FAUX PAS* I WAS MORTIFIED. WHAT DID SHE THINK WHEN SHE GOT IT, THAT I HAD BEEN KILLED IN ACTION? MUCH LATER, WHEN I GOT A CHANCE TO ASK HER, SHE BARELY REMEMBERED GETTING THAT LETTER. SHE DIDN'T KNOW WHAT THE BLACK BORDER MEANT EITHER. I WOULD HAVE THOUGHT SOMEONE WOULD HAVE TOLD HER.

There is a *Nazi* flag in the conference room too, with a big black swastika on it, but I leave it. To me it represents ugliness, evil. I don't want it on my person, I don't even want to touch it. But when I tell Sackett about the flag, he goes to the Town Hall and takes it for a souvenir.

Dinner at *René's*

On the main street of *Hayange* I meet a well-dressed dark-haired man, probably in his late twenties, and when he learns that I can speak some French he introduces himself as *René DeMuth*. He has a business of some sort, is obviously fairly well educated, and is clearly not one of the town's indigent.[5]

We talk easily together, he gracefully indulging my difficulties with the language, then he invites me to dinner with his wife, *Annette*. I accept. Six o'clock. We check our watches. He has a very nice watch, much nicer than my cheap Bulova, which miraculously still runs. Maybe I should have taken a watch from those German prisoners Sackett brought down from the mountain on the way to *Alençon*.

But dinner? How come all these French people have enough food to invite people for dinner? I thought they'd be having a hard time of it under the German occu-

[Notes for Chapter 20 start on p. 243]

pation. Out in the countryside I guess they had ways, and places, to hide things. And could catch, or keep, rabbits, and raise ducks and geese and poultry. Then I get an idea. We are far enough from the fighting, which has moved beyond us for the time being, to be getting hot chow, so I go through the line and take my serving of meat, which for a welcome change is sliced beef, not SPAM or S-O-S, but instead of eating it I put it in a waxed cardboard K-ration box, then go back for seconds.[6] I will take the meat as a gift for the *DeMuths,* a gift from the conquering *Américains* to one of France's deprived couples, living as they have been doing since the Germans first came, under the heel of the brutal *Nazi*.

When I arrive at the *DeMuth's* apartment with my gift I immediately wish I hadn't brought it. *Mon.* and *Mme. DeMuth* have a very nice apartment, and though very courteous about it, instead of adding my thin slices of meat to the meal we are about to eat, as I thought they might, he puts it in the refrigerator. The meat in the box looks like something for the cat. When we sit down to dinner it is a fine repast. Not lavish, not luxurious, but well prepared and presented, on nice dishes, with silver of a tasteful design, complete with a serving of meat, bread, potatoes, salad, some fruit, and a good wine. I don't know wines, but it tastes good to me.

I feel uncomfortably cloddish with my unclean clothes and GI boots. *Annette* is pretty and very charming. We have a fine time, she laughing at my mistakes with French, and flirting with me, at least enough to make me wonder what might happen if she weren't *Madame DeMuth*. As things progress I get better and better with the French. Or maybe I just think I am getting better because of the stimulation the circumstances and the wine provide.

I am not completely careless regarding the possible danger I might be in. My imagination is active, and I try to remember that it is to the advantage of these nice people to make friends quickly with *un Américain, un sergeant*, though they probably would rather have had *un lieutenant* instead.

As at the Frenchman's house back near *Reims* where they served me a rabbit dinner, I keep my M-1 rifle with me, and it is leaning against the wall behind me as I sit at the table. *René* had suggested that I could leave in the entrance hall, and had assured me that keeping it so close was unnecessary, and I agreed, of

[Notes for Chapter 20 start on p. 243]

course it was *pas nécessaire*, but you know about army regulations, *n'est-ce pas*? I could see that he felt a little hurt, maybe on behalf of *Annette*—having to look at an ugly weapon of death in her dining room—but we are fighting a war and there is no way of knowing what might happen in the next minute, or even the next second. Alf Green's death was a lesson I keep fresh in my mind. If a German combat column comes down the street I will need my rifle handy. The war is always close, even while having a private dinner with the *DeMuths*.

And I have taken another precaution. I asked Sackett to come to the *DeMuth's* apartment at seven o'clock to make sure that everything is OK. I tell my host and hostess that my assistant sergeant is coming up to meet them too, not saying when he is expected. Sackett does come, and I introduce him, and we sit around eating some *petit gateaux*—small cakes—and drinking some of the *DeMuth's* good wine. Sackett has no French to speak of, so I try to keep him in the conversation by translating back and forth, and we have a fine time.

René gives us both bracelets made, he says, of *ambre*, and I ask him if it's real amber, not expecting that it is, and it isn't, of course, because real amber is a clear fossilized tree gum, and is not at all plentiful, and not inexpensive. He wouldn't give us real amber even if he had any, and I don't think amber comes in chunks big enough to make one-piece bracelets out of. But surprisingly he says yes, the *ambre* is real, and then I have to diplomatically question his statement, and we have a polite argument until he says, no, I am right, rather yes, I am right, it is not really real *ambre*, not genuinely real, *pas vraiment*. He must have misunderstood me. He is a sales representative, he says, for the company that makes the bracelets.[7]

> I SENT THE BRACELET TO JEAN, TELLING HER THAT MON. DEMUTH HAD SAID IT WAS AMBER, ADDING A MAWKISHLY ROMANTIC THOUGHT: I WOULD BE "DRAWN BACK TO HER AS OBJECTS ARE DRAWN TO AMBER." IN HER ANSWERING LETTER SHE SAID IT WAS VERY SWEET OF ME TO SAY THAT. IN THE LIGHT OF MY LATER YEARS' CYNICISM, IT WAS CLOYINGLY SWEET. VERBAL TREACLE. BUT I'M GLAD I HAD THE OPPORTUNITY TO SAY THINGS LIKE THAT. HAVING A GIRLFRIEND BACK HOME WHILE YOU'RE FIGHTING A WAR IS AN IMPORTANT PART OF THE EXPERIENCE.

[Notes for Chapter 20 start on p. 243]

CHAPTER 20

We have more wine, and *René* says he has had military training and expresses interest in our M-1s. I can understand his interest. This is the first war the Garands have been used in, but they are already well known in military circles. We are standing now, and he says it looks heavy. How heavy is it? Under normal civilian circumstances you should always unload a gun before you hand it to somebody, but to unload it here would be as much as saying that I don't trust him. After enjoying his hospitality it would be an insult, and so with an alerting glance at Sackett, which I think he picks up, and with Sackett right there with his own M-1, I hand mine to *René*.

"*Caution!*" I say, giving the English word a French pronunciation, expecting that it means the same in French as it does in English. From *René's* perplexed look I can see that it doesn't. [IT MEANS "BAIL", THE KIND YOU POST TO GET OUT OF THE LOCKUP.] But in a moment he realizes my intent. "*Ah, précaution!*" But of course. At least I leave the safety on, though anybody with half a soldier's brain would figure out how the safety works in a second.

Immediately I feel I have made a mistake, letting my loaded rifle be finessed out of my hands like that. I have been living and sleeping with that rifle day-in-day-out for what seems like many months, and it has become a part of me. Even though it is now partially defective, operating only as a bolt-action weapon, I feel a bond of loyalty to it. For Alf Green's sake, to make his dying remembered, as a warning to the rest of us, I should be more careful.

The thought flicks through my mind that if the rifle is fired once, it won't fire a second time because of the defect, though a man who has had military training, which *René* says he has had, and who is used to bolt-action rifles, might instinctively work the bolt after firing a first shot and get another live round into the chamber without even understanding why it was necessary.

René hefts my M-1 and says it is too heavy for an Infantry rifle. Then he looks through the sights and says the rear peep sight is too awkward to use, and can't be used at night. Oh yeah? I say to myself, and reach out to take the rifle back. We're beating the Germans out of his country with this rifle, and I don't think it's too heavy, I think it's just fine. I may have thought it was too heavy once, but not

[Notes for Chapter 20 start on p. 243]

anymore. I like my M-1 just the way it is, peep-sight and all, though I've never used the peep-sight in combat, nor has anybody else that I know of. But I think this just to myself and don't make a big issue of it. *René* gives me back my M-1 without hesitation and when I have it in my own hands again I feel a lot better.

We have more wine, and *Annette* rejoins us after clearing the table, and we have some more wine again, *Moselle* wine they tell us, from the *Moselle* River Valley, which is just a few hills away. We had a glimpse of it from *Neufchef*. Then it is suddenly quite late.

"Why don't you stay here tonight," *René* offers, "We've got an extra mattress." He shows us to a store room with a twin-size mattress and box springs leaning against the wall, and in no time at all has them both on the floor, separately, with a blanket on each, and by golly, they look good, and I ask Sackett what he thinks, and he thinks it's all right, and after another glass of wine we're really floating high and we say we'd better hit the sack. We collapse—Sackett on the box springs, me on the mattress—room-spinning drunk. My last remembrance is *René* turning out the light and shutting the door as though he's putting a couple of children to bed.

We wake up very early in the morning, wondering where we are. We suddenly realize what we've done, and what might have happened to us, and grab for our rifles, but they are still right where we put them, still loaded, mine right under the blanket next to me, my faithful sleeping companion. We get up and I leave a note for *René* and *Annette*, thanking them for their hospitality and we sneak down the stairs as quietly as we can to the street level and get back to where we were expected to be sacked out, shamefaced but otherwise OK.

We stay in *Hayange* a couple more days and I am invited for a drink at the home of a dignified older man who seems to be a retired government official of some sort. *Oui*, he was in the government, he says, at the level of the *département*, years ago, between the wars. I ask if it's OK to bring my *lieutenant*, and he says of course, so I find Liebau and we go into the man's house, down a couple of steps into a sort of low-ceilinged study, and spend a couple of hours over some brandy which Liebau drinks slowly this time, and I am able to engage us all in a fairly philosophical discussion, about the war, and past wars, and international

[Notes for Chapter 20 start on p. 243]

politics, though it's lucky I can't speak better French because I would soon expose my ignorance and exhaust my ideas on these subjects.

Liebau can speak a little German; our host can speak both French and German. So the conversation is shared among us. With the low ceiling and dim light we look like three conspirators. The time and effort it takes to communicate any ideas other than the simplest ones makes the discussion seem much more thoughtful than it is. When we leave, Liebau seems impressed. "You know Wighty...," he says, "...you're a very smart guy." Well, it's about time.

The next day we get orders to pull back out the town—the same way we came in. The townspeople are visibly worried. We are leaving them open, they think, to the vengeance of the Germans, who, if they come back, will be told by their spies and *collaborateurs* which of the townspeople were particularly friendly with *les Américains*. They feel betrayed. They acted too soon with the American flags and their openheartedness. We tell them we don't think the Germans will be back, though we GIs don't really have any idea of what's going on in the bigger picture. Whether the other American battalions and regiments to the north and east of the town are leaving too we do not know. *René* and *Annette DeMuth* watch from their apartment window as we trudge off down the street, back the way we came. I give them a wave, and they wave back. Then we are gone. It is not our job to sort out the politics of *Hayange*.

No bridge to cross

We road-march for most of a day and go through a very small place called *Florange* and finally get an open view of the *Moselle* River. A little farther, at *Ukange* we are right on the river bank. Germans have been spotted directly across the river so we're told to keep out of sight. *Ukange* is strictly an industry town, and the factory buildings at the river's edge are dark and foreboding. The French countryside and its people were things we could comprehend. This industry, no doubt commandeered for the *Nazi* war effort, is something out of our ken, suggesting politics and power, things we aren't prepared to understand. But the products—whatever they are—aren't going to help the Germans anymore. The buildings are empty, like the town hall in *Hayange*, abandoned, spooky. I

[Notes for Chapter 20 start on p. 243]

crank up my alertness, watch carefully everywhere we go, look cautiously around every corner. But there is no resistance and not a soul to be seen.

> THIRD ARMY'S GAS SHORTAGE HAD GIVEN THE GERMANS TIME TO REGROUP. CROSSING THE *MOSELLE* WAS NOT TO BE EASY FOR US. 358TH REGIMENT GOT ORDERS TO TAKE *THIONVILLE*, A SIZEABLE INDUSTRIAL CITY SPLIT BY THE RIVER. THEY FOUGHT THEIR WAY INTO THE WESTERN HALF AND UP TO THE RIVER WITHOUT A LOT OF TROUBLE, BUT THE GERMANS BLEW THE LAST BRIDGE AND NO AMERICANS GOT ACROSS. XX CORPS' GENERAL WALKER ISSUED ORDERS FOR THE 90TH TO MAKE A NIGHT RIVER CROSSING, BUT AT THE LAST MINUTE THE PLAN WAS CALLED OFF.[8]

Notes for Chapter 20

1. Dozens of international agreements concerning the "proper" conduct of war have emanated from Geneva and the Hague. Keeping them up to date and sorting them out is somewhat problematical.

2. Battles are difficult to reconstruct. Sackett said he remembered that fight vividly. I remember it only as a lot of firing and confusion. We were told not to show ourselves over the top of the hill, and I was too busy digging my foxhole to look around, but years later Sackett said he did look over the crest of hill and saw the Germans getting pasted. He gave details—about our mortars, anti-tank guns and machineguns ripping into the Germans. I think he remembered what he read in Cole's *The Lorraine Campaign*.

   Major Hamilton was awarded a DSC for his actions at *Avril*. The citation is referenced at Web-link No. 11, Appendix C. It's not clear what it was for.

3. This was a division of ground troops made from *Göring's* command after Allied raids decimated the *Luftwaffe,* pounding German airfields and aircraft factories following the Battle of Britain.

[Notes for Chapter 20 start on p. 243]

4. Sgt. Barrett was new at the *St.-Germain* "Island" along with the other replacements. The action at *Mayenne* was his first combat experience. According to an account in Colby's *War From the Ground Up*, our Second Platoon balked when called on to cross the *Mayenne* bridge. My squad wasn't first in the platoon to go, so we didn't see what happened, but if our guys did hesitate, Barrett would have been involved. Add this to the incident at *Hayange*, and I wonder now if Barrett had a problem under fire. Assessing a man's combat competence is as much gut feeling as rational judgment. To me, Barrett always looked too clean to be a good combat soldier. But Sartori always looked clean, and he'd been OK in tight spots.

5. The name *Demuth*, for a German army cook, is found in Erich Maria Remarque's book, *The Road Back*, a sequel to *All Quiet on the Western Front*—evidence that *Lorraine* had a mixed German and French culture.

6. S-O-S is the universal acronym for a crude description of chipped beef in white sauce, served on toast. Hot, and with enough salt, it wasn't that bad.

7. Investigators are still looking for the legendary Amber Chamber, a complete room fashioned of amber that was a gift to the Russian royal family from Frederick of Prussia. The amber was supposedly taken during WW-II by the *Nazis*. A description of the room, written for the *Baltimore Sun,* and published also in the *Rochester Democrat and Chronicle,* November 19, 1995, did not give the dimensions of the largest pieces, but an article in *Mental Floss,* May, 2014, describing the American Museum of Natural History's amber collection, shows a piece about 2-1/2 by 3-1/2 inches.

8. Based on observed German activity on the east bank of the *Moselle*, the 90th's Commanding General, Leonard McLain, appealed to General Walker to rescind the order, and Walker did so. Colby, in *War From the Ground Up*, praises McLain for his courage in questioning his superior's orders. If McClain had followed orders, though, and secured a bridgehead across the *Moselle*, he would have been praised for his aggressiveness.

⊞

[Notes for Chapter 20 start on p. 243]

21

FÈVES RIDGE[1]

I, Platoon Sergeant [Foxholes 43, 44]

September 12

From *Ukange* we walk south, well back from the river so we won't be observed by the Germans on the opposite bank. We dig holes in the fields near *Homecourt* and Liebau stops by my foxhole to tell me that Sgt. Barrett and Sartori have been taken away from us to be MPs. Something in their records must have flagged them out as experienced in police work, or at least qualified for it.[2]

> AS WE GOT CLOSER TO THE GERMAN BORDER, MORE AND MORE OF THE RESIDENTS WERE UNSYMPATHETIC TO THE ALLIED CAUSE, AND A BEEFED-UP MILITARY POLICE PRESENCE WAS NEEDED TO HEAD OFF PROBLEMS WITH THE CIVILIAN POPULATIONS.
>
> ALSO, AS IT BECAME CLEAR THAT ALLIED VICTORY WAS INEVITABLE, MORE AND MORE AMERICAN GIS OPTED OUT OF THE FIGHTING BY DISAPPEARING INTO THE HINTERLAND OR THE BIGGER CITIES. PRIVATE EDDIE SLOVIK WAS SHOT BY A GI FIRING SQUAD FOR DESERTION, CLEARLY AS AN EXAMPLE TO DETER OTHERS. SEE ENTRY FOR *THE EXECUTION OF PRIVATE SLOVIK*, BY WILLIAM BRADFORD HUIE, IN THE *ANNOTATED BIBLIOGRAPHY*.

It's a good break for Sartori but it's a bad break for me. I will miss him, not only for his helpful attitude but for his coolness and competence in a pinch. He's not the bragging type like Lancaster—notorious for his night combat patrols [AT *PORTBAIL*], nor is he the professional soldier type like Seace, who takes a quiet pride in his military skills. But at *Avril* Sartori came through for us when he was badly needed, and that is the proof of the pudding. Just as we are learning how to be an effective combat squad we lose one of the three men I can count on. With more experience maybe some of the others will come around—if we all live long enough. And what will Browny do? Ever since the "Island" he's been Sartori's shadow.[3]

[Notes for Chapter 21 start on p. 265]

Sartori and Sergeant Barrett leave without even saying "So long." They're just not here anymore, the same way guys drop out of existence when they're hit. Liebau says he's putting me in for Platoon Sergeant to take Barrett's place. I don't know what a Platoon Sergeant's duties are. Nobody tells me and it doesn't occur to me to ask.

> I COULD HAVE ASKED SHAEFFER, THE PLATOON GUIDE. HE'D BEEN WITH THE COMPANY AS LONG AS I COULD REMEMBER. HE MIGHT HAVE WANTED THE JOB HIMSELF. BUT HE WAS A GOOD GUY DOING A CONSCIENTIOUS JOB. HE WOULD HAVE HELPED ME ANYHOW.

I'm pleased that Liebau thinks I'm qualified, and that Stevens, the Company Commander, now a Captain, must agree. I have never thought about being Platoon Sergeant, as I had never thought ahead of time of becoming a Squad Leader. Ever since I got to basic training at Ft. McClellan I've been trying to get an assignment where I can better realize what I think is my potential—just as a sort of duty to myself—but promotion up the military ladder has never been a conscious objective. Skills that I didn't know I had have come to me out of thin air, and a lot of things I've considered important aren't needed here at all.[4]

While I'm digging my hole in the soft dark soil in a field by a low hedge, Whitey Merrill comes by and says he thinks he should have been given the job as Platoon Sergeant. Merrill is Squad Leader of First Squad. He doesn't make a big thing of his beef, just squats down, states his feelings with a detectable hurt in his voice, then gets up and leaves.

I have nothing to say. It's the first clear instance I've seen in combat of anybody bucking for promotion, though Yensko at *Beau-Coudray* and the "Island" showed some signs of it.

Promotion in combat means more responsibility—and more risk.

I'm not sure that Whitey Merrill isn't a better man for the job. He's a couple of inches taller than I am, and seems to have more energy. And he might have been one of the already-experienced men when I came up on the line as a replacement. Maybe that's his beef, that he he's been with the platoon longer. The only

[Notes for Chapter 21 start on p. 265]

way I can see that his disappointment might affect me is if he isn't cooperative about following instructions.

And who will take my place as squad leader? Sackett? Considering his behavior at *Avril,* it would be a questionable choice.

> AT THIS JUNCTURE, THE 90TH HAD BECOME—IN GENERAL BRADLEY'S WORDS—"...ONE OF THE FINEST DIVISIONS...ON THE ALLIED FRONT".[5] AFTER *HAYANGE*, WE WERE ORDERED SOUTH TO RELIEVE THE 7TH ARMORED AND 5TH INFANTRY DIVISIONS, BOTH BATTERED AND WORN THIN FROM ATTACKING THE RING OF FORTS AROUND *METZ*. NO ONE HAD SUCCEEDED IN TAKING *METZ* BY DIRECT ASSAULT SINCE ATTILA THE HUN DID IT IN THE 5TH CENTURY.
>
> WHAT MADE THIS ATTEMPT ESPECIALLY DIFFICULT WAS THAT A GERMAN *SS* OFFICERS' TRAINING SCHOOL WAS LOCATED AT *METZ*, AND THE CADETS AND THEIR OFFICERS WERE PUT INTO THE FIGHT. THEY RELISHED THE ASSIGNMENT AND FOUGHT VIGOROUSLY.

September 15

We move out in the morning, south. As usual, we're not told where we're going, what we'll be expected to do, or what, or who, we'll be up against. We hike for an hour on a pretty good road, then turn into a side road that after a hundred yards splits into a road running east and another running west between two wooded ridges. There are no houses or buildings in sight. [MAP 12, P. 257]

At the Y in the road one of the guys spots a small metal object that seems to be protruding through the macadam surface and a half dozen of us form a circle around it, staring at it. I'm now the acting Platoon Sergeant, and I should be the one to decide what to do about it, if anything, but I find myself in decisional paralysis. I can't bring myself to the point of action.

The object could be the detonator for a mine, or it could be a metal fitting of some kind just lying on top of the road. If it's a mine it must have been buried there for quite a while because the macadam doesn't look disturbed. And the road isn't freshly paved.

[Notes for Chapter 21 start on p. 265]

A lot of traffic must have gone past on the road, so it's not likely to be a mine. But I can't move from thought to action—either to decide to leave it alone because of the possible danger, try to detonate it from a distance, or inspect it more closely to see what it is:

> A wrench tugging at a nut stuck
> with rust or grit, tight on its bolt, trying
> to loosen, questioning the act,
> questioning the hesitation, hesitating to
> question. The great torrent of
> Niagara once over the dolomite ledge continues to fall and will
> not be stopped by questioning. The rocks will shatter; I
> cannot stop the unstoppable. But I can
> stop the what-might-happen here. I
> can do, and say. Or can say: "Do
> nothing." Or: "Pick it up. Examine. Try its
> purpose." And then the
> Niagara will be upon us,
> mortar-pestling several of us with its dolomitic rush. Do, do
> something, speak, do, act. But
> I am halfway down Niagara's plunge, suspended unable to will my
> will to will. My life, my fate, our fate, stuck like a still-twitching
> butterfly on a pin. Or, to be Shakespeare (adding metaphor
> on top of metaphor): hung in frozen Niagara in full-midst plunge.
> But poetics do not occur to me.
> I stand, stare…

While my indecision hangs balanced, one of the guys from the platoon, not from my old squad, steps forward and kicks it away harmlessly into the ditch. I turn away without comment, as though that's what I expected, but the incident bothers me. In this small event my decisiveness, reliable up to now, reveals its fragile foundation. Just when I have been given greater responsibility, something has gone out of me. I feel very tired.

⊞

[Notes for Chapter 21 start on p. 265]

A half hour later we start moving up the ridge along the left branch of the road. Sankey has been sent ahead as scout. The slope is covered with trees, like a typical second growth of hardwoods back home in New York State. The largest are about a foot through. We get a hundred yards up the slope when a machine-gun up ahead lets go at us and drives us all to the ground hugging for cover. The hill is convex upward just enough to afford some protection if we stay very low, and the bullets come popping angrily over our heads, then after a couple of bursts, quit. The bursts aren't long and sustained the way they were at *Avril*. This German probably has a machine pistol rather than an MG-42, but it doesn't have the typical sound of a burp-gun. A burp-gun trails off in pitch at the end of each burst. He probably fired as soon as he saw the heads and shoulders of the first men coming up the hill. Where Sankey is we can't see. Another twenty seconds and we wouldn't have been able to get down below the up-swell of the hill. I'm with Liebau; my old squad is down flat on the floor of the woods just ahead of me, and Gervase is behind the trunk of a tree fiddling with his wrist again.

"Did Gervase get hit?" Liebau says.

"He gets hit a lot," I say. Liebau gives me a quick look but I don't say anything more, just let the thought hang.

An error in angles

Captain Stevens is near us over to our left a few yards and Liebau crawls over to him, then crawls back and starts calling in some mortar fire with his walkie-talkie to try to root out the machine-gunner. I'm right next to Liebau, and the first mortar round falls up the slope ahead of us but it is too close to us to be safe. Liebau calls in a correction, to lower the mortar's elevation. That doesn't seem right to me. It seems like lowering the barrel of the mortar will make the shells land even closer to us, and I voice my question without thinking: "Lower?"

Liebau stops a second, glances at me, thinks another second, then repeats the correction exactly as he had given it before but with a slight edge on his voice— the edge not for the mortar guy listening, but for me. Liebau doesn't say anything but I know I have spoken out of turn. If I'm right, that's one thing, but if I'm wrong it's just an irritating distraction. Liebau doesn't need distractions.

[Notes for Chapter 21 start on p. 265]

There is another *tunk* back of us from our mortars, and a few seconds later a bang up the slope that's farther away from us than the first one was. Liebau doesn't voice his irritation, doesn't tell me to shut up if I don't know what I'm talking about, but I am chagrined and subdued. My indecisiveness with the piece of metal on the road, and my mistake with the mortar settings, leave me with feelings that are not reassuring.[6]

After three mortar rounds for effect,[7] we start up the slope again. Whether the gunner was hit, or simply driven back we don't know, but the machinegun doesn't fire again. Liebau tells me to take my old squad straight up the slope while he takes the other two squads up to the right. When we get near the top of the wooded slope, a swath of daylight opens up and we see that there is a railroad going across our front. Ten yards short of the railroad we find the German's machinegun position. Branches, still fresh, had been bunched together into a sort of crude duck blind, and the ground cover is crushed from the German's lying down crosswise on the slope as he watched for us, and then fired. It's always eerie seeing where the enemy has been just moments before, somebody who was, and may again be, trying to shoot bullets into us. But we don't find the machine-gunner lying wounded, or his body, or his machinegun, and so far we haven't found Sankey.

Liebau will try to cross the railroad on the right; my old squad and I will try to cross it straight ahead. A low bank runs along the railroad, probably formed from earth removed from the bed itself, and bushes have grown up on top of the bank. Behind the bank we're protected, but to cross the railroad we have to go out in the open. I find a path that goes through the bushes and up over the bank. On the other side of the railroad the woods continue the same as on our side. Pausing behind the screen of bushes I hear a small metallic sound from across the railroad, like the bolt of a weapon being opened and closed. I think of Sankey. He's up here somewhere, maybe where the sound is coming from. I decide we've got to go across to keep up with the others on our right, and motion to the other guys to follow me. Browny is next behind me. I go through the path, up over the bank and into the bright daylight. The railroad is a single track and I pause in the very center of the tracks, looking and listening for any sign of what may be ahead.

[Notes for Chapter 21 start on p. 265]

My senses and instincts are at their quickest edge, bristling on the outside of me like a second skin; I am honed and poised, coiled, cocked like a piece of hard metal, completely given over to whatever clues I can pick up. I have been here for a second, or maybe two seconds—it is hard to measure time at moments like this—standing broad-open in the sunlight, taking in the surroundings and the look of the things ahead of me, tuned to the peripheral mode with every intuition at full scale, when I am hit by a very loud, very close, very powerful string of metallic sound ripping past my left ear so close the force of the air-splitting seems to impact on my head. But I am unhurt and without hesitancy of any kind I leap forward down the built-up bed of the railroad to the other side where there is a large steel vertical I-beam that supports the wires strung along the railroad. The hollow of the "I" is facing me, and I fit myself into it as deeply as I can.[8] It is not complete protection, but it is protection for part of me, and I crouch there perfectly still and quiet. I hear another small metallic sound in the bushes, and again I think of Sankey. The sound might be within range of a grenade, but the bushes and trees make it unlikely that a grenade would get through. It would hit a branch and drop short. And, the sound could be Sankey.

I wait absolutely quiet for probably five full minutes and then I hear a barely vocalized whisper from the other side of the railroad back where I came from:

"Wighty?"

It's Shaeffer, I can tell from his voice, but he is not visible.

"Yeah," I answer, also in a loud whisper.

"Are you all right?"

"Yeah."

"Browny got it," Shaeffer says. I cannot see Browny. He was next behind me and must have been hit when he came through the path. Was the string of bullets that went past my head meant for Browny? Or were they meant for me?

[Notes for Chapter 21 start on p. 265]

Shaeffer finds Browny at the railroad track on *Fèves* Ridge.

[Notes for Chapter 21 start on p. 265]

I BROKE AN INFANTRY FUNDAMENTAL BY GOING OUT THROUGH THE EXISTING PATH, BUT MAKING A FRESH OPENING IN THE BUSHES WOULD HAVE ALERTED AN ENEMY TO MY POSITION AND INTENTIONS. WHAT'S BEST TO DO IN EACH CASE IS A TOSS-UP.

ANOTHER QUESTION: DID THE GERMAN LET ME THROUGH INTENTIONALLY, PLANNING TO FIRE ON THOSE BEHIND ME? IF HE DIDN'T GET A SECOND CHANCE AT ME WHEN I TRIED TO RUN BACK, AT LEAST HE'D HAVE ME ISOLATED AND AT A DISADVANTAGE.

I hear Shaeffer going back to the right, and see Liebau and the other guys going across the railroad, and after five minutes, hearing nothing in my immediate surroundings, I slip out from the protection of the I-beam and move cautiously through the trees on my side of the railroad. It's like hunting in the woods at home, looking for a Ruffed Grouse before it bursts without warning into the air, or trying to see the fox cubs playing outside their den on the bank above the creek on my father's old-farm property before they, or their sly mother, see me.

I'm looking for both Sankey and the German machine-gunner, but I find neither. I do find where the German machine-gunner was when he let go that single shattering rip of bullets that went past my ear, and I find the weapon he was using: it's a GI M-3 "grease-gun", our stamped-metal counterpart of the German burp-gun, cast aside on the ground, empty of bullets, or jammed. I don't want to be burdened by carrying it, in case I have to use my M-1 quickly, but I know where it is and I leave it and continue moving very cautiously through the woods. Here there is no path for an enemy to be watching, so if there is someone there, we are on equal terms, except that, moving, I will be making some noise, but I encounter no one and after forty yards come to the upper edge of the woods. There's a shaley cliff about head high that I'll have to climb to go any further. Instead, I go right, and after a hundred yards find the rest of the platoon. Shaeffer has told Liebau about Browny. Liebau says in a loud voice:

"Goddammit, we gotta kill more of those bastards," his voice rising to the point of anger. I still don't know quite know what to make of his anger. Maybe it's his way of showing that he isn't unfeeling about Browny getting killed.

[Notes for Chapter 21 start on p. 265]

> THAT BROWNY WAS KILLED BY AN AMERICAN WEAPON IN GERMAN HANDS WAS A STRANGE CONFLUENCE OF EVENTS—REMEMBERING THAT BACK AT *STE.-SUZANNE* IT WAS BROWNY WHO SAID HE HAD ACCIDENTALLY SHOT THE GI ON THE TOWER.[9]

When Browny got hit, Sackett and the rest of the guys took off to the right to join the rest of the platoon. Shaeffer must have heard about Browny from them, and come back looking for me. Sankey was found crouching in the bushes on the same side of the tracks as the I-beam but farther to my right. He is OK. He says he heard the metallic noises too. When he first heard the noises he could have tossed a grenade without danger of hitting any of us, but it would have been a longer toss than from where I was at the I-beam. If he'd thrown it later it might have gotten me.

We climb the shaley bank and move across an open field dotted with a few small trees, and get up to another line of woods, and go fifty or so yards into the woods and see another open field like the first one on the other side with the ground sloping upward, but convex upward so we can't see what is farther up the hill. We stop there, then as the afternoon light shows signs of dimming, we get the word to fall back to the woods behind the shaley bank on the up-hill side of the railroad tracks. Someone has decided this will be a better place to spend the night. Maybe we have outrun the other companies on our flanks again.

We go back, post guards, one-on-two off, to keep watch over the bank and on the flanks, and dig in for the night. We can't dig deep. We hit shale after eight inches.

Before it gets really dark, I go back to where the German machine-gunner was, look out across the railroad the way he would have looked out, and I can see the path, but can't tell if he could have seen me when I was standing in the middle of the tracks. What I think happened was that at the moment I came through the path he was working on the grease-gun, not being thoroughly familiar with it, and that he didn't see me come out, or maybe just caught a glimpse of me, but wasn't ready to fire. Then I moved out of his view, to his left, blocked by the tall bushes on his side of the railroad. When Browny followed me out, the German was ready.

[Notes for Chapter 21 start on p. 265]

I cross back over the railroad track and step into the path. Browny is fallen forward in the path. I lift up the front of his helmet and there is a blue bullet hole in the center of his forehead. His rifle is still in his hands and I work it loose and take it from his fingers. Without Sartori to buddy up with, Browny turned to me. He was right behind me. I don't sense much feeling, I don't know what to feel, or how to express it, or whom to express it to. There isn't anybody here except Browny, and me, and he is completely quiet, completely still, completely dead. He can't hear me if I say anything or not. Saying nothing is as good as saying something, so that's what I do.

> He kept himself clean, I don't
> know how, when it was so easy
> to be dirty. He needed
> someone to follow. First it was
> Sartori; then Sartori got taken by
> the MPs (as one of their own); then
> for a while there was nobody; then
> when I stepped through the path
> out onto the railroad tracks at
> Fèves Ridge, it was me.
> A taut chain of steely lead laced through
> the space between my left ear and
> everything else in the world, closer to
> me than to anything else in the world
> as it passed, but not quite close
> enough to *be* me, to unite with me, and the
> chattering (though terribly-tight) metal stream
> glistened with
> fricative sound as it chased the
> air with its brilliant design of wanting, and
> seeking to install its special kind of
> deadness, missed finding a suitable
> place in me by the merest fractive of a
> second, or inch, or since we were in

[Notes for Chapter 21 start on p. 265]

France, centimètre. It wasn't until
later that I found that the steel-bright-
chain-of-ferocity had found the place it
sought, in another, in mine's stead.
Even as it lay in the path it looked
clean—the bullet went only into its forehead; the rest of it was still
neat, except that it had fallen forward and
crumpled itself upon itself, not even throwing
out an arm to catch itself because it didn't
know it was falling. What had been Browny's
rifle was clean too. In better working
order than my own I knew, so I took it and
left what was left, there in the path to the
railroad tracks on *Fèves* Ridge, in
France, in the September of
1944.

I take Browny's rifle, and my own rifle, and the grease-gun, and loaded down with all three—but trying to be ready for action if I need to be—I go back to the platoon. Liebau says he'll keep the grease-gun to carry, but reconsiders, and tells Shaeffer to turn it over to the weapons guys along with my defective M-1. I'm pretty sure Browny's rifle is OK. Maybe I didn't clean mine often enough. A lot of guys don't clean their rifles in combat. Other things seem more important—satisfying bodily urgencies, getting rations, staying dry, staying out of sight of the enemy, and being ready for the next move. I hadn't field-stripped my rifle since we had showers near *Sées*. The gas port is probably plugged.

It starts to drizzle and gets very dark. We huddle under our raincoats In our shallow foxholes and try to sleep.

Attack at *Kellermann* Works

In the morning we climb the shaley ridge and get back to where we were yesterday. We get to where we can see out over the open field on the other side of the upper wooded place. I get the guys spread out just inside the edge of the woods where Liebau said to put them, and some of them try to dig in but the soil is only a thin layer on top of rock. We aren't in a very good spot, but we're supposed to stay here and watch out front in case the Germans come at us across the field and try to drive us off the hill. Instead, they use mortars. They can't be very far, probably just beyond our line of sight over the upward curve of the hill. We can hear the *tunk* of the mortars when they fire.[10] At first the mortar rounds don't land close, and everybody seems to be OK. I go looking for Liebau and he's with Stevens in the company CP in a scooped out place on the hillside where it looks as though somebody once had excavated some stone or gravel.

> HUGH COLE, IN HIS BOOK, *THE LORRAINE CAMPAIGN*, SAYS WE WERE IN AN OLD QUARRY JUST BELOW THE *KELLERMANN* WORKS, ONE OF THE FORTS IN THE NORTHWEST SECTOR OF *METZ'S* RING OF DEFENSES.

Liebau and Stevens are in the only place that has any protection from the mortars, and I hang around for a few minutes, but Liebau says that I have to go back where I can check on the guys. There's a slight edge on his voice. He could just say it, and I'd do it, so I grouse a little to myself. I crouch along the line, not saying much. I have no idea what the plan is. One of our men has a .30-cal. machinegun at the right hand end of the platoon, aimed out across the open field.

I go back a few yards and lie on the ground where I can watch the guys up at the edge of the woods. More mortars come in and one lands right in our company area, and a guy is hit. Everybody can hear him: "Medic! Medic!" Somebody calls for a litter and after about fifteen minutes they come up and take the hit guy back.

Then another guy is hit. There is no protection from the mortars. The Germans have our range, and if anybody on their side climbs a tree they can probably see our guys lying just inside the edge of the woods because there are no bushes to hide behind. Some of our artillery goes over but it hits a good ways up the hill from where we are. Something bigger than our fight is going on, but we don't know what it is. We just have to lie here on top of the ground waiting for the next mortar shell to come down and explode among us.

[Notes for Chapter 21 start on p. 265]

Page 258 CHAPTER 21

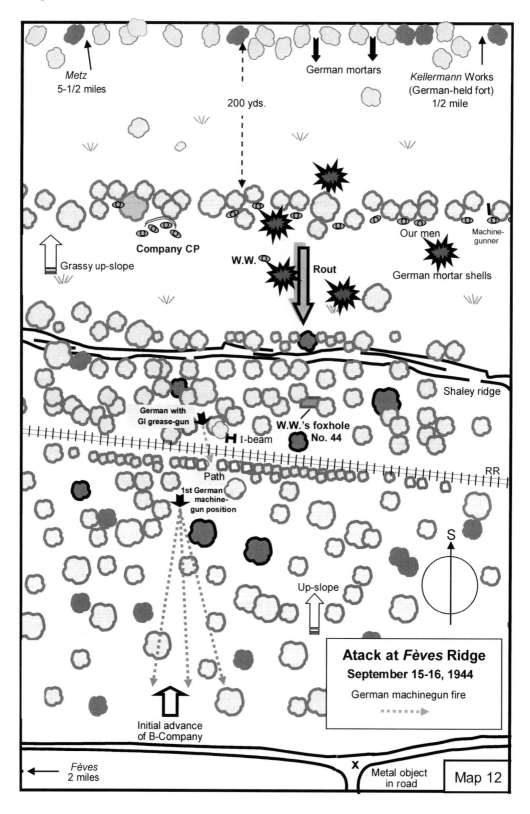

Rout

One of my old squad guys, Fullard, is up ahead of me a few yards and right after a mortar shell hits and goes off he turns around and says loud enough for some of the other guys to hear:

"Wighty, we gotta get off this damn hill before we all get killed!"

Fullard is the oldest man in the platoon, forty at least, and he has a mature heavy voice, and he is saying exactly what we all feel. What makes his words more effective is that Fullard hardly ever says anything at all.

Some more mortars fall among us, and suddenly up ahead a voice I don't recognize shouts, very loud: "Let's get outta here!" and then somebody is running back in my direction, and then all the rest of the guys are running back, past me, abandoning their positions without orders or permission, and some of them don't even have their weapons.

I lie on the ground a couple of minutes, not knowing what to do, then Liebau crouches over to me and says:

"Wighty, you gotta go and get those guys back up here!"

I have no idea how to accomplish what Liebau is asking me to do. But I get up, give Liebau a look, then start back through the wooded place, and come out into the open field we first went through on the way up the hill. I have been in a crouch, but here I stand up straighter, and keep walking back farther looking for the guys. I don't have a plan. I don't know how far back they ran. I keep going and then just above the shaley bank I see some of the guys, lying prone, only their heads and helmets showing, watching up the slope, watching me. I stand there for a few seconds, then without really knowing what I'm going to do, I say:

"We gotta go back up there." I recognize one of the guys, Russell. I single him out by name, and say as quietly and as calmly as I can and still be heard, "Come up behind this clump here," and I point to a clump of growth on a slight bump in the ground that affords a little cover, and, spoken to directly like that, there isn't much he can do but come, or not come. He decides to come. He comes up to the clump

[Notes for Chapter 21 start on p. 265]

in a deep crouch and gets down prone again, and then I point to the next guy, and he's another guy I can call by name, and I indicate exactly where he should go, and he gets up and comes up, and one by one I get them coming back up the hill.

Somehow I found the right thing to say and the right thing to do and they are coming back up. I am walking erect as though there is nothing to worry about, as though I am walking down the company street in basic training in Alabama on the way to the rec room for a game of pool. It is the old truth, discovered all over again: you cannot lead men in battle from a prone position. You have to get up on your feet as proof that it's safe to move, even if it isn't. You have to show them that you are not getting hit, and that you are confident and not scared shitless, and this is how, and why, so many officers and non-coms get killed in combat, because in the final shakeout, there's no other way to get guys to move up when they're getting shot at.[11] If the men don't come there's not much else you can do. I'm certainly not going to yell and curse and threaten them with a weapon the way officers are said to have done in WW-I and the Civil war [AND IN THIS WAR, TOO, IN OUR SISTER REGIMENT, 358, AT THE *SÈVES* RIVER "ISLAND"[12]].

Why am I even trying? Because I am imbedded in the great machine of war and acceptable alternatives are not available. Liebau said to get the guys back up on line, and I have to try to do it. I'm in the same position the guys are in, doing what I'm told. I'm just one notch up the ladder. The pressure is greater on me than it is on them. More is expected of me, as more is expected from Liebau than from me.

Once the guys get moving I get them leapfrogging themselves up the hill and then we're all moving and we get back to the wooded place and back up to the positions they were in before the rout. I was lucky. They'd had a few minutes to think about what they had done, and they were waiting for somebody to tell them what to do. Maybe they actually thought somebody in authority had given the order to go back. They didn't want to be guys who "ran back". Sure, they wanted to get away from the mortars, but they didn't want to be men who deserted their posts in the face of enemy fire. They still had the personal pride and dignity instilled in them since kindergarten, Sunday school and from the Army's ritual reading of the Articles of War, and all the other stuff at basic training and everything in the Army afterward. Inside they wanted to be able to do the right

[Notes for Chapter 21 start on p. 265]

thing, and they were ready for me to come back and tell them to do it, to rescue them from their predicament. I was lucky that I instinctively hit on maybe the only way to do it. And even luckier that no mortars shells came down on us while we were moving back up.[13]

> Each to himself, obeying the,
> pulled by the, strings of millennialized
> survival-trope: yanked, thrust, para-
> lyzed, out of thought's realm.
> Now the blood-
> rush quieted, now swirling in a
> stiller lagoon of doubt, each
> wishing to surmount his
> basal urge, to
> claim membership in a
> higher order of humanity—but
> doubting, too, now, humanity itself. "I am
> humanity," I must say. "Believe on
> me." I must say it, convey it, whether
> I believe, or not, myself, it...

But the mortar shells do start coming again. I am lying about where I was before, where I can see the guys up along the edge of the woods. I'm in as dangerous a place as anybody, because the mortar shells can land anywhere. I hear a *tunk*, then a second one, and then there is a wait of a few seconds as the shells arch overhead before plummeting down to earth. Just before the first one hits it makes a high-pitched hiss, a whine. You hear the hiss of a falling mortar shell only a half-second before it hits. When you can hear the hiss you know the shell is going to land close. I flatten myself on the ground and the first mortar shell hits about forty feet back of me and to the right, and sprays dirt on me but I am not hit, and then the second shell hiss-whines and hits twenty feet closer and I am hit on the thigh and the back and the buttocks. There is no sharp pain, just the sensation of being struck hard by something, the biggest one on the back of my right thigh, as though someone hit me with an axe-handle a hard sharp blow. After that there aren't any *tunks* for a while, and I get up half-way and try to assess the damage.

[Notes for Chapter 21 start on p. 265]

I can't see the back of my thigh but I pull my pant leg around so I can see the hole where a chunk went through the cloth. Not much blood, at least not yet. I can't see where the other pieces hit but I can feel them stinging. I can't be sure that they actually went into my back and buttocks or just sprayed me. On my thigh under my pants I can feel a swelling where the wound is, where a mortar shell fragment apparently buried itself in my leg, but I don't want to touch the wound with my fingers. I find I can still work my leg, and I can stand on it, at least so far.

I've been hit by a mortar shell but I don't know what to do about it. Am I a casualty now, a wounded soldier? I decide to tell Liebau, and I go over to the CP dugout where he is, and I see Shaeffer and tell him I was hit by a mortar, and he says to Liebau, "Wighty's hit," and Liebau wants to see where, and I show him the hole in my pants. Liebau doesn't want to lose his new Platoon Sergeant, I can understand that. At first he doesn't say anything. He doesn't know what to do either. He can't tell just by looking if it's bad enough for me to go back to the aid station. I seem to be walking on it OK. I stay there on the edge of the CP, and Stevens is talking on the phone to somebody—they've strung wires up to the company CP—and Liebau is listening to Stevens's end of the conversation, and it's obvious that there are things going on more important than one man getting hit with a mortar fragment. I go back where I was when I got hit, go down prone, and continue wondering what I should do. If it was an open bloody wound that everybody could see, the decision would be a lot easier.

Ten minutes later my leg starts to ache and I try to stand on it and it has started to get stiff. I can still get around on it, but it might keep getting worse. What will we be doing later in the afternoon? Another advance up the hill? Will I be able to function efficiently enough to do my job?

In everything before I have needed to be at my top effectiveness, just to do what I have been able to do. I go back to Liebau and I tell him my leg is getting stiff, and he shows a trace of annoyance, and I don't blame him. It's obvious that he doesn't want to do it, but he finally tells me to go back to the battalion aid station. Shaeffer tells me where he thinks the aid station is and I tell him I'll probably be back in a couple of hours and start back down the hill. I've gone only a hundred yards when a feeling of release hits me, like when I was tooling around alone in

[Notes for Chapter 21 start on p. 265]

the sports car at night with the bedrolls, and when I took the wounded guy back to the aid station at *Beau Coudray*. At least for a while the cables are cut, the ropes that tied me—like a mountain-climber—to the guys and the Army and the war.

I can still walk, but the leg is definitely getting stiffer and numb and I can't keep from limping. If I hang around, we might attack again and how can I do my job with a bum leg? Maybe I owe it to everybody to get out of their way, so they won't have to think about me, the way we have always put the dead and the wounded out of our minds as soon as they became dead or wounded.

Let the medics decide if I'm OK to go back up. Maybe the mortar fragment didn't actually go into my leg. They'll probably patch me up with a bandage and I'll be back up with the guys before nightfall. I'm already wondering how I'll find them, and what will have happened to them in the meantime, and who might have taken over my responsibilities.

I keep going back down the slope where we came up, and manage to slide down the shaley ridge on my left side without scraping my bad leg. Then German artillery starts coming in, over to the right of where our guys are, where C-Company is, or A-Company. They must be doing something the Germans are worried about and feel they need artillery for. It's big stuff. The shells land in the tall trees and some of them go off in the trees, and it's the loudest artillery I have ever heard. Maybe it's from the big guns at the forts we've heard rumors about. If the shells were landing anywhere near me I'd have to find a place to get down into, maybe even try to scrape out a hole, because it is hard angry stuff coming at us and going off like exploding cement mixers. But it isn't close enough to hit me, so I keep going and I come to the road, and follow it back and turn off where the piece of metal was sitting on the macadam, and a couple of hundred yards farther on I find the aid station.

I hobble up to the aid tent and go in and tell them what happened and they tell me to pull down my pants and shorts so they can see what the damage is. This time it isn't for a short arm inspection. They can see right away that it's not a terribly serious wound. Blood isn't spurting out of an artery, or the end of a bone sticking out. So everybody stays pretty relaxed. And there aren't any other guys there with

[Notes for Chapter 21 start on p. 265]

bad wounds, moaning or dying, but from the sound of that German artillery on my way down off the ridge there soon will be guys being carried in hurt really bad. I lie on my stomach on a cot and a medic pushes on the place where the biggest piece hit, and there's now a pretty good sized raised welt, and he scratches around on my buttocks and back, and picks out a couple of small pieces of metal and shows them to me, and swabs the skin with merthiolate. Then he says:

"You've got a penetrating wound in the thigh muscle. The shell fragment tore through the *fascia*, the muscle sheath. Might have nicked the bone. Probably cut some nerves. They'll have to dig it out and sew you back up at a field hospital."

They give me a cup of hot coffee and then put me on a litter and strap it onto a Jeep alongside a guy with a bandage around his head. The driver gives the medics a wave and heads back down the road.

> The grip of the claw on my
> throat, tautening, tightening: *You:*
> *must account for yourself. You:*
> *must be what those who know you, and*
> *of you, who begat you, expect of you, expect you*
> *to be, and to do. You: must show strong*
> *mettle. You: must*
> *represent us well.*
> You have been, and have
> done, all of this. Now
> the talons withdraw with only small blood. With
> every bump and Jeep-jolt the
> grip loosens.

Abruptly I am out of the fighting.

⊞

[Notes for Chapter 21 start on p. 265]

Notes for Chapter 21

1. The name, *Fèves* Ridge, for the hill where we started our attack, is of my own creation. An aerial photo shows the tiny village of *Fèves* down the road to the east, a mile or two from the Y in the road where we turned off to go up the hill. *Fèves* Ridge seemed a good name for the hill, but I haven't seen it identified that way on any maps.

2. Storing and retrieving personnel data in WW-II was crude. A serviceman's record was kept on an IBM card, approximately 12 X 14 inches, with small holes punched along all four edges, each hole representing an item of information. To enter data, a triangular punch was used to cut away selected holes to form open notches. The cards were kept in filing cabinets in stacks precisely aligned so that all the holes matched. To find a person with a certain combination of characteristics or qualifications, long rods like knitting needles were inserted by hand into the holes representing the qualifications sought. When the rods were lifted out of the stack, the men you were *not* looking for came out with the rods; the ones you wanted were the ones that were left.

3. There is no safe generalization to be made regarding a soldier's progress toward being effective in combat. Writers with a penchant for armchair wisdom—like Hastings, Keegan, and Ambrose—may even emphasize opposite aspects of the problem. Whereas one will tell, and document with facts and anecdotes, how green troops are initially terrified until they learn the basic facts—like the difference between incoming and outgoing artillery shells—others will say that green troops have an advantage, and may actually be bolder, because they don't realize how bad things can really get.

   For me, all such broad statements are bound to be flawed. Too much depends on the individual, on the leaders, on the interplay between them, and, of course, on the actual circumstances of the fighting.

[Notes for Chapter 21 start on p. 265]

Only one generalization rings true for me, and it should be obvious, that regardless of how he starts out—bold, or scared out of his wits—a combat soldier's chances of becoming a casualty, physical or psychological, increase as the length of his exposure increases. The logic of statistics is inescapable. True, a man can become more effective as he gains experience, but he can also become less effective as the rigors of combat accumulate. (See also Addenda, Item No. 1.)

4. I have commented previously about my being picked quite often for leadership positions in pre-army days—for responsibilities I was not qualified for. A high-school friend once said, with near scorn: "You don't even know *Robert's Rules of Order!*" He was right. I didn't know what to do in the positions I got elected to. I didn't even know how to conduct a meeting.

My ineptitude must have been pretty obvious but it didn't seem to make much difference—I kept getting appointed and elected anyhow. And there always seemed to be somebody around who was glad to help me—without trying to get the job away from me or show me up. It even happened in combat, as at *Mayenne.* I owe such people a lot.

5. Quoted from *Preparing the Army for Modern War*, by Henry Gole, Chaper 3. Only a few weeks later during the German offensive in the *Ardennes*, Eisenhower said he wished he had a few more divisions like the 1st, 9th, and the 90th. (*Eisenhower at War 1943-1945,* p. 637, by David Eisenhower). If Ike hadn't also included the 9th on his short list I'd be tempted to think he had made a mistake—confusing the 90th with the 9th.

6. It took me more time than it should have to realize why Liebau was right. Mortars are always fired at angles at or greater than 45° with the ground because the hand-loaded mortar shell must slide down the tube and fall by gravity to the bottom where it strikes the firing pin which ignites the propellant in the base of the shell. At angles less than 45°, the shell might not slide to the bottom with enough force to set it off. A shell stuck in a mortar tube is extremely dangerous. With a mortar's standard-issue bi-pod on level ground, it's probably impossible to set the tube at less than 45°. See photo, p. 44.

[Notes for Chapter 21 start on p. 265]

45° is the theoretical angle for maximum distance with any ballistic projectile. Increasing the angle greater than 45° brings the point of impact closer to the weapon's own position; lowering the angle of the tube—assuming it's not already at 45°—moves the point of impact farther away. For me to have been right, the mortar tube for the first round would have had to be already at 45°. If that had been the case, the mortar guy would have told Liebau that he was already firing at maximum range.

Things are the opposite with a howitzer, which can be aimed at angles of less than 45° because the ignition of the propellant is not dependent on gravity. Lowering the muzzle of a howitzer causes the shell to land closer to the howitzer's own position. At Fort McClellan I questioned the cadre lieutenant's judgment about the deflection needed for the mortar and I was right. At *Fèves* Ridge, with lives at stake, I was wrong—which speaks to the problem of getting adequate training. We should have had more.

7. The phrase "Fire for effect" is confusing. In military jargon it means the opposite from what it might seem to mean in everyday language, viz., just for effect. After bracketing a target for range—short and long—or creeping up to it, or back to it, and after doing the same for azimuth—right and left—shells are then fired "for effect," which means they are fired *to get the desired effect*, viz., to knock out the target.

8. Looking back on it, my actions, taken unhesitatingly, to move ahead rather than back, and to go to the only cover available, remind me of an incident with a pet snake that illustrates how animals sometimes act like pre-programmed computers, picking the best thing to do for their survival with very little time spent pondering the alternatives. Animals seem to have the ability to short-cut the reasoning process—which for them is limited anyhow—an ability which in some circumstances we humans seem to share.

Here's the story: When I was a kid I kept a small Red-bellied Snake in a terrarium until I became convinced he would not eat in captivity. I got him to go into a small glass jar, capped it, then put the open jar on its side on the ground in my back yard. In less than two seconds his head was out of the jar, tongue flicking, and in another second he spotted the only cover available, a very small pile of leaves six feet away. Without hesitation he slid out of the jar, made for the leaves and disappeared. When I looked for him a minute later, just to see how he was doing, he was gone—where, I never discovered.

Snakes have very small brains, but what brains they do have work very well for their purposes. Corresponding behavior in a human, like my actions on the railroad track, is probably controlled by the brain-stem, our own remnant of the reptilian brain.

9. It occurred to me years later that Browny might not have shot that GI after all. If the brass knew that he said he did, there might have been an investigation and he might have been taken out of the line pending some sort of resolution—maybe re-assignment, or even transfer out of the Infantry. If it was a dodge, my silence may have nixed it. (As far as I know, the term *friendly fire* wasn't used in WW-II.)

10. After experiencing enemy mortar fire in combat, I wondered why we didn't have triangulating range finders to locate enemy mortars. The technology was available and they wouldn't have been very expensive. Some such equipment was used by the British in the ETO in WW-II, and by the U.S. Army on Okinawa and in the Korean War, but we never heard about it.

Police in Rochester, NY are now using *ShotSpotters* to locate gunfire on the streets. Something similar, for mortars, would have been a great help to the Infantry in WW-II, and could have made a crucial difference in many situations, but as with flak jackets, the Infantry got last dibs.

11. The many accounts of the initial assaults on Omaha Beach bear this out, especially the one about General Cota walking around upright urging the men to move forward. But if the man who gets up gets hit, the attack is stalled worse than before.

12. Reported in Walter Brown's *Up Front With U.S. Day by Day in the Life of a Combat Infantryman in General Patton's Third Army,* and in Colby's *War*

[Notes for Chapter 21 start on p. 265]

From the Ground Up. (See ANNOTATED BIBLIOGRAPHY). S.L.A. Marshall also tells of several routs in *Men Against Fire* where non-coms or officers threatened to shoot men who were running back. And in Colby (cited above), a battalion medical officer at *Beau-Coudray* says he heard Col. Barth, Regimental Commander of 357, tell his officers to shoot any "cowards" who ran back. I doubt this story. It doesn't jibe with what I have read elsewhere about Barth. Also, some other things the same medical officer is quoted as saying make me suspect his facts.

13. Nothing was ever said in basic training about routs, or how to deal with them. Officer candidates In OCS may have been told what to do, or what to try to do, but none of us trainees even heard the word "rout". The Army was in denial; it couldn't happen with American troops.

    My coming up with a way to get the guys back up on the line by being very specific was pure luck, or maybe gut instinct. William DePuy, then our battalion Operations Officer, much later commented on the need for specific instructions in a manual on *Operations of Army Forces in the Field* which he authored. See Web-links 1 and 2, Appendix C.

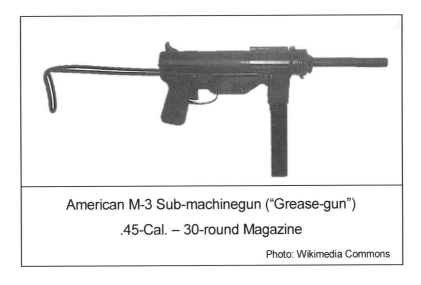

American M-3 Sub-machinegun ("Grease-gun")
.45-Cal. – 30-round Magazine

Photo: Wikimedia Commons

[Notes for Chapter 21 start on p. 265]

The need is not really for more brains, the need is for a gentler, a more tolerant people than those who won for us against the ice, the tiger, and the bear. The hand that hefted the ax, out of some blind allegiance to the past, fondles the machinegun as lovingly. It is a habit man will have to break to survive, but the roots go very deep.

Loren Eiseley, *The Immense Journey* [A3]

Afterword

No attempt at wise words. There was a big war and I was in it.

Why the series title, AN ALMOST PERFECT WAR? What could be, for me, a "perfect" war, and why didn't the one I was in fit that description?

As the country plunged into a desperate struggle to ensure the survival of entire nations and cultures I was torn between my feelings against doing the will of people I had never met—the government, the Army and the draft board, with the ultimate purpose of killing other human beings—and the need to meet the expectations of family, neighbors, friends, girl-friend, church, and myself.

And like many young men in every generation I was curious about how I would respond to the challenges of personal danger. As long as I had to be in a war, I felt I should take advantage of the opportunity to get a broad sample of what war was about, and in that respect I feel I succeeded.

For me, the war would have been "perfect" if I managed to fulfill everyone's expectations without personally depriving a fellow human of life. Still, I would have wanted to know if I could find the resolve to act decisively when lives were on the line. I found that I could summon that resolve.

And there is a small possibility that I did not take a life. When I fired at the German soldier on the hill near *Avril* he fell instantly. A few moments later Sankey said that he, too, had seen him, and that he had fired as he—Sankey—went down into a prone position. Did Sankey's shot hit the German, and could it have hit him first by a split second? The unanswerable question lets me have it both ways.

The title, '44 FOXHOLES IN FRANCE, refers both to the year 1944 and the number of foxholes I dug, slept in and/or fought from. The one at *Fèves* Ridge was barely a foxhole, scraped into the shallow soil that overlay the shale, but it was the last one before I got hit, and was, without fudging, number 44.

The German compass on the cover is the one I picked up during the fight for *Le Mans*. The fact that it is broken may to some readers be symbolic.

It should go without saying that the only perfect war would be one that did not need to be fought.

Appendix A

Primary References for '44 FOXHOLES IN FRANCE

Blumenson, Martin, *Breakout and Pursuit*, Washington: Office of the Chief of Military History, Department of the Army, 1961. Can also download from Internet. See Web-link No. 4.

Butcher, Harry C., *My Three Years with Eisenhower*, New York: Simon & Schuster, 1946

Colby, John, *War From the Ground Up – The 90th Division in WW-II*, Austin: Nortex Press, 1991

Cole, Hugh M., *The Lorraine Campaign*, Historical Division, Department of the Army, 1950

D'Este, Carlo, *Decision in Normandy*, New York: Dutton, 1983

Featherston, Alwyn, *Saving the Breakout*, Novato, CA: Presidio, 1993

Harrison, Gordon A., *Cross-Channel Attack*, Washington, DC: Office of the Chief of Military History, Department of the Army, 1950

Hastings, Max, *Overlord*, New York: Simon & Schuster, 1984

Leckie, Robert, *Delivered From Evil*, New York: Harper & Row, 1987

Regimental S3, *Operational Report 357th Infantry*, June through September, 1944

Von Roeder, George (Staff Sergeant), *Regimental History of the 357th Infantry*, Weiden (Bavaria): 1945.

Weigley, Russell W., *Eisenhower's Lieutenants*, Bloomington, Indiana: University Press, 1981

Note: Books shown in **Bold Type** are official U. S. Army histories known as *Green Books* because of their green covers. BOOK FOUR OF AN ALMOST PERFECT WAR, ANNOTATED BIBLIOGRAPHY, contains an extended list of references with comments by the author.

Appendix B

Operational Report 357th Infantry

Author's Note:

The "Op Report" that follows was scanned from photocopies of pages typed at regimental headquarters during combat. They were provided to the author by the National Archives.

Although this *Operational Report* is the most complete and perhaps the only record of where the Regiment's component units were located on a day-to-day basis, and what their missions were, and their outcomes, the "Op Report" cannot be taken as gospel. Even under the best of conditions, communication between regimental headquarters and those actually doing the fighting was distorted by the confusions of combat. Men below the level of Platoon Leader seldom knew what was happening beyond their immediate vicinity—a hundred yards or so—and reports back to Battalion and Regiment did not always represent actual events and circumstances of the fighting.

Communications was mainly by field telephone which was subject to noisy transmission, and the wire itself was vulnerable to damage by shell-fire, road traffic and enemy sabotage. In many situations wire could not be extended to the actual fighting areas. Walkie-talkie radios were used mainly to guide artillery and mortar fire. Back-pack radios were available for some purposes and there are a few entries in the Op Report where Regimental HQ communicated with Battalion HQ by radio.

Another consideration was that initially most high level officers were inexperienced in combat, having come from units of the Regular Army or the National Guard that hadn't been engaged with an enemy for decades—if ever. For several weeks after D-Day such officers' interpretation of what was happening was necessarily shaped more by discussions at West Point or in Officers' Candidate School than by first-hand knowledge of how the war was actually being conducted. Only those who had been in North Africa, Sicily or Italy, or, as with General J. Lawton Collins, the Pacific, had had any real combat experience. To my knowledge none from any of these theaters were in the 90th Division. New officers replacing casualties suffered from the same lack of experience. The gaps between front-line actualities and perceptions at division, regiment, and even battalion headquarters were significant, and in many cases led to problematic decisions.

Even men fighting side-by-side could have different recollections of what happened. Those of Sackett, a man in my own squad, differed from mine in important ways. After the war we met and corresponded, but disagreed on many points. So it is not surprising that I have found some discrepancies between what I personally experienced and events described in the 357th Op Report. Which representation is more accurate will probably never be resolved, and at this point it is of little consequence.

Notable omissions in the OP Report are any description of the largest assemblage of aquatic craft in the history of warfare—the invasion fleet—and the vast assemblage of bombers for the July 25th COBRA carpet bombing near *St.-Lo*. Omitted also is any overall description of trapping the German 7th Army in the "*Falaise-Argentan* Gap". The Op Report states how the regiments of the 90th were deployed at the Gap, and in a couple of instances the number of prisoners taken, but nothing about the encirclement itself or its strategic significance. Regiment 358's meeting up with a Polish unit at *Chambois* is mentioned, but its importance in closing the German 7th Army's escape route is not.

The American Third Army itself is not mentioned, nor is its Commanding Officer, General George S. Patton. Neither General Eisenhower nor General Bradley is mentioned. Corps Commanders are not mentioned. Replacement of the 90th Division's Commanding officers, Generals McElvie and Landrum, is not mentioned. Col. Sheehy is named when he became 357's Regimental Commander, but his death only a few days later is not mentioned. The attempt to assassinate Hitler is not mentioned, nor is Rommel's accident.

The Op Report is a nuts-and-bolts account relating almost exclusively to the details of the movements of 357's own regimental components along with any attached units such as tank platoons, tank destroyers, artillery batteries, assault guns, trucks, infantry units from other regiments, and in one case, French armor. Very few tactical details of the fighting itself are included, and I found no officers below Battalion level named except in one case, a company commander.

How the Op Report was actually written, and by whom, is, to me, not known. Was it typed by the Operations Officer himself, by a clerk from notes, or from dictation? Just getting it compiled and typed each day, with new information sometimes coming in by the minute, as at *Beau-Coudray,* must have been a difficult and daunting—even heroic—task.

As a historical document, the Regimental Op Report it is of questionable value because of the dense amount of detailed information that is not germane to the actual fighting. One wonders if anyone ever read it. It was primarily "yesterday's news". Following the geographical progress of the regiment on a map while referring to the report, furthermore, is extremely difficult, and my attempts at a concordance may in some cases be inaccurate.

The Op Report was not a document that conveyed official orders for movements and actions; it simply recorded them, and not verbatim at that. It does not contain casualty counts or personnel records, nor logistical data relating to ammo, rations and fuel. That it was produced during actual combat, however, does provide a unique aura of authenticity. The regimental CP was sometimes shelled, strafed and/or bombed (See entries for June 10, 24, and July 19), and in a couple of cases, overrun by the enemy—providing adequate excuse for the typing mistakes.

The notes and underlines added to the original Op Report by the author indicate entries especially pertinent to the book's narrative, with arrows referring to specific underlined material. Comments in rectangles are not related to specific entries in the Op Report but are inserted at the approximate dates. References to the author are made with the initials, "W.W."

Only a few items in the Op Report that are also mentioned in the text or chapter notes are included in the indices.

Operational Report, Annotated by the Author

DECLASSIFIED PER EXECUTIVE ORDER 12356, Section 3.3, /1617650
By RLB/JJO   NARA, Date 4-24-91

HEADQUARTERS 357TH INFANTRY
APO 90, U.S. ARMY

OPERATIONAL REPORT 357TH INFANTRY FOR MONTH OF JUNE 1944   UNCLASSIFIED

3 June 1944 – Advance elements of the regiment boarded ship off Cardiff at 1615.

5 June 1944 – The SS Explorer set sail from Cardiff and moved to anchorage at Swansea.

6 June 1944 – At 2000 the Explorer set sail for France.

8 June 1944 – Dropped anchor off Utah Beach on the Cotentin peninsula at 0930. Debarkation began at 1200. At 1246 the first elements of the regiment waded ashore on the beach. At this time the Regimental Commander was notified that the prearranged transit area had not yet been secured by the 4th Division, and that the regiment would move instead into an area in the Vic of LOUTRES. The CT closed in the area at 1910 less many of its vehicles.

(Regt. debarked)

9 June 1944 – At 2200 the regiment received the Division order to pass through elements of the 82d Airborne Division in the Vic of AMFREVILLE at 100515, seize and secure the crossings of the DOUVE RIVER W of ST COLUMBE until relieved by the Division Engineers.

10 June 1944 – At 0030 the regiment moved from its assembly area in the Vic of LOUTRES in the order– 3d, 2d, 1st Bns, and Spec Units. The 82d Airborne Division dispositions were somewhat altered from those reported the 9th of June 1944, and the passage of lines was not accomplished until 0545. The regiment suffered light casualties from an enemy 88MM A/T gun while crossing the bridge over the MERDERET RIVER at LA FIERE. The 3d and 2d Bns from R to L on line, moved forward against very light resistance until 1240 when the 2d Bn was held up. "A" Co of the 1st Bn was sent forward to support the 2d Bn and at 1530 the 1st Bn relieved the 2d Bn on the left of the 3d. At 2130 the regiment launched a coordinated attack in the direction of LES LANDES with the 3d Bn and 1st Bn on line from R to L. The attack was unsuccessful. At 2230 the regimental CP and adjacent area underwent a 20 Min bombing attack.

(Cross La Fière Causeway*)
(Attack failed. Rgtl. CP bombed)

11 June 1944 – At 0800 the regiment launched another attack in the same direction with no changes in orders. A gain of about 800 Yds was made by the 3d Bn. This gain was subsequently lost. At 1800 another attack was launched in the same formation with "C" Co moving wide on the left flank. "F" Co was attached to the 1st Bn, "E" and "G" Cos were attached to the 3d Bn. "C" Co reached the road running through LES LANDE at this point the attack was stopped by heavy enemy resistance.

(Attack failed)

12 June 1944 – At 1345 the regiment attacked again in the same formation supported by two platoons of medium tanks. The attack failed after two tanks were knocked out by German 88MM fire, and the rest withdrew. At 2130 another attack was launched with the same plan. The 1st Bn made a limited advance, but the failure of the 2d Bn to move forward stopped the advance of the regiment.

(More problems of 90th' Division)

SECURITY CLASSIFICATION CANCELED

---

* *La Fière* Causeway is where my childhood next-door neighbor, "Markie" Heim, earned a D.S.C. as assistant gunner on a bazooka team. The citation for the medal, and a photo of General Omar Bradley pinning it on, can be found by Googling for "Marcus Heim." His name is also listed in Gordon Harrison's *Cross Channel Attack*, one of the Army's *Green Books*.

DECLASSIFIED PER EXECUTIVE ORDER 12356, Section 3.3, /1617650.
By RLB/550 NARA, Date 4-24-91

Col. Sheehy made Rgtl. Commander.

13 June 1944- Colonel JOHN W. SHEEHY assumed command of the regiment. At 0700 the attack was resumed against the same line with 1st an 2d Bns abreast from L to R with the 3d Bn in reserve after being reorganized during the previous night. After a slow advance by both the 1st and 2d Bns, the 3d was moved to the R flank and crossed the AMFREVILLE-GOURBESVILLE road, with the mission of attacking GOURBESVILLE from the NW. This movement around the flank was not complete until after dark, and the attack on GOURBESVILLE did not materialize.

Problems at *Gourbesville*

14 June 1944- During the morning of the 14th, the 3d Bn was given several hours to prepare for a carefully coordinated attack on the town. At 1200 a bombing mission on the town was requested for 1400. At 1700 the bombing mission was finally called off because the artillery did not have the proper colored smoke shells to mark the target for the planes. The Asst Div Comdr planned an attack with the Div Arty in support for 1930. The attack moved forward into the town of GOURBESVILLE, but the force that finally got into the town was unable to hold it, and was withdrawn during the night.

15 June 1944- The 1st and 2d Bns were pulled back into the Vic of AMFREVILL into a defensive position and at 0700 the 3d Bn attacked the town of GOURBESVILLE and successfully took the town. The patrol action that preceded the attack and the actual attack itself, lasted all day, and the entry of the main portion of the Bn into the town was accomplished at 1930. At 1000 the 2d Bn relieved elements of the 359 Inf at MAGNEVILLE.

Col. Sheehy Killed

16 June 1944- At 0745 the 1st Bn moved to GOURBESVILLE to relieve the 3d Bn which was withdrawn slightly to the SW. The Regt remained in this defensive position for the remainder of the day. Col G.B.BARTH assumed command of the Regt.

Col Barth new Rgtl. Commander

17 June 1944- At 1600 the Regt moved to an assembly area in the Vic of HAUTEVILLE BOCAGE. Closed in at 2100. The 2d Bn remained in same location under division control.

357 ordered to *Portbail* area

18 June 1944- At 1400 the Regt'l Comdr received orders to move the CT to the Vic of PORTBAIL, relieving the 47th Inf with the mission of blocking the Germans from entering or leaving the Cotentin Peninsula in the bottleneck between hills 121-131, and the inlet at PORTBAIL. Attached: 345th FA Bn, Co B,899 TD, 1st Plat 90th Rcn Troop. The move to the Vic of PORTBAIL was made by motor. At 2030 Rcn by Bn Comdrs revealed thatthe 47th Inf was not on the objectives indicated in the relief or which necessitated a night relief in contact. The 1st Bn howe was able to relieve a Bn of the 47th Inf in the same position it was to occupy in the defensive plan. This position was N of the ST SAVEUR LE VICOMTE - PORTBAIL hi-way. Both the 2d and 3d Bns relieved respective Bns of the 47th well N and E of the final positions to be occupied. Orders were issued by the Regt'l Comdr for these two Bns to attack no later than 190630 to seize objectives S as per previously determined defensive plan.

19 June 1944- At 0630 the 2d Bn started its advance to its objective S of DUPREY, and the 3d Bn by 0730 had reached its objective. The 2d Bn was unable to fully occupy the position indicated in the order and finally stopped just N of YONS. During the entire day the Regt was harassed by 4 to 5 tanks probing at the position from the S and by German patrols working down from the N to escape the trap. One force of 299 Germans by

19 Jun - 1st Bn in Vic of PORTBAIL. This force and others of small
(Cont'd) number were taken under heavy Arty and mortar fire. Fighting
during the day took place on all sides of the Regt with the
main threat from the S where evidently the German was attempting
to break through and relieve units trapped on the N side
of the bottleneck. The 2d Bn 359th Inf was attached to CT
to cover the area from NEUVILLE EN BEAUMONT to the DOUVE
River S of ST SAVEUR LE VICOMTE. The platoon of the 90th
Rcn was relieved by this Bn and was employed on the N with
the mission of forming a warning net to protect the position
from infiltrating groups of the enemy trying to break through
the bottleneck from the N. During the day the 2d Bn attempt
to infiltrate forward onto the high ground in front of their
position in the Vic of RUE BATON. At 1700 this position was
attacked by the German with tanks and infantry, and F Co
was forced to withdraw to their previous position, thus
refusing the R flank of the Bn to a position bordering on
the inlet just S of ST LO D'OURVILLE.

20 June 1944 - During the day, minor readjustments were made in the position
and the German continued to harrass the Regt by Arty and
mortar fire, and a limited number of tanks in both the 2d
and 3d Bn areas. Tank action by the German in the L Co sector
near the bridge at ST SAVEUR DE PIERRE PONT, caused the Regt
to establish an A/T strong point at LA HARDELLERIE with one
Plat of Engrs and two 57MM A/B guns. 2d Bn 359 was returned
to 359th.

[W.W. still at repple-depple]

21 June 1944 - At 0530 the 1st Bn was engaged with a German force estimated
to be about 160 men and officers and accounted for all of
them, capturing 125 prisoners and killing or wounding the
rest. Minor readjustments in this position were continued
during the day. Improvements in position and defensive fires
were made.

22 June 1944 - 0800 the 2d Bn attempted to infiltrate forward onto the ground
lost by F Co. This attempt was unsuccessful. A Co, 315th Engr
was Atchd to the 2d Bn and employed to extend the L of that
Bn. By 1700 this relief and Atchmt was complete. At 1900
the 3d Bn 359th Inf was Atchd to the CT and was placed on
the L flank of the 3d Bn 357, which moved to the W and closed
the gap which was attached to the CT and relieved the 90th
Rcn Elms on the L flank of the position S of ST SAVEUR LE
VICOMTE.

[W.W. assigned to 90th Division]

23 June 1944 - At 1100, Troop B, 4th Cav and Co B, 607 TD Bn were Atchd to
the CT. Troop B and 90th Rcn Troop (-), were employed on
combat Rcn mission in area ST LO D'OURVILLE, BARNEVILLE,
BESNEVILLE, ST MAURICE. During the day and night, our troops
patrolled agressively in the Vic of YONS, ST SAVEUR DE PIERRE
PONT and the railway station named HALT. Patrols in the Vic
of PORTBAIL were consistently harassed by enemy fire from
the Vic of LA RIVIERE. It became evident by this time that
the German coastal defenses protecting the village of PORTBAIL
were located in this area and that a coordinated attack
would be necessary if the position were to be occupied.

-3-

DECLASSIFIED PER EXECUTIVE ORDER 12356, Section 3.3, NND17650
By RLB/JJO   NARA, Date 4-24-91

24 June 1944 – At 0500, 3d Bn 359th Inf reported an attack on the L Co outpost by a small enemy force. At 0800 all enemy patrol activity had ceased. At 1300 the 90th Rcn Troop was shifted to the L flank in the area held by Co B, 315th Engrs. At 1600 movement was initiated to reconstitute the sector on the W of the LA HAYE DU PUITS road into a two Bn sector. C Co relieved A Co. A Co was designated as Regt'l reserve in position astride the ST LO D'OURVILLE-PORTBAIL road with leading elements outposting ST LO D'OURVILLE with the mission of protecting dominant observation provided by the church tower in that town. [W.W.'s first day on line] B Co, released from 2d Bn control, relieved G Co. The latter Co moving into a Bn reserve position to reorganize. A Co, released from 2d Bn control. 1st Bn assumes responsibility for a designated sector on the R of the 2d. At 1900 the reserve Plat of B Co, 607 TD Bn given secondary mission of an indirect fire mission in conjunction with the harassing fire of the 343d FA. [Regimental CP shelled] At 2140 the Germans shelled the area of the Regt'l CP with 105MM Arty fire.

25 June 1944 – During the previous night all patrols from the CT reported enemy outposts dug in on the entire perimeter of the defense. At 1030 a situation developed in the 2d Bn sector wherein a greater share of a Bn of Georgians made arrangements through a previously captured prisoner to come into our lines and surrender. This arrangement was made by GEN S.T. WILLIAMS, the Ass't Div Comdr. At 1845 approximately 150 Germans approached the 3d Bn position and were dispersed and driven off by mortar and Arty fire. At 2230 a patrol was sent into the town of PORTBAIL to stay for a period of 24 hour By 2400 all enemy activity had stopped including mortar and Arty fire.

26 June 1944 – At 0730 a 30 minute mortar and Arty barrage was fired along the entire CT sector in simulated attack. During the day [W.W. patrol with Steel] small patrols of three to five men were sent into the area S of the 3d Bn and several enemy gun positions were discovered and thereafter fired on by both mortar and Arty fire.

27 June 1944 – During the previous night, 2 man patrols were sent out in the R sector by the 1st Bn and due to faulty signals [GI patrol killed by our own outpost] one of these patrols was killed by our own outpost when returning. This patrol was from B Co. At 1000 instructions were received from Div to govern the relief of the CT by the 79th Div and the return of the CT to the zone of Div Opns in the Vic of HOUTEVILLE. At 1300 quartering parties were sent to HOUTEVILLE At 1400 CT 315 from the 79th Div closed in bivouac N of the position. At 1600 F Co completed relieving E Co on the L flank of the 2d Bn. At 1800 a message was received informing the CT that the 501st Parachute Regt would relieve Co B of the Engrs in the L sector. At 2000 the Rcn Troop reverted to Div control in the Vic of ST SAVEUR. At 2400 Co B of the 315th Engrs reverted to Div control in same location.

28 June 1944 – At 0900 the following written order was issued: "COMPANY A 315TH ENGRS WILL RELIEVE CO L 359TH INF. C.O. 3RD BN 357 WILL

-4-

DECLASSIFIED PER EXECUTIVE ORDER 12356, Section 3.3, /1617650.
By RLB/JJO NARA, Date 4-24-91

29 June 1944- MOVE HIS RESERVE COMPANY TO E AND WILL TAKE OVER THE POSITION
(Cont'd) NOW OCCUPIED BY COMPANIES K AND I 359th INFANTRY. HE WILL
MAINTAIN ACTIVE PATROLLING TO THE E TO MAINTAIN CONTACT WITH
COMPANY A 315TH ENGRS. TROOP B 4TH CAVALRY WILL MOVE TO THE
VICINITY OF CARVILLE AND UPON ARRIVAL WILL BE ATCHD TO THE
3RD BN 357TH INFANTRY FOR USE AS BN RESERVE. AT 1000 THE
RELIEF OF THE 1ST BN WAS INITIATED BY THE 315TH INFANTRY.
RELIEF OF THE 1ST BN WAS COMPLETE AT 1300. RELIEF OF THE
2ND AND 3RD BNS WAS COMPLETE BY 2200. RELIEF OF THE ENGRS
AND OF L COMPANY, BOTH UNDER THE COMD OF CAPT ST CLAIR OF
THE ENGRS WAS COMPLETE BY 2200. THIS LATTER RELIEF WAS MADE
BY UNITS OF THE 134TH REGIMENT. THE REGIMENT MARCHED TO AN
ASSEMBLY AREA IN THE VICINITY OF HOUTEVILLE ON THE FOLLOWING
MARCH ORDER:

    1600 - Guide Party
    1700 - Quartering Party
    1800 - Field Train (-) kitchens
    1900 - A/T Co
    1930 - Headquarters Co
    2000 - Cannon Co
    2030 - Company A, 315 Medics
    2300 - 2d Bn
    2400 - 3d Bn
    0100 - 343d FA Bn
    0145 - Co A, 315 Engrs
    0410 - 1st Bn

[W.W. in 1st Battalion, B-Co.]

[Harmonica duet with Steel]

June 1944- Regiment closed in the new location at 0530. No activity
throughout the day of the 30th. The men were issued new clothing and were given an opportunity to bathe, wash clothes
and rest.

HEADQUARTERS 357TH INFANTRY
APO 90, U.S. ARMY

OPERATIONAL REPORT 357TH INFANTRY FOR MONTH OF JULY 1944

1 July 1944 - At 0830 a quartering party was sent to reconnoiter an assembly area South of BEUZEVUILLE. At 1300 orders were received from Division directing the 3rd Bn to relieve the 2nd Bn of the 358th Inf to readjust itself for an attack toward ST JORES. At 1800 the 3rd Bn went under Division control and relief of the Bn of the 358th was complete.

2 July 1944 - At 1200 the Regiment started its move by infiltration across the causeway at PONT L ABBE to an assembly area at 317884 and closed at 2000.

3 July 1944 - At 0515 the Division attacked to the Southwest with the 357th Inf in Div Reserve. At 1515 the 357th was ordered to move to the vicinity of PONT AUNY. Movement was initiated at 1630. At 1845 Fwd elements arrived at the new CP location. At 2000 the Div Comdr ordered the following disposition of the 3rd Bn: One Co (Subsequently designated as "L" Company) to remain in position in the vicinity of BAUPTE with the mission of securing the crossing of the Canal DU PLESSIS. Atchd to this Co was the 3rd Bn AT Platoon and one section of both 81mm Mortars and HMG's. The remainder of the Bn was given the mission of outposting the area between BAUPTE and PONT AUNY. At 2100 the Remainder of the Regiment closed at PONT AUNY.

4 July 1944 - The attack of the rest of the Division was continued at 0545 supported by 12 additional Bns of Arty. [*Artillery celebrates 4th of July*] At 1300 the 1st Bn 357 was alerted for movement. At 1345 "L" Company was released from Div control and rejoined the 3rd Bn. At 1420 Division ordered one Company, ("A" Company), into the town. At 1500 the remainder of the 1st Bn was ordered to join "A" Company in St. JORES and defend the town. At 1645 Major Hamilton was ordered not to move until 1730 due to a delay in the attack of the 358th. 1st Bn closed in ST JORES at 1800. At 2121 out of 26 mortar shells falling in the area of the Regimental CP, 18 were duds. At 2150 Company "D", 82nd Chem Bn (4.2 Mortars), was attached to the 1st Bn. [*Chemical mortars lay smoke screen*] At 2200 the following order was given to the 1st Bn: "At three hours after daybreak on the 5th of July, the 1st Bn with Cn Co, one platoon Co "D" 82nd Chem Bn, and Co "C" 712th Tank Bn Atchd, and with the 343rd FA Bn in support, will pass through the 1st Bn of the 358th and attack in the direction of BEAU COUDRAY, LES PLESSIS. [*Orders to attack Beau-Coudray*] The 2nd Bn will move into the position vacated by the 1st Bn at ST JORES. The 3rd Bn to remain in reserve in the present location in the vicinity of PONT AUNY.

At 0800 the Regimental CP was shelled for a very short time by 88mm fire. At 0930 the 1st Bn jumped off on time and advanced initially about 400 yards. At 1010 after the tanks had eliminated slight enemy resistance, the advance was resumed. The 3rd Bn was ordered to move forward on the left of the 1st Bn. At 1120 the 1st Bn advancing in Clm of companies [*1st Battalion leads attack*] with "A" Company leading, knocked out one 88mm gun and reached a point about 1000 yards short of the RJ leading into BEAU COUDRAY. At this time "B" Company, the 2nd Bn in Clm was committed on the right of "A" Company, and the tank support was shifted to that company. A 1330 "B" moved off on the pivotal movement to the right of "A" Company. At 1410 it was contemplated that the entire 1st Bn would clear the road and allow the 3rd Bn to start movement to the right of the 1st Bn in the area just

DECLASSIFIED PER EXECUTIVE ORDER 12356, Section 3.3, /16/7650.
By RLB/JJO   NARA, Date 4-24-9.1

North of Beau COUDRAY which was in the form of a bottleneck flanked by wide open marshy land on both sides. At 1600 Co "D" of the Tk Bn (712) was Atchd to the 3rd Bn and was to proceed "L" and "I" Companies who were to move abreast to the stream running E and W just S of the town of BEAU COUDRAY. At 1610 the 1st Bn of the 358th still under control of the 357th since being passed thru by the 1st Bn 357th, reported that there was no enemy activity to the S and SW along the W edge of the West swamp in the direction of the East nose of the FORET DE MONT CASTRE. At 1620 this Bn was ordered to move SW to the road from the FORET to BEAU COUDRAY at the W edge of the swamp adjacent to the forst. Due to heavy fighting, the 1st Bn failed to clear the road in time to get the 3rd Bn into the right sector. "B" Company ordered to change direction to the S and extend to the W to reach the open ground in order to protect the right flank of the Regiment from infiltration in that sector. "B" Company was unable to move far enough to the right to allow "C" Company to move in between "A" and "B", so the 1st Bn Comdr requested permission to move "C" Company to the right of "B" Company. Neither "B" or "C" Companies were able to make any appreciable gain toward the South. At 1835 the 3rd Bn had moved across the main road and was in position behind the 1st Bn and was ordered to make Rcn to determine the feasibility of passing through or relieving the 1st Bn. At 1940 the Regimental CP arrived in the vicinity of St JORES. At 2157 "B" Co had moved forward and had reached a point about 50 yards short of the Blacktop running thru the town.

> W.W. with B-A-R vs. German MG-42

> Our night attack back up hill

6 July 1944 - At 0930 "C" Co crossed the blacktop on the right of "B" Co. At 1000 the following plans were made: Co "C" to resume the attack to the South. Upon reaching a point about 300 yards south of the blacktop road, the 3rd Bn would attack in the gap between the right flank of "A" Co and the left flank of "C" Co. The 3rd Bn to attack with "L" Co on the left and "I" Co on the right, with "K" Co initially on the right rear and behind "C" Co.

> Smoke screen

The 4.2 mortars were to smoke the area of Le Plessis. Heavy enemy action developed on the right flank of "C" Co. At 1120 "C" Co reported reaching check point X and "K" Co which was filling the gap between "A" and "C" Cos, was shifted to the right and the 3rd Bn was ordered to move into the gap and attack toward the South and upon reaching the stream to hold and await orders. "K" Co was atchd to the 1st Bn and "A" Co was Atchd to the 3rd Bn. By 1520 the 3rd Bn had moved about 150 yards south of the blacktop and were overlooking the stream. Three enemy tanks were reported operating on the blacktop. The 3rd Bn had advanced ahead of "C" Co and therefore "K" Co was ordered to move up on the left flank of "C" Co. At 1700 "E" Co was ordered to move forward and take a defensive position astride the narrow part of the bottleneck. At 1900 the 2nd Bn was put under Div control as Div Res. At 2000 orders were issued to move "A" Co back to the vicinity of the bottleneck, to reorganize after dark and for "B" Co to move to the right rear of "C" Co. At 2315 the enemy counterattack against the position South of the blacktop, supported by heavy Arty and mortar fire. At 2330 "C" Company was forced back across the highway and was caught during movement by the counterattack, and "K" and "C" Companies became intermingled and completely disorganized, both companies dropping back to a position behind "L" and "I" companies, and had reached BEAU COUDRAY. at 2354 messages sent to "I" and "L" Companies to conserve ammunition due to expected resumption of German attack at dawn.

-2-

DECLASSIFIED PER EXECUTIVE ORDER 12356, Section 3.3, /161/1050.
By RLB/JJO   NARA, Date 4-24-91

> **Company Cdr. shot off tank**
>
> **W.W. splints man's knee**
>
> **W.W. finds wounded Co. Commander.**
>
> **Crying lieutenant**
>
> **Our tanks go up hill past W.W.'s hole**
>
> **Maj. Hamilton put in command**
>
> **W.W. in hole with Alf Green. Takes GI to Bn Aid-station.**

7 July 1944 - 0010 Bn Comdr of the 733d FA Bn reported at CP that his Bn is ready to fire support in morning. At 0050 an order was issued to the assault Cos to reorganize, redistribute and issue ammunition. At 0800 "B" Co was ordered to attack the town of BEAU COUDRAY supported by tanks to relieve the situation of "I" and "L" Companies, at that time cut off. At 0950, "B" Co launched its attack supported by two platoons of medium tanks. "B" Co reached a position overlooking the town at 1100. At 1130 "B" Co was one hedgerow from town and was suffering casualties from severe mortar fire. The tanks were put into action again at this time. At 1405 a strong force of German infantry was reported approaching the town. Arty and mortar fire was placed on the stream crossing consisting of WP and HE. At 1450 "B" Co was attacked on its right flank and the tanks successfully stopped the enemy action. "B" Company continued to suffer heavy casualties and were unable to advance. The tanks with the Co withdrew. By 1545 "B" Co at this time with no officers or NCO's left, withdrew into "A" Co's position. At 1550 the 2nd Bn took up a defensive position astride the highway at the bottleneck. "I" and "L" Cos at this time were unable to get ammunition thru due to German MG fire coming from the town of BEAU COUDRAY. At 1612 "C" and "K" Cos now formed into one force, reported repeated enemy attacks supported by tanks all of which were repulsed. At 1635 a carrying party from "I" and "L" Companies managed to get thru the German line with heavy losses, and the Bn Comdr would not allow them to go back to their companies. At 1740 "I" Co reported being attacked on the right flank. One Bn of Arty was immediately placed on the area. At this time the Medium tank Co was ordered to make an attack on the town supported by a small number of Infantry from the 1st Bn. At this time the Germans made the 14th counterattack against the right flank of "C" and "K" Cos. At 2100 radio communication was lost with "I" and "L" Cos, and a runner from "L" Co reported that "I" Co CP had been overrun by an enemy tank and had surrendered. "E" Co was ordered to attack at once supported by tanks to relieve the situation of "I" and "L" Cos. Lt Col Kilday was placed in command of the entire operation. Confusion prevented the attack of "E" Co from materializing and due to the approach of darkness, the Regtl CO ordered the attack to be organized during the nite and executed at the first light of dawn. Lt. Col Kilday reported to the CP at 2345 and stated that he believed "L" Co would infiltrate back to our lines during the nite. He was ordered to send an officer patrol to "L" Co, to order their withdrawal and to organize the attack of "E" Co in the morning. At 2359 the situation was as follows: Front: "L" and "I" Cos isolated to S of blacktop, "A" Co astride the NS Rd, one mile N of stream, "B" Co on the R flank of "A" Co with "K" and "C" Cos still holding same position just N of blacktop. "E" Co with the tanks behind "A" and "B" Cos. 2nd Bn in Div reserve.

8 July 1944 - At 0800 the 357th was ordered to continue the frontal pressure. At 0900 personnel from the field train and Regtl Hqwers formed into a provisional company to add depth to the position and protect the left flank of the sector. At 0900 six members of "L" Co returned to Regimental CP by way of the swamp on the left of the sector and told about the capture of killing of part of "L" Company. During the day a very few men of these organizations worked their way back to our lines. The contemplated attack of "E" Co was called off due to a failure to properly organize it, and also the failure of the 3rd Bn to send the officer patrol to "I" and "L" companies as ordered. Lt. Colonel Kilday was relieved of his command. Major Hamilton was placed in command of the combined force of the 1st and 3rd Bns with Major Mason as second in command. During the day, minor adjustments were made in the line, but very little activity was noted. At 1845 Captain Wilson was placed in command of the provisional company.

-3-

DECLASSIFIED PER EXECUTIVE ORDER 12356, Section 3.3, /1161 / (0)00
By RLB/JJO NARA, Date 4-24-91

9 July 1944 - Very little activity during the morning other than sporadic fire of mortars and artillery including 150mm howitzers. At 1030, by written field message Lt. Col. Kilday was officially relieved of command and Major Hamilton placed in command. At 1045 the I&R Platoon established an OP at BAUPTE, in the sector of the 4th Division. At 1330 the provisional company was heavily shelled by enemy artillery. Minor readjustments were made in the disposition of the provisional company, extending them farther to the left and tying them in by listening posts with the left flank of "B" Co, now astride the road leading to LE PLESSIS.

10 July 1944 - During the early morning from 0100 to 0500 the area from the 1st Bn CP to and including the Regimental CP was subjected to continuous shelling by 150mm German artillery. There was no front line ground activity during the nite. At 1145 reports from the right of the Corps sector indicated an enemy withdrawal and patrols were immediately sent out from the front lines. At 1200 all patrols reported the presence of enemy to the front and no evidence of withdrawal in the sectors patrolled. The Assistant Division Commander arrived at the CP and plans were made to exert pressure to aid the advance units on the right of the Division and Corps Zone. At 1300 the plans were complete and were as follows: "K" Company, with 5 tanks to move forward to the black top. "C" Company to move to the left of "K" to fill the gap between "B" and "K". "B" and "A" Companies to move forward to a line even with the present position of "K" Co and try to reach the town of BEAU COUDRAY. "B" Co to be supported by 5 medium tanks. "I" and "L" Companies reorganized to hold in present position, of (This position to right of NS Road just South of the narrow part of bottleneck.) At 1504 "K" Company started forward and immediately received MG fire from both flanks. "A" Company was unable to advance because of fire received from the left flank from positions evidently in the swamp. "B" Company, which was to move forward on the left of "K" Company, could not seem to get organized for any movement forward, and any gain made initially was counteracted by the prevalence of stragglers, which depleted the effective strength of the company to about ten men and two officers. "C" Company at no time during this action was able to move to the left of "K" Co, which exposed both flanks of "K" Co, which had reached a position just short of the black top. At this time "K" Company was ordered by Major Hamilton to turn to the left astride the black top and cut across in front of the town of BEAU COUDRAY. "K" Company by 2000 was not able to make this turning movement due to flanking fire from South of the road and the almost complete lack of control due to disorganization prevented any material assistance being given by other companies. The earlier advances of the left companies, "B" and "C", were subsequently lost and "K" Company was withdrawn just North of the road. The gaps which had appeared in the position were covered by patrols and the position became stablized.

11 July 1944 - At 0930 Division ordered the movement of the 2nd Bn to a position on the East tip of the FORET DE MONT CASTRE, prepared to attack in a Southeast direction in the vicinity of LE PLESSIS. The terrain in this area consisted of a continuation of the open swampy areas that were adjacent to the BEAU COUDRAY area and the most important terrain feature was a narrow neck of corridor which transversed the swamp at the Eastern tip of the Foret. This corridor contained a hedgerow pattern resembling a ladder. This formation canalized any attack through the ladder into a straight frontal action. In this corridor, the 2nd Bn of the 359th Inf had advanced about 300 yards. The plan of the Ass't Div Commander was to pass the 2nd Bn to the left of the 2nd Bn 359 as soon as the 359th had cleared the far end of the ladder and there was room for employment of additional troops.

-4-

DECLASSIFIED PER EXECUTIVE ORDER 12356, Section 3.3, /1061 /0250 /
By RLB/JJO   NARA, Date 4-24-9.1

11 July 1944 — However, the 2nd Bn 357th was ordered to move into the ladder on the left
(Cont'd) of the 359th, and did so in a column of companies with "G" Company leading.
At 1845 the decision was made by Division that the attack of "G" Company
would be suspended. At 1930 this decision was reversed and the company
moved forward and by very aggressive action forced the Germans to withdraw to the SE end of the ladder. During the night of 11-12 July, the German withdrew from this position.

12 July 1944 — At 0800 the 2nd Bn was moving forward with no opposition, and the 1st and
3rd Bns, previously organized into separate Bns, moved forward without
opposition and were halted at the stream just N of LE PLESSIS and placed
in an assembly area at 1310. The 2nd Bn meanwhile, had advanced to LE
PLESSIS. At 1400 the 2nd Bn, after having searched the LE
PLESSIS area, was ordered to move SE to the vicinity of LA COUTRIE. The
2nd Bn found that the 1st Bn of the 358th was in their assigned sector
and were unable to move into and occupy the position. At 1730 the CP was
moved to the vicinity of BEAU COUDRAY.

> Advance across open fields past Beau-Coudray

13 July 1944 — The 1st Bn of the 358th was ordered to shift to the South or right to allow
the 2nd Bn 357th to cross the cleared ground at the entrance to the stream
at LA COUTRIE. At 1100 the 2nd Bn crossed the stream at LA COUTRIE in a
column of companies with "E" Company making the crossing under heavy MG
fire. At 1210 "F" Company which was ordered to cross the stream and advance on the left of "E" Company, had only two squads across and had come
under heavy MG fire in the open ground on the left of "E" Company. At
1345 it was decided to move "G" Company into the area of the 358th in the
vicinity of GORGES to assist the attack of the 358th. At 1410 "E" Company
reported the enemy withdrawing from GORGES. Immediately time and WP fire
was placed on the area. By 1425 "F" Co had succeeded in crossing the
stream with the whole company and were deployed on the left of "E" Company.
This action entailed the elimination of several enemy MG positions in
open country which took some time. At 1945 after this action, "F" Company
still was not abreast of "E" Company At 2005 1st Bn 358th was was able to
enter GORGES without the help of "G" Company. At this time the Bn was
ordered to reconnoiter the road to LA STELLE to determine if the road were
under observation. By 2205 "E" Company with "F" Company echeloned to the
left rear and "G" Company with one platoon on the left of "F" Company and
one platoon on the right of "E" Company , and both refused back to the
river had reached a point just short of the blacktop where forward movement stopped for the night.

14 July 1944 — Summary of Division Order: 2nd Bn will attack at 1000, 1st and 3rd Bns
to be committed only on Division order. 0930 "E" Company began moving
forward with no contact. 1145 the I&R platoon operation on the left of
Regimental sector reached LA PLANQUETTE and found no resistance. 1220
the 358th Infantry with its right flank half way between GORGES and DUR-
A UVILLE reported mortar fire falling on them. At 1230 "F" Company was ordered to search the area to the north to VILLETOT. At 1245 the 3rd Bn
was moved from LA STELLE to LA BAGOTTERIE to block the main road at that
point. At 1445 the area between the 4th and 90th Divisions on the left
flank was reported clear of the enemy. At 1730 the CP was moved to the
vicinity of GORGES. At 2300 the following order was received from Division
"35th to relieve 358th by 150300 to be prepared to attack to South on
Corps order. The 359th was in position on the left.

15 July 1944 — During the nite the Regimental CP was shelled from the south and several
casualties were suffered in the Special Units. At 1000 the Regiment was
in the following position: Right flank at Rd crossing at 286766. 359th
extending to west. 1st Bn "A" and "C" Cos on line running to NE, along
blacktop road. "B" in reserve. 2nd Bn right flank at 293769. "G" and
"F" Companies on line, "F" Company in reserve. "E" Company left flank

DECLASSIFIED PER EXECUTIVE ORDER 12356, Section 3.3, /161/ /____
By RLB/JJO NARA, Date 4-24-9.1

15 July 1944 (Cont'd)	swings north following general line of SEVES RIVER. 3rd Bn in reserve in the vicinity and South of LE PLESSIS. At 1255 the 2nd Bn reports enemy visible across SEVES RIVER on the island of ST GERMAIN SUR SEVES. At 1415 the CP moved to the vicinity of DURAUVILLE. At 1800 patrols from "E" Company which had crossed the open ground of the SEVES RIVER bed met rather heavy resistance and were withdrawn.
16 July 1944	Positions remained unchanged, due to the open nature of the ground, patrolling was very difficult except at nite.
17 July 1944	During this period extensive training in infantry-tank coordination and mortar-artillery concentration was undergone by all units. In addition training in actual adjustment of Arty fire was undertaken by all officers. The enemy increased his mortar and artillery fire against the position during the day. 57mm and 3" guns were emplaced on the front lines and fired direct fire missions against enemy positions on the island. At 1545 the 3rd Bn started the relief of the 2nd Bn and completed it by 1800.
18 July 1944	At 1200 plans for an attack on the island by the 358th were transmitted to the Regiment. The attack was to jump off at 190530 supported by the fires of all weapons in the sector of the 357th. A detailed plan for the coordination of MG, mortar, 57mm fire was made. At 1330 the attack was cancelled for 24 hours. No activity other than sporadic shelling during the day.
	No change or activity took place during the morning. At 1500 two enemy planes strafed the Regimental area, neither causing any damage and one of them being shot down by the 537th AA Bn. At 1730 a strong combat patrol from the 4th Armored Division, operating without knowledge of our location, attacked the town of MAY, causing three casualties in the 3rd Bn. Identification was finally made and the firing ceased. Attack scheduled for the twentieth of July was postponed for the second time.
20 July 1944	At 1345 the first activity of the day was a shelling of the 3rd Bn position by the enemy lasting for about 20 minutes. The Division plan for attack still utilized the 357th in a supporting role and thence to Division Reserve. At 1950 the 4th Armored Division stated an attack to straighten out their lines and eliminate a pocket containing several snipers according to their version. The firing stopped at 2045.
21 July 1944	Very unfavorable weather delayed the attack of the Corps. At 1115 a stringent ammunition limitation was placed on mortar ammunition.
22 July 1944	At 0630 the limited objective attack of the 358th Inf to seize the island jumped off. The 357th, supported the attack by heavy fire on predesignated positions on the island. In return the Regimental position was heavily shelled by the enemy. Intense fog prevented the effective direct fire of A/T and TD guns on the island. At 1325 the 1st Bn of the 358th had crossed the river. At 2010 the 358th 1st Bn received a counterattack and withdrew about 200 yards. At this time communication with the Bn was lost and a few stragglers appeared in the front lines of the 1st Bn 357th.
23 July 1944	By 1120 it became evident that the 1st Bn 358th was no longer in an organized position on the south side of the SEVES RIVER. Disorganized groups had returned into our lines and into the area just to the west of the 1st Bn. At this time the 1st Bn was extended to the west to join the left flank of the 3rd Bn 358th, while the 1st and 2nd Bn 358th were withdrawn to reorganize. During the day the Regimental sector underwent increased enemy shelling.
24 July 1944	In conjunction with the Corps attack still postponed the Division revised its plan and called for the relief of the 357th by the 358th and the movement of CT 357 into the area between the 4th Armored Division and the 83rd Division along the PERIERS-CARENTAN Road. Reconnaissance was initiated in the early morning in this sector and the CT Commanders were briefed at 1145. At 2105 the German scored a direct hit on the house containing the

Margin notes:
- W.W. promoted to Sergeant. Replacements come up. W.W. to be Asst. Squad Ldr.
- W.W. sees German soldier on "Island"
- Rgtl. area strafed
- Attack across river by 358
- 358's attack routed
- 358 Bn Cmdr relieved. (Ref: Colby)

-6-

DECLASSIFIED PER EXECUTIVE ORDER 12356, Section 3.3, /N61 /0530
By RLB/JJO   NARA, Date 4-24-9.1

24 July 1944 - 3rd Bn CP.
(Cont'd)

25 July 1944 - At 1300 the 358th had begun the relief of our 3rd Bn and 1st Bn, and at the same time the 2nd Bn initiated its move to positions in the new sector. At 1345 the Regimental CP moved to the vicinity of N of RAIDS. At 1705 the 1st Bn was completely relieved and started movement to assembly area in rear of the 2nd Bn. At 1715 A/T Company closed in the new location. At 1800 Colonel Clarke of the 358th assumed responsibility for the sector being vacated by the 357th. Attack plan as coordinated with the 83rd Division called for column of battalions in the order, 2nd, 1st, 3rd. At 2100 the Regiment closed in the area.

[We watch COBRA carpet bombing.]

26 July 1944 - At 0530 the 2nd Bn jumped off in the attack. It was found during the morning after much reporting of position, which was obviously incorrect, that the LD reportedly held by the 83rd Division was actually well within German lines and that the advance of the 2nd Bn which reported itself on Phase line one, actually was very slightly ahead of the LD. At 1035 the attack was stopped completely and no further attempts were made to continue for the balance of the day. Plans were made for the next morning involving air support and heavy artillery preparation, the attack to be coordinated with a similar move by the 83rd Division. During the night heavy enemy artillery fire fell in the general area. Patrols were established to push out as far as possible to attempt to determine possible withdrawal during the night.

27 July 1944 - The attack, originally scheduled for 0700, was delayed until 0900. Weather was very poor, and the scheduled air support was cancelled. The patrols of the previous nite encountered small arms fire and were not able to accurately report any other enemy activity. At 0915 the 2nd Bn had moved off in the attack, following a fifteen minute artillery preparation, and by 0945 had advanced four hundred yards without encountering resistance. This advance opened a gap on the right flank, as 4th Armored was not attacking. The 1st Bn followed the advance of the 2nd, maintaining an echelon formation to cover the opening. The 3rd Bn executed a similar maneuver on the left flank of the 2nd Bn, and in this order the Regiment moved forward. It was obvious that there had been a major withdrawal, and Division ordered the Regiment to proceed, turning to the South and continuing across the TAUTE RIVER. At 1320 the advance of the 2nd was stopped to allow the 1st and 3rd Bns to close some of the gap which had developed. At 1415 General McLain arrived at the CP, and the 3rd Bn was ordered to move into route march formation with advance guard, going as far as possible toward the high ground just south of the highway running east-south-east out of PERIERS. 1st and 2nd Bns were assembled N of the TAUTE RIVER while the 3rd Bn passed into the lead. At 1740 the 3rd Bn crossed the TAUTE without resistance, followed by the 2nd and 1st Bns. The Regimental CP was moved forward to the vicinity of ST SEBASTIAN DE RAIDS. At 2220 the 3rd Bn encountered small arms fire which was eliminated after short engagement, continued its way south until dark.

[W.W.'s 1st experience as non-com]
[German withdrawal]
[Cross *Taute* River*]

28 July 1944 - At 0530 the 2nd Bn and 3rd Bns moved forward, meeting some small arms fire from small units which were dissolved without difficulty. By 0930 the 3rd Bn had reached ST MARTIN AUBIGNY, while the 2nd Bn advance was slowed down somewhat by mines which had to be cleared. At 1050 Division ordered the advance to hold up at Phalse Line "B", a line running approximately from ST SAVEUR LENDELIN east to MONTCUIT. It later developed that COUTANCES was in allied hands, that we could expect only isolated resistance and all units would proceed to approximately 5000 yards south of ST SAVEUR LENDELIN. Serious traffic congestion developed in the advance south and it was necessary to stop approximately 1000 yards south of ST SAVEUR LENDELIN. The

[St.-Sauveur Lendelin, Coutances]

-7-

* Have not been able to find the *Taute* River on maps.

DECLASSIFIED PER EXECUTIVE ORDER 12356, Section 3.3, /1617650
By RLB/JJO NARA, Date 4-24-91

28 July 1944 - Leading elements reaching this point at 2100. The Regimental CP was set
(Cont'd) up between BEUSEVILLE and LA GUESMONNIERE in a small town not named on maps.

29 July 1944 - The positions assumed at the close of the previous day's march, with the exception of setting up outposts to form a continuous line of contact, were maintained. This was to prevent possiblities of infiltration from the units which had been trapped in the armored thrusts by the 1st, 2nd and 3rd Armored Divisions to our south. The Regiment was out of contact with enemy at this time.

[Margin note: Alf Green killed by escaping Germans]

30 July 1944 - The situation remained unchanged with no prospect of immediate change. A full training schedule was instituted for all units to be followed as long as the Regiment remained in the area.

31 July 1944 - 357th was ordered by Division to be prepared to make reconnaissance for motor or foot move 1 August 1944. Training program was continued according to schedule. No further developments at the close of the period.

[Margin note: W.W. sick]

DECLASSIFIED PER EXECUTIVE ORDER 12356, Section 3.3, /16/7650.
By RLB/JJO   NARA, Date 4-24-91

HEADQUARTERS 357TH INFANTRY
APO 90, U.S. ARMY

OPERATIONAL REPORT 357TH INFANTRY FOR MONTH OF AUGUST 1944

1 August 1944 – Situation at opening of month: 357th Infantry located in vicinity LA SUESNONNIERE, in defensive position awaiting orders for further movement. At 1200 this day the 90th Division passed to the XV Corps, which had included the 83rd Infantry and 5th Armored Divisions. Div. Hq notified the Regiment of probable move 2nd August, to point approximately 15 miles to South. At 1230 the I&R Platoon was sent out to reconnoiter possible routes of the new location. The problem of routes was complicated because of the presence of armored units moving in the same direction, and reconnaissance was not completed until late afternoon. At 1530 a Division order called for the 1st Bn to be prepared to move out mounted on tanks. At 1645 plans were changed and further communication from Division placed Regiment on alert for move by trucks, setting PERRIER as location where trucks were to be picked up by Regimental representative. Possibility of move advanced to sometime during night. This represented change in objective and the earlier reconnaissance of the I&R Platoon was nullified by the new plans. A 2015 confirmation of movement was received, to be initiated at earliest possible hour, with objective ST HILAIRE DU HARCOURT, SE of AVRANCHES, and approximately 60 miles from present location. 358th Regiment was to proceed 357th on this move. Balance of the period was spent in organizing for move, with Battalion and Special Unit Commanders called for meeting shortly after midnight.

> 90th in XV Corps, 3rd Army
> Armored unit passed thru position at night
> W.W. told of map assignment

2 August 1944 – Briefing of Battalion and Special Unit Commanders began at 0030, calling for the following order of march: 1st Bn plus 1 Plat A/T Co, 1 Plat Engrs; 3rd Bn plus 1 Plat A/T, Regtl Hqs; Engineers; 2nd Bn; Cannon Company, A/T Co, 343rd FA Bn. The route was as follows: From present location to COUTANCES and S to AVRANCHES, then SE to LA SOURSERIE, at which point 1st Bn would detruck and proceed on foot to RJ at MONTHIE, then NW to area of REPTVILLE with the mission of blocking road net in the area. The 3rd Bn to follow the same route and program continuing through LA BOURSERIE to the SE to area of NAFTEL to block the road net in that area. The 2nd Bn was assigned as reserve, bivouacking in the area of LA MANCELLERIE. At 0410 the 1st Bn moved forward, followed by properly scheduled units. The convoy met with numerous delays because of very heavy traffic congestion. At 1230 the 1st and 3rd Bns were moving into their positions, and at 1415 the CP Staff set up in the vicinity of LA MANCELLIERE, 418106. At 1430 the 1st Bn reported that elements of the 1st Armored Division were going through its positions heading E. A rearrangement of territory to be defended by 357th left us with the following lines: 358th Regiment, previously assigned the South part of the area, was moved across the LE SELUNE to approximately 8 miles South. Our lines ran from the SELUNE RIVER on the South to LA SEE RIVER on the North.

> W.W. with map in lead Jeep of motorized column. Route choice countermanded.
> Gen. Patton said to have directed traffic at *Avranches*

3 August 1944 – During the morning positions were changed leaving the Bns located as follows: 1st Bn in vicinity POIRIER; 2nd Bn remained at LA MANCELLIERIE; 3rd Bn moved one company to LE PIGEONNIERE, NE of ST HILAIRE DU HARCOURT. These changes in position were completed by 1100. Following the visit of General Weaver at 1330, a further readjustment of positions was scheduled. 1st Bn was to move directly to JUVIGNY after the 1st Armd Div had cleared that area; 2nd Bn to move E to LA BAZOGE; 3rd Bn to move balance forward and S to LA PIGEONNIERE where "L" Company had been stationed.

> B-Co to *Juvigny*

DECLASSIFIED PER EXECUTIVE ORDER 12356, Section 3.3, /1601 /
By RLB/JJO   NARA, Date 4-24-91

3 August 1944 - This schedule was then modified, the 1st Bn was ordered to remain in
(Cont'd)   place because of the presence of the 1st Armd Div at JUVIGNY. This did
not seriously effect the purpose of the changes, which were designed to
facilitate a move to either E or S. The Regtl CP was moved to the E to
the town-hall-school building at LA BANCONNIERE. By 2000 the 2nd and
3rd Bns had assumed their new positions. The primary mission of the 90th
Division at this time was to provide security for the area in general;
[Germans preparing *Mortain* offensive] several Panzer divisions were in this sector and the British drive to
VIRES created the possibility of attempted breakthrough to the South.
In addition, the dam approximately one mile S of VEZINS ON THE SELUNE
River was an important factor in our supply line; destruction of the dam
would effectively cut this line, with serious consequences for the forces
S of the river. Because of this general situation, active pa-
trols were continuously maintained between units. Because of the possibility of tank action, each Bn was strengthened with one platoon of A/T
and one Platoon TD's.

4 August 1944 - Patrols of the previous night reported negatively. During the morning
General McLain made presentations of awards to the various units. At
[B-Co at *St.-Hilaire-du-Harcouët*. After-action report not mention route snafu.] 2145 Div Hq alerted the Regiment for possible move at 0600 5 August.
Several British tanks were reported to have reached "E" Co., apparently
broke through the VIRES salient. No furher identification was made.
Toward midnight 1st Bn reported that elements of the 9th Div were pas-
sing in front of its positions.

5 August 1944 - At approximately 0300 Div order was received, outlining mission of the
XV Corps now consisting of the 79th and 90th Divs, to attack S with the
mission of seizing and securing crossing of MAYENNE RIVER at MAYENNE.
[New objective: *Mayenne*] For this purpose "Task Force Weaver" was organized, consisting of Det of
Div Staff, 90th Rcn, 712th Tank Bn, 357th Inf Mtzd, 343rd FA Bn, Co "A"
315th Engrs, Co "A" 315th Medics, one Co 607 Tank Destroyer Bn, 1 Battery
537 AA Bn, Det 90th Sig Co, Det 90th MP's. Order of march for 357th Inf
was as follows: Flank Guard, consisting of "K" Co plus 1 Platoon TD's,
1 Platoon A/T, and I&R Platoon as point, to take route to left of main
body, through towns of BUAIS, FOUGEROLLE, DESERTINES, GORRON, and MAYENNE.
The flank guard left at 0530. The main body, in the following order: 1st
Bn plus 1 platoon Engrs and 1 Platoon A/T; 343rd FA Bn, Command Group;
3rd Bn; Hq Co; 2nd Bn; Cn Co; TD Hq; Med; Ser. Co; followed the route from
ST HILAIRE DU HARCOURT to LANDIVY, through LA TENIERE: ERNEE to MAYENNE,
which was approximately 50 miles from point of departure. The main body
was on the road at 0600 and proceeded without resistance to a point about
ten miles W of MAYENNE. Some resistance was met in MAYENNE, but was eliminated by the leading elements, prisoners taken, and the march resumed.
At 1430 the 1st Bn had entered the town, met considerable scattered resistance, including mortar and artillery fire from the E Side of the River.
During this period a temporary CP was set up approximately six miles W of
MAYENNE, while the balance of the main body was brought up and moved into
position. At 1600 message was received from the flank guard, giving its
position 2½ miles NW of enemy force just outside of GORRON. This enemy
force was reported by French underground connections and described as including one Tiger Tank, four A/T emplacements, one Co Paratroopers plus
some infantry. This information was reported to Division by the Regtl
CO, with the recommendation that a mtzd unit be sent to the flank guard
to add the support necessary to eliminate the enemy group. Because of
shortage in transportation facilities, the flank guard was instructed
to maintain its positions until furher notice, to not attack. At approximately 2000 underground connections provided the information that the
enemy force had withdrawn, and the flank guard unit occupied GORRON without

-2-

DECLASSIFIED PER EXECUTIVE ORDER 12356, Section 3.3, NND 750057
By RLB/SJO NARA, Date 4-24-91

5 August 1944 – resistance and was ordered to remain in that area overnight. In the mean-
(Cont'd) time the balance of the main body had moved into proper positions. The
1st Bn moved through the town, began crossing the MAYENNE RIVER with "B"

> B-Company crosses bridge

Company at 1810, after being held up by assault guns and mobile 88's from
the east side. The bridge was very heavily mined with 500 pound aerial
bombs, but had not been detonated. To the south of the town the 3rd Bn

> Mine wires had been cut by GI engineer

was preparing to cross the river on penumatic boats. This operation got
under way at 1920. At 2015 those crossings had been completed and the
2nd Bn was following the 3rd in the same manner. Reconnaissance was made
to the east of the river for CP location, the LA FERIGHARD HOTEL being
selected just at the edge of town on the main road running north.

> W.W. leads advance thru *Mayenne*

Following the crossing of the river, the 3rd Bn began moving into a defensive position, forming an arc beginning at the main road running east out
of town, and extending to the south of the river. At 2145 the temporary
CP was closed out and began moving forward to the new location. At this
time 88's were falling in the area; phone contact with the 1st Bn reported
that the source of firing was just ahead of its position, and an assault
was being made. This assault was successful, two guns being knocked out,
and three others withdrawing. The Command Group entered MAYENNE just at
dusk, quartering with the CP of TASK FORCE WEAVER. Shortly after dark,

> German vehicles entered town

at approximately 2300, two enemy scout cars came down the main road from
the north, followed by a truckload of troops. The two scout cars were
knocked out, the truck and occupants captured by the CP guards. Another
scout car drove in shortly after this incident and was knocked out. At
the time of these incidents, the 3rd Bn had not yet moved into its position which would block this road. Pending the arrival of the 3rd at that
point, "A" Company of the 1st Bn (Quartering inside the town of MAYENNE),
was brought North, supported by one 3" gun. Two TD's and two light tanks
also were placed in a position directly in front of the CP and to the
North and South, where the previous action had taken place.

6 August 1944 – At 0100 and 0250 enemy cars drove into town and were knocked out. During
this period the 3rd Bn was having similar experiences with its left flank,
(I Company), to the East of town. At 0200 the 2nd Bn was ordered to send
a platoon forward to contact the left flank of the 3rd Bn and offer support. Previous contact was not effected because of the 2nd Bn taking
its positions too close to the town proper.
While these contacts were taking place, enemy aircraft were dropping numbers of flares some distance to the west of MAYENNE, ignoring the town
itself, indicating that our crossing was not generally known by the enemy.
At 0250 message was received from the flank guard at GORRON, stating that
in addition to the occupation of that town, 1 platoon had occupied DESER-
TINES. At Approximately this same time, 357th was alerted by Division
for possible movement motorized, at 1200 this day. There was no further
activity during the night.
At 0900, elements of the 16th Infantry were arriving in MAYENNE to take
over the positions in the city and release our units for the new mission.
When our flank guard units arrived at MAYENNE at 1130, we were then prepared to undertake the new mission, calling for the seizing and securing

> New objective: *LeMans*

LE MANS and the bridges crossing the SARTHE RIVER. This attack was to be
made by the 79th Division attacking to the right of the 90th, with the 5th
Armored Division attacking to the right of the 79th. The plan called for
convergence of the three divisions at LE MANS, 90th coming from the West,
the 79th from the Southwest, and the 5th Armored from the South and Southeast. 357th Infantry was selected to spearhead for the 90th Division
attack, which was divided into two sections. Our 3rd Bn and Co "A" of
the 1st Bn were attached to Task Force Weaver, which was to initiate move-

-3-

DECLASSIFIED PER EXECUTIVE ORDER 12356, Section 3.3, /16/7650.
By RLB/JJO   NARA, Date 4-24-91

, August 1944 — ment on the right route, scheduled to go through the towns of AROM, JUB-
LAINS, EVRON, STE SUZANNE, ST DENIS, COULANS, CHAUFOR, and into LE MANS.
The balance of the 357th Infantry, with two platoons of the 712th Tank
Bn, two platoons of 807th Tank Destroyer Battalion, and the 695rd Field
Artillery Battalion, was assigned the route through the town of MOUAY,
COMMER, MONTSUR, STE SUZANNE (where the route crossed with that of Task
Force Weaver), VIVIERS, STE SYMPHORIEN, BERNAY, LA QUINTE, and into LE
MANS on the same road to be used by Task Force Weaver. Order of March
was as follows: I&R Platoon as point, medium tanks mounted with troops
of the 1st Battalion, balance of 1st Battalion on trucks; Command group,
2nd Battalion, Special Units. The TD and A/T elements were divided through
the column for flexibility in case of counter attack. Departure of Task
Force Weaver was held up by enemy tanks just outside of MAYENNE. Support
of the 9th Air Force was called in. Leading elements of the 357th Infantry moved out at 1430, followed by the mounted tanks and motorized 1st
Battalion at 1510. The movement of the 2nd Battalion was initiated on
foot, to be motorized enroute by trucks of the 5th Armored Division. These
arrived at the 2nd Battalion when they reached the town of COMMER. The
1st Battalion with its attachments proceeded forward, with frequent interruptions as the point and tanks cleared enemy resistance. This resistance
consisted mainly of small groups of enemy; the surprise of the attack had
made it impossible for the enemy to organize any effective strength. One
plane strafed the column north of MONTSUR, inflicting a few casualties.
Upon arrival at the intersection of roads, running from EVRON to LA CHAP-
ELLE RAINSANT just north of LE GRAND BOIS at 2030, the column was halted
and liaison sent back to start the 2nd Bn forward, which had not resumed
its march at COMMER on the impression that it was to await orders. The
1st Battalion proceeded forward after a short interval, clearing enemy
from STE SUZANNE and proceeding on to VIVIERS. The Command Group halted
at STE SUZANNE to await the arrival of the 2nd Battalion. At approximately 2230, radio message from the 2nd Battalion related that the enemy
had reentered MONTSUR, erected a road block, and that it would stop for
the night north of the town. **This resulted in the isolation of the command group at STE SUZANNE.** Task Force Weaver had been stopped approximately one mile southeast of MAYENNE by heavy enemy resistance. At the
close of the period, these widely scattered positions remained unchanged.

7 August 1944 — During the early hours of the day there was a great deal of enemy activity in the area surrounding STE SUZANNE. Shortly after midnight an enemy
vehicle drove into the square, unaware of our presence, and was knocked
out by the personnel with the command group, which consisted of three A/T
guns, 1 platoon of Infantry, Regimental C.O. and staff, 345th Field Artillery Battalion Commander, and Radio operators. It was obvious that
the enemy did not know the situation in the town, and during the remaining hours of darkness, the strength was built up to what seemed to be a
preparation for attack. At approximately 0500 an urgent radio message
was dispatched to the 1st Battalion to return to STE SUZANNE, AS THE
force in the town would force certain capture. Just as the enemy forces
were coming into the town, the two tank platoons rolled into the square,
followed by the balance of the 1st Battalion. The enemy was dispersed
after a brief engagement. Prior to this, the 1st Bn had been engaged in
a continuous counter attack during the night, inflicted very heavy casual
ties on

Margin notes:
- Command Group isolated
- TF Barth beats TF Weaver
- B-Company rides on tanks to the rescue

-4-

DECLASSIFIED PER EXECUTIVE ORDER 12356, Section 3.3, NND17650.
By RLB/JJO   NARA, Date 4-24-91

7 Aug 44 (Cont'd) — the enemy while taking very few. At approximately 0900 heavy enemy artillery began falling on the town, destroying an ammunition truck and a jeep in the square. The command Group was withdrawn to a point about two miles West of the town. The 1st Bn remained to hold the town pending the arrival of the 2d Bn which had resumed its advance from the bivouac area north of MONTSUR. General McLAIN arrived at the CP, reported that TWF had been forced to abandon its scheduled route because of heavy resistance at ARON, and was moving forward following our route to MONTSUR, then south to VAIGES, E through JOUE-EN CHARNIER, CHASSILE, COULANS. By 1200 the 2d Bn had reached the area of the CP, E Company was sent forward to relieve the 1st Bn at ST SUZANNE, to free that unit to continue its march toward LE MANS. Just about this time 15 enemy tanks were reported to the SE of town; heavy artillery was directed against their position by the 345th FA Bn, successfully holding the tanks off while the 1st Bn passed on to the East. E Comoany was relieved by the 358th Inf at approximately 1800 and rejoined the convoy east of ST SUZANNE. The march continued to meet interruptions caused by small enemy groups, and at 2200 halted in the vicinit of LA QUINTE for the night. There were no further developments for the balance of the period.

[Margin notes: Regimental CP withdrawn; B-A-R man Paull killed by mortar at Ste.-Suzanna]

8 Aug 1944 — The early hours of the day resulted in knocking out several enemy vehicles which came into the area unaware of the presence of our troops. A number of prisoners were taken and additional vehicles captured.
The march was resumed at 0940 in the same order. At the road junction where the two routes were to be consolidated, an enemy column was intercepted moving east toward LE MANS; this happened after the I&R Platoon and one platoon of tanks had passed this point. The remaining platoon of tanks knocked out the 1st ten vehicles of the column. B Company was deployed toward the west and in the ensuing engagement knocked out the two SP 75MM guns, two 88MM dual purpose guns. The balance of the column, stretched along the road to the southwest was destroyed by planes of the 9th Air Force. This action was completed by 1215. Further reports were received, indicating other enemy forces in area to south, so these positions were held and the march was held up until the situation clarified.
At 1545 radio message reported that TFW was approximately 7000 yards west of the road junction. After meeting with heavy resistance from MONTSUR forward. At 1600 B Company reported a column moving toward its position from the west, but could not identify because of distance. The artillery observer plane was requested to make a report, and at 1515 positively identified the column as enemy and all kinds of fire were brought on its position. Because of the difficulties encountered by TFW in its march toward this point, and the attempts of enemy columns to move to the east, the 1st Bn was relieved of its mission toward LE MANS to hold the intersection, while the 2d Bn took over the mission of going into LE MANS, picking up the attachments of the 1st Bn for this purpose. At 1300 the Bn was on the move, and at 1755 reported being held up just west of LES TERTRES by flat trajectory fire. In the engagement

[Margin notes: American and German columns converge; Pulczak hit, W.W. made Squad Leader.; Typical Op Report understatement; Observation plane seen over column]

DECLASSIFIED PER EXECUTIVE ORDER 12356, Section 3.3, /161/1050
By RLB/JJO   NARA, Date 4-24-9.1

which followed, two tanks were knocked out. At 1900 the Comd Gp moved Fwd, setting up in a field on N side of Rd near OSERA The progress of the 2d Bn was held up several times by Arty and mortar fire coming from unknown sources, and during this period, at 1930, the 315 Inf of the 79th Div was reported to have moved into LE MANS and had reached the river. The 2d Bn was ordered to proceed to the river and await orders As the period closed it was still on its way to the town.

9 Aug 1944- At 0300 the 2d Bn reached the SARTHE River in town, after knocking out two tanks on the approach. Crossing was delayed until daylight. At 1015 Gen McLAIN and Gen WEAVER arrived at the CP. Task force Weaver was coming up without resistance After the departure of Gen McLAIN and Gen WEAVER, the Comd Gp proceeded into Le MANS, crossed the SARTHE and arrived at the NE edge of town with the head of the 2d Bn. Reports of an enemy regiment to the north of the road proved unfounded and the Comd Gp proceeded on to CHATELET, Approx three miles from town on the rlad to SAVIGNE. Here Elms of the 5th Armored Div were met. CP was set up in the Chateau. All three Bns were brought forward and moved into assembly area NE of Chatelet. This move completed the mission of the Regt and the Div.

> Victory march thru *Le Mans*

> Helmet incident

10 Aug 1944- 357 was alerted for possible movement to N at 1500. At 1900 Opns order was received from Div outlining following Opn: At 080010 August the XV Corps Atkd to the N with two Divs abreast, the 2d French Armored and the 5th Armored. The 90th Div was to follow the 2d French armored on the Left, with the 79th Div following the 5th Armored on the right. 357 to follow 359 Mtzd in the following order of march: I&R Plat to maintain contact with CT9; 3d Bn as Adv Guard with transportation moving by bounds in Clm; CT Hq; 2d Bn and 1st Bn (Comd vehicles and rifle Co transportation); Hq Co, Engrs Plat; Cn Co; 343 FA Bn; Co A, 315 Med Bn. The A/T Co was to protect the Clm at main avenues of Tank approaches. Time of departure set 110630 August. Corps objective for this move was line from CARROUGES - SEES.

> W.W. drives sports car

> Objective: *Sées*

11 Aug 1944- Because of density of traffic, route of 357 changed to Adv in rear and between CT8 and CT9. The I&R Plat moved out at 0430 to mark the route, and at 0630 the 3d Bn crossed the IP, just NE of Chatelet. The Clm proceeded along the route LES FOURCHES-COURCEBOEUFS-ST MARS SOUS BALLONS-CONGE SUR ORNE without incident. In the Vic of this last town forward movement was halted because of confusion in routes between 2d Fr and 5th Armored Divs, and went into assembly area. Traffic confusion cleared and 357 was ordered to proceed forward into assembly area just south of RENE. This move was initiated at 1930 and completed without incident, Regt closing in at Approx 2300.

> Sackett takes prisoners

12 Aug 1944- Change in Corps plans cancelled further movement to N until 1100 when order was received to continue. At 1130 the 3d Bn initiated movement, on foot, with vehicles for Clm control only. Cn Co and one Btry Arty attached to 3d, followed by 2d and 1st Bns, less A Co which was in Div control with mission of guarding bridges crossing ORNE River; rejoined 1st Bn in assembly area at ALENCON. Route of march from RENE, left to CHANCE, N to BOIS MOCQUET, thru ROUESSE FONTAINBOURG LE ROI-CHAMPFLEUR-LEVX. BOURG-ALENCON. Clm was halted at

> W.W. & Sackett caught in flares

-6-

DECLASSIFIED PER EXECUTIVE ORDER 12356, Section 3.3, /16/7650

By RLB/JJO NARA, Date 4-24-91

> *Alençon* inspected by German Generals as possible route of withdrawal from failed *Mortain* Offensive

Clm was halted at intersection just S of ROUESSE FONTAINE to allow 359 to clear, also Elms of 2d French Armored. At this point all motors were routed W to La HUITE, then N to ALENCON. March resumed from intersection at 1640. At 2030 the Comd Gp reached Alencon, with the head of the 3d Bn reaching the city at 2045. Heavy traffic congestion delayed movement through city to assembly area to NW in immediate vicinity of Damigni, units closing in at Approx 2400, to await orders for further movement. Trip completed without incident.

13 Aug 1944-At 0800 357 was ordered to prepare for movement to CARROUGES, where French units were reported to have cleared. At 0930 this plan was changed, as the 2d French Armored had moved around intervening area. 357 mission to seize and hold 3 hills at W end of Foret DECOUVES. 3d Bn to take BUTTE CAUMONT, 2d LA ROCHE ELIE, 1st LE CRACHET. A later report indicated that 2d French was moving Elms along route of 357 and that they had encountered resistance Approx 500 Yds NW of LONRAY. Our move was delayed until Fr had moved Fwd. At 1230 3d Bn initiated movement proceeding to and occupying the hill without resistance by 1500. 2d Bn occupied Obj without resistance at 1645; 1st Bn closed in Approx 1900. I & K Cos were moved from BUTTE CAUMONT to NE to position at edge of woods just N of ERE AUX GALAIS. One Plat of 1st Bn was sent to occupy high ground at CORBINIERE, was blocked by enemy force reported as five tanks, 100 infantry plus anti-tank guns, and was withdrawn to allow use of Arty on this target. Main position of 1st Bn and 2d Bns had brief small arms exchange with small groups which were eliminated.

14 Aug 44 - At 0930 357 was given mission of clearing up section of Foret DECOUVES from main road to W and occupying CARROUGES. Co A of 315 Engrs replaced L Co at BUTTE CAUMONT, which rejoined 3d Bn for this mission, with Cn Co Atchd and 1 Plat TD in support. 1st Bn was given mission of clearing enemy at CARBONIERE with the Co. 2d Bn was given responsibility for blocking all roads to W of BUTTE CAUMONT and LA ROCHE ELIE, Co a, 315 Engrs Atchd to facilitate mission. When Co of 1st Bn had reached CARBONIERE resistance had dissolved. 3d B reached Obj at Approx 2000, when orders were received from Division to relieve 359 at main intersection N of Foret DECOUVES, Approx 2000 Yds NE of L'ETRE PIERREAUS. Motors were sent Fwd to expedite this removal which was initiated immediately. The Div order also called for the relieving of 358 and 359 at all posisions, the two Regts to go into assembly area for move to NE, this relief to be initiated morning of Aug 15. 2d Bn took Approx 240 prisoners today in area to N & W of positions.

15 Aug 1944-At 0530 readjustment of positions in line with Div order was begun and completed by 1200 resulting in the following dispositions: 1st Bn-A Co at ST DENIS SUR SARTHON, B Co just W of LA FERNIERE-BOCHARD, C Co in Res Vic CONDE SUR SARTHE. 2d Bn-occupying BUTTE CAUMONT & LA ROCHE ELIE (Co A 315 Engrs released to Div). 3d Bn-I Co reinforced with Hvy Wpns and A/T guns at intersection of main roads N of Foret DECOUVES, Bal of Regt'l Res between CUISSAI & forest NW on main road. At 2030 Div called for altering of I Co for possible move to COURRAGES to reinforce Fr garrison of tanks and TDs.

UNCLASSIFIED PER EXECUTIVE ORDER 12356, Section 3.3, /16/7650.
By RLB/JJO   NARA, Date 4-24-91

343d FA Bn ts were brought fwd to be n readiness for this move, which was ordered at 2155, and initiated immediatel The TDs and Cn Co were recalled to area of 2d Bn position for balance of night. I Co control passed to 2d Fr Armored.

16 Aug 1944 - During the morning of 2d Fr Armored was relieved of its mission in COURRAGES and I Co of 357 reverted to our control, moving back to its position N of the Foret DECOUVES, the area it had occupied prior to its move of the previous evening. This was the only activity during the day until 1700 when 3d Bn reverted to Div control to move to Vic N of SEES by Mtr. Prior to the move, I Co rejoined the Bn at 1800, the Bn getting underway to its Obj at 2045. Bal of the Regt was ordered to go into assembly area in Vic of LONRAY in preparation for move to NE in morning. CP closed in at chateau Approx 500 Yds SW of LONRAY at 1930, balance of Regt being closed in by 2200. Order from Div for 357 to relieve 359 in area N of SEES and assume all around defense position as Div Res, to be initiated as early as possible 17 Aug.

17 Aug 1944 - Quartering parties moved out at 0615, followed by the 1st Bn at 0700, following route LONRAY to NE through COLOMBIERS-RADON to main NS road; N through SEES to area N of CHALLOUE. [Gervase's horseback ride] The 2d Bn remained in position, awaiting the return of the Trks which had carried the 1st Bn. Relief of positions held by 359 was completed by the 1st Bn by 1200 with the following disposition, with mission of blocking roads to N and E: CROISILLES; LE TAILLIS; SOURERS; LE MERLERAULT and NONANT [Our roadblock at Le Merlerault] LE PIN. Co F of the 2d Bn was assigned with the same mission at GAPREE, occupying its position by 1430. In the meanwhile, 357 CP had closed in just N of CHAILOUE, 458344. These blocking missions were to protect right rear of Div Atk to N and W. At 1645 G Co of 2d Bn was ordered to relieve K Co of 359 at the town of EXMES, with further readjustment of positions to take place 18 Aug. By 1830 2d Bn had G Co in position, E Co in Res Approx 2000 Yds S. 3d Bn remained in its position just NW of NONANT LE PIN in reserve. These positions were maintained until 18 Aug. Atchmts were as follows: F Co, 1 Plat TDs; G Co, 1 Plat TDs (607 TD Bn).

18 Aug 1944 - In line with Div order 171800 Aug, which included Corps order calling for Atk by the Provisional Corps as follows: 2d Fr Armored, 80th Inf and 90th Inf Divs Atk to N at 0600 respectively left right. 90th Div Obj high ground N of Foret DE GOUFFERN from Vic ORENNES to NE thru BON MENIL to CHAMBOIS. 357 had mission of protecting right rear of corps w/following dispositions: 1st Bn- A Co at Rd intersection just NE of LE TAILLIS, B Co at LE MERLERAULT, C Co in Res at ST [Jeep patrol and firefight] GERMAN-LE CHAIREFEUILLE (NE of Nonant Le Pin); 2d Bn- G Co at EXMES, F Co at CROISILLES, E Co in Res; 3d Bn in Regt'l Res Approx 500 Yds NW of Nonant Le Pin, to N of Rd to LE BOURG-ST LEONARD. CP 357 just N of NONANT LE PIN (484400). The I&R Plat was given the mission of patrolling area E of Rd from SEES to NONANT LE PIN; S of Rd NONANT LE PIN to MERLERAULT; W of grid line NS thru latter town; N of line SEES-GAPREE. At 1200 Div order was received to occupy road junction SE of MONT BOUGON, N of EXMES. Patrol from E Co

-8-

was ordered to determine situation, since information in our hands indicated that this intersection was protected by dug-in enemy positions. This order from Div was later modified (1400) calling for occupation of the area without commitment. Reports from E Co patrol indicated that the intersection was held by enemy so the Div order was further modified calling for the placing of a combat patrol across the road at a point Approx 2000 Yds S of the intersection. This patrol was reinforced with A/T guns and Hvy Wpns and was in position by 2300. During the early evening A & F Cos reported receiving strafing and rocket fire from 3 ME 109's with Allied markings. These planes were observed from CP 357 and the identification was later confirmed by shell casings dropped during the strafing. Orders were received and execution initiated by 357 calling for the elimination of all captured vehicles not authorized for use by the various units.

Captured vehicles ordered abandoned

19 Aug 1944–Corps Atk to N continued at 0800 with mission of cutting off escape routes of trapped enemy forces W and N of CHAMBOIS. 357 was assigned to continue mission of protecting right rear of corps. A combat team of the 2d French Armored passed to the N through our combat patrol N of EXMES. The mission of the corps was effectively executed and the continuing attempts of the enemy to break through resulted in wholesale destruction of equipment and extremely heavy casualties. At 1345 our 3d Bn passed to Div control and began move to point 2000 Yds N of LE PIN AU-HARAS as Div reserve. 3d Bn of 358 was brought around the rear of 359 with the mission of attacking CHAMBOIS from the SE. The 2d French Armored began taking over parts of 357 areas, relieving G Co at EXMES and F Co at CROISILLES, both companies going into assembly areas alongside of E Co. 2d Bn was then placed on alert status for possible movement. The TD and A/T attachments reverted to their own units. Developments of the attack on CHAMBOIS caused rearrangement of 357 dispositions, initiated at 2100, resulting in following picture: 1st Bn- remained in place with exception of one rifle platoon supported by TDs, A/Ts and heavy weapons, taking over 2d French Armored positions at CROISILLES; 2d Bn- remains in place on alert for movement; 3d Bn- L Co moved N in reserve position behind 3d Bn of 358, which had gained outskirts at SE edge of CHAMBOIS, and was atchd to CT 357. Meantime 359 2d Bn had entered town from SW and the 3 Bn 358 made contact, with Polish troops, part of reconnaissan elements of Canadian forces attacking from N. The enemy continued suffering heavy loss of men and equipment in attempting to break out of the pocket. CP of 357 was set up approximately 2500 Yds west of EXMES, 500 Yds N of Rd to LE BOURG-ST LEONARD, grid 436469 in chateau.

357's mission to protect Corp's rear

358 to attack Chambois

French armored involved

Falaise-Argentan "Gap" closed

DECLASSIFIED PER EXECUTIVE ORDER 12356, Section 3.3, /1601 (...)
By RLB/JJO   NARA, Date 4-24-91

20 August 1944 - At 0850 Division assumed control of our 2nd Bn, moving by motor to SILLE-EN-GOUFFERN, just south of GOUFFERN FOREST, as reserve for 1st and 2nd Bns 358th Inf and 1st and 2nd Bns of 359th which were heavily engaged north of forest. At 0855 the 3rd Bn of the 357th, less "L" Company, was ordered to motorize and proceed to a point just outside of FOUGY to intercept enemy column which had broken through between right flank of 359th and left flank of 3rd Bn 358th. While our 3rd Bn was preparing to make this move, the enemy column was reported to be abandoning and burning its vehicles and dispersing into the woods. The objective of the 3rd Bn was then changed to occupation of the high ground 2000 yards NE of LE BOURG-ST LEONARD to cover secondary roads in that area. While moving to this area, several enemy half-tracks which had broken through CHAMBOIS block came within 200 yards of 357th Regimental CP, were knocked out or captured by miscellaneous elements of 357th Infantry and 2nd French armored. Numerous prisoners were being taken by troops in vicinity CHAMBOIS block ############ because of occasional infiltration of enemy personnel and some equipment, it was necessary to use the I&R Platoon as cover for trucks bringing prisoners to rear areas. At 1200 Co "C" of the 893rd Tank Destroyer Bn passed to 357th Regimental control.

> **Germans trapped in "pocket"**

21 August 1944 - Enemy pressure continues as attempts are made to break out of pocket. Our 3rd Bn was moved North in the morning to assume reserve and supporting positions behind 3rd Bn 358th and "L" Company 357th which were in CHAMBOIS blocking roads to E and NE.

> **357's L-Company at *Chambois***

Elements of the 11th British Armored were passing through our positions during this period, attacking to north and east of 1st Bn outpost positions. At 1530 90th Division prepared to go into assembly area to be in readiness for move to East. Assembly area move to begin 22 August. During the 48 hour period ending at 2400 today, approximately 1700 prisoners were taken by the 357th Infantry. 90th Division positions to be taken over by 50th British Infantry Division.

22 August 1944 - At 0800 the 2nd Battalion initiated movment into assembly area in vicinity NONANT LE PIN, was closed in by 1200. The 3rd Battalion was originally ordered to remain position until 50th British Division moved into area, this order recalled and 3rd Bn was enroute at 1200. 358th Infantry was relieved by the British at approximately 1700 and reverted to its own Regimental control. By 1500 the entire 357th Regiment, excepting 1st Battalion, which was to continue to outpost positions, was in assembly area, the CP set up in house at LA CHAUVIERE, just SW of NONANT LE PIN, 475390. The regiment was ordered to be on alert status for offensive or defensive action to North or East, and for this purpose Co "C" of 893rd Tank Destroyer Battalion remained attached, together with one platoon light tanks, which were placed in defensive positions with 1st battalion. All other attachments reverted to own units.

23 August 1944 - The situation remained unchanged during this day. Arms and vehicles inspections were instituted. "Critique After Battle" discussions resumed, reviewing past engagements.

24 August 1944 - At 1150 the 2nd Battalion relieved the 1st Battalion positions with "E" Company at LE MERLERAU, "F" and "G" Companies at LE TAILLIS. At 1530 Division notified of planned move to vicinity of ORLEANS, quartering parties were organized and had reached meeting place for quartering parties from 358th and 359th, when plans were cancelled. This was followed by an alert for possible movement to take place 25 August.

> **B-Co. leaves *Le Merlerault***

25 August 1944 - At 0915 the Regiment was notified of possible move to East at approximately 1530. At 1115 this was modified and no move was planned before morning of 26 August. The mission of outposting positions to the East and North was cancelled at 1115, relieving the 2nd Battalion which was ordered to go into assembly area and release attachments to their own

> **Showers and clean socks**

-10-

DECLASSIFIED PER EXECUTIVE ORDER 12356, Section 3.3, /16/7650
By RLB/JJO   NARA, Date 4-24-9.1

25 August 1944 - units. Confirmation of move was received from Division, to be initiated
(Cont'd)   at approximately 1200 August 26, with objective FONTAINEBLEAU, 175 miles
to the East. Upon arrival at this point, the 90th Division would pass
90th to XX Corps to the 20th Corps which consisted of the 7th Armored Division and the 5th
Infantry Division. Mission of the Corps on this move was to cross and
secure the SEINE RIVER at that point. 90th Division to be in Corps Reserve. The situation remained unchanged at the close of the period.

26 August 1944 - Order of march for 357th Infantry (following 358th): CT Hq & Hq Co, 2nd
Battalion, 3rd Battalion, 1st Battalion, 343rd Field Artillery Battalion,
A/T Company, Cannon Company, Engineer Platoon, Collecting Company, Service
Company. The first units of the convoy were scheduled to cross the Regimental IP at NONANT LE PIN at 1145. The advance unit quartering party
left at 0930 to faciliate the movement of the units into proper areas
at the objective. Route of march was as follows: NONANT LE PIN, SEES,
LE MESLE, MAMERS, CHAMPAISSANT, LA FERTE BERNARD, MONTMIRAIL, LA BAZOCHE,
Bivouac near Forest of Fontainebleau CHATEAUDUN, JANVILLE, PITHIERS, MALESHERBES, LA CHAPELLE LA REINE and to
area two miles SW of FONTAINEBLEAU. The units moved out on shoedule, a
slight interruption caused by traffic at NONANT LE PIN delayed the clearing of the last vehicle to 1350. The march was completed without unusual
interruption as scheduled. The leading elements of the column reached
the objective at 2200. At the close of the period the balance of the
column was closing in.

27 August 1944 - The last vehicle of the column closed in at 0030. At approximately 0300
a new XX Corps order was received, calling for resumption of movement to
New orders to Reims NE with Corps objective REIMS. The order called for spearhead by 7th
Armored, with the 90th and 5th Divisions extending and clearing bridgehead to left and right respectively. 357th was assigned to spearhead
for the 90th Division, and arranged the following order of march: 2nd
Battalion (1 Platoon mounted on light tanks), 1 Platoon Cannon Company,
Command Group, one battery 343rd Field Artillery Battalion, 1st Battalion,
Headquarters Company, 3rd Battalion, A/T Company, Cannon Company (minus),
and the Medics. The route for the first days operation was as follows:
See Palace of Fontainebleau through FONTAINEBLEAU, crossing SEINE RIVER into VULAINES SUR SEINE
MACHOULT, LES MONTILS, NANGIS being the objective for the move. Leading
elements left the assembly area at 0930; severe traffic congestion delayed
Cross the Seine River movement and the crossing of the SEINE by ponton bridge was not effected
by the leading elements until 1045. From this point on the march continued without interruption or resistance, the leading elements reaching
NANGIS at 1245, proceeding to north of town to await balance of convoy.
As the 2nd Battalion moved into the area, it took over the outposting
of the following towns to the north and east of NANGIS, JOUY-LE-CHATELET,
CHENOISE, MAISON ROUGE, GASTIN. "E" Company was left in NANGIS TO hold
the town. 1st Battalion moved into the area of LES PLESSIS HAINAULT; 3rd
Battalion vicinity ORBIS, balance of the Regiment just to the south.
All of these positions were approximately 1000 yards west of the FORET
DU JUOY. The presence of other units in the town of NANGIS made continued posting unnecessary, and "E" Company was relieved at 2000 and moved
into assembly area just west of the 1st Bn position. No further changes
took place for the balance of the period.

28 August 1944 - Continuation of the movement toward the objective was delayed to allow
the 7th Armored to clear the area; to further facilitate handling, the
march was broken into two routes, designated as "X" on the left, and "J"
on the right. Route "X" was to be followed by the left flank guard,
consisting of the 3rd Battalion, with the I&R platoon serving as point,
the 384th Field Artillery Battalion, one platoon Tank Destroyers, and one

DECLASSIFIED PER EXECUTIVE ORDER 12356, Section 3.3, /16/7650
By RLB/JJO   NARA, Date 4-24-9.1

28 August 1944 - platoon of A/T Company. In addition to serving as left flank guard it
(Cont'd) had the mission of maintaining contact with the 7th Armored to the front
and the 39th Infantry (9th Division) to the left. The route of march was
as follows: from PETIT PARIS north through CHAILLY EN BRIE, BOISSY LE
CHATEL, northeast, passing around REBAIS, rejoining at LE TRETOIRE, continuing northeast through BOITRON, PAVANT, NOGENT ARTAUD, CHEZY SUR MARNE,
into CHATEAU THIERRY. The main body was to move on route "3", in the
following order of march: 2nd Battalion with one platoon TD's, 1 platoon
A/T and 1 Platoon light tanks mounted as the point, Cannon Company, Command group, 343rd FA Bn, 1st Bn, Hq Company, balance of A/T Company and
TD's, and Medics. The route was as follows: Through JOUY LE CHATEL,
BAGNY, CHOISY EN BRIE, north through REBAIS, northwest through VILLENEUVE
SUR BELLOT, VIELS MASON to vicinity of MONTFAUCON. Just as the march was
to begin, Division ordered the return of all trucks not belonging to the
regiment. This did not effect the march of the 2nd Battalion which was
using kitchen trucks. However, it was necessary to limit the 3rd Bn's
use of vehicles until 1400 when they were to be returned. The 3rd Bn
initiated its move at 1115, the main body 1145. The march proceeded
without interruption according to schedule, excepting a deviation from
route by the main body which took it through the town of JOUY SUR MORIN,
which lay to the south of the planned march. The column then headed
northwest, coming back on the correct route at REBAIS. At 1530 the head
of the column arrived in the vicinity of MONTFAUCON, where it was decided
to halt for the night because of congestion caused by the 7th Armored
units just ahead.
The left flank guard was detrucked half way between LE TRETOIRE and BOITRON
proceeding on foot and arriving at CHEZY SUR MARNE at 1800. Here the column
was halted to await orders, and was instructed to continue on into CHA-
TEAU THIERRY. Movement was resumed at 2000, the column crossing the MARNE
just as darkness fell, moving into defensive positions north of the town
and relieving the 7th Armored.
Positions at the close of the day's operations were as follows: 1st Bn
in vicinity of COURBOIN, with the 343rd Field Artillery just to the South.
2nd Battalion in area northwest side of road, at intersection just northwest of VIFORT. The Regimental CP was set up in the chateau approximately 1000 yards southwest of the 2nd Bn position. 3rd Battalion remained
North of CHATEAU THIERRY, approximately six miles northwest of 2nd Bn.
Survey of crossing facilities over the MARNE RIVER revealed that other
than tactical transportation of units would have to cross at CHATEAU THI-
ERRY, the only other bridge available located at MONT ST PERE being of
six ton capacity.

29 August 1944 - The original mission of the Regiment to seize and secure crossing of LA
VESLE RIVER at FISMES and JONCHERY was extened to call for the same mission
at the AISNE RIVER at the towns of PONTAVERT and GUIGNICOURT. The 3rd
Bn as left flank guard began the march on foot at 0700 following route X
with the 1st Battalion taking the lead of the main body and moving motorized at 0730, crossing the MARNE at CHATEAU THIERRY, thence south through
MONT ST PERE nad JAULGONNE, there resuming its way on route "3" to the
north. The 2nd Battalion initiated its move on foot, other than tactical
transportation crossing behind the 1st Bn; foot troops and tactical transportation crossed at MONT ST PERE
Route of the 3rd Bn was as follows: Through VERDILLY, TRUGNY, BEUVARDES,,

> Cross the *Marne* at *Chateau Thierry*

to north of FRESNES EN TARDENOIS through NESLES, east to COULON north to DRAVEGNY, to NE through ST GILLES to FISMES, E and N through VENTELAY to PONTAVERT. At VEUVARDES the Bn was motorized and at 1800 arrived at the AISNE RIVER. The bridge was badly damaged so it was necessary to move across the AISNE on foot, leaving vehicles S of the river. At that point a defensive position was formed.

[Margin note: Ride tanks through Small town to tumultuous welcome]

The main body proceeded without incident from JAULGONNE through LE CHARMEL, RONCHERES, COUSSANCOURT, N through VEILLY. Just N of this point a confusion in routes developed because of inaccurate maps. The column moving S to ROMIGNY, turning N through LHERY, FAVEROLLES, SAVIGNY SUR ARDRE then to the NE through JONCHERY SUR VESLE, BOUVANCOURT then NE to CORMICY CONTINUING NE to AGUILCOURT. Approximately one mile S of LA VESLE River the kitchen trucks were sent back to motorize the 2d Bn. The 1st Bn proceeded on foot to a point S of BOUVANCOURT, where it was again motorized, using trucks of the 343d FA Bn and the 607 TD Bn. At AGUILCOURT the R was detrucked, proceeding on foot to GUIGINCOURT. Arrival at this point marked the completion of the 90 th Div Obj. Meantime the 2d Bn had moved into assembly area between GOUSSANCOURT and RONCHERES where it was motorized on the returned kitchen trucks at approximately 2000, moving Fwd on route B to go into assembly area at CORMICY. At the close of the period the vehicles were still enroute.

[Margin note: Inaccurate maps cause confusion]

30 Aug 1944- The last vehicles closed in at 0030. On completion of the move the dispositions were as follows: 1st Bn at GUIGINCCURT with Co C at EVERGHICOURT, 2d Bn in assembly area NW of CORMICY, 3d Bn N of L'AISNE River at PONTAVERT, less one Co which was left at FISMES as security. Special Units and the Regimental CP were located in CORMICY. In these positions the Regiment awaited further orders.

[Margin note: We See C-47s landing at Reims]

31 Aug 1944- No new orders for further advance were received, the only activity of the day being the dispatching of one Co of the 2d Bn N to provide cover for Engrs restoring the bridge over the AISNE at BERRY EN BAS. At 1745 the Regiment was alerted for movement to E approximately four miles from REIMS, the move to be made on order 1 Sep 1944. An additional order was received to have one Co prepared to move to XX Corps as Corps guard, the morning of 1 Sep.
No further changes at end of period.

DECLASSIFIED PER EXECUTIVE ORDER 12356, Section 3.3, 1161 1030
By RLB/JJO NARA, Date 4-24-91

HEADQUARTERS 557TH INFANTRY
APO 90, U.S. ARMY

OPERATION REPORT 357TH INFANTRY MONTH OF SEPTEMBER 1944

1 September 1944 — At 0900 the 1st Bn moved out, taking a route around REIMS into its assembly area between WITRY and BERRU. The 2nd Battalion moved out at 1000, taking the main road running Southwest, through REIMS, followed by the balance of the Regiment. The Regimental CP was set up in CERNAY, in chateau near the West end of town. By 1600 all elements of the Regiment had closed, the march being completed without incident. The Regiment then awaited orders for further movement.

[Moved near Vitry-les-Reims]
[W.W.'s "small revolt"]

2 September 1944 — No orders were received, the time being passed in cleaning of equipment shows were shown in the afternoon in the auditorium in CERNAY. Because of gas shortage, rigid restrictions were placed upon the use of all vehicles; trip tickets and permission of various C.O's being required before vehicles were allowed to leave the motor parks.

[Gas shortage]

3 September 1944 — At 1800 the Regiment was alerted for move east, scheduled for 4 September, to the vicinity of VERDUN. Details of the move were not available during the day. Restrictions on use of vehicles continued.

[Objective: Verdun]

4 September 1944 — The scheduled move to the East was postponed because of continued gasoline shortage. At 2000 orders were received to move as early as possible the following day, the time of departure dependent on the arrival of gasoline supplies. Battalion and Special Unit Commanders were assembled at the Regimental CP at 2130, and were given the plans for relieving elements of the 5th Division in area approximately 15 miles east of VERDUN. The 359th Regiment was to relieve the balance of the Division in the REIMS vicinity. The plans, order and route of march follow 2nd Battalion to leave on foot at 0730, proceeding to main road running SE out of REIMS. Just South of LE PATRON the battalion was scheduled to be motorized on 22 trucks furnished by XX Corps. One Company of medium tanks (712th Tank Bn) would lead the battalion, supported by 1 platoon of 607th Tank Destroyer Battalion, passing through the towns of ST HILAIRE LE GRAND, JOUEY SUR SUIPPES, SOMME TOURBE, SOMME BIONNE, VALMY, DOMMARTIN, STE MENEHOULD. At this last town the column was to stop to obtain information on reported group of enemy in the southwest section of the ARGONNE FOREST, the site of some 30,000 tons of enemy ammunition, according to the FFI in the area. In the following order, the balance of the Regiment and attachments were then to pass through the 2nd Battalion, continuing on the route through LES ISLETTES, CLERMONT, PARIOIS, DOMBASLE, FLERCOURT, VERDUN, ETAIN. The area to be taken over from the 5th Division was reported to lie East of road running from ETAIN north to VAUDONCOURT, south of line from VAUDONCOURT through HAUCOURT, JOUDREVILLE, south from that point to BOI COMMUNAUX. Total distance of the move, 85 miles.

[Through Argonne Forest]

5 September 1944 — In the following order the units moved forward on schedule: Company "C" 712th Tank Bn, 2nd Bn plus 1 Platoon TD's, 3rd Bn, motorized on its vehicles and those of Cannon and A/T Companies, 1st Battalion, motorized on vehicles of the 343rd FA Battalion, balance of TD's, Hq Co and Special Units, and 343rd FA Battalion. The 2nd Battalion left the road at STE MENEHOULD at 1330, the balance continuing on, passing through VERDUN at 1630. The Command Group stopped at ROUVRES at 1710 where the Regimental CP was set up, the balance of the Regiment continuing into positions previously assigned. It was found that the 5th was not in the positions reported, and there had been considerable enemy activity in the general area up to the day of arrival. Pending the arriv

[Through Verdun]

-1-

DECLASSIFIED PER EXECUTIVE ORDER 12356, Section 3.3, NLR1 /030
By RLB/JJC   NARA, Date 4-24-91

5 September 1944 - of the 358th Infantry Regiment, the 357th adopted the following defen-
(Cont'd) sive positions: 1st Battalion: "A" Company from North boundary at SPIN-
COURT to JOUDREVILLE on the South; "B" Company South to 3rd Battalion
sector at FLEVILLE. "C" Company in reserve. Tank destroyers were
placed at strategic position from FAUDONCOURT in the NW corner of the
sector to the South boundary. 3rd Battalion: "K" Company on line facing East, from one-half mile south of main road which bisects sector to
THUMMERVILLE, "L" Company balance of area to south. "I" Company still
serving as Corps CP Guard. The 343rd and 345th Fa Bns were placed in
general support of the area. Late in the evening, at 2200, an officer
from the 358th Infantry arrived at the CP stating that their 3rd Battalion was scheduled to arrive and take over north section of area occupied by our first battalion. Because our positions had been already
placed, and the difficulty in making changes after dark, it was decided
to allow the 358th 3rd Battalion to move into assembly area in the vicinity of BARONCOURT until the following day. During this period the
2nd Battalion was carrying on its mission of investigating and clearing
the southwest section of the ARGONNE FORET. The CP was set up at LES
ISLETTES. Inventory revealed 35,000 tons of ammunition, a good portion
of which had been equipped with demolition charges; another section had
been partially equipped, indicating that the abandonment of the area
was comparatively sudden. Approximately 300 FFI members were placed
along the east and north edge of the forest in this section, and the
search through the woods drove 50 enemy into their ranks, who were
taken as prisoners. The 2nd Battalion was notified that it would be
relieved of the mission by Engineers.

6 September 1944- The positions of the 357th Infantry were maintained during the day. The
I&R Platoon reported that the 7th Armored was heavily engaged at BRIEY,
directly to the east of our general positions, distance approximately
8 miles. This fighting continued until late afternoon, when the enemy
withdrew. Relief of the north area occupied by the 1st Battalion was
completed by the 3rd Battalion of the 358th during the early afternoon.
At 1400 the Regiment was alerted for move to northeast. In preparation
for this move the 2nd Battalion was relieved at the ARGONNE and moved
into assembly area with the balance of the Regiment by 2300.

7 September 1944 - Corps order received through Division at 0345. 8th Armored preceding
5th Division on right, 90th Division on left, to move NE, crossing
MOSELLE, SAAR And RHINE RIVERS, Objective FRANKFURT. 90th Division

Objective: Frankfurt

participation to be as follows: Initially to capture SAARBRUCKEN. Formation of the 90th Division: 357th on right of sector, to move from
present area at 070800 to assembly area on line running from ROSSELANGE
through FAMECK to the LA FENTSCH RIVER, from that point to reconnoiter
for crossings to the MOSELLE RIVER. 358th and 359th to move similarly
from left respectively, 358th to capture THIONVILLE. While the Battalion and Special Unit Commanders were assembling at the Regimental CP
the departure hour was changed on a two hour notice basis, because of
evidences of enemy resistance involving the north part of the Division
sector. At 0845 order was received to start move as early as possible,
and our first elements were on the road at 0914.
The march was divided into two routes, the north going through FLEVILLE
ANOUX, MANCIEULLES, through BOIS D'AVRIL to the assembly area. This
route was followed by the 1st Battalion, the balance of the column consisting of 1 platoon of TD's, Hq Co and Special Units, and 343rd Field
Artillery Battalion. The south route passed through OZERAILLES, LUBEY,
LANTEFONTAINE, MANCE, then East through FORET DE MOYEUVRE, N to AVRIL,

DECLASSIFIED PER EXECUTIVE ORDER 12356, Section 3.3, /1/61/1030
By RLB/JJO   NARA, Date 4-24-91

7 September 1944 - thence to assembly area. The 3rd Battalion started its movement at
(Cont'd) 0914, a last minute change resulted from the report that enemy had re-
occupied BRIEY, the 2nd Battalion being changed from the north to the
south route, to continue straight into BRIEY to eliminate the enemy
concentration. All elements were on the road by 1030, first enemy contact was made by the 1st Battalion when its advance guard captured an
enemy staff car which drove into the column at MANCIEULLES, this occur-
ing at 1110. At 1300 the 1st Battalion had moved to the high ground
NE of MANCIEULLES, and called for artillery fire on a column of enemy
horse drawn artillery, which was quickly dispersed. The column continued on its route, through the woods, reaching the clearing on the east
side at 1330. From this point roofs of buildings in the town of AVRIL
were seen to the right, to the left of the town of TRIEUX. Company "B",
leading, crossed the open area and occupied hill 303 without resistance,
while our artillery was firing on enemy targets on the road running north
from AVRIL. TD's were brought forward to cover this road, faced to the
north. At this same time the 3rd Battalion was approaching AVRIL from
the west. A motorized patrol was sent forward, and received fire from a
tank located just west of the town. One jeep was knocked out, the occupants of four others forced to abandon their vehicles by concentration
of small arms and artillery fire. While the 1st Battalion was occupying
the open area north of AVRIL, the balance of the column waited in the
woods for the situation to clarify. Enemy artillery fire began falling
on the woods, coming from the direction of TRIEUX, so it was necessary
to reverse the route and the vehicles were brought back to the south
of MANCIEULLES. By this time it was obvious that enemy resistance was
general along all points of advance and the Special Units, together with
the Regimental CP was set up in MANCIEULLES, closing in at 1530. The
343rd F.A. Bn had set up positions just to the northeast of the town.
Meantime, the 2nd Battalion was heavily engaged at BRIEY, the town occupied in strength by the enemy. Pressure by the 1st Battalion from
the north and the 3rd Bn on the south resulted in the elimination of
enemy resistance at AVRIL, and at 2045 the 3rd Bn occupied the town.
Positions at the close of the day's operations were as follows: 1st
Battalion, Main body on Hill 313, 2nd Battalion to the west of BRIEY,
still engaged, and the 3rd Battalion physically occupying AVRIL, with
A/T defense around the town.

8 September 1944 - At 0730 the 1st Battalion moved on to the northeast, being replaced by
the 3rd Battalion in its outpost positions north of AVRIL. The march
met with minor small arms interruptions until a message from General
McLain ordered its return to the positions of the previous evening,
because of reported enemy concentrations to the north in the area of
AUDUN. While the Battalion was carrying out this order, the Regimental
CP and Special Units were brought south east to AVRIL closing in at
1410. Shortly after this the 1st Battalion had resumed its defensive
positions to the north of town; at 1610 the outpost on hill 303 was
receiving an attack which grew in proportions. Enemy equipment included Self Propelled TD's and a number of other vehicles and infantry.
TD's and A/T's were moved into position and were successful in knocking
out two tanks and by 1730 the attack had been repulsed. Just after this
attack opened, message was received from the 2nd Battalion at BRIEY. The
deploying of one company to the south and one to the north, continuing
the pressure from the west, had been successful and the enemy had surrendered. Total prisoners taken in the capture of the town numbered

-3-

[Margin notes:]
- W.W.'s squad on battalion point
- W.W.'s squad fights off German attack
- This was Major Hamilton's idea
- W.W. asked to volunteer for recon patrol

8 September 1944 (Cont'd) — approximately 400. With the exception of the erection of a road block at the edge of the woods east of ST PIERREMONT by the 1st Battalion, to close the gap between 357th Infantry and 358th, the situation remained unchanged for the balance of the period.

9 September 1944 — Because of heavy resistance in front of 358th and 359th, forward movement of the 357th Regiment was delayed, with the exception of reconnaissance parties. "B" Company less one platoon was given the job of patrolling to NEUFCHEF at 1800, which was reported clear after encountering some small arms fire and road blocks of felled trees. The 1st Battalion followed, being replaced by "K" Company of the 3rd Battalion with 4 TD's as support, and occupied NEUFCHEF prior to dark. Following success of 358th and 359th in their attacks which were initiated at 1100, taking the towns of FONTOY and AUDUN, preparations were made for continuing to the east the following morning.

[Through woods to *Neufchef*]

10 September 1944 — Company "A" 315th Engineers relieved 2nd Battalion in BRIEY at 0800. 2nd Battalion was ordered to move by foot through MAYEUVRE GRANDE to occupy a defensive position on the high ground 3000 yards SE of RANGEVAUX and north of VITRY. The Battalion moved starting at 0900. The 1st Battalion was ordered to occupy the town of HAYANGE on the high ground to the north. The 3rd Battalion remaining in AVRIL. The 1st Battalion entered HAYANGE unopposed initially but at 1400 a brief engagement took place between "B" Company and a small enemy force on the high ground north of town. Tank fire effectively eliminated this resistance. At 1500 the 2nd Battalion which was just arriving in position was ordered to move immediately to a defensive position north of MORLANGE leaving one Company ("G") in RANGEVAUX. At 1700 the 3rd Battalion was ordered to move immediately and relieve "G" Company at RANGEVAUX. The 2nd Battalion (- "G" Company) arrived in position at 2000. The 3rd Battalion relieved "G" Company at 2100. "G" Company rejoined the 2nd Battalion by 2400. The Regimental CP closed at NEUFCHEF at 1700. At 2300 "A" Company minus one platoon which had moved north of HAYANGE to the crest of the high ground, was receiving MG fire on fron and both flanks.

[B-Company to *Hayange*]

[W.W. and Sackett have dinner at *DeMuth's*]

11 September 1944 — The Machine gun fire directed against "A" Company at midnight developed into a counterattack, and the company was forced to withdraw back to HAYANGE after two platoons had been overrun. "B" Company was also withdrawn into town because of unfavorable defensive positions. At 0830 "C" Company was given the assignment of retaking the hill; when reports of withdrawal were received from the 358th through Division, the attack was cancelled and patrols were substituted to determine the situation in the general area to the north and east. These patrols returned with the report that the withdrawal did not extend as far south as our sector, and "C" Company was again ordered to attack the hill and move to the crest, which was accomplished without resistance by 1500, the enemy apparently withdrawing in the interim. 2nd Battalion patrol made reconnaissance of the area in the north regimental sector to the MOSELLE without encountering any enemy resistance. The patrol of the 3rd Bn on a similar mission in the south sector, reported enemy in the forest just to the southwest of UCKANGE and the 3rd Battalion was ordered to clear this area and to proceed into UCKANGE. It reached the edge of the town by 2100, encountered considerable small arms fire and was ordered to tie in around the town for the night. During the evening, "G" Company was ordered to serve as cover for the 282d FA Bn which was moving into vicinity of ERZANGE; "E" Company was sent forward to occupy FLORANGE to block any possible enemy activity in that sector. These moves of the 2nd Bn were completed by 2000

[B-Company pulls out of *Hayange*]

12 September 1944 – Beginning at 0900 the 3rd Battalion completed its occupation of UCKANGE, the enemy had withdrawn to the east side of the MOSELLE during the night, blowing the bridge after the withdrawal had been effected. During the day the 3rd Battalion received continuous heavy artillery fire but took few casualties. During this time careful observation of the ground to the east side of the river indicated it was heavily fortified by a number of dug in positions, including pill boxes, some camouflaged as hay-stacks. An intercommunicating trench system made defense of the area comparatively easy. These positions were seen to be occupied, and PW information substantiated that heavy resistance could have been offered at this point. The position of the 3rd Battalion was under continuous observation from the east bank, and it was necessary to arrange for supply movement after dark. The balance of the Regiment maintained positions during the day.

13 September 1944 – Reconnaissance of the area to the MOSELLE was continued during the day. The I&R Platoon reported encountering small arms fire in the southeast sector; other than that the area was cleared. An air mission requested by the 3rd Battalion was not successful as the planes limited their use of weapons to MG's. In order to handle the increasingly difficult problem of Nazi party members now beginning to show up after occupation (NEUFCHEF was the first town in LORRAINE to be occupied by the Regiment), The Commanding Officer ordered the formation of the Regimental MP's, made up of 25 men from each of the battalions and 25 from the Special Units. This group was assigned the job of searching houses, checking civilian activity, enforcing curfew, etc.

> Sartori and Barrett taken for MPs. Liebau picks W.W. as new Platoon Sgt.

Plans for the crossing of the MOSELLE RIVER by the 358th on 14 September were set by Division, involving deceptive thrusts by other Regiments to cover the real site of the proposed crossing. The 358th Infantry had occupied THIONVILLE to the river. At 2330 these plans were cancelled and the Regiment was alerted for movement to the south to assemble in the area of HOMECOURT, southeast of BRIEY, to await orders.

> Moselle crossing at Thionville cancelled

14 September 1944 – During the early morning of the 14th, the 3rd Battalion left UCKANGE moving into the woods southeast of the town so that its departure would not be observed by the enemy on the east bank of the MOSELLE. At 0900 the 1st Battalion moved out, followed by Hq Company, TD's, A/T, Service Company and medics, 2nd Battalion, 343rd Field Artillery, following the route southeast of NEUFCHEF, through AVRIL, BRIEY, and south to AUDOUE, where the column was halted at 1020 to wait for orders. The mission was then received to relieve elements of the 7th Armored and the 5th Infantry Divisions in the area southeast of HOMECOURT, to attack the fortified positions between this area and METZ. By 1800 the battalions had closed in the southern portion of FORET DE JAUMONT, the 1st on the right, 2nd on the left, and the 3rd centered to the rear of the others. The Division order covering this move called for the 358th to take over the balance of the Division area in the territory left by 357 and 359. 359th was assigned to attack the METZ area from the West the relieved 7th Armored to move south of METZ, cross the MOSELLE, and continue the expansion of the bridgehead previously effected. Information regarding the enemy defenses in this area were provided from captured enemy maps and the Commander of the Task Force previously in the area. A concrete wall, 20 x 30 feet, formed the first fortification line, running from just northeast of AMANVILLERS to the area just SW of FEVES. In front of this wall, south of the FORET de JAUMONT, a strong outpost line was maintained, manned by troops made of OCS members. Attempts of the previous American forces to penetrate the

By RLB/JJO   NARA, Date 4-24-9.1

14 September 1944 - outpost line resulted in heavy casualties and were unsuccessful. Our
(Cont'd)   attack was to be initiated at 0715, 15 September, against that section
                where wall was broken by road running to the southeast.

15 September 1944 - Supported by one platoon of Engineers (315th Bn), the 1st Battalion
moved off to the attack on schedule, with "B" Company on the left,
"C" on the right, moving against the quarry which was reported to
mark the left flank of the enemy outpost line. While this advance
was being made in the face of some small arms fire, a report was received indicating possible withdrawal. The quarry was occupied by "C"
Company by 1125; a five man patrol was sent to the southeast to determine whether report was accurate. Just short of the intersection of
the railroad and road, the patrol was fired upon by machine gun and
retired to the balance of the company at the quarry. At this time
"C" Company took up positions in the gully just east of the quarry,
staying in that position while "B" Company moved directly south, preceded by a strong patrol. In the face of heavy small arms and mortar
fire, the company continued its advance to relieve the patrol which
had been cut off and pinned down at 1345. By 1630 the patrol had been
able to withdraw to the balance of "B" Company, which had continued its
slow advance. At 2000 one platoon had crossed the railroad tracks, at
this time the company was ordered to halt the advance for the night.
Because the company was unable to offer effective support for the platoon which had crossed the tracks, it was withdrawn. While "B" Company
was moving to the south, "C" Company left its position in the gully,
moving southeast and taking position off the right flank of "B" Company
"A" Company was then brought from its position as reserve and moved behind "B" and "C" Companies with an ouspot in the quarry. These position
were maintained for the balance of the night. At 1700 the 3rd Battalion
was moved to the North. "C" Company had suffered two casualties from
booby traps in houses just south of the quarry. The I&R platoon which
had the mission of contacting the 90th Rcn to the left of the 357th
sector, was unable to locate the Reconnaissance. Later in the day this
area was taken over by "I" Company of the 358th under Division control.
The 2nd Battalion had remained in the BOIS DE JAUMONT, holding only
the dominant observation during these operations, with the exception of
one patrol which was dispatched to feel out the situation at the northeast end of the fortified line. It worked south from the north section
of the BOIS DE L'ABBE, bypassed a road block approximately 1200 yards
south. Results of the patrol indicated that this open country was controlled from the high ground in the vicinity of FÈVES, to the southwest,
and was considered impractical from an attack standpoint.

16 September 1944 - The attack was resumed on schedule, "C" Company passing behind "B" and
moving to the left flank. The weather favored the attacking force,
visibility being very limited. By 1000 the companies had reached a
point 150 yards short of the fortified line. Although at the time the
companies could not locate their positions exactly, plans were then made
for advancing into the opening at the roadway, calling for "B" Company
to go forward and block to the south while "A" and "C" Company would
pass to their right into the fort for mopping up. During this time the
3rd Battalion was to be moving forward to complete the block to the
south and be ready to resume the attack. While these preparations were
going on, at 1230 a counterattack was directed against "B" and "C"
Companies, and was repulsed after heavy exbhanges of small arms, artillery and mortar fire. Sporadic artillery had continued throughout the
day; in addition the casualties from the attack and counterattack nec-

-6-

DECLASSIFIED PER EXECUTIVE ORDER 12356, Section 3.3, /76/7650
By RLB/JJO   NARA, Date 4-24-9.1

> Reorganization may have been due to Liebau's being killed by a mortar.*

16 September 1944 – essitated reorganization, which was completed by 1700. The attempted
(Cont'd) advance at that time was stopped completely by all types of fire, and
the Battalion was ordered to dig in for the night.

17 September 1944 – Resumption of the attack was delayed by enemy artillery fire; however,
at 0745 "B" Company had reached the openings between the walls where
it was stopped by heavy wire entanglements, covered with machine gun
and mortar fire. This action made it advisable to relieve the 1st
Bn by the 3d Bn. At 1330 General WEAVER arrived at the Regt'l CP
to discuss possibilities of further attack, and asking that a conclu-
sive decision be given Division on the situation in 24 hours.
   To get all possible information on the picture, the 2d Bn was
ordered to send a patrol to determine feasibility of attacking across
the open against west of the fort, while other patrols from the 3d Bn
were sent to various points along the fortified line.
   K Company completed the relief of B and C Companies and the 1st Bn
passed into Regimental reserve at 1900, in the area N of the quarry.
   During the early part of the night there was considerable enemy
activity and movement on the east side of the MOSELLE, on which Arty
was directed. Because of poor visibility, it was not practical to
determine results of the fire.

18 September 1944 – The 2d Bn was alerted for possible attack around the W side of the Fort
to begin sometime after 1300. During the morning further study of
the situation continued, reviewing the results of patrols. During
the morning the 3d Bn simulated an attack on the fortified position
with full Arty, using screening smoke. The cross fire of enemy
machine guns continued right through the barrage, indicating that
their positions were too well dug in to be effected by Arty screening.
   At 1330 Col BARTH and Maj DE PUY went to division to report their
conclusions and as a result further attempts to take the fortified
positions were postponed.
   At 1640 I Co of 358 was officially attached to 357 and its positions
were rearranged around the road net in the HAGONDANGE area, and Cn Co
of 357 was sent to the area for support, going into position across
the RR west of the NW overpass at HANGONDANGE.
   At 2100 the 90th Rcn reported that a patrol had crossed the
MOSELLE and occupied RICHEMONT.

19 September 1944 – At 0630 the I & R Plat was ordered to make Rcn to RICHEMONT,
contacting the 90th Rcn before going into town. On that contact it
developed that the Rcn had had the report from civilians. The I & R
proceeded into town and found that the enemy had been in the afternoon
previous, but had withdrawn.
   Because of continuous patrol activity along the MOSELLE front, the 2d
Bn was ordered to move to that area at 0810, with one Plat of Med
tanks and 1 Plat TDs in support, this support was later increased to
include the Cn Co, which had been released from its assignment when I &
of 358 was returned to the control of its own regiment.
   At 0900, while the 2d was preparing to make its move, a counterattack was directed against the L flank of the 3d Bn, and A Co was
ordered to move up to be available in case needed. By 1030 the
counter-attack was repulsed and there was no further enemy activity
in the regimental area for the balance of the day.

-7-

* W.W. evacuated to field hospital 9/16/44 (See Morning Report in Addenda), then to hospital in Paris, then to England. Learned of Liebau's death from another patient.

Appendix C

WEB-LINKS TO THE INTERNET

Web-link No. 1

Soldiers not participating in fighting:

The following is an excerpt from *Leavenworth Papers Number 16*, by Major Paul H. Herbert, Infantry, Fort Leavenworth, Kansas, 1988, with comments by William DePuy, our battalion Operations Officer (S-3) in Normandy.

Chapter 2, p. 11:

> Convinced by his experience in World War II that only a small percentage of combat soldiers actually participated in the fighting, he [General William DePuy] believed in dominant decisive leaders and frequent, clear, simple, and direct instructions to keep an organization functioning.

http://usacac.army.mil/cac2/cgsc/carl/download/csipubs/Herbert.pdf

Web-link No. 2

Need for specific instructions to soldiers in combat:

Ibid, Chapter 2, p. 16:

> DePuy was not impressed with the initiative and aggressiveness of American soldiers. He perceived them as inherently reluctant to take risks and, because of inadequate training, unable to take charge in the absence of orders from a superior. On the other hand, he believed that they were willing to carry out specific instructions and orders and that only specific personal orders could overcome their natural fear in combat.

Herbert was referring to DePuy's field manual, *FM-100-5, Operations of Army Forces in the Field.*

Author's note: In regard to initiative, we trainees were told in basic training that American soldiers had an advantage over German soldiers because Americans were used to thinking for themselves in a free society, whereas Germans were used to knuckling under to authority and not doing anything on their own. My own take on this is that the U.S Army itself trained initiative out of its own troops. We were instructed to do everything in a certain way or risk being gigged. I remember questioning a bayonet instructor on which direction to turn, left or right, when approached by the enemy from the rear. When I demonstrated that it was just as effective to wheel to the right as to the left, he refused to admit that it could work and stuck to his original regimen. He had been taught to teach it by the book and couldn't allow any deviations.

Another example: Firing our weapons on the range was so closely supervised, with every action requiring a specific instruction, that it's no wonder that when soldiers got in combat they didn't feel they should fire their weapons unless given direct orders to do so. Somewhere along the line we should have been told that, unless instructed otherwise, it was OK to decide for ourselves when to fire at the enemy. It seems hard to believe, but this was never done.

Ibid, Chap. 2, Note No. 16: (Herbert):

> DePuy recounts that, on at least one occasion, he took the principle of specific orders to squads to an extreme by walking along a river bank and personally ordering each squad into its boat for crossing, threatening some with a pistol.

Author's note: When I read this, my respect for DePuy took a nosedive. If an officer can't motivate men without threatening to shoot them, he's obviously lacking in leadership skills.

Web-link No. 3

Frontal assaults:

DePuy went on to command the 1st Division in Vietnam, and later became the first commanding general of TRADOC (Training and Doctrine Command) where he authored manuals of doctrine for the army's in which he disagreed with the

frontal attack approach. His work and opinions are reported in LEAVENWORTH PAPER NUMBER 16, WRITTEN BY MAJ. PAUL H. HERBERT, 1988, which can be found at: http://usacac.army.mil/cac2/cgsc/carl/resources/csi/Herbert/Herbert.asp
or at: http://usacac.army.mil/cac2/cgsc/carl/download/csipubs/Herbert.pdf

The following is an Excerpt from Chap. 2, p. 15:

> One problem the 90th Division had, at least until it became part of Patton's Third Army, was that of attacking directly into German defenses. Whether the enemy was in hedgerows, behind river lines, or on hill masses, the 90th plunged directly ahead and took the casualties. Only when confronted with the fortified defenses around Metz did the division seek an alternative to the head-on assault. The success of such attacks, as the one at *Maizières-lès-Metz* where squads infiltrated through the enemy lines, seized key positions, and then took out the defenses from the rear, all according to a centralized plan, convinced DePuy of the value of the indirect approach. When in later years he assailed tactical problems that required the attacking force to seize an enemy-held hill directly ("That's wrong...you want to go around behind it."), he was remembering World War-II.

Web-link No. 4

Juvigny and *St.-Hilaire,* roles in *Mortain* Offensive:

Described in detail in a chapter of Martin Blumenson's Breakout and Pursuit, a complete download of which is available on the Internet at:

http://www.ibiblio.org/hyperwar/USA/USA-E-Breakout/USA-E-Breakout-24.html

Web-link No. 5

Barth and Weaver Task Forces, *Mayenne* and *Ste.-Suzanne*:

http://www.archive.org/stream/breakoutpursuit00blum/breakoutpursuit00blum_djvu.txt

This website provides a complete text download of Blumenson's *Breakout and Pursuit*, an official Army "*Green Book*". It is the best source of details about our actions in Normandy. See *Primary References,* Appendix A. The next *Green Book* in the series, Hugh Cole's *The Lorraine Campaign,* takes up where Blumenson leaves off.

Web-link No. 6

Mauldin and Patton:

http://en.wikipedia.org/wiki/Bill_Mauldin

Web-link No. 7

Failed attack by 358 at the *St.-Germain-sur-Sèves* "Island"

Described in detail at the following web-site: http://www.historynet.com/us-armys-90th-Infantry-division-the-tough-hombres-battle-in-normandy.html

The German side of the battle, also included, reveals the surprisingly thin German defenses that repelled the American attackers. After capturing some American officers, the German commander invited them for tea!

Another account is given in Blumenson's *Breakout and Pursuit,* pp. 202 ff. at address shown in Web-link No. 5, above.

um/breakoutpursuit00blum_djvu.txt

Web-link No. 8

Early problems of the 90th Division, a good summary:

Leavenworth Paper Number 16, by Maj. Paul H. Herbert, 1988, pp. 12-14.

http://usacac.army.mil/cac2/cgsc/carl/resources/csi/Herbert/Herbert.asp

Web-link No. 9

Infantry weapons, specs and photographs:

The following is one of several websites describing WW-II Infantry weapons:

hhttp://en.wikipedia.org/wiki/List_of_common_World_War_II_infantry_weapons#.C2.A0United_States

Web-link No. 10

German V-Weapons, details:

HTTP://EN.WIKIPEDIA.ORG/WIKI/V-2#TECHNICAL_DETAILS

Web-link No. 11

Citation for Major Hamilton's DSC, for actions near Avril:

HTTP://MILITARYTIMES.COM/CITATIONS-MEDALS-AWARDS/RECIPIENT.PHP?RECIPIENTID=33382

Web-link No. 12

GI jargon not limited to terms used in this book:

HTTP://WWW.WW2TALK.COM/FORUM/GENERAL/6586-AMERICAN-MILITARY-SLANG-WWII.HTML

APPENDIX D

Correspondence with Robert Patton

Author's letter to Robert Patton:

November 10, 1994

Mr. Robert H. Patton
c/o Crown Publishing Group
201 E. 50th Street
New York, NY 10022

Dear Mr. Patton:

I recently read your book, *The Pattons,* and want to express my profound appreciation for what you have done for me personally.

I fought in the Third Army in WW-II during its drive across Northern France, from June to September, 1944. I started as a reluctant Infantry draftee, then by virtue of others getting killed or wounded, got to be the Platoon Sergeant of a rifle company in the 90th Division. That was the division General Patton called a "bad" division when he saw us on the road between Avranches and *St.-Hilaire-du-Harcouët* shortly after he took over the Third Army on August 1.

I never saw the General, and never met anyone who did. But I never saw our Division Commander either, and didn't even know his name. I saw our Regimental Commander only once—when he informed our group of replacements that the 90th had earned a very poor reputation in the fighting around St.-Mère-Église—that men had run back in the face of the enemy—and that he intended to make sure such behavior did not happen again.

When the 90th became part of the Third Army on August 1, 1944, we were told, by word of mouth, that General Patton was the Commanding General, but at that time the name meant nothing to me. That was the only time his name ever came up in my entire experience with the Third Army. I was still in college during the North African and Sicilian campaigns, and don't remember hearing about the "slapping" incident when it was in the news. So I can bear witness to the falsity of the myth that anyone who ever served under Patton "never wanted to serve under anyone else". The fact was that most of us who did the fighting on the line didn't know who we "served under". I didn't even know the name of the company First Sergeant.

After the war I began hearing about General Patton, of course, but it wasn't until 1988 that I started looking into the war in Europe, and my part in it. I read several of the books about and/or by your grandfather, and saw the movie with George C. Scott, and developed a growing confusion about General Patton–trying to decide if I approved of him or not. I really had decided that I did not, that he stood for a lot of things I was passionately against. I especially resented authors (some of them Generals, like Lawton J. Collins who glossed over his transgressions as minor flaws.

The most enlightening, and healing part of your book, for me, was the combat fatigue slap-ee's remark that he thought the General might be suffering from combat fatigue himself. That is a marvelous moment–for the insight the GI showed regarding the pressures on a man in Patton's position, and for showing a brand of compassion the General himself was not able to display.

The overall effect of your book, of course, is to transform the Great General into a human being, to report him honestly from an intimate inside view that is not available elsewhere. That alone is a valuable contribution to the literature.

When I was first reading about the General, long after the war, I built up an intense distaste for him and his philosophies which he expressed so vividly on so many occasions. Though I never had any personal contact with him of any kind, I despised him. He was one of the enemy for me, almost as much as the Germans I had fought, and in some ways more so, because he had worked from within and sullied our own system with a warlike fervor unbecoming to an American military leader–at least in modern times.

But now that I have read your book, I no longer despise him. In fact, I can almost feel some affection. He was caught up in the Patton military myth that he inherited; he embraced it fully, embellished it, and pushed it to new extremes. I don't mean to say I think that was good, but he was clearly a product of the mystique–a fate you escaped by making a free personal choice–for which you have my admiration.

When I was drafted, I almost applied for conscientious objector status, but in the end did not. I allowed myself to be drafted, and managed to "do my part" in a rifle company, and got out of it with only a minor wound (physically, at least). But I've been trying to sort out my feelings toward war and military matters ever since. I empathize with your somewhat ambivalent view of your grandfather's life, and toward your own choices.

I especially enjoyed the descriptions of "Georgie's" Mexican and WW-I experiences, heightened by his disarmingly honest, even humorous self perception. He seemed to have no illusions about himself. He was worried about his own personal courage, and had to prove himself, and admitted it. He also became aware of his ability to motivate his subordinates, and treated his persuasive skills in an objective, pragmatic way–an attitude that I decry, since the success of his methods had to be proved ultimately by the troops, of whom I was one.

"His guts and our blood" had a real meaning for me (in retrospect, when I knew he was the one in charge) because of his refusal to keep the troops around Metz in a defensive posture as he was ordered to do, insisting that they continue to probe Metz's defenses. Risking lives to feed his appetite for action, I think, was not morally defensible–if that was his reason for doing it.

What your book does for me is make the General humanly vulnerable, uncertain of himself as most of us were–a person I can understand and relate to. I feel much better about my entire combat experience because of your book. Our fate was not in the hands of an American version of Hitler, and to that extent my mind is eased considerably.

It also helps me to know of "Georgie's" poetic inclinations. Some of his efforts were pretty bad, as you say, but here and there some talent shines through. The idea that a man of his military bent would like to write poetry is especially interesting to me. I have always been a nature buff, a bird watcher and botanizer, but found little room in the military mind or life for such "gentle" interests. Farley Mowat had the same problem, as he relates in his book, *And No Birds Sang*.

In *The Pattons*, you manage to tread a fine line between encouraging a familiarity bordering on disrespect (especially by using the diminutive "Georgie" throughout–a master stroke) and upholding the reputation of a forbear who is an important figure in our history–as a driven but essentially honorable man. I think you did a marvelous job.

I am writing a book myself, about my experiences in France. General Patton figures in it occasionally, mostly in retrospective inserts, endnotes, and an ANNOTATED BIBLIOGRAPHY in which your book has an important place.

In *The Pattons* you have done us all, and me in particular, a great service.

Sincerely,

Warren J. Wightman
P.O. Box 44, Fairport, NY 14450

Robert Patton's reply (handwritten):

December 6, 1994

Dear Mr. Wightman–

    Your letter about my book, The Pattons, was most lovely and most appreciated. To have touched someone with my attempt to write a human portrait of my grandfather is very gratifying to me. Thank you for conveying your reaction to me. I've passed your letter on to my father (the General's son). I think he too will appreciate it.

    With best wishes,

    Robert H. Patton (signature)

Author's Note:

    General Collins's name is incorrect in my letter. It should be J. [Joseph] Lawton Collins. Also, the place where the 90th made a poor showing early on was probably *Gourbesville*, not *Ste-Mère-Eglise*.

    In the letter I say we GIs heard that General Patton had taken command of the 3rd Army, but in a note in the text I say I never heard Patton's name while I was on the European Continent. I believe the latter statement is correct.

Appendix E

GI Terms used in this book

Words <u>underlined</u> in the definitions are also in the main list, or in Foreign Terms (Appendix F). For a more comprehensive list of GI jargon, see Web-link No. 12.

ack-ack	Anti-aircraft <u>fire</u>.
across the pond	Euphemism for any foreign locale, usually with the implication of combat, as: "When the chips are down *across the pond*..."
ammo	Ammunition.
ammunition belt, M-1	Wide canvas belt with pockets for <u>M-1</u> <u>clip</u>s. Various other items of equipment were hung from, or clipped to, the belt.
APCs	Pills containing **A**spirin, **P**henatecin and **C**affeine. Standard treatment for "what ails you".
armor	Generally, tanks. Also the heavy metal protective sheath on the excterior of any vehicle.
artillery	Large-caliber surface-to-surface, or surface-to-air weapons fired at greater distances and with flatter <u>trajectories</u> than <u>mortars</u>.
automatic	Requiring only one pull of the trigger to fire multiple <u>rounds.</u>
AWOL	**A**bsent **W**ithout **L**eave — Off base without a pass; generalized to mean away from any <u>duty</u> position without permission.
azimuth	Angular direction measured horizontally, right or left, in degrees away from North, or in the case of <u>mortars</u> or <u>artillery</u>, degrees away from the compass bearing of the last-fired <u>shell</u>.
ball ammo	Regular .30-cal. <u>ammo</u> for the <u>M-1</u> rifle. <u>Bullets</u> copper-sheathed with rounded tips.
ballistic	Un-guided, as a <u>projectile</u> moving after its propellant is expended.
bandolier	Light-weight cloth <u>ammo</u> holder with multiple pockets for <u>M-1</u> <u>clip</u>s, usually looped over the shoulders so that it hung diagonally across the chest. Supplemented <u>ammunition belt.</u>
B-A-R	**B**rowning **A**utomatic **R**ifle. .30-cal. weapon capable of accurate <u>automatic</u> <u>fire</u> at 550 rounds per minute.
basic	short for <u>basic training</u>. Sometimes capitalized: Basic.

basic training	Initial training in military discipline, physical fitness, and military skills. In 1943 our basic Infantry training was for 13 weeks.
battalion	Three rifle companies plus a headquarters company.
battery	Group of two or more artillery pieces.
bazooka	Technically, a recoil-less rifle. Fired self-propelled rockets from an open-ended steel tube held on the shoulder. Main purpose was anti-tank. Rocket had a shaped charge that focused explosive on small area making it capable of penetrating armor. Named for musical instrument made from stovepipe by comedian Bob Burns. The German *Panzerfaust* was copied from the American weapon.
bivouac	Open-air encampment, usually not under enemy fire.
bolt	The sliding part of a weapon's firing mechanism that contains the firing pin and which picks up the rounds from the clip or magazine and pushes them into the chamber.
bolt-action	Descriptive of a rifle with a manually operated bolt.
brass (1)	High-ranking officers or civilian visitors
brass (2)	Empty shells and cartridges from small-arms or artillery
bullet	The projectile fired from a small-arms weapon; the entire round with its brass casing.
burp-gun	GI term for German MP-40 machine pistol.
buzz-bomb	German flying bomb propelled by ram-jet. See V-1.
cadre	Officers and non-coms at a military training base.
caliber	Also calibre. Diameter of a projectile in decimal inches.
carbine, M-1	A light-weight .30-cal. semi-automatic rifle carried by officers, mortarmen, machinegunners, artillery crews and some other rear-echelon personnel. Cartridge not necked-down.
cartridge	A bullet and it's brass casing, before being fired
casing	The brass part of a round.
chamber	The cylindrical space into which a round fits when ready for firing.
chickenshit	Excessive emphasis on authority and bureaucratic details.
chow	Food.

chow hound	A GI obsessed with food and eating.
clip	Metal ammunition holder that fed rounds into receiver of small-arms weapons. See also magazine.
CO	**C**ommanding **O**fficer of an Army unit.
CO	**C**onscientious **O**bjector. A person excused from military service because of religious or personal beliefs against war. COs were usually sent to special camps to perform non-combat duties.
combat pack	A field pack reduced to a minimum for use in combat.
commission	Authorization from Congress designating a person an officer.
company	A Rifle company consisted of three rifle platoons plus a weapons platoon (60-mm mortars or .30-cal. machineguns).
concussion grenade	A grenade with a relatively thin metal case intended to incapacitate the enemy by the shock of the explosion.
Corps	Sub-unit of an Army, usually made up of three Divisions.
cover (verb)	Provide backup for another man exposed to enemy fire.
cover (noun)	Any object or terrain feature that offers protection from enemy fire.
CP	**C**ommand **P**ost — headquarters for a field unit.
C-Rations	Individual meals in small cans.
D-Rations	Hard chocolate bar fortified with other nutrients, for use in situations where other rations could not be brought up to the line.
deflection	Left or right adjustment when aiming a mortar.
dog-face	A GI. Equivalent to *doughboy* in WW-I. Not a pejorative term.
division	Three regiments. Approximately 10,000 men.
duty	Any assignment or work in the military. *Good duty* had perks.
elevation	Angle measured in degrees upward from the horizon.
enlisted man	(Also EM and em.) Any non-commissioned soldier; including NCOs. The term is somewhat of a misnomer in that *enlisted men* did not necessarily enlist, i.e., volunteer.
entrenching tool	Small shovel or pick for digging foxholes and slit-trenches. Some models were folding, used either as a shovel or a pick.

ETO	**E**uropean **T**heater of **O**perations
fatigues	Green herringbone twill work clothing. Pants had cargo pockets. Jacket was fingertip-length worn outside pants. Some combat fatigues were impregnated with chemicals for protection against poison gas.
"Fix bayonets"	An order meaning to attach <u>bayonet</u> to rifles. The order implied that there might be a need to use them against the enemy.
field jacket	A tan waist-length cloth jacket worn both in <u>garrison</u> and combat. A later green finger-length version had a drawstring at the waist.
fire	Verb: Shoot a weapon. Noun: ammunition of any type shot from weapons. *Take fire* – be fired at.
fire for effect	<u>Fire</u> a weapon, such as a <u>mortar</u> or <u>artillery</u> <u>piece</u>, to accomplish its intended purpose after getting the correct <u>range</u> and <u>azimuth.</u>
flying bomb	Also *buzz-bomb*. See *V-1*.
foxhole	A usually rectangular hole dug in the ground for one or two men, sometimes more. Foxholes made it possible to get below the <u>trajectories</u> of <u>bullet</u>s and <u>shell</u> fragments.
fragmenta-tion grenade	A hand-thrown cast-iron grenade that broke up into segments when it exploded. Weight: 1 lb.- 5 oz..
Garand rifle	The <u>M-1</u> rifle, standard .30 <u>caliber</u> Infantry rifle in World War II. It was <u>semi-automatic</u>, firing 8 <u>round</u>s by pulling the trigger eight times without re-loading or re-cocking. <u>Necked-down</u> rounds were held in a <u>clip</u> that was inserted into the top of the <u>receiver</u>. Muzzle velocity was approximately 2,700 ft. per sec. Named after its American inventor.
garrison	Camp or base away from combat areas. Daily routines and military discipline increased as the distance from combat increased.
gas mask	Rubberized mask with goggles that fitted closely over eyes and face with an air intake that had a filter for certain gases.
gear	A <u>GI</u>'s individual military equipment.
Gerry	GI term for a German soldier; sometimes spelled *<u>Jerry</u>*.
Gerrycan	A flattish, ribbed, rectangular metal gasoline can with a handle, painted green, copied from, and named after, its German counterpart. Also used to carry water. Also spelled *<u>Jerrycan</u>*.

GI	1) **G**overnment **I**ssue. 2) An Army enlisted man; 3) Adj: Strictly according to the rules; 4) plural (the GIs): diarrhea.
GI can	A large metal can shaped like a garbage can, used for dispensing food in the field. Also for washing mess kits, and for garbage.
gigged	Required to perform some disagreeable or onerous task as punishment for a minor offense.
"got it"	In combat, usually meant "was killed", as in: "Johnson *got it* last night."
grease-gun	GI term for American made M-3 sub-machinegun.
grenade	Short-range explosive device thrown by hand or propelled from a rifle by a powder charge. Hand grenades were of two types: fragmentation and concussion.
grunt	A term used in WW-II for a Marine enlisted man, not an Army GI.
HE	**H**igh **E**xplosive.
increment	A packet of powder clipped to a mortar shell's fins to increase the shell's range. The mortar-man added one or more increments as needed according to his firing tables.
Jerry	Variant spelling of *Gerry*.
Jerrycan	See Gerrycan.
K-Rations	Single meals in cardboard boxes. Dry except for small cans of scrambled eggs or hash. Standard combat chow.
latrine	In garrison, a building with toilets, showers and wash-bowls. In the field, a narrow slit-trench serving as a toilet.
LCI	**L**anding **C**raft, **I**nfantry.
leaf sight	A fold-up rear rifle sight adjustable for both elevation and windage, standard on the '03 rifle and the B-A-R. Though considered to be more accurate than the Garand's peep sight, it could be damaged and/or knocked out of adjustment by rough treatment.
long Tom	155-mm artillery piece.
looey; looie	Lieutenant, as in *second looey*.
M-1	1) The first model of anything in the Army; 2) When used alone, the Infantryman's Garand rifle.

M-3 sub-machinegun	American .45-caliber sub-machinegun modeled after the German *Schmeisser* Machine Pistol. Both were manufactured largely with stamped rather than machined metal parts, which greatly reduced manufacturing time and costs. See also: grease-gun.
machinegun	Belt-fed weapon capable of sustained automatic fire.
magazine	Metal cartridge holder for small-arms that attached to a weapon and fed rounds into receiver. Held more rounds than a clip.
mess	Relating to food or meals, as *mess* hall, *mess*-kit, *mess* call.
mess-kit	Oval-shaped aluminum dish with cover and utensils.
mop up	Clear an area of possible enemy rear guard and/or stragglers.
mortar	A weapon that fired fragmentation or chemical shells in a high-arcing trajectory. Mortar shells contained their own propellant, expended on firing. They were fired by dropping them by hand into a metal tube set at a high angle. A firing pin at the bottom of the tube set off the propellant charge. American mortars were 60-mm, 81-mm, and 4.2 inch (used for smoke or chemicals). 60-mm mortars were used as "company artillery".
MP	**M**ilitary **P**olice
musette bag	A carryall canvas bag worn like a back pack. Standard equipment for some non-Infantry units.
necked-down	Descriptive of a cartridge or shell with a base section of greater diameter than the end section that holds the bullet or projectile, allowing a larger powder charge. M-1 30-cal. rifle ammunition was necked-down. .30 cal. carbine ammo was not.
non-com	A non-commissioned officer (NCO). In WW-II Infantry non-com grades were: Corporal, Sergeant, Staff Sergeant, Technical Sergeant, First Sergeant, Master Sergeant, plus several *Tech* grades for specialties.
NCO	**N**on-**C**ommissioned **O**fficer; non-com.
OCS	**O**fficer **C**andidate **S**chool.
OD	1) **O**live **D**rab; 2) **O**fficer of the **D**ay — An officer designated to be in temporary command of a unit, usually in garrison.
ODs	**O**fficial **D**ress uniform — In garrison usually wool OD pants, dark wool OD blouse (jacket with lapels), OD wool shirt, and sun-tan

	tie. The uniform of the day could vary, substituting an <u>Eisenhower jacket</u> or <u>field jacket</u> for the blouse, and a cotton sun-tan shirt.
officer	When used by itself, a <u>commission</u>ed <u>officer</u>, eg., Lieutenant, Captain, Major, Colonel, General.
0h-three; 03	Model 1903 infantry <u>bolt-action</u> Springfield rifle of WW-I. Sometimes used as a sniper rifle in WW-II because of its precisely adjustable rear <u>leaf sight</u>.
order	An instruction to do something from a <u>commission</u>ed <u>officer</u>, backed by the authority of the U.S. Army and Congress. Disobedience to a direct order was punishable by court martial.
orderly room	<u>Company</u> office in <u>garrison.</u>
peep sight	Rear rifle sight with a small round fixed-diameter aperture to sight through. Standard on the <u>M-1</u> rifle. Though adjustable for <u>elevation</u> and <u>windage</u>, it was not considered to be as accurate as a <u>leaf sight</u>. At night any peep sight was almost useless.
piece	Firearm. Rifle or pistol. Also <u>artillery</u> *piece*.
possible	A "possibly" perfect target with all <u>round</u>s in the black (bull's-eye). <u>Bullet</u>s sometimes went through previously-made holes so possibles had to be checked and OK'd by the <u>range</u> <u>officer</u>.
potato-masher	German <u>hand-grenade</u> with a long handle that resembled the old-fashioned wooden kitchen implement of the same name.
platoon	Sub-unit of a rifle <u>company</u>; three <u>squad</u>s.
projectile	<u>Bullet</u>, <u>shell</u> or <u>rocket</u> fired from a weapon.
propellant	Explosive material that forces a <u>projectile</u> into its <u>trajectory</u>.
Purple Heart	Medal given for being wounded by, or as a result of, enemy action. Often misrepresented in the media as being awarded for valor or courage in combat.
PX	Post Exchange. On-base store selling snacks and sundries.
ram-jet	Pulsing jet engine used on <u>V-1</u>s (<u>buzz-bombs</u>). When the fuel was exhausted the bomb plunged to earth and exploded.
range	Distance to a target; maximum distance a weapon could deliver a <u>projectile</u>. Firing <u>range</u>: area used for target practice and training.

rations	Packaged food issued to soldiers in the field. K-rations – 1 meal in a green, waxed cardboard box. C-rations – Individual portions of canned food. D-rations – Nutritionally-fortified, hard, unsweetened chocolate.
rear-echelon	To a GI, any area out of the range of enemy fire.
receiver	The part of a weapon that *receives* the rounds from the clip or magazine prior to their being pushed into the chamber by the bolt.
recoil-less rifle	See bazooka.
regiment	Made up of three battalions; three regiments made a division.
rocket	A projectile containing a propellant charge expended in flight.
round	A projectile fired from a weapon. Also an unfired cartridge.
S-1, etc.	Battalion and regimental staff designations. S-1 (Personnel and Administration); S-2 (Intelligence); S-3 (Operations); S-4 (Supply); S-5 (Civil / Military Relations).
scabbard	Protective sheath for a bayonet or trench-knife. Used on fixed bayonets in training to prevent injury.
screaming meemie	German rocket (*Nebelwerfer*) fired from multi-tubed launcher; name derived from the sound of approaching rockets.
semi-automatic	Capable of firing one round with each pull of the trigger without reloading or re-cocking.
shaped charge	Arrangement of HE in a rocket that focused the explosive force to a point; enabling penetration of armor. See also bazooka.
shell	Artillery or mortar round.
shell casing	The brass part of a round or shell.
shelter-half	A sheet of canvas which, when joined to another like it formed a two-man tent. It was seldom used in this way in combat because a tent required poles and stakes—which were usually thrown aside.
short-arm inspection	Examination of male genitals for evidence of venereal disease. Sometimes conducted while in formation.
shrapnel	Technically not correct for shell fragments but the term has come to be generally accepted. Shrapnel was originally round shot con-

	tained inside an explosive <u>shell</u>, named after the British general who first used it.
slit-trench	Field latrine. Many writers use this term incorrectly for <u>foxholes</u>.
small-arms	Weapons that fire ammunition of .45-<u>caliber</u> or less, i.e., rifles, <u>machinegun</u>s, <u>sub-machinegun</u>s, pistols and revolvers.
SNAFU	Acronym for: **S**ituation **N**ormal, **A**ll **F**ouled **U**p.
S.O.P.	**S**tandard **O**perating **P**rocedure.
S-O-S	Acronym for crude term describing chipped beef in white-sauce, served on toast. Term also widely used in civilian diners.
squad	Sub-unit of a <u>platoon</u>. In a rifle <u>company</u>, 10–12 men.
sub-machinegun	Light-weight <u>machinegun</u> intended to be fired while carried. Fed by <u>clip</u> or <u>magazine</u> rather than by cloth or metal belt.
tank	Enclosed armored, tracked vehicle fitted with with large-caliber weapons.
TOT	Acronym for **T**ime-**O**n-**T**arget. <u>Artillery</u> <u>fire</u> from several different batteries timed to hit the same target at the same time. Perfected by the American <u>artillery</u>, it was much feared by the Germans.
trajectory	The path of a <u>projectile</u>. A *ballistic* trajectory results from a projectile after its propellant has been expended.
trench-knife	A dagger-shaped double-edged knife often worn strapped on the ankle, the word *trench* a carryover from WW-I.
ULTRA	Allied code-breaking group at Bletchley Park, England, and the intelligence produced therefrom. Some field commanders downplayed ULTRA's usefulness, preferring to rely on their own battle savvy—or at least pretending to. Information from ULTRA was not always used for fear it would tip off the Germans to its success in cracking the German codes.
V-1	German <u>ram-jet</u>-propelled <u>flying bomb</u>; *buzz-bomb.*, Called by the British, *doodle-bug* and *diver*. The "V" stood for Vengeance Weapon (in German: *Vergeltungswaffen*).
V-2	A German <u>ballistic</u> <u>rocket</u> with an explosive warhead that rose 60 plus miles into the upper atmosphere, then turned downward to fall un-guided at four times the speed of sound, exploding on impact. V-2 development was headed by Wernher von Braun at

	Peenemünde on an island in the Baltic off the northern coast of Germany. After their fixed pads were bombed out, V-2s were launched from mobile pads. Primary targets were London and Antwerp. See also: V-Weapons, details, Appendix B, *Web-links.*
V-mail	Miniaturized pages photocopied from regular-sized paper provided to the troops to reduce the bulk of the mail to and from overseas.
VD	**V**enereal **D**isease. WW-II era term for STD (**S**exually **T**ransmited **D**isease).
windage	When aiming a weapon, the allowance made for the wind's effect on the projectile.

Appendix F
Foreign words and phrases used in this book

French

à	to, till, as in *à demain* – till tomorrow
absolument	absolutely
Allemands, les	the Germans
Allemagne	Germany
Américains, les	the Americans
au gratin	food prepared with cheese
avez-vous	do you have
beau (masculine)	good (in appearance); handsome
belle (feminine)	pretty, beautiful
bocage	literally, *thicket.* The hedgerows
Bosche, les	the Germans
bois	woods
bon	good, OK
bonjour	hello, good day
certainment	certainly, of course
c'est	it is
château	chateau
chocolat	chocolate
cognac	cognac
collaborateur	collaborator (masculine); feminine: *collabaratrice*
de la, des, du,	of, some (singular feminine, plural, masculine)
défendu (à)	forbidden (to)
départment	administrative division of France within a *région*
Dieu	God
elle	she
en Français	in French
est	is
faire	to make; to do (plus several other idiomatic usages)
forêt	forest

Page 328

fromage	cheese
gateau	cake
hôte	host
il	he, it
Jeanne d'Arc	Joan of Arc
jeune fille	girl, young woman
kilometres	kilometers (1 kilometer = 0.62 miles)
la, le, les	the (feminine, masculine, plural)
lapin	rabbit
meilleur	better
le plus meilleur	the best
Madame, Mme.	Mrs.; *une Madame*: a married woman
Mademoiselle, Mlle.	Miss (title)
(une) mademoiselle	a young woman
mais	but
mais oui	but yes; of course
manger	to eat
Monsieur, Mon.	Mr.
ne	not; negation
nécessaire	necessary
n'est-ce pas?	Isn't it? Isn't that right? Don't you agree?
non	no
oui	yes
palais	palace
parlez-vous?	do you speak?
pas	not
petit, petite	small (masc., fem.)
promenade	walk
région	one of 27 administrative divisions of France
régulations	regulations, rules
savoir faire	worldliness, sophistication, knowing one's way around
s'il vous plait	please; if you please

vache	cow
venez	come
voulez-vous	do you want?
vous	you
vraiment	really

German

[In the German Language, Nouns are always Capitalized]

Kamerad	Comrade, friend
Luftwaffe	German air force
Mauser	Standard German Infantry bolt-action rifle. *Mausers* with special sights were used as sniper rifles.
MG-42	Fast-firing German machinegun (1200 rounds per min.).
Nebelwerfer	Rockets, usually armed with HE, launched from multiple-tube rocket launchers. Dubbed "screaming meemies" by GIs.
Panzer	German word for tank.
Panzerfaust	German version of American bazooka. More effective than ours against tanks. The Germans copied ours which they picked up on the battlefields in the Mediterranean campaigns, and improved on them.
Schmeisser (machine pistol)	German sub-machinegun (called burp-gun by GIs). Used as model for American M-3 .45-caliber sub-machinegun. (called grease-gun by GIs).
Spandau	GI term for German machinegun
SS	Short for *German word Schutzstaffel* defense echelon. An elite *Nazi* military unit that served as Hitler's personal guard and as security forces in Germany and occupied countries. Specially trained, they had a reputation for ruthlessness.
Vergeltungswaffen	Vengeance weapon. The V-1s ("buzz-bombs") and V-2s (ballistic rockets).
Völkischer Beobachter	*Nationalist Observer,* the newspaper of the *Nazi Party* (National Socialist German Workers' Party).

Acknowledgments

First, I respect fully the efforts of my fellow platoon members to perform effectively under the circumstances we found ourselves in. We were asked to be more than we were, and to do more than we knew we could do, and we barely succeeded. Some of us died trying.

For steady encouragement with the book I am indebted to military buff and bibliophile, Mike Crough; to inveterate motivator, George Cronin; and to my nephew, Larry Wightman. Without the help of platoon-mate Alva Lumpkin I probably would never have begun to probe into our mutual war experiences. "Lump" clued me in to key reference books, reminded me of several places and names I had forgotten, and after five decades gave me the will to dig into the long-buried past.

An unlikely series of events led to a Silver Star fifty years after the war. Mike Crough saw an ad for John Colby's book, *War From The Ground Up;* I read it and recommended it to Lumpkin; he wrote to our Battalion Commander, Major Ed Hamilton who remembered watching our squad through binoculars in the fire-fight on the hill near *Avril*. Lumpkin suggested the medal and Hamilton put me in for it. I'm not sure I deserve it, but thanks, guys.

I applaud the competence of (most of) our governmental leaders and military commanders—especially Ike—who engineered the defeat of the Nazi in Western Europe. The cadre at basic training deserve credit for making fairly good soldiers of most of us. And I appreciate the contribution of the civilians at home who provided our weapons and equipment. No thanks, however, to the leaders and diplomats who allowed Germany to rebuild its military might under the Nazis.

Recently I have been in contact with Messieurs Fabrice Avoie and Vincent Orrière of *Le Mans*, and *Mayenne*, France, respectively. *Merci* for the helpful *témoignage*. I'm especially grateful for being put in touch with the family of Alf Green.

Thanks to the Fairport and Penfield public libraries for use of their resources and facilities, and to their staffs—especially librarians Kristin Gallagher and Todd Randall for their helpful computer tips. Thanks to Sonny Kompanek and Gail McKay for tweaking the cover art, and to poet Kathleen Wakefield for her willing midwifery—though approval of the final product should not be assumed.

Photos of weapons are from the *Wikimedia Commons* website. The *Operational Report* (Appendix B) was provided by the National Archives.

Whatever fortitude I discovered within myself came, or course, from my parents.

INDICES

There are separate indices for **Places**, **Military Units**, **People**, **Authors** and **Periodicals**, followed by a **General Index**.

Places

Adirondacks 98
Agincourt 2
Aisne (River) 202
Alabama 4, 98, 103, 110, 259, 331
Alaska 137
Alençon ....
.... 173, 174, 175, 188, 190, 212, 237
   map 170
Alsace 235
   map 216
Antwerp 326
Ardennes 266
Argentan 12, 174, 176
.... 177, 178, 190, 191
   map 170, 192
Argonne offensive, WW-I 210
Argonne Forest 208, 211
   map 192
Avranches 134, 135, 152, 174, 188, 315
   map .... iv, 192
Avril .... i, 221, 229, 231, 232, 243
.... 245, 249, 269, 313, 331
   map 216, 230
Baltic Sea 326
Barneville 54
Basse Normandie
   map iv
Beau-Coudray ..... i, 43, 55, 56, 66, 68, 87
.... 89, 91, 97, 100, 101, 102, 103, 108
.... 111, 114, 118, 119, 130, 131, 144
.... 223, 230, 246, 263, 269, 275
   map .... iv, 62
Belgium (map) 192
Belleau Wood 197, 210, 213
Berlin 26, 137
Better 'Ole 10, 14
Bletchley Park 155
Brest 135, 203
   map 192
Bretagne (Brittany) 135
   map 192

Briey 217, 228
   map 216
Bristol Channel 11
British beaches 54
   map iv
Buffalo, NY .. 14, 39, 99, 149, 150, 163, 331
   University of 331
Caen 9, 141
Camp Upton, New York 14
Cardiff (Wales) 106
Carentan 54
Chambois 170, 187, 274
   map 170
Champagne (Region) 179, 200, 213
Chartres 193
   map 192
Chartres Cathedral 193, 211
Château Thierry 197, 210
   map 192
Cherbourg 12, 14, 25, 26, 42
.... 47, 51, 54, 108, 203
   map .... iv, 192
Cherbourg Peninsula . i, 9, 16, 25, 54, 126
.... 128, 134, 138, 174, 188
.... 197, 203, 209, 212
   map .... iv, 192
Compiègne 197
Cotentin Peninsula 134, 135
Coutances 126, 131, 134, 219
   map iv
Dover (England) 137
Dulverton (England) 9
England ... 1, 9, 10, 13, 14, 16, 90, 118, 125
...... 126, 136, 140, 141, 155, 188, 197, 331
   map 192
English Channel 3, 4, 11, 14, 190, 331
   map 192
Étain 217
ETO 11, 13, 137, 268, 321
European Continent 1, 12, 168
Fairport, NY 331
Falaise 12, 174, 176, 178, 191, 194
   map 170

Falaise-Argentan Gap ("Pocket") 12, 178, 192, 212, 274
    map... 170
Fère-en-Tardenois................................ 197
Fèves .... i, 254, 255, 258, 265, 266, 269
    map.......................................216, 257
Fèves Ridge 245, 256, 263, 267
    map 258
Fléville 217
Florange 242
    map... 216
Fontainebleau .... ii, 196
    map... 192
Forêt de Fontainebleau .... ii, 194, 195
Frankfurt (Germany)............ 137, 208, 235
Fredericksburg, U.S. Civil War 67
French coast................................... 4, 125
Fort McClellan, Alabama.........................
    .... 4, 20, 23, 26, 68, 106
    .... 112, 175, 246, 267, 331
Genesee River gorge, NY State 228
Germany 326
    map..192, 216
Gondrecourt 217
Gourbesville................................10, 317
    map.. iv
Guignicourt 202
Gulf of the *Seine*, map iv
Hayange.................... 155, 234, 235, 236
    .... 237, 241, 242, 244
    map..192, 216
Hayangen (See also: *Hayange*)............ 235
Hill 317 (*Mortain*) 152
Homecourt 245
Isle of Wight 13
Italy.. 53
Japan.. 122, 331
Juvigny 135, 152, 311
    map.. iv
Kellermann Works 256, 258
L'Aigle 178
    map..170, 184
La Fière causeway.............................. 154
Lackawanna, N.Y..................................... 41
Lake Ontario (New York State) 23
Le Mans............. i, 157, 162, 163, 166, 167
    .... 168, 173, 174, 205, 212, 269
    map.......................................156, 170

Le Merlerault................................i, 178
    map..170, 184
Le Plessis 55, 107
Lessay 128, 135
    map.. iv
Letchworth Park, NY State 228
London.. 326
Long Island, NY State 14
Lorraine......... i, 83, 85, 153, 200, 217, 225
    .... 228, 232, 235, 244, 271, 312
    map... 216
Luxembourg 234
    map... 216
Maginot Line 51
Mansfield, Ohio 212
Marne (River) 67, 197, 211, 213
Marye's Heights (U.S. Civil War)........... 67
Mayenne.................... i, 141, 142, 147, 152
    .... 158, 161 174, 184
    .... 212, 230, 244, 266
    map ....iv, 142, 170, 192
Mayenne River 141, 142
    map... 142
Merderet River 11, 26, 154
    La Fière Causeway 26, 154
Metz................. 85, 247, 257, 258
    .... 311, 316, 331
    map 192, 216, 257
Meuse River 210
Meuse-Argonne Offensive, WW-I. 208, 209
Mexico .... See Grant, General Ulysses S.
Mortain Offensive 152, 155, 174, 311
    map.. iv
Moselle (départment) ....i, 241, 244
    ....231, 233
    map... 216
Moselle River........................ 85, 203, 234
    .... 242, 243, 244
    map..192, 216
Moselle Valley 228, 234, 241
Mt. Castre 55, 56, 103, 108
    map.. iv
Munich.. 137
Neufchef....................................233, 241
    map... 216
New York State....... 18, 150, 163, 178, 249
New York World's Fair 49
Nogent 196

Normandie 14
    map .... iv, 192
Normandie, on *Michelin* map
    and "St.-Pierre-Église" 14
Normandy 9, 11, 12, 25, 40, 41, 42, 50
.... 51, 52, 65, 121, 154, 191, 196
.... 206, 212, 271, 309, 312, 331
    Hitler thought invasion a feint 125
    Norman Conquest of England 13
North Africa 13, 117, 140, 166, 273
Northern France (map) 192
Nôtre Dame Cathedral 202
Oberlin College 99, 112, 117, 122
.... 128, 202, 331
Ohio 18, 117, 212
Okinawa 268
Omaha Beach 43, 54, 268
    map iv
Orléans 193, 194
    map 192
Paraclete (Abbey of) 196
Paris 190, 194, 197, 200, 202, 213
    map 184
Pas de Calais 125
Peenemünde 326
Périers 125, 129
    map iv
Pontaubault 135
    map iv
Portbail .... i, 42, 57, 74, 245
    map .... iv, 33
Prairie Marécageuses 55
    map iv
Provins 196
Raids 129
Reims 201, 202, 203, 205
.... 207, 208, 213, 238
    map 192
Reims Cathedral 202
Rhine River 137, 203
Rochester, NY 331
    City Schools 331
    City Newspaper 331
    Democrat and Chronicle 331
    Gannett Newspapers 331
Rouen 197
    map 192
Sarthe River 162, 174, 175

Sées 175, 176, 177, 178
.... 193, 199, 255
    map 170, 192
Seine River 187, 194, 196
    map 170, 192
Sèves River 126, 137, 139, 148, 175, 259
    map 120
Sicily 13, 53, 107, 140
Somerset, England 1, 10
Southampton, England 3, 7
    map iv
St.-Germain-sur-Sèves .... i, 105, 122
    "The Island" at 105, 109, 111, 112
.... 113, 117, 118, 119, 123
.... 126, 129, 139, 148, 161
.... 164, 175 188, 219, 230
.... 244, 245, 246, 260, 312
    map .... iv, 120
St.-Hilaire-du-Harcouët 135, 141, 152
.... 311, 315
    map iv
St.-Lô 120, 125, 129
    map .... iv, 122
St.-Mihiel 191, 208, 210
St.-Pierre-Église 13
St.-Pierremont 219
St. Sauveur-Lendelin 130
    map iv
Ste.-Mère-Église 7, 14
    map iv
Ste.-Suzanne 147, 148, 149, 155
.... 199, 254, 311
    map 170
Switzerland 234
    map 216
Syracuse University 331
Talladega National Forest . 23, 46, 98, 103
.... 110, 205
Tarawa 213
Taute River 129
Thionville 243, 313, 306
    map 216
Tyrol, German 234
Ukange 242, 245
    map 216
Upstate New York 18
Utah Beach 4, 14, 49, 54, 126, 331
    map .... iv, 192

Verdun 67, 138, 209, 210, 211, 214, 217
    map..192, 216
Vesle River..................................201, 213
Vismes... 201
Washington, DC..................... 17, 214, 271
West Point... 213
Witry-les-Reims 203
Ypres 210

Military Units

101st Airborne..................................... 11
1st Battalion, 357th 55, 113, 217, 230, 281
2nd French Armored Division 171, 175, 188
30th Division 152
357th, 358th & 359th Regiments
    ....see 90th Division
3rd Armored Division....................126, 134
4th Armored Division........... 126, 128, 134
4th Infantry Division 51, 54
5th Infantry Division 247
8th Infantry Division 126, 128, 138
9th Infantry Division 51
35th Infantry Division 155
79th Infantry Division .42, 51, 54, 126, 128
82nd Airborne
    .... 7, 11, 54, 126, 138, 147, 154, 213
90th Division
    author assigned to............................ 16
    debarkation at Utah Beach............. 276
    division's early problems . 276, 277, 312
    357th Regiment........ i, iii, 26, 49, 50, 55
        .... 105, 107, 113,121, 141, 155
        .... 217, 268, 271, 273, 274
    Regimental MPs 245
    B-Company........ i, 107, 113, 144, 147
        .... 148, 153, 164, 176
        ....201, 217, 232, 234
    358th Regiment........... 49, 55, 119, 137
        .... 139, 233, 243
        .... 260, 274, 312
    Bn. Cmdr. Relieved 286
    359th Regiment..........................49, 233
Allied Command 1
Allied Expeditionary Forces..................... 2
Deuxième Blindée 197
FFI, French underground, *Maquis*
    .... 197, 190, 198

First Army....... 40, 51, 53, 54, 55, 105, 140
    .... 152,155, 176, 191
French Armored Division 275, 171, 175
FUSAG............................... 125, 140, 141
    commanded by Patton, McNair 125
German 7th Army............... 128, 130, 166
    .... 171, 176, 274
    map 170
German war machine 2
Luftwaffe....................135, 233, 243, 328
Maquis .... See *FFI*
Marines, U.S. 53, 213
Panzer Lehr Division (German).......53, 126
Pathfinders, Airborne 11
Red Ball Express 207
Seabees.. 83
SHAEF (**S**upreme **H**eadquarters,
    Allied **E**xpeditionary **F**orces)
    .... 12, 193, 203, 208
SS (Elite German Unit) 247
Third Army 125, 134, 135, 140, 141, 152
..... 171, 187, 190, 191, 194, 203, 207, 208
..... 212, 217, 243, 267, 274, 311, 315, 331
    General Patton and insignia.......... 25
Tough 'Ombres (90$^{th's}$ nickname) 312
ULTRA (Code breakers at
    Bletchley Park) 155, 174, 188
VII Corps......................126, 138, 176, 185
VIII Corps...54, 56, 126, 128, 138, 211, 212
XV Corps.......................155, 194, 211, 212
XX Corps......................194, 210, 212, 243

People

Ambrose, Stephen......................191, 265
American Indian(s) 228
    stereotype... 39
Attila the Hun..................................... 247
Bailey, Donald (Bailey bridge) 212
Barker, General Raymond
    Ike's Deputy Chief of Staff 11
Barth, Colonel George
..... 141, 147, 148, 155, 157, 268, 269, 311
Bayerlein, General (German)................. 53
Beany, Major Roy 137
Bob Burns (Comedian)
    and origin of word "bazooka" 106
Bonheur, Rosa (French painter)....189, 196

Bradley, General Omar
 .... 9, 40, 51, 54, 55, 66, 136, 152
 .... 174, 187, 188, 190, 191, 192, 247
  and head-on assaults 138
  not mentioned in *Op Report* 274
  reason for not pushing
   past *Argentan* 190
Bromfield, Louis (Author) 212
Butcher, Commander Harry 12, 13, 65
Charlemagne 202
Charles II 202
Choltitz, General (German) 197
Churchill, Winston 137, 193
Clark, General Mark 12
Collins, General J. Lawton ....
 .... 42, 126, 134, 138, 155, 176, 184
 .... 190, 209, 213, 215, 274, 315, 317
  broke out of hedgerow stalemate,
   (not Patton) 190
  dislike of close-order drill 213
Cota, General Norman 268
d'Artagnan 9
De Gaulle, Général Charles 13, 190, 197
Demuth (as a German name) 244
DeMuth, René ....
 .... 237, 238, 239, 240, 241, 242, 304
DePuy, William
 .... 85, 138, 191, 268, 309, 310, 311
Der Führer (Hitler) 118
Duke of Normandy
 .... see William The Conqueror
Eberbach, General (German) 174, 175
Eddy, General Manton 25
Eisenhower, David 214, 265
Eisenhower, General Dwight D.
  and British Air Marshal Leigh-
   Mallory 11
  and carpet bombing 136
  and familiarity with French terrain .. 214
  and head-on assaults 137
  and *Mortain* offensive 152
  and Patton's outburst at Monty's
   slowness at *Falaise* Gap 190
  and praise of 90th Division 266
  and Self-Inflicted Wounds 54, 65
  at *Argentan-Falaise* Gap 177
  backing up Bill Mauldin's cartoons .. 169
  Butcher's book about 271
  D-Day message to troops 1
  Falaise Gap Order of the Day 12
  favoring Transportation Plan
   (bombing of roads, bridges
    and railroads) 196
  Ike not mentioned in 357th
   Operational Report 274
  orders from General Marshall 51
  pistol, gift from Patton 84-85
  reference to doubts about troops 65
Frederick of Prussia 244
Fussell, Paul 229
Gavin, General James
  and holding territory 147
Göring, Hermann
  German head of *Luftwaffe* 243
Grant, General Ulysses S.
  first battle in Mexico 82
Green, Major (in basic training) 49, 103
Hamilton, Major Ed 131, 133, 212, 218
 .... 219, 229, 232, 243
 .... 313, 304, 332
Hansen, Chester (Gen. Bradley's
  aide) 66
Haislip, General 194, 211, 212
Héloïse and *Abélard* 196
Hemingway, Ernest 43, 73, 84
Henry V, Shakespeare play 2
Herbert, Major Paul H. 311, 312
  Leavenworth Papers 309
Hitler 118, 188, 204, 316
  assassination attempt 119, 175
  not in *Op Report* 274
  and *Compiègne* 197
  and FUSAG 125, 141
  and *Mortain* offensive 152, 155
  and *SS* (glossary) 329
  author rips photograph of 236
  forbidding German 7th Army
   to give ground 174
  rumor of death 118
Homer, Winslow (painter) 196
Horace (Odes) 82
Ike .... See also Eisenhower
  and D-Day failure notes 3, 13
   Fussell's comment about 13
  and Leigh-Mallory 11
  and praise of 90th Division 265

(Ike, cont.)
    and pre-war trips to France 214
    and Transportation Plan 212
    yen to command troops 214
    author's loyalty to 2
    D-Day message to troops.............. 2, 12
    Letting *LeClerc* "take" Paris............. 197
    David, Ike's grandson..................... 265
    message real thing,
        not Shakespeare........................... 2
    use of overwhelming force 51
indian(s) 28, 29, 31, 33, 48, 51, 55, 58
    why not capitalized........................... 28
Javert, Inspector...................................... 9
Jean Valjean 9
Jennings, Alfred (author's
    great grandfather)............................ 67
Joan of Arc . (*Jeanne d'Arc*)...194, 197, 202
Kaiser, The.. 211
Kilday, Lt. Col................................... 283
Landrum, General................ 155, 209, 274
Le Clerc, *Général* (French) 175, 197
Leigh-Mallory, Trafford.......................... 11
Liebau, Lieutenant Chuck
    first of 56 mentions........................ 114
    picks W.W. for Platoon Sgt......... 306
    killed by mortar shell...................... 308
Marshall, Douglas..........................85, 229
Marshall, General George Catlett.......... 51
Marshall, S.L.A............... 85, 176, 191, 229
Mauldin, Bill 169, 312
McConville, Lieutenant..............57, 78, 89
McDonald, Lieutenant 228
McElvie, General 155, 209, 274
McLain, General Leonard
    .... 126, 147, 155, 209, 212, 244
McNair, General
    and FUSAG 125, 141
    death of 125
    secret burial in France 125
Middleton, Drew
    (war correspondent) 73
Middleton, General Troy.........54, 211, 212
Millet, Jean François
    (Impressionist painter) 195
Montgomery, Gen. Bernard Law
    ....9, 51, 84, 174, 187
    .... 190, 192, 203

Monty (see also: Montgomery)..9, 14, 141
Napoleon Bonaparte 200
Nick Adams (Hemingway
    character) 84
Olivier, Laurence 146
Patton, General George S. ....
    3rd Army's early gains 190
    advice to subordinates on
        importance of appearances........ 214
    attempt to cut off Germans escap-
        ing from *Falaise* Gap at *Seine* 188
    and Bill Mauldin 169, 312
    and cleanliness of troops 166
    and direct frontal attacks................ 311
    and FUSAG 125, 140
    and hedgerow stalemate................ 190
    and helmet chin-straps............167, 169
    and "kitchen cavalry" 203
    and momentum in combat 184
    and movie, *Patton*........................... 135
    and North Africa campaign 140
    outburst at Monty's slowness......... 190
    and his revolver(s)....................167, 169
    and sense of destiny....................... 208
    and his treatment of poorly-
        performing subordinates............ 139
    and ULTRA/*Mortain* info................ 155
    as post-war icon 315
    at *St.-Mihiel* in WW-I 191, 210
    author not hearing name while
        in France 317
    author's ambivalence toward 315
    author's comment on 53
    awarded DSC in WW-I 208
    in doghouse over *Argentan*
        outburst...................................... 190
    "Blood-and-guts" soubriquet........... 168
    calling 90th a bad division....................
        .... 135, 188, 315
    command of 3rd Army kept
        quiet 125, 141
    denied perfect rifle score.................. 68
    directing traffic at *Pontabault* 135, 289
    frustration at gas shortage.............. 203
    giving pistol to Ike 85
    myth about serving under 315
    not following own rules about
        GI equipment 166

(Patton, cont.)
    not mentioned in *Op Report* 274
    only two days combat in WW-I 208
    ordering death penalty for
        troops 83
    orders to wear insignia of rank 188
    pressures on; slapping incident 316
    retreating on a slant for
        appearance's sake 214
    stopped by Bradley at *Argentan* ....
        .... 190, 191
    strictness about proper uniform 166
    takes command of 3rd Army ....
        .... 25, 140, 190, 315
    The Pattons (Grandson's book
        about the family) 315–317
    turned loose with 3rd Army 190
    using *Michelin* road maps 209
    wounded in WW-I 139
Patton, Robert 139, 154, 169
    .... 190, 210, 215
    Author's correspondence with 315
Ridgway, General Matthew ... 154, 166, 169
Robin Hood 9
Rommel 117, 118, 119
    accident 117, 125
    not in *Op Report* 274
    and speed of rumors 122
    as "Desert Fox" 117
    respected for military abilities 118
Shakespeare 2, 248
Sheehy, Colonel John W. 274
Shrapnel, General Henry 83, 325
Slovik, Private Eddie 82, 121, 197
    .... 213, 245
Spaatz, General Carl A. "Tooey" ... 196, 212
Stevens, Lt. Burrowes .. 114, 158, 218, 230
    .... 147, 155, 246, 249, 256, 261
Von Braun, Wernher 326
von Schlieben, General (German) 108
Walker, General Walton 194, 243, 244
Weaver, Gen. William ... 147, 155, 168, 311
Wenner (squad-mate in basic) 20
Werrenrath, Reinald 136
William the Conqueror 13, 155
Williams (troop-ship acquaintance) 22
Yensko, Sgt 95, 97, 112, 113, 115
    .... 116, 120, 121, 230, 246

Authors

Altsheler, Joseph 31
    Keepers of the Trail 28
Ambrose, Stephen 264
    D-Day 52
    The Supreme Commander 191
Astor, Gerald
    June 6, 1944 – Voices of D-Day 68
Beevor, Antony
    D-Day, The Battle for Normandy
    .... 25, 154
Blair, Clay
    Ridgway's Paratroopers 154, 169
Blumenson, Martin
    Breakout and Pursuit (Green Book) ....
    .... 106, 107, 108, 122
    .... 128, 138, 271, 311, 312
Bradley, General Omar
    A Soldier's Story 65
Brown, Walter
    *Up Front with U.S. Day by Day in
    the Life of a Combat Infantryman in
    Patton's Third Army* 268
Butcher, Commander Harry
    My Three Years with Eisenhower ....
    .... 12, 271
Cain, Charles
    Fighters of Wold War II 137
Clayton, Tim; and Craig, Phil
    Finest Hour, The Battle of Britain 137
Colby, John
    War From the Ground Up –
    The 90th Division in WW-II . 106, 107
    .... 122, 147, 155, 230, 232
    .... 233, 243, 244, 268-9, 271
Cole, Hugh
    The Lorraine Campaign (Green Book) ....
    .... 83, 85, 153, 225, 228, 232
    .... 233, 243, 257, 271, 312
Collins, General J. Lawton
    Lightning Joe 138, 209, 213, 215
Crane, Stephen
    The Red Badge of Courage ....
    .... 17, 42, 67, 72, 73, 80
Daley, Robert
    Portraits of France ....
    .... 1, 38, 210, 213, 214, 215

Dank, Milton
- *The Glider Gang* 25

D'Este, Carlo
- *Decision in Normandy* 14, 192, 271
- *Patton, A Genius for War* 83

DePuy, William
- *Operations of Armed Forces In the Field* 269

Eiseley, Loren
- *The Immense Journey* 268

Eisenhower, David
- *Eisenhower at War 1943-1945* ... 11, 266

Ellis, John
- *The Sharp End of the Fight* 26

Featherston, Alwyn
- *Saving the Breakout* 152, 271

Fussell, Paul
- *Doing Battle* 168, 229
- *Wartime* 3, 12, 53, 84, 168

Gavin, General James
- *On to Berlin* 26, 147

Grieg, Edvard
- Music for *Brothers Sing On* 213

Harrison, Gordon
- *Cross-Channel Attack (Green Book)*. 271

Hastings, Max
- *Overlord* ....
- 52, 65, 85, 108, 121, 265, 271
- soldiers not firing weapons 85

Hemingway, Ernest 43
- *A Farewell to Arms* 42, 81
- *Big Two-hearted River* 84
- *By Line* 43
- *The Nick Adams Stories* 84
- *The Old Man and the Sea* 43

Horace
- *Odes* 215

Hugo, Victor
- *The Hunchback of Nôtre Dame* 202

Huie, William Bradford
- *The Execution of Private Slovik* ....
- 82, 122, 213

Ingersoll, Ralph
- *The Battle Is the Payoff* 140

Jones, James
- *WW-II* 53

Keegan, John
- *The Mask of Command* 82, 265

Kennett, Lee B.
- *G.I.* 83

Kilmer, Joyce (Poet)
- *Trees* 197

Leckie, Robert
- *Delivered from Evil* 271

Liebling, A. J. ....
- column in *New Yorker* 43

Marshall, Douglas
- *Reconciliation Road* 85, 229

Marshall, S.L.A.
- *Men Against Fire* ....
- 26, 50, 85, 191, 229, 269
- *Night Drop* 25, 26

Middleton, Drew 43
- *Our Share of Night* 42, 81

Monroe, Vaughn
- *Racing with the Moon* (song) 99

Mowat, Farley
- *And No Birds Sang* 53, 215, 317

Nez, Chester and Avila; and Schiess, Judith
- *Code Talker* 137

Noyes, Alfred
- *The Highwayman* 99

Owen, Wilfred
- *Dulce et Decorum Est* 215

Patrick, Stephen A.
- *The Normandy Campaign, June and July 1944* 66

Patton, Robert
- *The Pattons* 139, 154, 169
- 191, 214, 215
- 315, 317

Pyle, Ernie 53, 73, 136
- *Brave Men* 66
- *Ernie's War* (Ed.: David Nichols)
- 73, 136

Regimental S-3
- *Operational Report 357th Infantry* ....
- .... i, 51, 84, 102, 105
- 107, 120, 271, 273, 274
- 275, 122, 139, 148, 153
- 1st page of Report 276

Remarque, Erich Maria
- *All Quiet on the Western Front* ....
- 42, 244
- *The Road Back* 42, 244

Robert, Brig. Gen. Henry Martyn
   Robert's Rules of Order 266
Shane, Ted
   These Are the Generals 68
Skavlan/Dalmas
   Lyrics for *Brothers Sing On* 213
Tennyson, Alfred Lord
   Flower in the Crannied Wall 155
U.S. Army
   Green Books (Official Army Histories) ...
   .... 83, 271, 312
Wagner, Richard
   Die Meistersinger 136
West Point – *Military History*
   Series Second World War:
   Europe and the Mediterranean 65
Von Roeder, Staff Sgt. George
   Regimental History of the 357th
   Infantry 271
Weigley, Russell
   Eisenhower's Lieutenants 271
White, Stewart Edward
   The Long Rifle 38
Wightman, Warren
   ANNOTATED BIBLIOGRAPHY
   .... 14, 50, 53, 66, 80, 82, 83, 106
   .... 138, 152, 169, 176, 192, 213
   .... 214, 215, 229, 268, 271, 317

Periodicals

American Heritage magazine 85
Baltimore Sun 244
Colliers 43
   Fighting Words 80
Democrat and Chronicle
   Rochester, NY 244, 331
New York Times 42, 73
New York Times
   World Atlas 13
New Yorker 43
Saturday Evening Post 38, 68
Stars and Stripes 9, 169
Time-Life
   The Second Front 13
Völkischer Beobachter
   (*Nazi* newspaper) 103

General Index

.30-caliber ammunition 40
.45-caliber pistol 27
.50-cal machinegun 132
105-mm artillery (American) 81
105-mm artillery (German) 65
105-mm artillery shells 19, 26, 66, 71
155-mm "long Tom" 48, 66, 81
2-1/2 ton trucks 139
240-mm artillery 48, 56, 66, 102, 119
4.2 chemical mortars 56, 66
60-mm mortar(s) (American) 69
6-by-6 trucks .... See 2-1/2 ton trucks
88-mm German dual-purpose
   artillery 1, 119, 153, 154
   .... 158, 160, 167
ack-ack 124
adrenaline 229
aid station, battalion
   .... 59, 98, 106, 130, 212, 227, 261- 263
air bursts (artillery) 90
Amber Chamber 244
anonymity 6
anti-aircraft (Allied) 8, 135
anti-aircraft (German) 123, 136
anti-tank gun(s) (American) 243
anti-tank gun(s) (German) 218
anti-tank weapon(s) 96, 190
APCs (pills) 130
Armistice (WW-I) 197, 208
armor-piercing (AP) ammo ....
   .... 61, 68, 69, 182, 190
Articles of War 16
   read to recruits 75, 83, 260
assault guns 153, 274
atheists in foxholes 74
atomic bomb(s) 331
B-17 Flying Fortress 123, 136
B-24 Liberator 4, 136
Bailey bridge 196, 212
ball ammo (for M-1) 69
bandolier (ammo) 83, 84, 115
B-A-R (**B**rowning **A**utomatic **R**ifle)
   1st of 45 entries 19
   photo 69
barrage balloons 4

basic training
- aircraft recognition 13
- and dead bodies 106
- and German multi-engine planes 7
- and routs 268
- author not buck for promotion 246
- author's B-A-R "possible" 68
- author's sketch of terrain 110
- B-A-R man assignments 115
- brush fire on bivouac 103
- chickenshit 166
- crudeness of cadre 145
- hand-to-hand combat....................... 22
- hitting ground rolling...................... 183
- initiative, GIs and Germans............. 310
- keeping heads down....................... 228
- mortar training................................. 69
- overhead artillery exercise............... 19
- patrols.. 39
- reading of *Articles of War* 75, 83, 259
- realities of combat............................ 49
- rifle-grenade safetys....................... 153
- scouts... 42
- seeing 105 artillery shells.................. 66
- training in first aid, splints................ 92

battalion headquarters 46, 219, 231
Battle of Britain 137, 243
bayonet(s) 7, 14, 21, 46, 91, 236, 310
bazooka................ 45, 92, 93, 96, 106, 107
beachheads 9, 54, 135, 212
Bedcheck Charlie 7
berms................................. 30, 31, 33, 34
Big Bertha (WW-I cannon) 211
bipod (for B-A-R)..........................59, 67, 68
body count 42
bombing (by Germans) 166, 202, 275
bombing (by Americans).................52, 196,
booby-trap(s) 187
Burgundians (and Joan of Arc) 197
burp-gun (German)................82, 103, 107
.... 131, 145, 173, 183, 230, 249, 252
C-47(s)................................ 1, 11, 202, 301
camouflage........... 115, 120, 132, 201, 221
camouflage netting (for helmets)........ 115
canteen(s) 46, 76, 91, 102, 111
carbine, .30-cal................................ 3, 230
carpet bombing ....See COBRA
cartography (college course)........100, 131

cartridge belt..................... 21, 45, 91, 115
casualties in hedgerows........................ 54
casualty, chances of becoming............ 265
cathedral towns.................................. 200
Catholic mass 205
champagne (wine)............... 179, 200, 213
chickenshit.................... 18, 163, 166, 168
Civil Rights movement 39
Civil War (American)............ 17, 49, 72, 82
..............................83, 122, 139, 154, 260
civilian problems and casualties,
  in Beevor's book (see Authors)....... 154
close-order drill 205, 206, 213
COBRA (carpet bombing)....... 52, 123, 125
......................................126, 136, 137, 138
.....................................185, 190, 208, 274
- short bombing 136
- map iv

combat course, in Basic 38
combat fatigue 54, 65, 315, 316
Combat Infantry Badge......................... 48
command car(s)............121, 130, 131, 134
Communists 204
compass, German................. 160, 161, 269
compass, lensatic (GI)..................160, 161
correspondent(s), war 42, 43, 73
cosmoline... 3
cover (noun)...................................30, 35
cover (verb)...................... 28, 37, 39, 129
crap games... 3
C-Rations.. 65
D-Day
- and hedgerows, in Ambrose
  book, *D-Day* 51
- and inexperienced officers............. 273
- and paratroopers at *Merderet* R. 155
  at *Ste.-Mère-Église* 7
- and radio announcements of............ 12
- and V-1 casualties, comparison......... 14
- availability of Bailey Bridges 212
- beaches crowded 54
- Ike's message to troops 1
- Ike's reference to doubts re troops... 65
- Rome's capture preempting
  D-Day headlines 12

DDT... 108
dead bodies (location of) 108
DSC 153, 208, 214, 229, 243, 276, 313

Dienstglas (German binoculars) ....
.... 91, 102, 109, 149, 167, 218
dogfight(s) 125, 137
doughboy(s) 211
D-Rations (chocolate bars)
.... 55, 65, 102, 207
enfilade fire 60
entrenching tool(s) 7, 17, 76, 91
existentialism 136
fatigues, gas resistant 4
field exercises (in Basic) 22, 66
field hospital 98, 263
fighter bombers (Allied) 117, 136
.... 137, 167, 176, 177
fire for effect 250, 267
First World War 14, 52, 154, 191
.... 208, 209, 210
first-aid 92
flare(s) 41, 173, 174
floating steel pier 5
flying bomb (V-1, buzz-bomb) 9
Fourth of July celebration 55
frontal assaults 51, 128, 138, 210, 310
Garand rifle (M-1) .... 14 (photo), 240
gas masks 4, 55
Geneva Convention 231
German capitulation, WW-II 202
Gerries (German soldiers) ....
.... 1, 19, 30, 45, 64, 207, 223
Gerrycan 207
GI Terms, Appendix E 319
     Web-link 313
GI Bill 331
gig (punishment) 28, 31, 38
glider(s) 1, 10, 11, 16, 25
grapevine 122, 125
graves registration 106, 108
grease-gun 107, 252, 253, 255
.... See also M-3
grenade, fragmentation 76, 78, 83, 96
.... 101, 102, 160, 181, 187, 190
.... 195, 194, 222, 227, 233
grenade-launcher 115, 153, 181
guard – one-on-three-off 26, 233
     – one-on-two-off 20, 175, 253
halftrack(s), American 130
halftrack, German 112, 120
hand signals 32, 41

hand-to-hand combat 22
harmonica duet 47
HE (**H**igh **E**xplosive) ... 69, 83, 189, 322, 328
Horsa (British glider) 25
horse(s) 11, 34, 139, 177, 189, 193, 199
howitzer(s) 26, 267
Hundred Years War 197
hunting knife 4, 7, 21, 24
IBM card(s) 265
In Flanders Fields (poem) 211
Indian Love Call (song) 48
indian (why not capitalized) 39
Infantry weapons, Web-link 312
infantryman's crouch 111
infiltration (by enemy) 21
infiltration course, Basic 31
initiative (soldiers taking) 130, 131, 141
.... 177, 206, 309, 310
insignia of rank 25, 188
     and General Patton 188
intelligence (military)
.... 11, 29, 51, 155, 185, 236
invasion fleet 4, 274
invasion money 3, 13, 179, 201
iodide-treated water 10, 16
Jeep 63, 81, 99, 130, 131, 132, 133, 180
.... 181, 183, 193, 195, 232, 263
Kentucky muzzle-loader 38
K-Rations 46, 65, 173, 198, 238
La Plume de MaTante 10
landing craft 4, 43
landing nets 4
LCI (**L**anding **C**raft **I**nfantry) 4
leggings 31, 76, 210
lice 79, 103, 108
light armor, American 203
Lusitania 211
M-3 sub-machinegun (U.S.) 107, 253
machine-pistol (German) 77
machinegun fire (American) 41, 82, 89, 92
.... 96, 103, 132, 144, 243, 256
machinegun fire (German) 45, 60, 61
.... 63, 67, 68, 74, 75, 78, 81, 87, 89, 90, 92
...... 107, 132, 145, 157, 183, 219, 220, 224
.... 226, 249, 250, 252, 253, 262, 267
Mademoiselle from Armentiers
     (WW-I song) 211
map-reader, author as 130

Mauldin and Patton 169, 312
    Web-link.. 312
Mauser (German rifle) 77
ME-109 (German fighter plane) ...125, 133
medic(s) 79, 88, 90, 92, 94, 95
    .... 97, 98, 106, 130, 220, 232, 262
Messerschmitt .... 126, and see ME-109
MG-42 (German machinegun)
    .... 74, 81, 82, 145, 220, 249
Michelin Green Guide 155
    re map of *Normandie* 14
    road maps used by Patton 209
mines, minefields 5, 128
Miniéball 67
mink (alert as a...) 21, 26
morphine 98, 225, 226, 227
mortar fire American 3, 69, 63, 110
    .... 111, 115, 120, 143, 224, 225
    .... 227, 229, 230, 257, 243, 249
    .... 250, 265, 266, 273
mortar fire (German) ....
    .... 4, 50, 62, 63, 64, 75, 83, 107
    .... 109, 148, 158, 219, 257, 258
    .... 259, 260, 261, 267
    maps 62, 257
Mosquito bomber 4, 13
MP(s) 75, 163, 164, 245
MP Line 75
mulberries (artificial harbors) 13
muzzle velocity (M-1) 40, 228
muzzle velocity (German 88) 167
Nazi 2, 59, 172, 204, 208, 222
    .... 237, 238, 242, 244, 332
negro(es) 127, 207
    why not capitalized 39
Nescafé 46, 201
oblique tactics (vs. frontal
    assault) 138
observation plane, artillery 157, 167
OCS 269, 273
oil-and-thong kit (for M-1) 58
orders, military, legal force of... 226
"Over the top" 67
Over There (WW-I song) 211
P-38 Lightning (plane) 4
P-38, Walther (German pistol) 224, 230
P-47 Thunderbolt 4, 125, 136, 137, 171
P-51 Mustang 4

Panzerfaust (German bazooka) ....
    .... 107, 126, 131
parachute silk 201
paratrooper(s) 7, 11, 12
    and Thompson sub 38
password(s) 29, 46, 47, 64
patrol(s) 28, 29, 30, 34, 37, 38, 40
    .... 41, 42, 45, 46, 48, 57, 58
    .... 65, 83, 89, 90, 112, 113
    .... 115, 116, 120, 171, 180
    .... 183, 191, 193, 226, 245
    GI patrol killed by GI outpost 46, 279
Peabody Award 331
Platoon Guide 113, 246
"possible" (perfect target) 68
potato masher (German hand-
    grenade) 77, 103, 107, 111, 114
prisoner(s) (German) 29, 34, 35, 40
    .... 47, 59, 77, 79, 91, 108,
    .... 171, 172, 173, 217, 237, 274
prisoner(s) being taken, taking 29, 39
promotions (of author) 48, 113, 246
Provisional French Government 13
rabbit(s) 178, 206, 207, 226, 238
Red-Ball Express 207
Red-Cross arm bands 90
regimental headquarters 120, 273
reinforcements, term substituted
    for *replacements* 25
reorganization (after military
    action) 105, 308
replacement depot .... See repple depple
replacement(s)
    for casualties 16
    and chickenshit Looey 166
    and readiness for combat 189
    and reorganization 105
    appearance of... 101
    Browny as 150
    green officers leading seasoned
        troops 168
    how to spot 114
    Sackett as... 173
    many not infantry trained 120
    new B-A-R man's lack of caution 127
    new men told of 90th's
        poor performance 16, 315
    riflemen needed 121

(replacements, cont.)
    Sartori as.. 164
    Sgt. Barrett as.................................... 244
    terminology changed to
    reinforcements 25
repple depple 9, 10, 15, 16, 21, 99
reptilian brain...................................... 267
rifle grenade(s) 115, 143, 153, 160
....181, 182, 189, 190
roadblock(s) 57, 58, 64, 65, 89
....91, 112, 132, 171
.... 178, 180, 184, 186
.... 223, 232, 233
rotating bands (on artillery shells) 66
routs 26, 137, 258
.... 268, 269, 286
rout (GIs) at *Fèves* Ridge 258
rubber-band-gun(s) 99
rumors 10, 21, 49, 55, 95
.... 121, 125, 176, 262
Russians 67, 68, 204
S-5, Civil/Military relations...........190, 204
saturation bombing ....See COBRA
scabbard 21, 24, 31
Schmeisser (German machine
    pistol) 77, 82, 107
scout(s) 51, 97, 115, 116, 121, 122
.... 161, 173, 218, 233, 249
searchlight(s).................................... 6, 8, 10
self-inflicted wounds (SIWs)............. 54, 65
self-propelled guns............................. 131
shaped charge (bazooka)............. 106, 190
shelter-half... 169
Sherman tank(s) 92, 148, 154, 158, 178
short-arm inspection 264
ShotSpotters 268
shrapnel................................. 5, 14, 76, 93
    not correct for shell fragments 83
    origin of term 83
    use in American Civil War 83
Signal Corps.. 24
Silver Star medal (author's) 332
SIW ....See self-inflicted wounds
small-arms fire (German)...................... 47
smoke screen 56
smokeless powder................................. 68
    in Astor's book, *Voices of D-Day* 68
snap shooting... 38

sniper(s) 21, 24, 29, 30, 34, 36, 37
...........................40, 41, 42, 45, 48, 61, 101
.....................109, 143, 149, 150, 202, 226
souvenir(s) 167, 201, 213, 224, 227
.... 229, 230, 237
Spandau (German machinegun) 81
Spencer Lens Company......................... 39
Spitfire (British fighter plane)................. 4
SS Explorer (troop ship) 276
stragglers 102, 114, 127
superstition.. 74
swallows 96
swastika 237
tactical critiques (after-action)............ 134
tactics 138, 252, 253
Tank Destroyers (TDs) ....
....1, 3, 6, 7, 9, 15, 274
tank(s) (Allied)..................................... 212
tank(s) (British).................................... 154
tank(s) (American).. 54, 75, 92, 95, 96, 126
.... 127, 130, 131, 140
.... 141, 144, 148, 154
.... 158, 167, 201, 202
.... 203, 274
tank(s) (German) 34, 96, 107, 119, 132
.... 133, 134, 140,141, 143
.....................144, 145, 146, 153, 154, 167
    map 142
tank(s) in WW-I 208, 210, 214
The Great War
.... see World War One
Third *Reich* 82
Thompson sub................27, 28, 30, 35, 37
.... 38, 40, 41, 46, 57
.... 65, 89, 90, 107
thousand yard stare 53
time-fire (artillery)..........................87, 90
toilet paper 3, 103
Tomb of the Unknown Soldier 211
Tommy-gun.. 38
TOT (Time-On-Target) 66
tracers 8, 10
TRADOC
    Training And Doctrine Command..........
.... 85, 310
Transportation Plan (bombing
    bridges, roads and RRs)............196, 212
tree bursts 71, 113

trench knife 24, 31, 46, 180, 225
trenches (of WW-I) 15, 42, 209
troopship 4, 22, 121
Typhoons (British fighter-
　　bombers) 122, 136
ULTRA (code breakers) 152, 155, 174, 188
V-1, ... 9, 14
V-2 14
Valentine's Day massacre 38
vengeance weapon(s) 14
　......... See also *V-1, V-2* and V-Weapons
Vichy Government 190
V-mail 112, 176, 2337

V-Weapons, Web-link 313
Waco (U.S. glider) 25
wagons, German horse-drawn 34
walkie-talkie 224, 225, 249
War to End Wars .... See World War One
West Point 65, 125, 154, 273
white phosphorous
　(rifle grenade) 142, 143, 153, 189
World War One. 14, 139, 197202, 235, 260
　............... See also First World War, WW-I
WW-1 .... 67, 137, 138, 191, 197
　............................ 208, 209, 213, 214, 260
　........................... . 315, 319, 323, 325, 345

ADDENDA

The following material was added after final edit:

Item 1)   Page 189 – Chapter 17, Note 4:

Since writing this I have learned of NASA's marked success in screening astronauts for personality traits that could predict effectiveness under stress, and for compatibility of crew members on space missions. Their selection program is described in Christopher Steiner's book, *Automate This*, Chapter 7, published by Portfolio/Penguin, New York, 2012.

Item 2)   Page 190, Note 11:

One of the very few books that details the destruction left by the war in Europe, by both sides, is Keith Lowe's *Savage Continent,* published by St. Martin's Press, New York, 2012. I would suggest that *Savaged Continent* might be an equally apt title.

Item 3)   Page 270

Quote is from Loren Eiseley's *The Immense Journey*, p. 140, published by Random House, New York, 1957 (reprinted by permission).

Item 4)   Chapter 12, The Shelling

In 2014 a lot of attention is given to concussions, both in the military and in sports. In WW-II I never heard the effects of concussion mentioned. "Shell-shocked" was a term used in WW-I, but not in WW-II. "Combat fatigue", which supplanted it, did not necessarily relate to concussions.

Item 5)   Chapter 18, Page 212

The 2014 movie, *The Monuments Men,* tells how the Allies tried to preserve the art and cultural artifacts of the countries we fought through. The *Chartres* Cathedral windows may have been part of their mission.

Item 6)   The following are not in the main index:

Page in this book

Afghanistan	53
body armor	53
Donald, Aida: *Citizen Soldier*	213
El Alamein	117
flak jackets	53, 268
Gole, Henry: *Preparing the Army for Modern War*	266

ADDENDA (cont.)

(Not in Main Index, cont.)

> Iraq 53
> Korean War 53, 268
> *National Geographic Atlas of the World* 13
> ossuary (at Verdun) 214
> Truman, Harry S. 213

Item 7) Letter from Congresswoman Louise Slaughter, N.Y., to veteran constituents about body armor (used by permission):

April 15, 2014

Dear Warren,

When we send our young men and women into harm's way, it's our duty to make sure they are provided with the best life-saving equipment available.

The National Academy of Sciences (NAS) recently released a report on the safety of military combat helmets, which was commissioned by the Department of Defense (DoD) after I sent a letter to Defense Secretary Leon Panetta challenging an unacceptable new standard for testing helmets. The NAS report, which was released after a 14-month examination, validated my concerns and issued 30 recommendations to improve helmet safety and test protocols. On April 3, 2014, I sent a letter to Defense Secretary Chuck Hagel and Secretary of the Army John McHugh urging them to consider and quickly adopt the recommendations of the study.

Throughout my career, I have been working to protect American troops from faulty equipment and weak test protocols. After reading in 2006 that 80 percent of Americans killed in the Iraq War from upper body wounds died from the result of faulty body armor, I waged a five-year campaign to improve body armor safety standards and in 2009, secured the recall and replacement of 16,000 pieces of unsafe body armor from the front lines. My effort led to improved armor test protocols and ended the practice of outsourcing testing to private companies.

You can count on me to continue fighting to improve the quality of the protective equipment that our troops and their families rely on.

Sincerely,
Louise M. Slaughter

ADDENDA (cont.)

Item 8)   B-Company Morning Report for 9/16/44

```
COMPANY
MORNING REPORT        16 Sept    4
STATION  Malancourt V-7870   Nor De Guerre Zone
ORGANIZATION  Co B   357th Inf Regt   Inf

SERIAL NUMBER         NAME              GRADE  CODE
O-1287049    O'Brien, James P.            1 Lt
   Dy to Sk LD Clrg Sta (Not Hospitalized)
   15 Sept 44.
O-1287049    O'Brien, James P.            1 Lt
   Sk LD Clrg Sta (Not Hospitalized) to
   Hospitalized LD 104th Evac Hospital.
   Non-battle casualty, Slightly sick.
   Dropped fr asgmt (1542).
34777916    Hamilton, Fred R.             Pvt
   Dy to LWA (Hospital unknown) Dropped fr
   asgmt. 745.
35734866    James, Wilbur M.              Pvt
   Dy to LWA 12th Ev. Hosp. Dropped fr
   asgmt. 745.
32836007    McCrary, Ruben R. Jr.         Sgt
37575956    Lutjen, John A.               Pfc
   Move 2 Ll Dy to LWA. (Not Hospital-
   ized). 315th Clrg Sta.
42025717    Wightman, Warren J.         S Sgt    ← W.W. evacuated
   Dy to LWA 104th Evac Hosp. Dropped fr
   asgmt. 353.
37190246    Youngswander, Theodore H.    Pfc
```

About the Author

In October, 1943, after attending Oberlin College for three and a half years, the author was drafted into the Army and assigned to the Infantry. Following 13 weeks of basic training at Fort McClellan, Alabama, he shipped out to England, then across the English Channel to France. He debarked at Utah Beach with a group of replacements for infantrymen who had been killed or wounded in the first days of the Normandy invasion.

Wightman served in a rifle company in the 90th Division, Third Army until mid-September when he was wounded near *Metz*, France. While recuperating in the States, the Atomic bombs were dropped on Japan, effectively ending the war.

After discharge from the Army in February, 1946, the author earned a B.A. in Psychology from the University of Buffalo, and an M.S. in Broadcast Media Communications from Syracuse University, both on the "GI Bill". As a TV writer/producer he shared a Peabody Award for the 1953 season of *The Johns Hopkins Science Review*, the first TV science series aired on American networks.

Following several years as production manager and art director at a commercial TV station in Rochester, N.Y. the author took a position with the Rochester City School District as Administrator and Department Head for Televised Instruction.

As a freelance contributor he wrote a *Science and Nature* column for Rochester's *City Newspaper*, and reviewed books for Gannett's *Democrat and Chronicle*.

The author currently lives in Fairport, NY where he is working on the other four books of AN ALMOST PERFECT WAR. Other projects in progress are an art book for elementary schoolchildren, a Broadway-style musical, and a cartoon series based on the extravagant language of music critics.

Comments are welcome at wjw90@live.com

✤ ✤ ✤

Made in the USA
Middletown, DE
17 June 2015